£2.—

THE COMPANY

THE COMPANY

LAW, STRUCTURE AND REFORM
IN ELEVEN COUNTRIES

Edited by
Charles de Hoghton

PEP
12 Upper Belgrave Street

London

GEORGE ALLEN & UNWIN LTD
Ruskin House · Museum Street

Printed in Great Britain
in 10 on 11pt Times
by Alden & Mowbray Ltd
at the Alden Press Oxford

PREFACE

This book is intended as a contribution to the debate on the reform of company law that has been going on in most industrial countries for a decade or more. This debate (discussed in general terms in the Introduction) has led to new laws and new proposals which reflect dissatisfaction with the ways in which companies are structured and organised. In all the countries dealt with in these pages the facts of political, economic and social life are different; consequently, the need for change is felt with different degrees of urgency and the forms in which change is being or is likely to be embodied will also be different. But in all of them there is a growing awareness of the fact that enterprise, private as well as public, because it both contributes to and benefits from its society (local, national or larger), can be said to have rights and duties *vis-à-vis* that society in *somewhat* the same way as has an individual.

It is this theme of status and accountability that binds together the various contributions to this book, which is essentially a symposium resulting from an international seminar on 'The Future of the Enterprise and the Reform of Company Law' organised by PEP in April 1967. It is, in fact, an example of theme and variation form—a form which, as lovers of Bach and Beethoven will agree, may well be daunting but rich in final rewards. The businessmen and academics from eleven countries who attended the seminar (see list of contributors on p. 11) had been asked to base their contributions on a questionnaire, similar in organisation and content to Parts I, II and III of this book, and dealing with specific aspects of company law, structure and reform. The relevant points of the questionnaire are summarised at the head of each chapter. (The essentially comparative nature of this book called for a 'subject-by-subject', rather than a 'nation-by-nation', treatment.)

The responses to this questionnaire (which, apart from the Introduction, make up the entirety of this book) differed greatly in style and length; they were, in fact, as varied as human nature itself—a good augury for the future but something which made the editors' task difficult. The latter recognise but make no apology for unevenness (nor, of course, for disagreement) between the contributions of one country and another.

Any unevenness is attributable to three factors, of which the first is the most important—namely, the different stages which various countries have reached in the process of company reform. There are countries in which the matter is debated, certainly, but in which the process is, in essence, one of spontaneous evolution. The most obvious example of this category is the United States. Then there are countries in which formal proposals for reform

7

have been put forward but no legislative action so far taken: for example, Belgium, Italy and the Netherlands. Finally, there are countries where new Companies Acts have come into force, either as major landmarks (as in West Germany and India) or as the first stages of a kind of instalment plan (as in Britain and France). The other factors which have obviously differentiated the various contributions are the personal proclivities and interests of the authors and (even) their national characteristics. (The point at which this unevenness was most pronounced was in the response to Part IV of the questionnaire, 'General Proposals for Reform'. This was so varied that such replies as were received have been either incorporated in the Introduction or reproduced as Appendices.) Because of the special circumstances, the contributions of three countries—India, Japan and Yugoslavia—have been grouped together in Part IV and not dissected according to the 'subject-by-subject' treatment of the original questionnaire and the seminar discussions.

All contributions have been recently checked and revised by their authors to take account of developments since the seminar was held. PEP expresses its warm appreciation and thanks to all the contributors for their original work and their continuing collaboration and interest. (The views expressed in these pages are, of course, the authors' own and not necessarily those of PEP.) The Editor wishes to record his own gratitude to Professor Michael Fogarty and Mr Andrew Robertson for their advice and assistance in the final stages of assembling this book.

It should perhaps be emphasised that this book deals with two aspects only of 'company reform': the legal status of firms and their relationships with certain individuals (defined by role) or groups of individuals. Our contributors discuss the relationship of 'direction' to management but they were not asked to consider the third aspect of the evolution of the modern enterprise, the development and application of refined management techniques. Such an omission, it is plain, needs no excuse in this context; but the point is worth making that what is here only occasionally referred to is just as much a part of 'company reform' and that 'efficiency'—the goal of management science—*can* be as great a contributor to the social value of an enterprise as its awareness of a concept of accountability. The modern firm will not be able to fulfil its triple role (admittedly not yet achieved) of economic unit, social environment and, indeed, cultural vehicle until much more has been done, in thought and deed, to resolve the three aspects of its functioning and harmonise them one with another. Our French and American contributors (in particular) make their recognition of this point quite clear.

PEP organised the seminar that was the origin of this book shortly after the then President of the Board of Trade announced that the British government intended, before the end of the present parliament (i.e. early 1971 at the latest), to introduce a new Companies Bill that would 're-examine the whole theory and purpose of the limited joint stock company, the comparative rights and obligations of shareholders, directors, creditors, employees and the community as a whole'. He called for a 'systematic review of all these issues' and invited opinions from 'all those expert or less expert . . . who are interested'.[1]

[1] *House of Commons Debates*, 14 February 1967, col. 359.

It cannot be said that this appeal has been responded to with any great enthusiasm. Nor does it seem at all possible that the government will be able to bring in a comprehensive and 'fundamental' bill by the date set. The issues are so complex and the interests involved so many that this is one case where the principle of *festina lente* is justified. Nevertheless, such a bill will have to come sooner or later and the greater the range of arguments deployed in the meantime—from every shade of opinion, foreign as well as domestic—the better the bill is likely to be. Conversely, a debate in Britain may well be illuminating for people in other countries.

This book, therefore, is multinational in both origin and aim. Confident in the expertise of our contributors, we publish it in the belief that comparative studies of how different countries tackle similar problems can be fruitful for all.[2]

[2] PEP is also undertaking a separate study (to be published in 1970) of the actual ways in which British boards reconcile the various claims made upon them.

CONTRIBUTORS

BELGIUM

The Belgian contribution was written by a group from the Catholic University of Louvain, consisting of Professor Dr E. de Jonghe and Professor Dr V. van Rompuy (of the Faculty of Economic and Social Sciences), Professor Dr R. Blanpain and Professor Dr W. van Gerven (of the Faculty of Laws) and Dr J. P. Timmermans (of the Centre for Economic Studies, Institute for Economic, Social and Political Research).

BRITAIN

The sections dealing with Britain were written by T. C. Drucker, Barrister-at-Law. PEP wishes to acknowledge the valuable advice and assistance of R. S. Nock, of the Faculty of Laws, Queen Mary College, University of London, in the final preparation of the British material.

FRANCE

Three contributions were received from France. A detailed reply to the PEP questionnaire was written by Philippe Heymann, Deputy Chief Editor of the magazine *Entreprise*, and a paper considering the questions at issue from a more strictly legal viewpoint by Professor Jean Schmidt, of the Faculty of Law and Economic Sciences at the University of Lyon. The French sections of Parts I, II and III of this book are based on these two contributions. The third French paper (a sociological view) appears as Appendix D. This was written by Henri Le More, of the Centre de Recherche sur l'Evolution des Entreprises, Paris, in collaboration with Patrick Festy and Christian Vulliez. These authors wish to acknowledge the advice and assistance of Jacques Lautman (of the Centre National de la Recherche Scientifique) and Jean-Daniel Reynaud (of the Conservatoire National des Arts et Métiers and the Institut d'Etudes Politiques de Paris).

GERMANY

The German sections of Parts I, II and III of this book were written by Lothar Kühl, a Frankfurt lawyer specialising in company law. Appendix E was contributed by Joachim Willmann, at that time Director of the German branch of the Comité Européen pour le Progrès Economique et Social (CEPES), Frankfurt-am-Main.

INDIA

The chapter on India was contributed by D. L. Mazumdar, Director of the India International Centre, New Delhi. Mr Mazumdar was formerly Secretary of the Department of Company Law Administration (now known as the Department of Company Affairs) in the Ministry of Commerce and Industry, Government of India.

ITALY

The Italian sections of this book were written by Dott. Diego Corapi, Professor of Commercial Law at the University of Rome.

JAPAN

The chapter on Japan is the joint work of Professor Hiroshi Kato, of the Department of Economics, Keio University, Tokyo, and Dr Shozo Akazawa, of Tohoku Gakuin University, Sendai.

NETHERLANDS

The sections of this book concerning the Netherlands were contributed by Professor C. Æ. Uniken Venema, Professor of Law at the University of Groningen. In addition, use has been made of material received from the Dr Wiardi Beckman Foundation.

SWEDEN

The Swedish sections of this book are the joint work of Professor Knut Rodhe, of the Stockholm School of Economics, and Lars Lidén, Director of the SLT Group, Stockholm. PEP wishes to acknowledge the assistance of the Studieförbundet Näringsliv och Samhälle in the preparation of the Swedish contribution.

UNITED STATES OF AMERICA

The American sections of Parts I, II and III of this book and Appendices F and G were written by Professor Richard Eells, Director, Program of Studies of the Modern Corporation, Graduate School of Business, Columbia University in the City of New York.

YUGOSLAVIA

The chapter on Yugoslavia is the work of Professor Josip Županov, of the Faculty of Economics, University of Zagreb.

The majority of the contributors listed above attended the PEP seminar which was the origin of this book. Also present at the seminar were: *Belgium*: Professor P. van Ommeslaghe (Faculty of Law, Brussels University). *Britain*: R. Davies (Director, Finance and Administration, PEP); C. de Hoghton (PEP); Professor M. Fogarty (PEP); G. Goyder (Chairman, British International Paper Corporation, London); J. B. H. Jackson (Secretary, Philips Industries Ltd., London); J. Pinder (Director, PEP); Mrs B. Shenfield (PEP and University of London); Professor K. W. Wedderburn (Cassel Professor of Commercial Law, University of London). *France*: F. Bloch-Laîné (Director General, Caisse des Dépôts et des Consignations, Paris); M. Massonaud (Secretary General, Centre de Recherche sur l'Evolution des Entreprises, Paris); Professor J.-D. Reynaud (Institut d'Etudes Politiques, Paris). *Germany*: Baron F. von Loeffelholz (then Deputy Director, CEPES Deutsche Gruppe e.V., Frankfurt-am-Main).

CONTENTS

CONTENTS

[1] For *Germany*, see 2, Section C of this Part.

14

CONTENTS

INTRODUCTION

This Introduction is based on various contributions to the PEP seminar mentioned in the Preface and on parts of Professor Michael Fogarty's PEP broadsheet *A Companies Act 1970?* which was written shortly after the seminar at which he was himself a participant. Somewhat greater prominence is given here to countries in which reform is still at discussion or proposal stage (e.g. Belgium and Italy) than to those which have progressed farther. These latter receive fuller consideration in the body of the book.

In the last few years the functions and foundations of corporate enterprise have been analysed and questioned to an extent not seen for decades. The debate has spread across the world and the 'preservationists' are as vigorously engaged as are the 'reformers'. Indeed, as is so often the case, new thinking has encouraged the former to re-examine and strengthen their ideas without retreating from their main positions.

The reform movement is based on a conviction that much of the legislation now in force is out of keeping with contemporary conditions and ideas and that private enterprise ought, in some way that leaves its dynamism unimpaired, to be made more readily accountable for its decisions and actions. The practical terms in which this notion of accountability is expressed vary, of course, from one country to another. This book attempts to illustrate this variety and, by so doing, to make the fairly obvious point, so often obfuscated by ideology and idleness, that we can all learn from one another. It ranges over a spectrum from Yugoslavia, whose economy it is easy to label *dirigiste* and state-controlled (although the reality, as our Yugoslav contributor reveals, is far more complicated) to the United States where state activity, superficially, is minimal. Between these extremes are various types of 'mixed economy', from Japan, with state 'guidance' but relatively little state activity, to countries like Britain and Italy where large-scale nationalised industry co-exists with a strong and vigorous private sector. But there is also a more subtle spectrum that runs from the 'neo-liberal' Federal German Companies Act of 1965 (if the USA had a federal company law it would probably be quite similar) to the 'neo-socialist' views of the majority of the Dutch committee on company law reform. (Our American contributor uses the spectrum analogy in yet a third sense. See Part I, Chapter 1, pp. 51 ff.)

It is, indeed, within the second spectrum that the chief part of the current debate between 'preservationists' and 'reformers' lies. (It is also, certainly as far as Western Europe is concerned, the area in which actual changes in the law have been or are likely to be decided.) Both camps are concerned, in their own estimation at least, with bringing the company up to date. The former puts the greater emphasis on 'tidying up' the company as it is now—with regard, for instance, to the powers and position of shareholders or chief

17

executives. It may go a long way, as the German law of 1965 shows, but it is essentially bent on improving present structures, not on changing them. The 'reformers' go further: they question the relationship of the company with its environment and the modes by which this relationship is expressed and call for a fundamental review of its internal mechanism and external role. Both these points of view are well represented in this book, the former particularly clearly by the German contributions. (Who is in which camp is often surprising—a point taken up at the end of this Introduction.)

The materials of this debate are of fairly long standing, albeit the debate itself has in recent years become more intensive. A new element has, however, been introduced by the emergence of multinational companies, the majority of which are, of course, American. They are increasingly becoming the most suitable type of organisation for dealing, on a really large scale, with modern technical and market conditions. On the other hand, they raise new and special problems both of efficient management and of adaptation to the interests and needs of the countries in which they establish themselves or acquire subsidiaries. In doing so, they have widened the context of the notion of social responsibility. In the European Community, the long debate continues on the question of harmonising codes of company law or setting up a statute for a European Company valid throughout the Community. (It should be noted that the contributions to this book were written before the publication of the Sanders proposals for a European company statute. These are discussed in a paper in the joint Chatham House/PEP European Series, by D. Thompson, published in 1969.) Problems of multinationality are examined, in particular, by the American and German contributors to this book. (See Part III, Chapter 3, and Appendix G.) The heart of the matter, however, still remains at the level of national law, though certain aspects (notably the role and accountability of company managers) have been or are likely to be deeply affected by measures which are themselves not part of company law as such.

NEW LAWS IN FRANCE AND GERMANY

Under the French 'Plan', for instance, a new co-operative relationship has been developed between companies and the state. In German labour law employee representatives have a third to half the seats (depending on the industry and size of company) on the supervisory board which appoints a company's executive board. In a number of countries employees have been given stronger statutory rights to representation below board level, including rights to information and to appeal to outside arbitration. German legislation on works councils in effect fuses together (though not completely) the machinery for consultation and negotiation at plant and enterprise level. There is a debate in several European countries, on lines surprising to British or American observers accustomed to the role of the shop steward and district union officer within the plant, about whether unions should be allowed to negotiate at plant level or only to try to secure influence through works councils or (in France) 'employee delegates'. A related approach to 'participation through conflict' is being discussed in France. French firms, whether companies or not, which employ over a hundred, are now required, under a Decree of August 1967, to distribute to their employees, in the form of their own shares or obligations or of investment trust certificates, part of their profit after providing a minimum return to shareholders.

This requirement is the high-water mark, so far, of developments in France which can be traced back to the war-time years when people of very different persuasions were brought together in the harsh comradeship of the Resistance or the concentration camps. In the immediate post-war Gaullist period, several new lines of thinking emerged (often stimulated by the influence of the French communists), leading to the establishment of works committees, large-scale nationalisation and the setting up of a commission to study the reform of the commercial code and company law in 1947. Business reform as a whole, however, did not come into the limelight until the Pleven Commission (1962) and the publication of François Bloch-Laîné's book *Pour une Réforme de l'Entreprise* in 1963. The new law on commercial companies (frequently referred to by our French contributors) and the reform of works committees were the most important events in recent years and before the present controversies began. It is interesting to note that in France (as elsewhere) the most fervent advocates of business reform are becoming more flexible in their attitudes; above all, it is increasingly recognised that the way to reform does not lie in law alone but that other questions, such as advanced management techniques, are of paramount and parallel importance.

While the question of company law reform is still in the melting-pot in France, kept particularly warm by the turmoils of the spring of 1968, West Germany, with notable innovations to its credit, has reached something of a plateau since the new Law of 1965 came into force at the beginning of 1967. The intention of its drafters was to promote the involvement of larger sections of the population in the production of wealth and to check the concentration of capital into fewer and fewer hands. To this end it has enhanced the power of the shareholders' general meeting (at the expense of that of the directors), tightened up auditing requirements and attempted to protect minority shareholders by modifying the voting position of the banks. It has improved and clarified the rules relating to disclosure (as did the British Act of 1967) and facilitated the issue of shares to employees. West German opinion has generally welcomed these provisions as going some way towards meeting a demand for the wider distribution of property; but there has been disappointment in some quarters that the new Law has not done anything to widen the concept or practice of co-partnership. All these questions are fully discussed in the French and German sections of this book.

If Germany and France are the leading examples among Continental European countries of those that have put some, at least, of their aspirations into effect, three others—Belgium, Holland and Italy—appear to be on the way to enacting new legislation, with the two former moving towards the German two-board system.

BELGIAN LAW AND PROPOSALS FOR REFORM

Belgian legislation on limited liability companies dates back to as long ago as 1872 and has not been changed since. Management has, however, been restricted in its freedom by later social and economic legislation and by agreements reached in the 'National Joint Committees'[1] concerning, for instance, works councils, union representations, collective agreements, social security, shut-downs, accounting and auditing. It is now generally believed that company law as such has been overtaken by events and has become out of date. Some people consider that the most serious problems stem from the fact that the present law considers the enterprise as a capital association and that as a result the entire management structure is looked at from a capitalistic viewpoint. The new outlook of the second half of the twentieth century would stress the importance of the people who devote the greater part of their lives to the company that employs them and would change the law accordingly. The legal status of the enterprise should be reconsidered in its fundamentals, the essential structure of its functions and purpose; new legislation should give proper attention and recognition to all parties involved. The opposing 'neo-liberal' view is not, of course, without its spokesmen in Belgium. The proposals of the company law reform committee are generally of this persuasion. (See below, pp. 21 and 22 and also Appendix A.)

Several attempts at reform were made following the depression of the 1930s. These proposals were particularly concerned with the structure and competence of a firm's managing bodies, auditing, the protection of minority shareholders and disclosure. Because of the war the proposals came to nothing. Nevertheless, the debate on the reorganisation of the economic system continued during the wartime years and led to a so-called 'Social Pact'. With the coming of peace several legislative measures were introduced, concerning the legal recognition and general application of social security for workers and employees in the private sector (1944); the establishment of the 'joint committees' and collective agreements (1945); the setting up of the Central Economic Council (*Conseil Central de l'Economie*), committees for specific sectors of industry (*Conseils Professionnels*) and works councils (*Conseils d'Entreprise*) (1948), and the National Council for Labour Relations (*Conseil National du Travail*) (1951).

A Bill on the revision of company law was introduced in July 1947 by the then Chairman of the Christian Democratic Party. Some of its proposals were embodied in new legislation on auditing in 1953; but the rest of the Bill met with considerable opposition from the employers' organisations, while the trade unions showed an unexpected lack of enthusiasm (see Appendix A). The Bill as a whole failed to win a parliamentary majority.

There has been much evidence of new interest in the last few years. Its origins can be traced to a number of factors. The falling growth rate of the economy and high unemployment from 1955 to 1960 highlighted the role and responsibility of business in the economy. Secondly, there has been time to assess the results of the first reforms of the post-war years, the value of which, particularly those concerning works councils and the new auditing

---

[1] These committees consist of an equal number of employers and employees. Their terms of reference cover broadly the field of wages and working conditions. No agreement can be reached without the consent of all the members. The eighty committees set up after the war cover the most important sectors of the economy.

system, has been questioned. Thirdly, quite apart from serious concern over obsolete Belgian legislation, the need to harmonise the company law of the EEC member states has stimulated further thinking.

Although no parliamentary initiative has been taken, a company law reform committee (made up of lawyers) has been sitting since 1952. The subcommittee in charge of the reform of the limited liability company has completed its report and some of its thinking has emerged in the publications of one of the committee members. Among the more important proposals and attitudes are the following:

(i) The legal form of limited liability would be required only in the case of companies with a capital of more than BFrs. 1 mn.

(ii) Co-management within the statutory directing bodies of the company—the management board and the supervisory board (*Conseil de gestion* and *Conseil de surveillance*) (see (iv), below)—is rejected. Co-management could be considered only at plant level, since the company's functions are limited to the raising of capital, its appropriation to specific ends and its administration. The committee appears to think that interests within the company are never really at loggerheads and that existing administrative managements are capable of ironing out any conflicts that may occur. Those in charge of the company's management are accountable to capital suppliers only.

(iii) The committee nevertheless recognises that interests of employees and the company are not the same and are often quite opposed to each other. If representatives of both groups are to meet to discuss their problems, such confrontations should be organised not within the legal framework of the company but through official industrial organisations and works councils.

(iv) Following the example of certain foreign legislations, a distinction between 'active' and 'passive' directors is recommended. The former would be fully engaged in the management of the company, while the latter would have a supervisory or advisory function, representing some financial interests only. The active directors would form the management board (*conseil de gestion*) and the passive the supervisory (*conseil de surveillance*). The composition, appointment procedure, competence and remuneration of these boards would be different.

(v) The management board would consist of one or more members and would possibly take collegiate form. Its members would be in charge of all acts necessary to attain the objectives of the company, which they would represent. The law or the company's articles could determine the acts which could be performed by the management only with the approval of the general meeting of shareholders which could have certain powers reserved to it. (The general meeting, however, would no longer be the most important company organ as it still is under the present law.) The number of these 'administrative' directors would be fixed by the company's articles or by the supervisory board. They would be appointed by the supervisory board, or, at the formation of the company, by the memorandum of association. Their remuneration would be decided by the supervisory board; they could perhaps receive a share in net profits. Simultaneous membership of both boards would be illegal.

(vi) The supervisory board would consist of at least three members, appointed by the general meeting of shareholders, or, at the formation of the company, by the memorandum of association. It would supervise the management board but would not have the right to interfere directly with the running of the firm. In some cases it would have to authorise acts *a priori* or approve *a posteriori*.

(vii) The committee proposes no important modifications with regard to the general meeting of shareholders—an omission significant in itself. A number of technical improvements are, however, suggested, concerning, for instance, the nullity of general meeting decisions. The restriction of single shareholder voting rights to those holding one fifth or two fifths (see reference to Art. 76 of the Commercial Code at p. 179 below) of the votes would be dropped, as would the present ban on voting agreements between members of the general meeting. The powers of the general meeting to modify the company's articles would be extended to make possible (under certain conditions) a change in the company's form without interruption of its incorporation, the transfer of its registered office to another country, its merger with a foreign company and insertion into its articles of provisions limiting the transfer of shares. The committee has also proposed that shareholders representing at least one twentieth of the paid-up capital should be able to lodge a complaint against the management board on the grounds of error in management; and that information provided for shareholders and the general public should be broadened and improved by: (*a*) definition of the principles of accountability for acts done by the company; (*b*) regulations concerning the drawing up of the balance sheet and the profit and loss account; and (*c*) an obligatory statement and justification of the method used to determine the balance sheet items and the calculation of the provision for depreciation and of the reserves. The committee has clearly pinned a great deal of faith on revitalising the shareholders' general meeting which, it obviously believes, would be better able to hold the balance between the various parties concerned if the proposed reforms were put into effect.

IDEAS FROM THE NETHERLANDS

A committee, under the chairmanship of Professor Verdam, was set up by the Dutch government in 1960 to go into the question of whether the legal form of enterprises in the Netherlands needed to be reformed. It was asked to pay special attention to the management and supervision of large enterprises and to the public accountability of firms. The Verdam Committee reported in 1964 and among its proposals were a draft bill to provide for broader disclosure provisions and legal methods whereby interested parties could compel companies to improve their presentation of accounts in accordance with the law. The committee also looked at wider questions: by a bare majority, it decided in favour of employee representation on supervisory boards, while a minority of its members thought that the supervisory board should include at least one representative of the public interest. There is not much support for this latter suggestion; some form of external public control is acceptable, within limits, but public opinion seems to be wary of internal control being wielded by outside appointees. Accordingly, the committee put forward suggestions for widening the present right to demand a public enquiry into the conduct of a business by its management and for setting up a special division of the Court of Appeal (an *Ondernemingskamer*) to hear disputes about annual accounts. The committee's specific proposals are outlined in the relevant Dutch sections of this book. Its approach has been noticeably speedier and more radical than that of its Belgian neighbour.

LAW AND REFORM IN ITALY

The 'sovereignty of the shareholder' is clear from any study of Italian company law. It is equally clear that this principle is not reflected in current practice. Over the years shares have been widely spread among small investors and it has become common to give proxies to the bank where the shares are deposited. This has encouraged the formation of controlling groups which can govern a company with only a small percentage of shares—statistics show that from 11 to 15 per cent is enough. The majority principle is adulterated: the shareholders who need protection are not a minority but a majority, by number and by amount of capital subscribed. Moreover, it is evident that the division between shareholders as mere investors and those who want some control of the company and its directors calls for a reconsideration of the shareholders' role. More generally, many Italians believe that the place of the company itself in the economic and social setting and its objectives and structure must be looked at afresh. There is much criticism of the fact that both large and small joint stock companies (*Società per azioni*) come under an identical regime. It is thought that any reform of the SpA must start by distinguishing between the two classes of firms and resolving the different problems that occur. In addition, a rethinking of company organisation, even if strictly limited to internal problems, cannot avoid taking into account other types of enterprise and, in general, the economic system in which companies work—above all a system like the Italian, where there is a large and powerful public sector. The possibility of future EEC legislation has also undoubtedly influenced the debate on company law reform in Italy. Some people think it would be wise to delay reform until Community decisions can be taken into account; but the majority view is that an uncertain prospect must not hold up any moves for reform in Italy, any more than it has in Germany or France, whose example has also swayed Italian thinking. France and Germany are traditionally the two countries which have most influenced Italian legislation and what is done there is always followed with great interest.

This does not, of course, mean that the Italian debate started only after the French and Germans got to work. Nearly fifteen years ago Professor Ascarelli anticipated most of the solutions now generally accepted: the need for more disclosure and a tighter check on the activities of directors, stiffer control of holding and financial companies, modernisation of the stock exchange, and so on. He acknowledged the decline of shareholder democracy, but—although his political views were radical—he thought the best solution was to try to halt the decline and to keep the power to govern the company in the shareholders' hands. He also believed that, although the gap between large and small companies was increasing, their basic problems were still common and that a reform should consider the matter as one. His writings and activities[2] were important factors in the company reform debate. He and the political and cultural groups he took part in (especially the small republican and radical party, the socialists, and the *Amici del Mondo* group) organised many meetings and study groups, and directly or indirectly inspired a series of parliamentary projects on SpA reform,[3] although, together with others in a narrower field,[4] they never won parliamentary approval. The writings of Professor Ferri[5] were influential in advancing other opinions, especially on the need to distinguish between the problems of the large and small SpA. There was also a general feeling that more thought should be given to small investors and the spread of share ownership at all levels of society.[6]

At this point of the debate, the government began to pay more attention to the matter and a committee was set up in 1959 by the Ministry of Industry to prepare a draft on company reform.[7] Nothing happened until the centre-

[2] Prof. Ascarelli's writings include: 'Proprietà e controllo della ricchezza', in *Studi di diritto comparato e in tema d'interpretazione*, Milan, 1952; 'Considerazioni in tema di società e personalità giuridica', *Rivista di diritto commerciale*, 1954, I, p. 426; 'Disciplina delle SpA e legge antimonopolistica', in *Problemi giuridici*, Vol. II, Milan, 1959; 'I problemi delle società anonime per azioni', *Rivista delle società*, 1956, p. 3. Professor Ascarelli founded the *Rivista delle società*, a publication entirely devoted to the problems of corporations, in 1956. He died in 1959.

[3] The most important, presented by the deputies Sig. La Malfa and Sig. Lombardi in September 1958, was published under the title *Riforma della società per azioni* in *La Riforma delle società di capitali in Italia, Progetti e Documenti*, S. Scotti-Camuzzi (ed.), Milan, 1966.

[4] Also published in Scotti-Camuzzi, op. cit.

[5] Professor Ferri's writings include: 'Potere e responsabilità nell' evoluzione della società per azioni', *Rivista delle società*, 1956, p. 35; 'La tutela dell' azionista in una prospettiva di riforma', ibid., 1961, p. 177. Professor Ferri, who teaches commercial law at the Law School of Rome University, was also a member of the Commission which drafted the reform project in 1964 and his views strongly influenced the Commission. For an, opposing, re-statement of Ascarelli's opinion, see Oppo, 'Prospettive di riforma e tutela della società per azioni', *Rivista delle società*, 1961, p. 361. See also: Auletta, 'L'ordinamento della società per azioni', ibid., 1961, p. 1; Ferrara, 'Sguardo generale sulla riforma della società di capitali', ibid., 1966, p. 1; and Visentini, 'Evoluzione e problemi della società per azioni e i lineamenti generali della riforma', ibid., 1967, p. 1.

[6] This led to some proposals with regard to the so-called *azionariato popolare* and for introducing an institution similar to investment trusts into the Italian system. A govern-ment-sponsored draft bill (*Disciplina dei fondi comuni di investimento mobiliare*, Senate, No. 763) was put forward in September 1964 but its content was later absorbed into the more general reform draft. It should be noted that the concept of *azionariato popolare* (i.e. a diffusion of shares throughout society in order to encourage small investors) is a policy quite separate from that of employee participation or co-determination; see *La diffusione della ricchezza mobiliare: investment trust e azionariato popolare*, Atti del VI convegno di studi di politica economica e finanziaria, Ancona, September 1962, organised by the Centro Italiano di studi finanziari, Milan, 1963.

[7] Among the literature published as a result of these debates, the following may be noted. Consiglio nazionale dei dottori commercialisti, *Appunti e lineamenti per la riforma della*

left government came to power in 1963; the reform of the SpA found a place in its programme. The following points were considered suitable matters for reform: the minimum capital provision (to be raised to a more realistic figure); the company's objectives (specifically, to sanction their limitation to economic activity); cross-shareholding; the regulations for shareholders' meetings; shareholders' information and disclosure in general; the protection of minority shareholders; the independence of *sindaci* (see p. 47) and the effectiveness of their control; the protection of the 'patrimonial' rights of shareholders; and the regulation of bond issues.

It was proposed that a new authority for control over quoted companies should be established, with regard to disclosure and the protection of small shareholders and investors. This authority would be dependent on the Banca d'Italia, which already has authority for the control of banks and other credit institutions. For the first time a distinction was made between large and small companies. Other proposed reforms were directed at holding companies and combines, including the introduction of an institution similar to investment trusts to overcome the difficulty of fitting the 'trust' device into the Italian system. In order to encourage wider share ownership, a special type of security was to be introduced, the so-called *azioni di risparmio* (i.e. non-voting preference shares; see p. 194), which only quoted companies would be able to issue.

The task of translating these proposals into a draft Bill was carried out by another group (the de Gregorio Committee), which eventually produced a draft extending and modifying the present legislation. This was approved by the Cabinet and examined by the Consiglio Nazionale dell' Economia e del Lavoro, which gave its opinion as required by the Constitution. Progress was delayed in 1968 following the fall of the centre–left coalition government in May of that year; but company reform again became a top priority during 1969.

The provisions of the reform draft have been thoroughly discussed by various social and economic groups and the general reaction has been favourable. In broad outline, the draft covers the areas specified in the government programme. Its 130 articles are grouped under the following headings: provisions on *società per azioni*; provisions on quoted *società per azioni*; provisions on *società a responsabilità limitata*; provisions on holding and investment companies; criminal offences; tax provisions; and temporary provisions.

legislazione delle società per azioni, Rome, 1964; Consiglio del notariato, *Studi del notariato sul progetto di riforma delle società per azioni*, Rome, 1966; *La riforma delle società per azioni*, Atti del centro italo-statunitense di studi giudiziari, Vol. I, Como, 1965 (a symposium on SpA reform held at Ravenna in September 1964); *Profili giuridici della riforma delle società per azioni*, Atti del convegno di studi economici e sociali dell' Università internazionale degli studi sociali, Rome 1963; *Problemi e prospettive delle società commerciali*, Atti del convegno indetto dall' ISLE (Rome, 16 November 1965), Milan, 1965. Reports of an Italian–German meeting on the protection of minority shareholders have been published in *Rivista del diritto commerciale*, Nos. 8–9, 1966. A very important meeting organised by the Associazione tra le società italiane per azioni (a branch of the employers' association) was held in Venice in October 1966 and was attended by Italian and foreign experts and observers of all the groups interested in the reforms. Its proceedings have been published in three volumes, *La riforma delle società di capitali in Italia: studi e dibattiti*, Milan, 1968.

In its general approach, the draft regards company law exclusively as the law governing a private group's organisation for economic activity. Very much like the Jenkins Committee in Britain, it takes the view that the only matters with which company law reform is concerned are the problems of the position of shareholders and directors within the company. Nevertheless, a certain appreciation of the market forces which may be interested in the activities of a company is evident in some of the draft's provisions. The proposals do not go beyond the existing framework of company law, which considers the company essentially as an organisation managed on behalf of its shareholders; but there is an attempt to give new strength to their position in the light of recent economic developments. Wider problems, such as the relationship of companies to public enterprises, national planning or the EEC, are not dealt with in the draft, though their existence was recognised by the authors. Nevertheless, although there is general agreement that the proposed reforms should now go through the parliamentary process as quickly as possible, there has been a revival of interest in the more general and fundamental problems of the enterprise. The Italian debate is now going beyond the reform draft.[8] (The draft's specific proposals are discussed in the Italian sections of this book.)

THE DEBATE IN BRITAIN

Britain till recently was rather slow to take part in this reconsideration of corporate enterprise. There was of course much debate about the role and control of nationalised industry, but as a thing apart rather than as one type of corporation among others. Some more general discussion took place at the end of the second world war. The Cohen Committee on Company Law, which was set up during the war, was instructed: 'to review the requirements prescribed in regard to the formation and affairs of companies and the safeguards afforded for investors and for the public interest.'[9]

The reference to the public interest is particularly striking. The Committee made far-reaching proposals, particularly on disclosure, which are now incorporated into the Companies Act of 1948, and its work was widely acclaimed as bringing in a new era in company law. The Trades Union Congress proposed that trade unionists be appointed to the boards of nationalised industries, though not as union representatives; that Industrial Boards 'composed of representatives of workpeople and employers in the industry in equal proportion' and with a government-appointed chairman, be set up to guide and regulate privately owned industries; and that consultative machinery be strengthened in public and private industry alike.[10]

Even at that time, however, reforms in the structure of private corporations were not in the centre of the political picture, nor were these corporations' traditional principles challenged. Indeed, when a further committee on company law, the Jenkins Committee, came to be appointed in 1960, company

---

[8] See Minervini, 'Società per azioni: riforma anno zero', *Rivista delle società*, 1967, p. 1280.

[9] *Report of the Committee on Company Law Amendment*, Cmd 6659, 1945, p. 2.

[10] TUC, *Postwar Reconstruction*, 1944.

law seemed to need no more than a technicians' tidying-up. (The views of the Jenkins Committee are discussed in the British sections of this book.) The 'preservationists' still held the centre of the stage. The TUC was concerned with influencing companies through consultation and negotiation or with regulating them from above, not with direct participation in their control. National planning was out of favour in the 1950s, and debates on collective bargaining and employee participation were carried on without much originality or force. Isolated voices such as those of George Goyder and L. G. B. Gower called for fundamental rethinking of the company's role and constitution; but few listened to these prophets in the wilderness and new ideas and experiments abroad were often either unknown or misunderstood. This now has changed. One factor has been better knowledge of new thinking in other countries. Another has been the sheer pressure of facts in two areas: industrial relations and national, regional and local planning.

British industrial relations have a long history, and many of their historic features have proved irrelevant to the world of fuller employment, higher educational standards and new patterns of management which emerged after 1945. Innovations made during and just after the war, for example the development of joint production committees or the provisions on consultation and employee welfare written into the post-war nationalisation Acts, have proved on the whole disappointing. By the early 1960s criticism had accumulated to a point at which change was clearly pressing and new ideas began to break through. A Royal Commission on Trade Unions and Employers' Organisations was appointed in 1964 and reported early in 1968. The whole question of the unions' role and responsibilities is now in the forefront of the British debate.

The discussion of industrial relations in the UK has tended to turn in three main directions. The first is more careful protection, if necessary by law, of employees' rights to representation and in case of dismissal or of merger and takeover. The second is 'participation through conflict': the idea of bringing together the present machinery of negotiation and consultation and strengthening it to provide at plant and enterprise level a single channel through which employees can take a more positive as well as a more powerful part in shaping their firm's policies, in the wide field traditionally open for consultation as well as the hitherto narrower field of bargaining. The TUC has been hesitant about this. The Labour Party's June 1967 report on 'Industrial Democracy', on the other hand, presents its demand for 'a single channel of representation' in capital letters and heavy type. (See also p. 204.)

Thirdly, there have been proposals for direct participation in management by employees or their representatives. These proposals come not only, as in the past, from isolated thinkers or experimenters and from the Liberal Party, but from major sectors of the labour movement. The TUC, for instance, going well beyond its proposals of 1944, has proposed to the Royal Commission on Trade Unions legislation to encourage, though not compel, the appointment of trade unionists to private as well as nationalised boards, and has pressed strongly for participation by trade unionists in bodies responsible for managerial decisions at lower levels.

The craft unions in the steel industry proposed that employee representatives should sit on the industry's management committees after nationalisation at all levels from the plant to the national board. The British Steel Corporation in due course proposed to appoint up to three part-time employee directors, nominated by the TUC after consultation with the steel unions, to the Group Boards by which the industry was to be run. These directors would serve in a personal capacity, not as union representatives, and would not be appointed to the group board by which they themselves were employed. The unions objected to both these limitations, and the Corporation agreed to drop the ban on employees serving in their own groups. On this basis the Corporation's proposal was adopted. (The final structure of the BSC is still being debated.)

Interest in concerted planning by government and industry for growth and regional development faded in the 1950s but revived at the beginning of the 1960s. It has taken shape in a number of new institutions—NEDC, Economic Development Councils for individual industries, regional Economic Councils —and in a more positive, less arm's-length working relationship between government and industry.

The implications for company law of developments in planning and industrial relations are drawn together from the Labour point of view not only in the official documents of the Labour Party and the TUC but in K. W. Wedderburn's Fabian pamphlet *Company Law Reform*, which has had a wide influence in both the Labour Party and the unions. 'The real need is for some focus of accountability for management other than the shareholder.' The shareholder in a public company should no longer be treated 'as a proprietor entitled to control', though in some companies he may still have a function in promoting efficiency and controlling management. Employees should be allowed to appear officially on the company scene: company law 'surely cannot be allowed to go on pretending that the worker is not there'. Professor Wedderburn is hesitant about employees on boards, but argues that disclosure should be extended to provide data for collective bargaining, company law should include an obligation to bargain collectively, and the pace of development of works councils should be forced. 'Among the techniques that should be investigated is the extent to which a bridgehead of employees' rights might be established in the midst of company law itself, something which might mark a new beginning in the democratisation of power.'

National economic policy (including the consumer interest) should also have its recognition. Disclosure should be designed to provide data for national policy on prices, incomes and productivity. Among methods to consider for achieving these purposes might be compulsory efficiency audits, tough enquiry powers for the Board of Trade, state-appointed directors, a special public body to regulate top management remuneration, and more effective reporting on and control over the relations between holding companies and their subsidiaries, as well as more conventional ideas for defining directors' duties and disclosing their remuneration and transactions on the lines developed in the United States by the Securities and Exchange Commission. A number of Professor Wedderburn's points are met by the Companies Act of 1967 (which is dealt with in the British sections of this book), but his suggestions about a 'focus of accountability other than the shareholders' and a 'bridgehead of employees' rights' reach well beyond the Act's scope.

The 'fundamentalist' attitude is perhaps most soberly expressed (though with no lack of vigour) in the writings of Professor Fogarty. His views have been summed up in his PEP broadsheet *A Companies Act 1970?*, written with the materials of this book to hand. He outlines a form of corporation law that would be both more unified, in that it would abolish the distinction between state and non-state enterprises, and more diffuse in that it would classify firms into three groups: 'giants', ordinary public companies and 'small', with a clear demarcation between those companies that function as single units and those that have many units, including branches or subsidiaries abroad. This would make it possible, Professor Fogarty argues, to take account of the special problems of the multi-unit firm and to protect the shareholders of subsidiaries against the misuse of controlling interests. He also advocates the setting-up of a Capital Market Commission which would go further than either the Council of the London Stock Exchange or the American SEC (for instance) in supervising the capital market and in 'providing the hard facts on which sound judgment about the general management of the capital market needs to rest'. It could also act as an 'investors' Ombudsman'. Professor Fogarty's thought appears to be something of a synthesis of the 'preservationist' and 'reformist' strands, particularly in the way he takes up the especially strong points of the former attitude and remoulds them within a generally reformist conception.

On the side of employers and managers, a sign of the times is that by 1966 a number of businessmen and industrial consultants felt the need to set up an Industrial Educational and Research Foundation specifically:

'To enable directors and senior managers to examine the principles, concepts and responsibilities underlying business decisions. Much existing management training is concerned with creating higher standards of management within the organisation. The Foundation's work will supplement this by exploring the crucial factors affecting the long-term success and status of industry and its relationship to Society.'

The Foundation's first public manifestation was a striking re-examination by the then Director-General of the Confederation of British Industry of the relationship between industry and government.[11] This is being followed by a series of seminars under the general title 'The Company and Its Responsibilities—Towards a Business Philosophy'. The programme has aroused widespread interest among businessmen and senior civil servants, on a scale which would certainly not have been found a few years ago.

The government, for its part, announced in February 1967 that it intended to bring in a new Companies Bill before the end of the present parliament. The Bill, it was said, would cover some classical issues of company law, such as the protection of minorities or the power of the Board of Trade to investigate company affairs—the Labour Party's *Industrial Democracy* proposes that Courts of Enquiry should be set up on the application of employees or

[11] J. Davies, *Industry and Government*, Sir George Earle Memorial Lecture, Industrial Educational and Research Foundation, 1966.

others as well as of shareholders, and in cases of ordinary mismanagement as well as of those approaching fraud—but possibly also the question of whether employees 'ought not to have a more settled place or places on the board of directors of the company by which they are employed than English law allows them now'.[12] As mentioned in the Preface, such a 'fundamental' Bill can now scarcely be put to the present parliament though there are signs that a great deal of thinking (prompted, in large part, by the continuing stream of mergers, proposed and effected) is going on, both in Whitehall and in the Labour Party. The response to the government's call for a general debate on the matter has been disappointing. Nevertheless, it is striking that whereas a few years ago, at the time of the Jenkins Committee, the fact that a proposal for company reform was novel or fundamental was enough to rule it out of consideration (even on the Left), today this is ceasing to be so. Proposals for fundamental change, whether in the interests of the efficiency of firms and the economy or of the satisfaction of employees and the community, are now taken more seriously by more people.

NEW THOUGHTS FOR OLD

Fresh approaches are found in the newer as well as the older industrial countries, and in the East as well as the West. In Japan many major companies grew up under a combination of state direction and protection and tight family control. Now their managements are coming out from under the umbrella and learning to live, though as yet with no very clear view of where they are going, in a world of freer competition, widely dispersed shareholding, greater labour mobility and effective trade unions. In India the Companies Act of 1956 contained new and to Western eyes startling provisions for public control over the appointment and remuneration of managing directors and agents. The socialist countries have been moving from a centrally directed, autocratically managed economy towards one which relies much more on the market and leaves workers with more freedom to bargain with management or, as in Yugoslavia, to control it directly. This has begun to throw up problems of corporate organisation and finance of a sort hitherto more familiar in the West. A manager's role is of one kind in a 'command' economy and of quite another in an economy like that of Yugoslavia where he has to meet the competition of a relatively free market and to conciliate the interests of employees and local authorities who have the power and freedom to make their influence felt. In a command economy the state directs investment and can bring political power to bear if it thinks invested funds are misused. In an economy like that of present-day Yugoslavia something much more like a free capital market emerges. A good deal of cross-investment is needed between enterprises and public authorities below the level of the state. In a market economy it has to be induced, not commanded, and investors cannot automatically bring state power to their aid. If they are to invest with confidence in risky enterprises they must have rights of oversight and control of their own. In these circumstances there are signs that a relationship may emerge between socialist investing institutions and socialist

[12] Lord Chancellor, *House of Lords Debates*, 22 November 1966, col. 136.

firms very like that between private investors and firms in the West, and this quite apart from any question of attracting the interest of private investors from within the socialist countries or from abroad.

These developments, whether in the East or the West, have of course given rise to much controversy as well as being the outcome of it. Many of them have been coloured with ideology, history, or a mixture of the two. Special pleading by particular interest groups is as common in this field as in any other. Those for whom the shoe pinches hardest or who are closest to a problem tend to lead in calling for solutions. Trade unions are naturally more likely than shareholders' associations to call for more employee participation. Company lawyers show an interest in the refinements of *ultra vires* which few others share.

On the other hand, it is noteworthy that pressure for change in the law and practice of corporations has come from many different sources, conservatively minded lawyers and economists, shareholders' associations, radical politicians, trade unionists and, in some countries, the clergy. One cannot say that it is the Right and the employers who put forward 'preservationist' reforms such as the technical tidying up of traditional company law while the Left and the trade unions press for more far-reaching measures of employee participation and public control. In France the most radical thinking about employee participation and public control, and indeed about the reform of classical company law itself, has come not from the Left and the unions but from the technical and managerial elite, whether in business or in the civil service, and from nationalist politicians supporting General de Gaulle. German employers' associations part company with German unions on the question whether employees should have equal representation with shareholders on supervisory boards, but otherwise hold views about employees on boards, about statutory works councils, including councils' rights to information and to appeal to outside arbitration on issues such as major redundancy, and about employee shareholding, which would seem decidedly left-wing elsewhere in the West.

It may be, when everyone has had his say, that what will finally emerge will be not a distortion of the development of the corporation by this or that interest or ideology but the progressive adaptation of businesses and of those who manage, regulate and influence them to the actual logic of a mixed economy in which many interests have to be reconciled and both competition and planning have a part. Certainly, East European businesses have moved towards a more Western pattern, not because their leaders have turned capitalist, but because a market economy has proved useful in a socialist as well as a capitalist framework and its logic has to be respected. Similarly, American corporations are recognising a distinct 'public affairs function' not because they have turned socialist but because a large corporation in a modern economy inevitably develops a network of relationships with governments (at home or abroad), local authorities, and a wide range of other social institutions. These relationships like any other branch of management must be handled in an expert and organised way. They have also to be co-ordinated, for a company, whether it intends to or not, develops an overall image which influences customers, recruits and its own standing with public authorities.

In neither the East nor the West is the move towards more participative forms of management simply or even primarily the outcome of a battle for control between opposing classes and groups, though this has played its part. It rests on a new valuation of autonomy and self-administration as against bureaucracy and as a factor essential to long-term efficiency in a rapidly changing economy.

It would be comforting if one could be confident that such a new evaluation would lead to a humane and rational convergence of capitalism and socialism, a best of all possible business worlds. There are, to be sure, signs of a new flexibility on both sides and of moves in this direction. But men (fortunately and usually foolishly) always believe they are witnessing the dawn of a new era and that the answers are within their grasp. The truth of the matter is, indeed, that answers are within our grasp—but that the debate will never be over. The 'spectrum' will last as long as the rainbow and the red shift and in the years to come there will be scholars and 'men of action' as learned, eager and imaginative as those whose writings fill the many pages that follow.

Part I

CORPORATE DISTINCTIONS

Chapter I

THE DIFFERENT FORMS OF PRIVATE ENTERPRISE

What distinctions are made between different forms of private enterprise with regard to objectives, constitution and the degree of external control? Should companies be classed according to their size? How is it determined which enterprises are more suitably organised as companies and which in other forms such as partnerships or public corporations? What changes in current law and practice have been advocated?

BELGIUM

Lines between different classes of company are not drawn on the basis of objectives, size or external control, but mainly on the purely legalistic grounds of the limited or unlimited liability of the shareholders and of the restricted or unrestricted transferability of shares. Moreover, the differentiation between companies and partnerships under civil or commercial law is based on the legal distinction between acts which are deemed 'civil' and those deemed 'commercial', the latter being defined in Arts. 2 and 3 of the Code on Commercial Companies. In short, a company whose purpose is the accomplishment of commercial acts is a commercial company.

The present legal form of the Belgian limited liability company (*société anonyme*) is briefly as follows.

The general meeting of shareholders (*assemblée générale*) is its most important organ. Powers not given by law or by the articles to any of the other organs remain with the general meeting which has the widest power to carry out or ratify all acts concerning the company. (Code on Commercial Companies (CCC) Art. 70.) The company is managed by a board of at least three directors (*administrateurs*) directly accountable to the general meeting. This board has the power to accomplish all acts for the management of the company and to represent it before the courts. (CCC Art. 54.) The daily management of the company, and the power to represent it in respect of such

35

daily management, may be entrusted to managers (*directeurs*) whose appointment, dismissal and powers are regulated in the company's articles of association. (CCC Art. 63.) At least one auditor (*commissaire*) must be appointed by the general meeting to supervise the accounts (CCC Arts. 64 and 65) and in quoted companies at least one auditor must be a member of the Institute of Company Auditors (*Institut des reviseurs d'entreprises*). (For the reality, as opposed to the form, see p. 143 below.)

Employees are represented within the enterprise through works councils (*conseils d'entreprise*) set up by the law of 20 September 1948. A council is obligatory in all firms which regularly employ 150 people. Its main aim is to promote a spirit of collaboration between employer and employees. It is entitled to receive regular information on the position of the firm and is also authorised to decide on certain matters relating to working conditions. In all companies regularly employing fifty people a health and safety committee (the full title is *comité de sécurité, d'hygiène et d'embellissement des ateliers*) must be established by the employer. (Statute of 10 June 1952 and Art. 832 of the General Regulations on Labour Protection.) Like the works councils, these committees are composed of an employers' delegation and elected representatives of the employees. Trade union representation within the firm was settled by the National Agreement of 17 June 1947. The actual setting up of the union delegations in each firm is organised by the National Joint Committee of each individual sector (see Introduction, p. 20 above). In principle, a body of union representatives may be established in any firm which meets the requirements for the establishment of a health and safety committee. Its main task is to negotiate with the management on wage problems and related issues and to represent employees as individuals or groups. (Questions arising from these arrangements and proposals for their reform are dealt with in the Belgian sections of the chapters that follow. The suggestions of the company law reform committee are summarised in the Introduction, pp. 21 and 22 above.)

BRITAIN

British law has a wide variety of forms of business organisation. Palmer's Company Law[1] lists ten types of company permitted by the Companies Acts, as well as a variety of companies created in special ways.[2] Of these forms the most important are companies limited by shares. Since the Companies Act 1967 came into force, there remain only two types of such companies—'public' and 'private'. This distinction is not the same as that between a 'quoted' and an 'unquoted' company, since there is no legal compulsion on any company to seek a Stock Exchange quotation for its shares. The main differences are those of restrictions on the size of membership and limited transferability of

---

[1] 21st ed., p. 20. Before the abolition of the exempt private company by the Companies Act 1967 Sec. 2, there were eleven types of company available; see Palmer, *Company Law*, 20th ed., p. 20.

[2] Of the companies created in special ways those created by Royal Charter, known as common law corporations, are perhaps the most important. It appears that there are 46 such companies still trading, some of great significance such as the Hudson's Bay Company and the British South Africa Company.

shares. The qualification for the status of a private company are set out in Sec. 28 of the 1948 Act[3]—the company must contain in its articles of association a limitation on the maximum number of shareholders to fifty, with exceptions for employees past and present, a restriction on the transferability of shares, and a prohibition on invitations to the public to subscribe for shares or debentures. Any company whose articles of association do not contain these restrictions is a public company.

The idea behind this distinction appears to have been to provide a comprehensive set of rules to protect shareholders in companies, but to exclude from such regulations small family companies, formed largely for tax purposes, where matters are dealt with on the basis of mutual trust and understanding and where observance of the rules might prove unduly burdensome and expensive. However, it is now generally accepted that this distinction is unsatisfactory and does not provide an adequate dividing line between large and small companies, especially as there is no restriction placed upon the capital of a private company. Many companies with fewer than fifty members have large resources and employ large numbers of people, and cannot be regarded as 'family companies'. The feeling appears to be growing that it is time for a fundamental reconsideration of this problem. It is not satisfactory to have only one set of rules for all companies with certain companies having exemptions from complying with certain rules. It is probably more appropriate to have a variety of companies each type being governed by its own laws, thus providing a more flexible framework for the development of rules, instead of one general law complicated by arbitrary and unsatisfactory exceptions and limitations.[4]

Under the present law a private company is under the same obligation as a public company, except that it need have only two shareholders instead of seven, one director instead of two; its directors are not subject to compulsory retirement at seventy years of age; it does not need a trading certificate to commence business; it need not hold a statutory meeting; and proxies may speak as well as vote at its meetings.

All companies, with limited liability, whether public or private, must prepare an annual return which must be sent to the Registrar of Companies within two days after the annual general meeting. To this must be attached a profit and loss account, a balance sheet and reports by the directors and by independent auditors. The purpose of these regulations is to reveal to members, creditors and the public the financial state of the company, and the information which must be revealed has been extended by the Companies Act 1967.

The annual return[5] must set out the address of the company's registered office, a summary of its issued and nominal capital; a statement of the total indebtedness of the company where these debts are secured by charges; a list of persons who have ceased to be members and of shares transferred during

---

[3] See Companies Act 1948 Table A Part II.

[4] To some extent it might be said that this need has been recognised in the development of special rules for companies engaged in banking and insurance. But even here the special rules are grafted upon the general structure without any attempt to create a wholly separate body of law for such companies.

[5] Companies Act 1948 Sec. 124 and Sixth Schedule.

the year; and every third year a full list of the names and addresses of all members of the company and the number of shares that each of them holds; and details of the names, addresses, nationality of directors and secretaries.

The profit and loss account[6] is designed to reveal the company's income and expenditure. The 1967 Act provides that it must set out the company's turnover where this exceeds £50,000 in the year and the method by which it is calculated. Loans to certain officers must be disclosed. The chairman's emoluments must be stated, as well as income of employees receiving more than £10,000 a year. The aggregate amount of remuneration paid to directors must appear as a scale dividing directors' remuneration into bands of £2,500 and showing the number of directors whose emoluments fell between the upper and lower limits of each band. The company's income from quoted and unquoted investments from land must be stated separately for each source. Expenditure must include hire charges for plant, depreciation, corporation tax and interest on loans, overdrafts and so on. Dividends must be shown before deduction of tax. Details of shareholdings in subsidiary companies must be made known, but the Board of Trade may consent to the withholding of this information if the subsidiaries are incorporated or carrying on business abroad and disclosure would be harmful to the group; and where the details would be of excessive length.

The balance sheet requirements are designed to reveal the net worth of the company. It must set out under separate headings fixed assets with details of their acquisition and disposal during the year, and a note if they will not realise a sum equal to their value as shown in the balance sheet; current assets such as stock and work in progress, and assets which are neither fixed nor current; together with details of quoted and unquoted investments with a note of their current market value; of land held; of loans other than from banks and of tax reserves.

The directors' report[7] must include details of any significant changes in the fixed assets of the company or of any of its subsidiaries in the year, and the market value of each asset if it differs substantially from the value stated in the balance sheet, the reasons for making any issue of new shares or debentures during the year, the number issued and the consideration received; particulars of any contract significant to the company's business entered into by the company during the year; and details of shares acquired by directors or arrangements made to enable them to acquire shares. It must also reveal the different classes of business carried on by the company during the year, and the proportions in which the turnover is divided among the classes, and the extent to which each class contributed to the profit or loss of the company during the year. If the turnover exceeds £50,000 during the year, the directors' report must state the value of goods exported from the United Kingdom by the company and its subsidiaries; and where more than 100 people are employed it must state the average number of employees in Britain each week, and their aggregate remuneration per week. Political and charitable

---

[6] Companies Act 1948 Sec. 197 and Eighth Schedule and Companies Act 1967 Sections 6–9 and Second Schedule. If these matters do not appear in the accounts, there must be annexed to the accounts a document setting out this information.

[7] Companies Act 1967 Sections 16–18.

contributions exceeding in aggregate £50 must be disclosed. Most of these facts require disclosure under the 1967 Act which significantly extended the requirements.

The only means of avoiding this comprehensive disclosure and retaining the advantages of corporate form is to go 'unlimited' (as the retail group C & A has done) or to give up the corporate form and make use of one of the other forms of business organisation. In practice most companies will submit to the new requirements since these, on the whole, merely bring the law into line with the recommendations and requirements which the Stock Exchange Council had already imposed upon public companies quoted on the London Stock Exchange.

Apart from the limited liability company, there remain as forms of private enterprise in Britain the sole trader, partnership and the retail cooperative society.[8] The first of these is *ipso facto* a very small undertaking with few if any employees other than relatives. Partnerships may take either of two forms—an ordinary[9] or a limited partnership.[10] The former of these is rare apart from professional activities such as solicitors, chartered surveyors, consultant engineers, architects or accountants where professional etiquette forbids the use of the corporate form, although the changes in the tax structure under the Finance Act 1965 has resulted in a slight increase in this form. The limited partnership has never been popular although it offers the benefits of limited liability. The reasons for this lack of interest appear to be that there must be at least one partner whose liability is not limited, and that any partner whose liability is limited cannot participate in the management of the business and should he do so he loses the benefits of limited liability.

The co-operative varies in size, although the organisation controlled by the Co-operative Wholesale Society is large enough to deserve the name of 'big business'. However, because of their constitution their affairs are made known to every member but no member may exercise more than one vote no matter how many shares he may hold.

The sole legal criterion for deciding whether the corporate form is necessary is that it is unlawful for twenty or more persons to carry on any business with a view to gain unless it is registered as a company under the Companies Acts.[11] To this general principle there are two exceptions: certain professions may be carried on by more than twenty persons[12] and in the case of a banking business the maximum is ten persons.

For the purpose of this book the private enterprise company, both public and private, and the public corporation or nationalised industry form the only two constitutions in business that come under scrutiny. The latter is discussed below in Chapter 2 (pp. 61 ff).

---

[8] During the late nineteenth century there appears to have been an embryonic form of mutual trading fund or trading trust; see, e.g., *Smith v. Anderson* (1880) 15 Ch. D 247. But there appears to have been some doubt as to the legality of such associations; they were wound up and the experiment has not been repeated.

[9] Partnership Act 1890.

[10] Limited Partnerships Act 1907.

[11] 1948 Act Sec. 434.

[12] 1967 Act Sec. 120; these are partnerships of solicitors, accountants and stockbrokers.

French legislation on commercial companies, as amended by the new law of July 1966, distinguishes between five different basic forms:

(i) The *société en nom collectif* (SNC). This may be formed by two partners only. No capital minimum is laid down. The partners are left in great freedom to nominate executives, whose powers are fixed by the statutes and who can never be said to have acted *ultra vires* with regard to third persons. Precise methods of control of the administration of the company have been instituted under the new law. The partners are all entirely, indefinitely, jointly and severally responsible for the company's debts.

(ii) The *société en commandite simple* (SCS). This also may be formed by two partners only and is not kept to any minimum capital. The financing partners are solely and indefinitely responsible for the company's debts, any sleeping partners' liability being limited to the amount of their own contributions. The partners' right of control over company documents is now regulated.

(iii) The *société à responsibilité limitée* (SARL). This must have at least two partners and, under the new law, 50 at the most. Its minimum capital is fixed at Fr. 20,000 (formerly Fr. 10,000). Control and publicity have been reinforced. Above a certain capital the presence of an auditor is necessary. Many features are borrowed from the joint stock company.

(iv) The *société anonyme* (SA). The joint stock company. There is a distinction between quoted and unquoted companies. In the first case, the minimum capital is set at Fr. 100,000 and in the second at Fr. 5 million. At least seven persons must always be involved. Under the law of July 1966, an SA may adopt either a single-board or two-board structure. (See pp. 151 ff).

(v) The *société en participation* is secret and does not in principle have to be revealed to third persons. It exists only in the reports which the partners circulate among themselves and does not have to disclose anything about itself.

The French debates and proposals on company reform have been largely concerned with *sociétés anonymes*. This type of company, however, represents only a minority of French businesses: there are about 60,000 SA as against approximately twice as many limited liability companies (SARL) out of more than 770,000 industrial establishments all told. In terms of labour force, the SA employ about 4,700,000 persons, private companies some 2,440,000 and SARL and other forms of company around 2 million. (There were altogether 14,071,000 wage-earners in France according to figures quoted by the Mathey Report in 1966.) In order to improve information and control, J. Dubois[13] has proposed making the status of joint stock company (SA) and a stock exchange quotation obligatory for every commercial company employing more than 500 persons. The CJP (see Appendix C for French abbreviations) would like to see the same regime applied to family and joint stock companies.[14]

[13] *Perspectives*, No. 977, 7 May 1966.

[14] M. Brissier, *Réflexions et propositions sur le livre de M. Bloch-Lainé* Pour une réforme de l'entreprise, Bureau d'Etudes du Centre des Jeunes Patrons, October 1963.

(a) *The commercial company in German company law*

Whenever labour or capital is pooled in order to accomplish tasks beyond the personal or economic capabilities of an individual, the participants may resort to various organisational forms provided for by the law. They may choose to avail themselves of a form of law concerned with a common purpose applying to all the members in common, without a new legal entity being set up, or of a form which goes further than the separate legal realm of the individual members and establishes a corporate body independent in its own right. The legal organisation of common interests thus determines whether the new 'community' has a separate personality or not.

The open trading company (OHG), the limited liability partnership (KG), the shipping company and the older unions laid down by General Prussian Land Law are economic 'communities' without legal personality. The joint stock company (AG), the limited liability partnership issuing shares (KGaA), the limited liability company (GmbH), the co-operative society, the insurance company and the newer unions of the General Prussian Mining Law are among the communities which have legal personality.

This important distinction is, however, only one of many. In the commercial field, where the OHG, KG, AG, KGaA and the GmbH are easily the most important forms, the distinction between 'private' and 'capital' companies is especially important from both the legal and economic points of view. It must not, however, be overlooked that these are ideal stereotypes, which may take various hybrid and marginal forms according to whether 'private' or 'capital' elements are in the ascendant. German company law is extremely flexible in its differentiation.

At the centre of the private company stand the individually responsible partners, whose membership is essentially not transferable without the approval of the other partners. The partners have, severally, rights and duties and for this reason the private company is usually a company in the narrower sense and dispenses with a legal personality. Its purest form is the OHG. Private companies, together with one-man businesses, account for more than 90 per cent of German commercial firms. Their significance lies not only in their numbers (which proves, as Bühler writes, how very much the 'personal, wholly involved and fully liable element . . . is still intact in the German economy'), but also in the fact that they provide for the livelihood of a good two thirds of all employed persons.

Despite this, these remarks will be limited to 'capital' companies which account for only some 7 per cent of the overall number of firms and not quite 30 per cent of employees, because it is these which 'are particularly characteristic of the economy in the modern industrial state and are to a certain extent its representative phenomenon' (Hueck). Increasing concentration and the growth of international links are taking place almost exclusively between capital companies, whose form emphasises not the personality of the individual partners but the sharing of capital and is therefore best suited to satisfying the growing need for capital in modern industrial conditions. The capital company is most clearly embodied in the AG, which, with the GmbH, plays a dominant role in the life of the German economy, while the KGaA has not made much headway.

(b) *The legal nature, history and economic significance of the AG*

According to the definition of Sec. 1 of the Company Act, the AG is a company with its own legal personality, whose partners have made a contribution to the basic capital, which is itself divided into shares. The liability of the company to its creditors can be guaranteed only by the property of the company. For this reason one of the most important principles of company law is to secure the preservation of company property which is commensurate with the basic capital. This means primarily that pure profit is shown on the balance sheet only when the sum of the assets exceeds that of the debts and basic capital. The quoted sum of the basic capital thus symbolises a guarantee to the creditor, who runs relatively greater risk with a juridical body than he would with a private company. As a juridical body the AG needs specific organs for the exercise of its appropriate independent rights. While the shareholders, as a rule, can exercise their rights only at the general meeting, the AG itself is managed both externally and internally by its board of directors (*Vorstand*), which has both representative powers and administrative authority. Between the general meeting and the directors is placed a third organ, the supervisory board (*Aufsichsrat*), whose chief tasks are the appointment and dismissal of directors and the continuous supervision of their activities. The three organs are established by law; but the actual outcome of the relationship between them will vary from company to company and will depend very largely on the allocation of the share capital dividends and the various constellations of power which result. In addition, it is one of the essential guiding principles of company law to face up to the difficulties which may possibly arise from this situation and to give appropriate protection to recognised interests within the firm and to its shareholders.

It has, moreover, taken a century of legal and economic development to bring, by strict regulation, the always vulnerable rights of shareholders, creditors and other interests within the firm as a whole into a stable relationship. Although the legal origins of the AG go back to the rise of the great trading companies in the seventeenth and eighteenth centuries, the business with a hugely increasing need for capital made its appearance only at the time when industrialisation was beginning in the early nineteenth century. As parliament was reluctant to intervene, abuses spread and much harm was caused to gullible or inexperienced investors. The first comprehensive codification of company law was introduced within the framework of the *Allgemeines Deutsches Handelsgesetzbuch* about the middle of the nineteenth century. The state concession system, which had applied until then, was dissolved by the company law amendment of 1870 and replaced by the observation of minimum legal requirements. But even after this, the history of the AG, especially in its early years, remained the history of its scandals. For this reason, the amendment of 1884 brought in more specific provisions for founding firms and a considerable strengthening of the influence of the shareholders. This was done by means of the general meeting, which it was intended to make the highest decision-making body in the firm. The principle of the separation of functions between the capital contributor and the entrepreneur, which was built into the idea of the AG, prevented this intention from being put into practice. The Act of 1937 once again transferred the *de jure* administration of the firm to the directors and this principle was not affected by the company law reform of 1965. The economic necessity of leaving the management of a big modern firm to experts and people acquainted in detail with the many-sided problems involved was reflected in the strong legal position of the directors. The desire to make the supervisory board effective and to give a little more weight to the general meeting also paved the way towards a balance of functions appropriate to contemporary economic and social conditions.

The economic significance of the AG lies in its basic purpose of raising a large fund of assets by the contributions of many shareholders, in order to bring them into a capital unity for profitable ends. This applies equally to capital appeals to the general public and to the combination of economically linked businesses. The legal nature of the share, with its double function as an instrument for raising money and as a bearer of rights of control, is of decisive significance.

From this basic conception the AG has progressively emerged as the typical form of the large modern capital-intensive business. It was only natural that many provisions of the new Act of 1965—those for example, concerned with balance sheet audits or the need for greater disclosure—should be directed at big firms. A glance at the development of investment in Germany reveals, however, that the tendency of the AG to grow large began relatively late—after the world economic crisis of 1929–31—and has since gathered momentum. It has continued, uninfluenced by political or economic changes. Symptomatic of this is the decrease in the number of AG and a simultaneous increase in their total capital. If there were still about 11,000 AG in 1930 with a total capital of some 24 milliard RM and an average nominal capital of 2·2 million RM, the number fell steadily during the 30s and 40s to reach 2,673 by 1954 when the total capital exceeded 20 milliard DM and nominal capital averaged 8 million DM (Bühler). At the beginning of 1965 the number of AG in the Federal Republic (including West Berlin) had fallen to 2,541 while their total capital, averaging 16·5 million DM, had grown to 41·8 milliard DM. In 1960 (according to Hueck) there were among the 100 largest businesses, on a basis of turnover, 79 AG, 13 GmbH, three KG, one OHG and one individual business; of the 1,000 largest businesses the corresponding figures were 440, 229, 143, 36 and 38. True, the smaller AG has not completely disappeared but its economic significance has much diminished—a development, incidentally, which has taken place in all Western countries. In Germany, however, it is expected that the capital significance of the AG will continue to grow, while the most important amalgamations will take place, for the most part, between AG. Since the promulgation of the new Act there has been a tendency for the small AG to convert into a GmbH or a KG; this will further decrease the overall number of AG and makes it still clearer that this is the legal form appropriate to big and 'mammoth' businesses. Similarly, the position of the second most important capital company, the GmbH, will also become clearer as it emerges as the typical form for small and medium-sized capital companies.

(c) *The legal and economic characteristics of the GmbH*

Unlike the AG, which is the result of historical development, the GmbH was established by parliament in 1892 without any historical model, although some of its elements were taken over from the AG (cf. Hueck). The legal provisions for investment, much tightened following the experience of the early years, and a series of strict regulations concerning the annual balance sheet, were already in existence for businesses which appealed to a wide public for funds and which were also in a position to carry the burdens and costs involved. On the other hand, there was a great need to cater for smaller numbers of participants, none of whom wished to assume the unlimited liability necessary in the case of the private company, yet who wished to found a commercial company. The GmbH was the legal answer to this economic necessity. It differed from the AG, for instance, in a simplified procedure for foundation, a constitution requiring only two organs (the head of business and the partners), the absence of the AG's obligation to call in a notary or judge at the passing of a resolution (Sec. 241 of the Company Act) and looser provisions concerning the annual balance sheet. Furthermore, the flexible regulations of the law relating to the GmbH allow the partners to decide for themselves whether their company should be 'individual' or 'capital' in make-up. Thus, one type of GmbH corresponds to a simplified AG and the other to an OHG without personal liability. The final decision-making body of the GmbH is, in any event (unlike the AG), the collectivity of the partners, although only the head of the business may represent the company legally.

In contrast to the AG there is no embodiment of membership in proprietary or other stocks. Membership rests solely on a share in the central capital of the business, the purchase or transfer of which requires legal or notarial certification in order to protect the public interest. The GmbH law is also concerned to protect creditors: when the profit is calculated, payments may be made to the partners only when the company assets exceed the basic capital, which must, by law, be at least 20,000 DM. This protective device is a very sound measure, considering the high proportion of one-man companies (probably about a third of all GmbH) and also the large number of companies with two or three partners only. Indeed, an important problem of the present GmbH law is the misuse and exploitation of the one-man company in order to obtain limited liability.

The economic significance of the GmbH is shown by its wide extent and considerable total basic capital. GmbH were most numerous (71,000 companies) in the 1920s, when a corporation tax, then highly favourable in comparison with income tax, was introduced. In 1954 there were some 30,000 GmbH with a total basic capital of about 6·8 milliard DM. According to the Federal Statistical Office there were at that time nine main sectors in which the GmbH, along with the AG, had great importance. In wholesaling, housing, foodstuffs (excluding brewing, sugar and margarine) and in the construction industries the total nominal capital of GmbH exceeded even that of the AG in the same sectors. In chemicals the medium and small firms had widely chosen the form of the GmbH. In power production the GmbH was important in the municipal concerns where company form has been adopted. Today, too, the

GmbH has its main field of activity in these areas but it also plays a considerable part in the composition of cartels and combines. At the beginning of 1965 the number of GmbH in the Federal Republic was 50,300 with a total capital of 23·8 milliard DM. In view of the great importance of the GmbH, which these figures reflect, it seems especially desirable, following the company law reform, to adapt the law on GmbH to the changed economic circumstances and to work out legal solutions to the problems and abuses that remain. In spite of exploratory discussions that have begun it is still not possible to predict whether the planned reform of the GmbH law will be taken up in the foreseeable future.

ITALY

(a) The role of the SpA

The *società per azioni* (SpA) has become more and more important in the Italian economic system as a result of the great industrial development of recent years. The total nominal capital of such companies is some 8,808,000 million lire, about 25 per cent of the gross national product.[15] Their number increased from 379 in 1873 to 41,205 in 1965. More than 84 per cent are less than twenty-five years old and more than 80 per cent have been established during the years since the end of the second world war. This suggests that the SpA is the legal form best suited to corporate enterprise in Italy.

Another important aspect is the size distribution of SpA. Only 28·6 per cent of these firms have a nominal capital of more than 50 million lire but this group disposes of 95·9 per cent of the total nominal capital. The bigger the companies, the more impressive is this disproportion. SpA with a nominal capital of more than 100 million lire represent 18·6 per cent of the total number and 92·9 per cent of the total nominal capital. Those with a nominal capital greater than 200 million lire comprise 10·7 per cent of the total, yet they dispose of 88·4 per cent of all SpA nominal capital. These figures (which relate to 1965) reflect the intense concentration of big firms and, on the other hand, the wide dispersion of small enterprises in independent corporate units. The large SpA are merely a mechanism for collecting money from small investors and employing it in an industrial or commercial enterprise. The small are mostly family or personal enterprises or (even more often) a device for gaining limited liability toward creditors and for separating assets for tax purposes.

It is very significant, however, that most of the smaller SpA are located near the larger, in areas where economic life is more active and where there is a greater possibility of complementary activities. Thus, there are more small SpA in northern than in southern Italy, where industrial development started more recently and where it is chiefly sustained by big enterprises favoured by legislation or by direct state intervention. The average nominal capital of an SpA in northern Italy, moreover, is 214,400,000 lire, as against 180,700,000 and 241,600,000 in the central and southern regions, respectively.[16]

[15] Statistical data in this section are taken from *Le società per azioni nel 1965*, Rome, Associazione fra le società italiane per azioni, 1966. (This publication appears every three years.)

[16] The distribution of SpA is as follows (percentages):

45

The problems of the social and economic roles of the SpA thus appear to be of two kinds. In the first place, there are issues concerning the use of this legal form for the big enterprise, similar to those encountered in most European or industrialised countries. Companies are structures, neutral in themselves, but their organisation may vary according to the balance of interests represented by them. It is very important, therefore, to make clear what kind of objectives the SpA must pursue and whose interests it is meant to satisfy. The second set of problems concerns the small SpA, which are often not even engaged in an enterprise or a productive activity. These are not met with either in Britain, where a line is drawn between private and public companies, nor in Germany, where the GmbH is clearly distinguished from the AG and accounts for many smaller enterprises. To understand these two kinds of problems we must necessarily take a brief look at the legal framework of corporate enterprise in Italy.

(b) *The position of the SpA in Italian law*

The *società per azioni* is regulated by Art. 2325 to 2641 of the Civil Code of 1942. The other types of company regulated by the Code are the *società a responsabilità limitata* and the *società in accomandita per azioni* which, like the SpA, have a corporate entity, and the *società in nome collettivo*, the *società in accomandita semplice* and the *società semplice* which cover the area of the English partnership.[17]

The general framework is provided by the concepts of *impresa* ('enterprise') and *imprenditore* ('entrepreneur') laid down by Art. 2082 of the Code. This Article defines the purpose of an *impresa* as the 'exercise of economic activities organised for the production and exchange of goods and services'. (See also Part II, Chapter 1, p. 85 below.) The *impresa*, as a productive organisation, and not the *atto di commercio* (in an objective sense), has been the focal point of commercial law since the commercial code was merged into the civil in 1942. The concept of *impresa* was closely associated with the 'corporative' tendencies of Fascist ideology but is nevertheless broadly suited to the needs of a modern economy which places the 'enterprise' in the centre of the productive system. It is for this reason that while 'corporative' theories (according to which the *impresa* should be considered an institution, a community of capitalists and workers) were definitely set aside after the war and the fall of the Fascist regime, the concept of *impresa* has kept its value as a general framework for the legal discipline of industrial and commercial

	Land area	Inhabitants	Number of SpA	Amount of SpA capital
Northern Italy	39·8	45·8	71·1	71·9
Central Italy	19·2	18·3	18·1	15·8
Southern Italy	40·9	36·2	10·8	12·3

[17] The main authorities on the SpA are as follows: Ferri, *Manuale di diritto commerciale* (2nd ed.), Turin, 1962; Ferrara, *Gli imprenditori e le società* (5th ed.), Milan, 1965; Frè, Della società per azioni, in *Commentario del Codice Civile a cura di Scialoja e Branca*, Bologna/Rome, 1960, sub Art. 2325 ff; Graziani, *Diritto delle società* (5th ed.), Naples, 1962; Greco, *Le società nel sistema legislativo italiano*, Turin, 1959. A comparative study is to be found in Van Ommeslaghe, *Régime des sociétés par actions et leur administration en droit comparé*, Brussels, 1960.

organisations. Consequently, questions related to the place of companies (and particularly *società per azioni*) in the economy and in society are, to some extent, seen as aspects of more general problems concerning the *impresa* and are deliberately ignored in discussions on the reform of company law.

The *società per azioni* is considered by the civil code as a legal entity (a 'juristic person'), separate from its shareholders but having its origin in a contract between them. Its full existence as an entity does not begin until this contract, stipulated under seal, has been checked by a judge in its formal requirements and has been registered in a public register held by the clerk of the court. This contract is generally divided in two parts, the memorandum of association and the by-laws. The memorandum must include (Art. 2328 of the Civil Code):

(i) The name and residence of shareholders and the number of shares underwritten by each of them.

(ii) The name and head office of the company.

(iii) The objective of the company. (This is a limit placed on the directors' powers but not on the company's ability to make any transaction—i.e. the *ultra vires* transaction is valid but the directors are liable to the company. Cf. Art. 2298.)

(iv) The amount of nominal capital and the number and value of shares. The nominal capital is a fixed figure, which must correspond to the total of shares. Shares cannot, therefore, be issued at no par value. To ensure the existence of assets at least equivalent to the amount of nominal capital, all shares must be underwritten and at least 30 per cent of their value cashed and deposited in a bank. (The code also contemplated bearer shares but subsequent legislation forbade them for tax reasons, though regional laws allow them in Sicily, Sardinia and the Val d'Aosta.) The minimum capital was fixed in 1942 at one million lire and the figure has never been revalued, despite post-war inflation. This is why the SpA is today a legal device available to practically anyone.)

(v) The value of credits or goods paid in by shareholders.

(vi) The criteria for the distribution of profits.

(vii) The proportion of the profits which the promoters may reserve to themselves. (This is limited in amount and duration by Art. 2340.)

(viii) The number of directors and their powers. (See Part III, Chapter 1, p. 156.)

(ix) The number of members of the *collegio sindacale*. (This is a supervisory organ, with powers comparable with those of an auditor.)

(x) The duration of the company.

The organisation of the SpA is based on the shareholders' meeting. Shareholders elect directors and *sindaci*, approve the balance sheet and the distribution or the ploughing-back of profits and may change the memorandum of association or the by-laws. The majority principle governs the company but every shareholder has a range of weapons with which to protect himself. He can, for instance, bring the shareholders meetings' decisions to court if they are not regularly taken (Art. 2377). He can also quit the company and obtain a liquidation of his shares when the majority makes important changes in the memorandum of association (Art. 2437.) A minority of one tenth of the share-holders may ask for the intervention of the court when there are serious irregularities in the management of the company. The court may dismiss the directors and *sindaci* and appoint a judicial director to serve until the situation is back to normal. (Special requirements and controls are laid down for banks, insurance companies and certain other types of enterprise.)

The *società a responsabilità limitata* (SRL) differs little from the SpA.[18] Its minimum capital is set at 50,000 lire; its shares are not represented by a certificate, so that it is more difficult for them to circulate. When the nominal capital is less than 1 million lire, *sindaci* are not obligatory and each par-ticipant has some rights of control. The SRL is a form much used for small family enterprises but can also be used for larger firms. On the other hand the difference between SpA and SRL is not great enough to prevent the SpA being used for small enterprises as well as large. Hence, the problems of the small SpA and those of SRL coincide.

(c) *Proposals for reform*

The proposals of the company law reform committee (see Introduction, p. 25 above) attempt to draw a line between different classes of companies and different kinds of *società*. The minimum capital requirement for the SpA (now one million lire, the same as in 1942) was set at 200 million lire in Art. 2 of the draft and, though this figure was reduced to 100 million lire in the debates that followed, it still makes clear the intention to limit the company device to industrial or commercial enterprises of a certain minimum size, and to prevent family enterprises taking company form. The draft proposes raising the capital limit for the SRL from the present 50,000 lire to 20 million lire and also laying down a capital ceiling of one billion lire (Art. 51). The theory behind this is that the benefits of limited liability and market finance should be granted only to enterprises of a certain importance. The same idea lies behind the express restrictions of the use of company structure to the organisation of an 'enterprise'.

Another distinction introduced by the proposed reform is one between listed and non-listed companies. Only the former would be able to issue *azioni di risparmio* (see p. 194) and they alone would be subject to the stricter forms of public authority control. However, in order to prevent subsidiaries or linked companies slipping through the net, Art. 47 of the draft provides that the public authority should extend its powers over non-listed companies which control or are controlled by a listed company. (The intention is to avoid abuses similar to those that may occur under English law, when a

---

[18] See Santini, 'Società a responsabilità limitata', in *Commentario del Codice Civile* (op. cit.), sub Art. 2472 ff. With regard to the regulation of the SRL, the Code refers back to the articles concerning the SpA; only those rules applying exclusively to the SRL are laid down in full. The third type of company is the *società in accomandita per azioni*, which differs from the SpA in that the directors are also shareholders and personally liable beyond their share-holding. With the one big exception of Pirelli, this type of company is not much used. (In Germany, under the form of the KGaA (see p. 41), it is rather more common.) For its problems, see Ferri, 'Accomandatari e accomandanti nella società in accomandita per azioni', in *Rivista di diritto commerciale*, 1963, I, 15.

public company forms a private subsidiary in order to evade disclosure obligations.)

The principal forms of business enterprise in the Netherlands are the following:

(i) co-operative associations, regulated by the Co-operative Associations Act of 1925;
(ii) open partnerships (under Arts. 16–18 and 22–35 of the Commercial Code);
(iii) limited partnerships (Arts. 19–21);
(iv) limited companies (Arts. 36–56).

Dutch law makes no distinction between 'open' and 'close' limited companies, except (under Arts. 42(3) and 42c of the Commercial Code) with regard to annual reports and the obligation to publish annual accounts, as discussed in Part III, Chapter 2, Section A (p. 173 below). The Verdam Committee (see Introduction, p. 22 above) proposed that this situation be maintained apart from a minor amendment. More recently, however, in connexion with developments in the field of European company law, there has been some Dutch support for separate legislation for the close company. The government appointed a committee in 1968 to study, among other subjects, the desirability of introducing a separate type of close company. The first Directive of the EEC Commission under Art. 54(3)(g) of the Treaty of Rome, which came into force in March 1968, provided that Dutch close companies which fulfilled certain requirements listed in the Directive would be exempted from the obligation to publish annual accounts if the balance sheet did not exceed a certain amount. (The actual amount is to be established in a later Directive, to be issued before March 1970, and until this comes into force the obligation to publish under the first Directive is suspended.) The present situation in the Netherlands, under which practically no distinction is made between open and close companies on grounds of size, will not last much longer as EEC member states are obliged to amend their national law in accordance with the Directives of the Commission. (See also pp. 144, 158, 162, 165 and 174.)

Which of the legal forms mentioned above is adopted by an enterprise depends on many factors, including questions of finance and taxation and also considerations of continuity and liability. Many enterprises begin as one-man businesses, grow into the form of a partnership and then, after further expansion, are converted into limited companies. The last form is the normal one for an enterprise of any size.

The current Swedish Companies Act was passed by parliament in 1944 and came into force at the beginning of 1948. Unlike many other countries, Sweden has only one company law applicable to private and state-owned enterprises. The legal distinction between types of firms is based on the way they raise their capital, not on size nor on the identity of the owner. The main part of Swedish industry is in private hands. This is especially so in manufacturing industry and services, although the state owns a big proportion of the transport industry as well as some natural resources. With one exception the banks are privately owned, while enterprises owned by associations such as consumers' and producers' co-operatives, trade unions and the like are regarded as being, also, in the private sector.

At the moment there is little discussion on amending the Swedish Companies Act as such. One main reason for this is that Denmark, Finland, Norway and Sweden are engaged in an attempt to draw up a companies act common to the four countries. Trying to harmonise four acts on their present bases is difficult enough and the legislation committees involved can hardly be expected to take on the additional burden of putting forward radical long-term proposals for company law reform. Moreover, the composition of the committees is such that they would be unlikely to want to do so; their members are mainly jurists, experienced in the 'technical' problems of company law, and there are no representatives of radical, 'political', opinions. Furthermore, the acts in force are of varying age. In the case of the Finnish, for instance, which is the oldest act of the four, to adjust it to the more advanced solutions of the disclosure problem, which the other countries have adopted, is quite a radical step forward.

On the other hand, the question has been raised of whether there should be one form of company law for big firms, the shares of which are widely spread, and another for small. This, in turn, might bring up separate issues not always clearly distinguishable. One differentiation, for instance, may be based on the size of the company, another on the number of shareholders.

As far as size is concerned, the greatest emphasis has been given to questions of disclosure and the protection of creditors' interests. Some people believe that small firms should be subject to a simplified type of company law providing for less stringent public supervision. Parliament, however, has so far held that strict rules on disclosure and auditing should come into operation as soon as the owners' financial commitment to the company is limited to the capital they have raised. Consequently, no special act for small companies has yet been passed and (with some minor exceptions) Swedish law makes no distinction between large and small firms.

As regards the number of shareholders, the important issues are mainly of organisation—the protection of minorities, for instance. In companies owned by a few stockholders there is an obvious danger that the majority holding may misuse its power and therefore a special need for rules designed to protect the minority. The Swedish Act contains provisions the intention of which is to protect a minority against (for instance) a majority granting the directors exorbitant fees. Such provisions are, however, of little practical import as there are none regarding any right of minority shareholders to receive information about abuses of this sort. Again, the act (which obliges a company to distribute to its shareholders nothing but earned profit) gives minority shareholders the right to claim a distribution of profits. However, this provision also has little significance, primarily because majority shareholders, in practice, are able to draw up the final accounts in such a way (through depreciation and other dispositions out of profits) that prevents the declaration of any profit at all from which minority shareholders would be able to claim a distribution.

These problems could be taken care of either by a new legal definition of enterprises with few owners or by special arrangements within the framework of the law as it now stands. However, parliament has given scant attention to the particular problems of companies with few owners and it is in this area that one of the most serious and obvious deficiencies in current Swedish law is to be found.

Finally, it may be briefly noted here that the Swedish Act allows a company to donate money for purposes of public utility (e.g. education, research and charity) within a limit set in the interests of creditors. The amount put aside for donations of this kind must take account of profits available for distribution and be reasonable as regards the financial standing of the company.

AN AMERICAN VIEW: A SPECTRUM OF COMPANIES[19]

The unqualified term 'the modern corporation' is nowadays too wide to be useful to either the scholar, the investor or the administrator. This section discusses the major categories into which corporations may be divided according to the part they play in the rich brew of modern capitalism. Such a discussion is a helpful preliminary to the consideration of corporate social responsibilities which is undertaken in Part II of this book, since the categories (and the subtypes within them) will respond to the notion of these responsibilities in different ways.

The structure of American capitalist society involves about six grades or types of company, which fall into two general categories.[20] In the first category there are companies that can be designated 'public corporate capitalism' or 'democratic capitalism', as distinguished from nineteenth-century bourgeois family-owned personal capitalism. In the second category is the true private capitalism most people have in mind when they speak of the economy in terms reminiscent of Adam Smith, a capitalism that does not fit the realities of the first category but which, none the less, still exemplifies a large number of the business units in the United States.

Public corporate capitalism

The differentiating mark of public corporate capitalism is the separation of ownership and control among stockholders, management and directors. This is the characteristically organisational type of corporate business in which the executive managers and directors have to go before the stockholders at least once annually to justify their stewardship. In this general category one finds

[19] A substantial part of this section is taken, by permission of the publisher, from the author's *The Corporation and the Arts*, New York, The Free Press (a Division of The Macmillan Co.), 1967. The relevant pages (157–166) from this book are reproduced here with the permission of the copyright owners, the Trustees of Columbia University in the City of New York.

[20] The author is indebted to Armand G. Erpf, General Partner in Loeb, Rhoades & Co., for his ingenious concept of a 'spectrum of companies' used in this section.

the very large institutional companies. The question of social responsibility weighs heavily in their executive decision-making. The criterion of profitability is not their sole test of good business performance. And because they have criteria other than profit, it is in these companies that one is more likely to find attention given to such issues as patronage of the arts and sciences, not only as a matter of social responsibility, but more broadly as a facet of the institutional company's 'fit' into a society moving towards higher cultural goals.

Yet this broad category of publicly owned companies contains some that are not so institutionally and socially oriented. At least three subtypes can be distinguished: the great multibillion dollar corporations; large companies in the range of perhaps several hundred million dollars in market value to a couple of billion; and medium to large, professionally managed, service-type corporations. To some extent the social attitudes of managements in all these companies may be expected to vary with size of assets. A rough and ready basis for classification, size is nevertheless relevant, because the emphasis, in general, on social responsibility as compared with profitability has seemed to be in inverse ratio to size. There are notable exceptions, of course, but this rule of thumb may be used at least tentatively.

(i) The great multibillion dollar corporations have become institutions of the country. These are old-established companies, many having had their origins in the economic activity that followed the Civil War, and then again around the time of World War I. We all know these companies. They encompass the railroads, steel, automobiles, mass retailers, oil, communications, non-ferrous metals and many types of manufacture. These are the huge companies characterised by a large number of stock-holders, in many cases more stockholders than employees; by professional management teams, many echelons deep; and by boards of directors, usually culled from outstanding names and owning minor or negligible percentages of total shares. Such directors tend to think of themselves as trustees and conservators and are no longer doers or creators.

These companies, because of their size, must operate under bureaucratic procedure, and, to the extent that they are big, they are subject to the threat of antitrust law. Social pressures are put upon them to stabilise employment, and they proceed cautiously in the development and unfolding of their long-term plans. Perhaps because of their gigantic size and the dominance of their position in their respective markets, perhaps because many phases of their operations are mature, their growth rate is more consistent with the growth of the country as a whole than superior thereto. The upsurge of business from 1946 to 1958, during a period of shortages the world over, engulfed them in an atmosphere of dynamism that in many cases was temporary. In any event, whatever the bold and aggressive developments in one or another of their many activities, the impact has to be related to a multibillion dollar base. The shares of these companies, with important exceptions and leaving out the revaluation of the post-war decade, move in price occasionally, gradually, and in general not as dynamically as newer segments of the economy.

(ii) Next, there are large-sized companies, many of which moved out of the private sphere only in the last few decades, and which represent the corporate organisation outside the heavy sector of industrial activity. It is perhaps possible to characterise them as more aggressive, not yet the full target of government antipathy. A number are growing faster than the economy as a whole.

(iii) In a third layer, there are companies largely of the service type, many of which represent new industries as far as the marketplace is concerned but old in their activity or history; some are new institutions in their particular fields and are not infrequently dominant in their respective markets.

These three types of layers constitute our public corporate capitalism. There is some concern for social responsibilities in all of them but coloured by anxiety about what the stockholders may think of new departures in external relationships, especially in areas that may seem to some quite unrelated to business. There is also the development among professional managers, especially younger men with widened cultural horizons, of keener interest in a 'great society' and their companies' part in the 'cultural boom', but at the same time aware of the pull of their economic interests in other directions. Finally, there is a willingness in the larger companies to push out the frontiers of managerial discretionary authority into unexplored terrain, whether for reasons of social responsibility, a sheer spirit of adventure or 'business statesmanship'—qualities often evident in the new breed of big business executive.

Private capitalism

Turning now to the second broad category of 'private capitalism', three subtypes are discernible: 'enterprises' in the more traditional sense of the term; 'ventures'; and 'wildcatters'.[21] All three fit more clearly into the older genre of capitalism than the public-capitalistic companies just described. The characteristics of these private-capitalistic companies may be summed up briefly as follows. The 'enterprises' do have public stockholders, professional managers and directors, but there is no such separation of ownership and 'control' as is evident in the first general category of companies. The ownership, the direction and the management are all much more coincident. The driving hand of a management-ownership is much more evident. Tension between managerial concern about social responsibility and stockholder reluctance (real or imagined) to move into new areas of corporate activity is absent. The 'ventures' are a group of companies in which capital and management combine to explore or exploit a business concept or concession. Here,

---

[21] In oil, wildcatting means sinking a well in unproven acreage and either finding the oil or losing the money, all of this taking place in a brief period of time. The business may be a wildcat, however, even if the period of experiment may be prolonged. There may be large selling for up to $100 million. But there are wildcatters in other fields besides minerals. In all such ventures, the investor takes a calculated risk on the breakthrough either in the markets to which they aspire or in the technological supremacy that they hope to achieve for a manyfold return.

again, there is not the separation of ownership and 'control' that one finds in the general areas of public corporate capitalism. Public stockholding is not so widespread. Finally, the 'wildcatters' are those enterprises which engage in radical speculation and have little or no interest in those external corporate relationships that characterise the great institutional companies.

In the enterprises, ventures, and wildcatters one sees the ferment of private capitalism. Here is the field for bold exercise of intuition, for adventuresomeness and for agility. Risks are recognised and undertaken with the aim of becoming bigger, stronger and finding a firm position in the industrial structure either through growth or combination. Ultimately, many of these companies find safe harbour as divisions of the great institutional organisations which, for one reason or another, have not moved into their areas.

These three subtypes of companies in the category of private capitalism engage in activities that are distinctive but they blend into each other and their borderlines are blurred. A mark of distinction might be their relative degree of fragility. In all three, however, the private stockholders, to a large extent, ride along on the coat-tails of the dominant managerial ownership who determine the policy, constitute the decisive force and have no qualms as to the predatory pursuit of their profit objectives. For this reason many investors prefer such managements if their objective is speculation, while other investors, of a more conservative bent, may lean towards the companies in the general category of public corporate capitalism.

The corporate reach for new values

It is frequently said that today's corporate managements go their own way regardless of the will of the stockholders—those 'ultimate owners' of corporate capitalism who seem to have less and less to say about the use of their money by corporate managements. The probable fact is, however, that there is equal concern among management about the preferences of investors and the financial community. But the differences among the six subtypes of companies mentioned above constrain corporate executives to different kinds of policies in their external relations. The differences affect the social relationships of these companies in interesting ways. These differences are best seen in historical perspective.

In the multibillion dollar corporations, and even in many of lesser size, the corporate concept has reached a high stage of maturity. In these corporations, the principle of perpetuity prevails; there is a strong desire to maintain personnel and talents intact; there is a constant search for new outlets for the company's energies and resources, the replenishment of its depleted or obsolete assets. In line with this concept, the modern corporation attempts to create a continuing institution that has stability and growth, that can assure more or less constant employment, and where the equity constitutes a gradually rising reservoir of value for the savings of the nation. When such an institution has achieved adequate strength and standing in the economy, it has access to capital markets—whether from retained earnings or from its ability to issue capital stock that will be sought by investors—so that it can undertake new enterprises.

Such institutions often comprise a major segment of the country or of the society in which we live. They are manned by officers of merit with broad managerial staffs two and three echelons deep in key functions. They plan and undertake long-term programmes of capital expenditure to maintain, to renew and to expand their corporate activities. They undertake research to keep abreast of technological and other developments, to create new values, to improve old values and to obtain optimum efficiency. The modern corporation thus has a strength and continuity that frequently, if not generally, was absent from older enterprises, where the mortality rate seems to have been much greater.

The mature giants no longer benefit from an appreciable per capita expansion in demand for their products. (From the investors' point of view they must be distinguished from some of the electric utilities that can serve as a standard in judging other equities, and from established growth leaders operating in industrial and other competitive markets and that register sustained growth rates ranging from that of the average utility up to the phenomenal near 15 per cent of one or two outstanding cases.[22]) All these companies, together with some smaller ones that are institutions in their own particular fields, fall into the general category of public corporate capitalism. Investors can assess them somewhat differently from those enterprises, ventures, and wildcatters that are the true private capitalism of the nineteenth-century type.

Whereas the great corporate institutions have won their race, the speculative companies of private capitalism are often striving and struggling to hack their way upward. These more venturesome companies cannot be satisfied with the sedate rates of growth of the institutional corporations, whose safety and impregnability stand in decided contrast. Nor can they afford the 'luxury of cultural uplift', as a manager of one of these marginal operations once put it, that seems to the venturer the only reason for a corporate relationship with the arts. They do not have that sense of security against the chaos of the market which the great institutions more nearly attain. Nor do they have the advantage of planned operations in known areas of administered prices and markets. Their exposure to the risks and perils of business is different both in degree and in kind.

The large number of business units in the general category of private capitalism, leavened by the yeast supplied to the entire economy by enterprises, ventures and wildcatters, is an impressive reminder of the continued vitality of a competitive system that tends to rule out the cultural activities of company managements. If, on the basis of nineteenth-century models of the economy, we were to assume a continuance of corporate shunning of social responsibility except for narrowly expedient aims, there would be little point in a protracted consideration of the interplay between corporations and cultural institutions. But the emergence of a new kind of modern, scientific corporate capitalism, bearing the stamp of the great institutional companies,

[22] In most of the very large, mature companies the growth of sales is not usually expected to exceed that of the overall economy, about 3 to 4 per cent a year, and this may or may not be translatable into equal earnings growth. Growth at the rate of 8 to 15 per cent has been seen in the utilities, the process food companies, the mass production and mass distribution companies, education, life insurance and others. This is exceptional in the category of public corporate capitalism.

opens up new horizons for this interplay. With their extraordinary stability, these great institutions can afford to try out new paths. With their staffs of specialists they can explore the potentialities of the term 'corporate enlightened self-interest' in this particular field of company external relations. With their access to available new knowledge, and their capacity to enlarge the store of knowledge, concerning the cultural ecology of institutional growth and survival, these companies can soberly engage in the search for new values that would generally be closed to companies in the category of private capitalism.

There are of course important exceptions on both sides of the line. The purely private capitalistic sector sometimes turns up outstanding examples of companies that make imaginative forays into the field of corporate external relations, especially in the development of the arts and culture. On the other hand, the great institutional companies are sometimes the most conservative and their managers seldom seem to grasp the opportunities open to them, as potential leaders, to become standard-bearers of the new capitalism.

The corporate reach for new values today is to be seen, however, mainly in the general area of the great institutional companies that have established foundations or have undertaken to push out company operations into new fields. This reach, it should immediately be added, is not away from the proper area of business activity, but rather an enlargement of the vision of the businessman to encompass functions that had been hidden from view by outmoded economic doctrines. The growth rate of the economy depends to a large extent on this widened vision on the part of corporate management. Among labour leaders, politicians, publicists and academics it has gradually been realised during the past few decades that the forward movement of the economy depends on the private as well as the public sector and, perhaps as important as any, on that intermediate sector described here as 'public corporate capitalism'.

The executive leader of the great institutional company, shaking off the nostalgia of the politics of a bygone agrarian age and of economic systems which have now the characteristics of myth rather than reality, must face the future of an urban age, in terms of the political economy as a whole. The dominance of the 'entrepreneur in blinkers' will decline as the voice of the 'public corporate capitalist' is heard and heeded more clearly in the marketplace.

A survey by the National Industrial Conference Board provides evidence of a trend that has been emerging for some time: the nation's leading corporations increasingly consider 'public affairs' to be an important responsibility of management.[23] Over 80 per cent of more than 1,000 firms surveyed had a

[23] See 'Playing a Civic Role', *Business Week*, 30 April 1966, pp. 100–102. 'Of 1,033 US corporations, in the largest sampling ever taken on this subject, 815 have some form of public affairs function. That is a tremendous upsurge from the handful of companies in the 1950s.' The report of the National Industrial Conference Board notes, however, that only 172 of the companies have written policies on corporate public affairs. But 309 had public affairs programmes that were regarded as 'significant' by NICB public affairs research division head Thomas J. Diviney. A 'significant' programme would contain most of these elements: legislative relations, political and economic education of employees, contributions to and participation in community affairs and a written policy.

public affairs function, embracing such activities as relations with legislators, political and economic education, community relations and corporate philanthropy. The top issues that the companies regarded as 'urgent' were inflation, taxation and labour relations; near the top came a host of socio-economic problems, including air and water pollution, poverty, civil rights and urban renewal. Only a small minority of the companies said it was not their business to solve the nation's problems but simply to produce and sell goods. This evidence points to some remarkable and intriguing reconsiderations of the long-debated issue of the businessman's social responsibilities, particularly in the interplay between the worlds of business and those of education, science and the arts. Some of the implications of this development are discussed in Part II of this book (pp. 124–137, below).

Chapter 2

PUBLIC AND PRIVATE ENTERPRISE

---

*How do the general objectives, constitutions
and external controls of nationalised and other
public enterprises differ from those of private
firms? Are the differences between public and
private enterprises widening or narrowing?*

The debate on public and private enterprise in Belgium has emphasised that the two differ in far more than locus of ownership. In the first place, a private enterprise has as its main objective a return on capital or an income on all its productive factors; its social objectives are secondary. A public enterprise, on the other hand, exists primarily to meet social needs and as far as it is concerned the profit motive is totally or partially lacking. Secondly, the main responsibility for taking decisions in a private firm is with the board of management or the representatives of capital; in a public concern, government intervention is of much greater importance and may even be dominant. Thirdly, private companies are subject to the sanctions of the market; if they do not cover their costs and gain a normal return on their investment they will founder. The sanctions upon a public enterprise are political in character; economic factors are of secondary importance or even of none at all.

The public sector in Belgium is not large; purely public enterprises or mixed enterprises (in which the state participation is at least 50 per cent) employ not more than 8 per cent of the working population. Nationalisation has not been favoured as a solution to problems because of a fear that government management would be inefficient, the high costs to the state of compensating private shareholders and a conviction on the part of the unions that their members would not be better off in publicly controlled concerns (see Appendix A)—not to mention a lasting attachment to private property. In those instances where the state has intervened, preference has been given to *mixed enterprises* (the Banque Nationale, the Société Nationale du Crédit à l'Industrie, the Société Nationale de l'Investissement and certain urban transport undertakings are examples of this form); to *government control,* as is exercised through the Coal Industry Directorate; and to *joint control*, as in the Gas and Electricity Agreement.

The Coal Industry Directorate was set up in 1961. It is a public corporation and has five members, appointed by the Crown, who must have no connexion with mining companies or with employers' or employees' organisations. In accordance with government policy and the rules of the European Coal and Steel Community, the Directorate has authority in the following areas: setting prices and sales conditions; foreign trade; production programmes; the co-ordination and financing of investment programmes; accounting; shut-downs; mergers and other corporate changes; and social affairs. The Directorate can take decisions (binding in their totality); make recommendations (binding as far as aims are concerned but leaving to companies a free choice of means); and give advice (not binding). All these measures may be general or individual. Legally binding decisions and recommendations by the Directorate are issued through the Ministry of Economic Affairs and Power, which can veto them. Attached to the Directorate is a National Consultative Council, on which employers, employees, distributors, consumers and the government are represented. The Directorate is obliged to seek the Council's advice about any decision or recommendation of a regulating character. Since its formation, events have shown that the Directorate has significantly influenced management decisions in the coal industry.

The Gas and Electricity Agreement was concluded with the aim of reaping the advantages of unified overall management (as would be gained by nationalisation) while maintaining the existing structure of private, mixed and public enterprises. The arrangement was set up not by law, but through agreements between the companies and employers' and employees' organisations. The government has approved these agreements, helped to put them into effect and is to some extent represented in certain organs of the new structure (see below).

The first agreement was concluded in 1955, under the supervision of the Ministry of Economic Affairs, between the three main trade union organisations—the FGTB, the CSC and the CGSLB (see Appendix A)—the Federation of Belgian Industries (FIB) and the private companies which generate and distribute electricity. It aimed at the co-ordination and rationalisation of electricity production and distribution in order to cut customer prices. To achieve these ends a managing committee representing the private firms and a supervisory committee representing the unions and the FIB were set up. The success of the 1955 agreement led to its extension in 1964 to public enterprises producing and distributing electricity, to enterprises which produced their own electricity and to private gas distributors. Management is now the responsibility of a committee representing private electricity enterprises; another committee representing the public electricity sector; and the FIGAZ subdivision which co-ordinates the transport and distribution of gas. The supervisory committee retains its original composition, although the government now has certain privileges (see below) and the union of municipal managers of the mixed intercommunal electricity companies is also represented on it.

Under the agreement the supervising committee has authority over the

59

entire electricity sector and the private gas transport and distribution sector, in collaboration with government and municipal authorities. In dealing with private firms, it has co-ordinating organs at its disposal to ensure that its policies are put into effect. Its duties are to control the application of the agreement; to assess the working of the managing committees; to keep the agreement under review and make, if it sees fit, recommendations for its improvement; to study investment and other plans put forward by the managing committees; and to publish an annual report on the situation in the Belgian electricity and gas sector and all aspects of the agreement. The managing committees are obliged to supply the supervisory committee with information, including particulars about individual firms, periodical reports and studies. The supervisory committee, which has a permanent secretariat, meets as such, or with delegations of one or both of the managing committees. Its budget is fixed by the managing committees. A government delegate may attend any supervisory committee meeting and may ask questions and suggest studies concerning the aims of the agreement; he also has the authority to postpone a recommendation made by the committee in so far as it concerns the structure of the gas and electricity sector.

The managing committees consist of representatives of the enterprises concerned. Their authority extends, broadly, to the co-ordination of investment; production; transport and distribution tariffs; accounting; and obligatory publicity. Decisions made by the managing committees are binding on the enterprises involved, although the latter may appeal to a board of arbitration.

The agreement has yielded handsome results in the electricity sector, particularly with regard to the co-ordination of the activities of the private concerns. The institutional structure, however, leaves something to be desired: the respective authorities of the supervisory and managing committees have not been clearly enough defined, there are no sanctions that can be applied and the government role might well be strengthened.[1] It has been suggested that a similar arrangement might be worked out for the steel industry.

Public and private enterprises in Belgium have been slow in harmonising their aims and ways of working. More recently, however, there have been some signs of convergence. Private enterprise seems gradually to be changing its outlook, spontaneously through the influence of new ideas about the concepts and practices of management and the role of the company in society, together with representatives of employees in joint agreements that have led to new attitudes to planning, and under government compulsion through the extension of social and economic legislation. Moreover, the dominant influence of purely market sanctions has been weakened by government

[1] For the working of the gas and electricity agreement, see: J. Henrard, 'Une réforme dans l'industrie électrique: les accords de la table ronde et leurs resultats', *Revue de la société royale belge des ingénieurs et des industries*, No. 11, November 1959, and 'Le contrôle de l'électricité et du gas: un cas de coopération', *Annales de sciences économiques appliquées*, 1965, No. 2 (available as offprint); J. Merchie, 'Réalisations du comité de gestion des entreprises d'électricité en matière comptable', *Electricité*, No. 119, October 1964, pp. 1–12; and 'Les travaux de la deuxième table ronde de l'électricité', CRISP, *Courrier Hebdomadaire*, No. 210, 13 September 1963.

measures to strengthen or encourage industry in difficult circumstances while public concerns have been obliged by the government to pay more attention to economic criteria.

BRITAIN

Public enterprise in Britain has a long history. One of the world's oldest state institutions run for profit is the Post Office, which dates from the reign of Charles II. (It was reconstituted in 1969 as the Post Office Board to bring it into line with other public corporations.) However, it is since the election of the Labour government in 1945 that public corporations have expanded at a rapid rate and developed into a major part of the economic life of the country. The last fifty years have seen the creation of the National Coal Board, British Rail, the London Transport Board, the Electricity Council, the Gas Council, British Overseas Airways Corporation, British European Airways Corporation, the British Airports Authority, the United Kingdom Atomic Energy Authority, British Road Services, the Inland Waterways Authority, the British Broadcasting Corporation and, recently, the British Steel Corporation. This list is not exhaustive and does not include some public enterprises that are not clearly autonomous, such as the Forestry Commission, which has more of the status of a government department.

Effectively, the distinction between one type of public enterprise and another is the degree to which the directors are answerable to Parliament.[2] Public corporations are allowed to behave as monopolies, their chief executive is not elected but appointed and their capital is part of the public funds. In these ways they are quite different from the privately funded company, whose board of directors is elected by the shareholders, and which is not allowed to exercise monopoly powers without coming into conflict with the Monopolies Commission. Moreover, the absence of shareholders renders inapplicable a large amount of company law. There is no need to consider the relationship of members with the management—this problem is replaced by questions of the relationship of the board with the Minister. For these reasons a single law—called 'enterprise law' by Professor Michael Fogarty in his book *Company and Corporation—One Law?*—does not seem appropriate, although there is something to be said in favour of a codification of company law which would distinguish between large companies, whether nationalised or private enterprise, and small family businesses where the economic power is slight and distinctions between shareholder and employee are somewhat vague.

In 1954 a Select Committee of the House of Commons was set up to consider the existing methods by which the House was informed of the affairs of the nationalised industries and to make suggestions as to improvements. As a result of their report[3] a Select Committee on Nationalised Industries was established in 1955 'to examine the Reports and Accounts of the nationalised industries established by Statute whose controlling Boards are appointed by Ministers of the Crown and whose annual receipts are not

[2] See the *Report of the Select Committee on Nationalised Industries on Ministerial Control* (1968).
[3] (1955) H.C. Paper No. 120.

wholly or mainly provided by Parliament or advanced from the Exchequer'. The Committee has investigated the Scottish Electricity Boards, the National Coal Board, the Air Corporations, British Rail and the Gas Industry. Thus through the Select Committee and control over Ministers, Parliament exercises some degree of control over public enterprise.

As in the case of a private company, the powers and responsibilities of a public corporation are governed by its constitution which is usually set out in the nationalising Act creating it. For example, the Coal Industry National-isation Act 1946, which set up the Coal Board, imposes upon it a duty to supply in quantities and sizes and at prices that will be in the public interest. In addition the Board is required by the Act to consider its obligations towards its employees as regards their safety, health and welfare. Such a provision is fairly typical of nationalising Acts, and contrasts sharply with the absence of any similar stated objective on the part of private enterprise, except as regards obedience to controlling statutes such as the Factory Acts, the Alkali Acts and similar restraints upon all employers whether companies or not.

Finally, the National Coal Board has the obligation of attracting revenue adequate to meet outgoings on an average of good and bad years. A provision of this type is common to most public corporations and, according to the White Paper *The Financial and Economic Obligations of the Nationalised Industries*,[4] this represents a minimum performance not a maximum. It is not sufficient that such industries should 'pay their way' or 'break even'; they are expected to show a profit after the payment of interest on capital borrowed and after making allowance for depreciation. Although this White Paper, prepared by a Conservative government, recognised these 'industries have obligations of a national and non-commercial kind' it went on to state 'they are not, and ought not, to be regarded as social services absolved from economic and commercial justification'. This meant that the return on capital should not be the same as that obtained by private enterprise but a profitable return is expected. In fixing their prices the nationalised industries should give great weight to considerations of the national interest; but, since to supply goods and services cheaply might have adverse effects on the national economy through the artificial stimulation of demand, the government must take an interest in the prices of basic goods and services, especially where there is a monopolistic element. As regards capital expenditure, this should, if possible, be self-financed, and there should be annual discussions with the government to arrange plans for development over the five years ahead. In these discussions the government must keep public sector investment within the national resources.

These arrangements are designed to achieve flexibility in the running of nationalised industries, and to allow Parliament a close scrutiny of their affairs. It has, however, been argued[5] that the distinction nowadays should not be between public (nationalised) and private enterprises, but by way of size. The 'giants' such as Unilever, ICI, the National Coal Board and British Rail have 'special' constitutional needs, whether their capital is publicly or

---

[4] (1961) Cmnd 1337.
[5] By Professor Michael Fogarty in his PEP broadsheet *A Companies Act 1970?*

privately owned. It is their very size that makes them vital to the economy and therefore gives them an influence over the economic health of the country that makes it essential for all of them to be in close direct 'partnership' with the government. The power over the national economy of such companies is such that it is questionable whether decisions as to development and reduction of enterprises should be left to the board of directors alone; this should perhaps also involve representatives of the general public or the government, and employees whose livelihood may be affected.

FRANCE

French nationalised enterprises are generally under the control of a government department. Although employees and consumers or users are in principle sometimes represented within their administrative boards, the real power remains in the hands of the publicly appointed chief executives.

It cannot be said that the 'nationalisation solution' has evoked much enthusiam in France. René Capitant has stressed[6] that, by itself, it cannot be the whole answer to the problem of company reform. Spokesmen of the Club Jean Moulin, which cannot be suspected of liberal extremism, have maintained[7] that power is not more widely shared in the public than in the private sector and that in many cases the opposite is true. In wage disputes, public enterprises do not seem to have any better record than private firms. In 1963 M. Pompidou, then Prime Minister, wrote: 'It has been clear for some years that the present bargaining procedures do not allow a true dialogue between the state and the government department on the one hand and the union organisations representing the employees of the big public enterprises on the other.' M. Toutée, in his 1964 report on the nationalised industries, stressed that the union representatives were all more or less at one in their anger. 'The history of their relations with the public authorities with regard to wages seems to them to be one of patience exhausted, confidence misplaced, contracts not to put into effect and promises not kept. Their attitude ranges from indifference to bitterness and even indignation.'[8] It must be admitted, however, that the climate has slightly improved since the introduction of the 'Toutée Procedures'. At the level of the Plan, the Club Jean Moulin believes that it is better followed in the private than in the public sector and recalls that few private activities yielded such poor results as the 20 per cent shortfall in the Fourth Plan in agricultural equipment and industrial plant.[9] (These remarks, however, concern the overall public sector and not the nationalised industries alone.)

Influential people increasingly believe that the nationalised industries should be managed according to the same principles as private enterprise, chiefly for reasons of efficiency and because of their concern at the threat to the

[6] *La réforme de l'entreprise*, Colloques de l'Institut des Etudes Coopératives, Royaumont, 2–3 May 1964.
[7] C. Bruclain, *Le socialisme et l'Europe*, Paris, Editions du Seuil, 1965.
[8] 'Mission sur l'amélioration des procédures de discussion des salaires dans le secteur public', a report by M. Toutée, CREE Document No. 111, 1964.
[9] Bruclain, op. cit.

private sector of 'false' competition from the public. The recent Nora Report, prepared at the government's request, broadly supports the thesis of managerial autonomy for public enterprises. (See also p. 230.)

Public enterprise in Italy may take various forms. In the first place, there are economic activities directly run by a public body (with more or less independence) such as the railways, the post office and, since the nationalisation act of 1963, electricity. This kind of quasi-independent organisation is not even considered to be a real 'enterprise' as it has to pursue not only economic but also 'political' and social objectives. Then there are the *enti pubblici*, completely independent organisations expressly set up to pursue an economic activity. Although organised under public law, these *enti pubblici economici* have the status of *imprenditori* (see p. 46 above) and act in the market under the same kind of regime as private enterprises. Most of them are grouped together under the control of the Ministry of State Participations (set up in 1956) and must follow the same *criteri di economicità* ('economic criteria') as any private firm. This ambiguous formula has generally been interpreted in the sense that state enterprise, like private, must be profitable and competitive: the public interest that justifies the intervention does not justify a wasteful use of capital and labour.

IRI (Istituto per la Ricostruzione Industriale)[10] and ENI (Ente Nazionale Idrocarburi) are examples of this type of public enterprise. Both are holding companies, investing capital in and controlling a wide range of firms in different sectors. It is important to note, however, that the legal status of the subsidiary companies, even when the public holding is 100 per cent of their share capital, is that of a private enterprise concern. (A striking recent newcomer to this class is Montedison.) This means that a private SpA does not lose its private character because of state participation, although this participation may be majority or controlling. The articles of the civil code which deal with public participation in an SpA concern only minor differences in such a company's organisation. The state may, for instance, be given the right to elect one or more directors or *sindaci* (auditors) even if it has only a minority interest. Any other minority shareholders may, however, be granted this right in the memorandum of association, the only difference being that in the case of the state there is no need for a special clause and that these directors or *sindaci* can be dismissed only with the consent of the state. (Arts. 2458–2460 of the Civil Code.) Thus, the objectives of an SpA may be private or public, according to the identity of its shareholders. This gives the state a subtle instrument for intervention in the economy, which has been used very widely and with remarkable success.[11]

[10] See Franceschelli, 'Natura dell'IRI e posizione del capitale privato nelle sue aziende', *Rivista di diritto commerciale*, 1954, I, 466.

[11] On the legal problems of state intervention in the economy, see the following: Bracco, *L'impresa nel sistema del diritto commerciale*, Padua, 1960, pp. 388 ff; Cassese, *Partecipazioni pubbliche ed enti di gestione*, Milan, 1962; D'Albergo, *Le Partecipazioni statali*, Milan, 1960; Ottaviano, 'Sull'impiego a fini pubblici della società per azioni', *Rivista delle società*, 1960, p. 1013; C. Ducouloux, *Les sociétés d'economie mixte en France et en Italie* Paris, 1963; F.

If the present discipline of *società per azioni* and *impresa pubblica* adequately solves the problem of state intervention in a particular sector, it offers no solution to the wider problem of policy for national economic development. The new centre–left coalition government is taking up its predecessor's programme for the national planning of capital allocation and the development of resources. As in other Western democratic systems, the planning provisions will be compulsory for the government and other public authorities, while for private institutions and enterprises they will be indicative. With this intent, a draft has been prepared and is now being examined by parliament. In this document, known as the Pieraccini Plan from the name of the minister who proposed it,[12] there are specific provisions concerning the co-ordination of the activity of public enterprises and the position of private firms, with special regard to SpA and the protection of investors and consumers. How far these provisions directly affect company law and to what extent they should be dealt with in a reform of company law is a subject of intense discussion. (The reform draft made no specific references to public enterprise and has been somewhat criticised on this score.) The prevalent opinion, however, seems to distinguish sharply between problems of company organisation, to be dealt with by company law reform, and problems of the economic behaviour of firms, to be solved otherwise.

THE NETHERLANDS

A Dutch commerical enterprise may be run directly by the public authorities —i.e. by a particular government service—without being given any separate legal form, or under a particular legal form, especially that of a limited company. Examples of direct commercial enterprise by the state are the Staatsdrukkerij en Uitgeverijbedrijf (the official printing and publishing organisation), the Staatsmuntbedrijf (the mint), the Staatsvissershavenbedrijf (the national fishing ports organisation) and the PTT (Post Office). The management of these enterprises is appointed by the Crown or by a minister authorised by the Crown. The minister usually draws up directives indicating the managerial policy to be followed. In some cases it is laid down in these directives that the enterprise should be managed as far as possible on the

Bloch-Laîné, *L'entreprise remise en question*, Paris, 1964. For the history of state intervention in Italy, see: M. S. Giannini, 'Le imprese pubbliche in Italia', *Rivista delle società*, 1958, p. 226; Ottaviano, *Considerazioni sugli enti pubblici strumentali*, Padua, 1959; D'Albergo, 'Impresa pubblica', *Nuovissimo Digesto Italiano*; Treves, 'Azienda pubblica', *Enciclopedia del diritto*; Roversi-Monaco, *Gli enti di gestione*, Milan, 1967; Votaw, *The Six-Legged Dog—Mattei and ENI: A Study in Power*, Berkeley and Los Angeles, University of California Press, 1964. The constitutional problems raised by the establishment of the Ministry of State Participations were examined by the Constitutional Court in its decision of 26 January 1960, published in *Rivista di diritto commerciale*, 1960, II, p. 161.

[12] The Pieraccini Plan (*Programma di sviluppo economico per il quinquennio 1965–69*) was intended to be passed into law by the end of 1964 but subsequent parliamentary delays have led to its modification. The modified text (*Testo unificato del programma di sviluppo economico per il quinquennio 1966–70*) has been discussed by parliament. Parts of these two documents and of the Saraceno Plan and the Giolitti Plan, dealing with company law reform, have been published in *La Riforma delle società di capitali in Italia, Progetti e Documenti*, S. Scotti-Camuzzi (ed.), Milan, 1966. NOTE. Since this was written there has been a change of government.

same lines as a private enterprise. These state enterprises are supervised by the Government Audit Department (an independent government organ which supervises public finances) and by parliament. The lower government authorities at provincial and local level also run commercial enterprises directly—gas and electricity, for instance.

Examples of state enterprises operated under the legal form of a limited company are the Netherlands Railways and many public utility corporations. Indeed, there is an increasing tendency for Dutch public enterprises to be given the form of a limited company, as the Staatsmijnen (Dutch State Mines) recently were.

SWEDEN

It has already been mentioned (see p. 50) that nationalisation has been the exception in Sweden but that the state and local communities have often found it suitable to use the joint stock company as a legal framework for their activities—an arrangement that allows more flexibility than direct public administration. With a few exceptions the charters of public enterprises have no special rules allowing the authorities to interfere in their day-to-day activities; public influence is normally exercised at shareholders' meetings.

There is, of course, a fundamental difference between the objectives of public and private enterprises. To quote an official statement:

'The primary objective of a private firm is to make a profit. This gives the main incentive for rational administration and technical development, notwithstanding the fact that a private company must consider its relations to industry as well as its social responsibilities. For the state, on the other hand, it is impossible to allow economic considerations to be its sole guide. The authorities must always reserve the right to consider the wider financial position of the nation and of local communities.'

Nevertheless, there is general agreement in Sweden that the difference between private and public enterprise is diminishing. On the public side there is a growing interest in efficiency and rationalisation. It is not unusual now for managers to move from public to private enterprises and vice versa, especially in the manufacturing field. Government, parliament and other interests demand good economic results and this pressure may be considered as influential as profit expectations in privately owned companies of a similar size. The situation is somewhat different in the case of a public monopoly, such as that producing and selling alcoholic beverages, which is conducted through a joint stock company. Fiscal considerations play a decisive role here and it is for such practical reasons that the legal form of a joint stock company has been adopted. The same goes for certain cultural activities such as the Royal Opera, the Royal Theatre and the Swedish Broadcasting Corporation. Some enterprises with clear-cut non-economic objectives are consequently joint stock companies. Other public concerns have obvious economic objectives—those responsible for forest resources, electricity and the state railways, for example. There has also been a proposal to put all public enterprises under the central management of a state-owned holding company.

Part II

THE OBJECTIVES OF THE COMPANY

Chapter 1

OBJECTIVES IN GENERAL

---

*What are the purposes for which a company
exists? Has it responsibilities that can be
defined? If so, should they be defined in legal
form? What is the position of the doctrine of*
ultra vires?[1]

BELGIUM

There is much debate in Belgium about business objectives, both in academic circles and among businessmen. Notable among the academics are Professors Ph. de Woot de Trixhe and E. de Barsy.

De Woot starts from the proposition that a company has a threefold reality—economic, human and public—each with its own internal logic. He argues that the reality of the company is much broader than that of an association of capital; it is a human working community that performs a collective action for the common good.[2]

According to de Barsy it is no longer possible to maintain that the idea of 'the company' is closely related to, or even coincidental with, the individual ownership of capital goods. He holds that economists nowadays agree with the more advanced jurists in acknowledging the company to be a community of material and human elements, with convergent interests, which should be ordered towards a common goal. Being a community, the company cannot be reduced to its material capital goods, but neither can it be identified with the totality of the workers. Its reality is wider. Its autonomous goal is the continuity of its existence. In this view the 'company-community' resembles the 'social institution'—a concept that transcends the personality of its agents. This idea expresses the duties which should be fulfilled. The company must therefore be defined as an 'institutionalised social function ... an

---

[1] Only the British contributor has fully discussed the doctrine of *ultra vires* in this Chapter· Other contributors deal with the matter in Part III, Chapter 1, in the context of the powers of chief executives with regard to third parties.

[2] Ph. de Woot, 'Croissance et progrès des entreprises', *Industrie*, No. 5, May 1963, pp. 300–312; and *La fonction de l'entreprise: formes nouvelles et progrès économique*, Louvain, Nauwelaerts, 1962, p. 23.

economic task'. De Barsy asserts that the idea of the 'economic institution' excludes neither the rule of competition nor economic efficiency, but that it changes their connotation, as it does the definition of the status of goods and persons.

De Barsy sees the genesis of the 'company-institution' as the consequence of two events. First, a capital association is founded in order to achieve a particular industrial purpose. This association is merely a juridical institution, a corporate institution of secondary importance, and without 'inspiration'. After this first stage, the 'company-institution' gradually comes into being as a result of human efforts which give a new meaning to the goods brought in and processed. From the idea of 'company-institution' de Barsy logically deduces who is to be regarded as being part of the enterprise—the 'inside human forces'. These are the founders and all those who join with them to support the undertaking, who necessarily and *ipso facto* form 'the community'. Those who merely provide capital and receive some rights in return are not part of the 'community' in the same way. They will not or cannot make the enterprise live by total personal involvement. Full membership of this 'community' will be granted only to those who accept the full consequence of failure.[3]

A number of leading businessmen have also tried to define the specific function of the company. Business today regards its economic activity as a contribution to general progress. Businessmen seek to promote the welfare of their employees and the big company tends to harmonise its power with that of the government. Profit is regarded as a yardstick of a company's economic success, and the traditional concept that a company has no other goal but its pursuit is gradually giving way to the idea of a more comprehensive purpose. De Woot has shown how the search for this purpose has now taken the three aspects of the company (the economic, the human and the public) into account. Each aspect has an internal logic which may often conflict with those of the others. The task of the company, then, will be the optimal realisation of its economic purpose (its creative economic activity, its contribution to economic progress) without neglecting its human and public ends. This comprehensive goal 'will be the pursuit of economic progress within the limits of human equilibrium and public integration, such as the present-day state of society defines them'.[4]

De Barsy singles out social progress as the most important of the elements of this comprehensive goal. He sees the company indirectly serving social progress by the large-scale production and distribution of goods. A more direct contribution would seem possible under institutional conditions that reflected the hierarchy of values accepted by society as a whole. For this reason, claims de Barsy, the purpose of the company must be subservient to the social or wider common purpose. He lays particular stress on one important aspect of 'social purpose'—the desirability of employee participation in management, since only thus can the self-realisation of all the members of

[3] E. de Barsy, *Raisonnement sur l'entreprise*, Société d'Economie Politique de Belgique, No. 312, December 1965, pp. 19–20 and 28–29; and *De Onderneming en de sociale vooruit-gang*, Brussels, 1963, pp. 47–48.

[4] Ph. de Woot, 'Croissance et progrès des entreprises', op. cit., p. 311.

the 'institution' be achieved. The desire to participate in management meets two fundamental moral aspirations: the wish to go beyond the limited field of a particular job or function in order to attain a higher level of knowledge and understanding; and the demand for greater responsibility which looks for fulfilment through participation in leadership. Upon this natural desire for knowledge and responsibility, de Barsy founds the right to participation in management. For if the right to found an enterprise is a natural right, so is the right of participation. Both are fundamental human aspirations which must be taken fully into account when they meet in the same institution.[5] The right of participation is also the ground upon which a discussion of profit-sharing can be based. In this context the company, as an institution, would recognise the workers, the management and the providers of capital as partners of equal importance.

Apart from some radical proposals which are very unlikely to make any headway, the question of the legal definition of company objectives has not been a matter of important debate.

BRITAIN

The objects of a company are set out in the 'objects clause' of its memorandum of association.[6] An example is given in Table B of the 1948 Act which contains a Form of Memorandum of Association of a Company Limited by shares: 'The objects for which the company is established are, the conveyance of passengers and goods on ships or boats between such places as the company may from time to time determine, and the doing of all such other things as are incidental or conducive to the attainment of the above object.' The subscribers of the memorandum are free to choose any objects which are not unlawful under the 1948 Act or the general law—an object in restraint of trade or to promote an illegal lottery,[7] for example, would not be lawful under the general law. The power of the Registrar to refuse to register a company with unlawful objects appears to be the only control over the choice of purposes. It seems that the Registrar has no power to refuse to register a company because he regards it as economically undesirable or reckless. Should he fail to register a company with lawful objects, the promoters may apply to the court for an order of *mandamus* to secure registration.[8]

Objects clauses define the area within which a company may act; the company cannot exceed those powers and any *ultra vires* act is void and creates no rights against the company. Such a transaction cannot be ratified, even by all the members,[9] and it appears that the company cannot enforce the contract against the outside party,[10] although some writers support the

[5] E. de Barsy, 'Raisonnement sur l'entreprise', op. cit., pp. 16–17, and *De Onderneming en de sociale vooruitgang*, op.cit., p. 43.

[6] Companies Act 1948 Sec. 2(1)(c).

[7] *R. v. Registrar of Joint Stock Companies ex parte More* [1931] 2 K.B. 197.

[8] *R. v. Registrar of Joint Stock Companies ex parte Bowen* [1914] 3 K.B. 1161.

[9] *Ashbury Railway Carriage Co. v. Riche* (1875) L.R. 7 H.L. 653.

[10] *Bell Houses Ltd. v. City Wall Properties Ltd.* [1966] 1 Q.B. 207, reversed on other grounds [1966] 2 Q.B. 656.

view that the outsider is bound by an *ultra vires* contract.[11] This restraining effect of the objects clause has led to the modern practice of having much wider objects clauses than the example contained in Table B of the 1948 Act. The courts have long disapproved of this practice as being inconsistent with the policy behind the doctrine of *ultra vires*[12]. The answer of the courts was to develop the 'main objects' rule of construction which provides, that when the main objects were specified and were followed by wide powers expressed in general words, the latter should be construed so as to cover their exercise only for the purpose of carrying out the main objects. This was countered by the practice of inserting in the objects clause a provision that each of the specified objects or powers should be regarded as independent of each other and not restricted by or subordinate to any other object. In addition, the recent decision of the Court of Appeal in *Bell House Ltd v. City Wall Properties Ltd.*[13] has suggested that there may be yet another way of easing the restrictive effect of the *ultra vires* doctrine. Here the objects clause provided that the company was authorised, *inter alia*, 'to carry on any other trade or business whatsoever which can, in the opinion of the board of directors, be advantageously carried on by the company in connection with or as ancillary to any of the above businesses or the general business of the company'. The Court of Appeal held that such words meant that any act is within the company's powers if the directors are honestly of the opinion that it can be advantageously combined with the other business of the company, even though they are mistaken in this opinion. Such 'subjective' provisions, should they ultimately prove to be valid, raise questions as to whether the *ultra vires* doctrine can survive in its present form as a meaningful policy. However, there is authority[14] which suggests that an objects clause which merely states that the company may 'carry on any business that the company may think profitable' would be unacceptable, thus restricting these clauses to being one of several objects which are more specific.

Moreover, a company is not restricted to its original objects clause. Under Sec. 5 of the 1948 Act the company, by special resolution, may alter its objects clause for one of the seven specified purposes. However, holders of not less than 15 per cent of the company's issued shares may apply to the Court within twenty-one days after the passing of the resolution. If such an application is made, the alteration takes effect only to the extent that it is sanctioned by the Court. But such protection for minority shareholders is largely illusory in view of the reluctance of the Court to interfere with decisions of shareholders concerned with the management of their company provided that the formal requirements have been satisfied.

The *ultra vires* rule has, however, led to occasional unjust results. A decision often cited in this connexion is *In re Jon Beauforte (London) Ltd.*[15] where the objects of the company were to carry on the business of costumiers and gown-makers. The company decided to produce veneer panels and erect

[11] Furmston, 'Who can Plead a Contract is Ultra Vires' (1961) M.L.R. 175; see also Salmon L. J. in *Bell Houses v. City Wall* [1966] 2 Q.B. at p. 656.
[12] *Cotman v. Brangham* [1918] A.C. 514.
[13] [1966] 2 Q.B. 656.
[14] *Re Crown Bank* (1890) 44 Ch.D. 634.
[15] [1953] Ch. 131; see on the same problem, *Re Introductions Ltd.* [1969] 1 All E.R. 887.

72

a factory for this purpose, although this activity was not within the objects clause. When the company went into liquidation claims were brought by the builder of the factory, a firm which had supplied veneer and a company which had supplied coke to the factory. All claims were rejected, and this rejection upheld by the Court of Appeal. The claimants knew the purpose for which the goods were required, they were deemed to know that the purpose was *ultra vires* and so could not claim against the company.

The main purposes of the *ultra vires* rule was to ensure[16] 'that an investor in a gold mining company did not find himself holding shares in a fried fish shop and [to give] those who allowed credit to a limited company some assurance that its assets would not be dissipated in unauthorised enterprises'. However, recent judicial utterances[17] have suggested that the principal functions of the rule is to protect shareholders by informing them of the business in which their money may be used and that any protection that creditors received is purely coincidental. Moreover, the Cohen Committee concluded in 1945[18] that in consequence of the width of modern objects clauses 'the doctrine of *ultra vires* is an illusory protection for the shareholders and yet may be a pitfall for third parties dealing with the company', as the *Jon Beauforte* decision illustrates. The Cohen Committee recommended that a company should have the same contractual powers as an individual, and that the powers of a company stated in its memorandum of association should take effect solely as a contract between the company and its shareholders as to the powers exercisable by the directors, and could be altered by a special resolution without the necessity of obtaining the sanction of the court.

The Jenkins Committee[19] accepted the grounds for non-implementation of this recommendation which were set out in a memorandum of evidence submitted by the Board of Trade.[20] This memorandum stated that third parties would not be placed in a better position by the implementation of the recommendation since the objects clause would affect them with notice[21] of the limitations on the authority of the directors and *ultra vires* difficulties would enter at a lower level. An alteration in the rule that the memorandum of association constitutes a public document of the company would be necessary to avoid this result. Such an alteration might incidentally lead to sweeping changes in the power of directors to bind their companies, since these agency powers are restricted by the provisions of the memorandum and articles of association and the doctrine of notice of the company's public documents. Moreover, the recommendations would not avoid the prolixity of modern objects clauses, and might lead to even wider clauses as directors sought to protect themselves by attempting to provide in advance for any possible mistake by them as to their powers.

[16] Gower, *Modern Company Law* (2nd ed.), pp. 82–83.
[17] For example, *Anglo-Overseas Agencies Ltd. v. Green* [1961] 1 Q.B. 1.
[18] *Report of the Committee on Company Law Amendment*, Cmd 6659, paragraph 12.
[19] *Report of the Company Law Committee* (1962), Cmnd 1749.
[20] *Minutes of Evidence*, Vol. 20, p. 1566.
[21] The doctrine of constructive notice provides that a person is treated as having knowledge of the contents of a company's registered documents whether or not he has taken the trouble to read them, at least where he is seeking to enforce against the company a right which is inconsistent with the provisions of those documents.

The Jenkins Committee pointed out that the *ultra vires* rule rarely led to unjust results. But the fact that this is a rare occurrence is no consolation to the few individuals affected. Nevertheless they concluded:[22] 'It seems to us that the best course will be to attempt no general repeal of the existing law of *ultra vires* in relation to companies registered under the Companies Acts but to provide protection to third parties contracting with companies (i) against the unfair operation of the *ultra vires* rules, and (ii) by abrogating the rule already mitigated by the decision in *Royal British Bank v. Turquand*,[23] that parties are fixed with constructive notice of the contents of a company's memorandum and articles of association.'

In the light of this conclusion the Committee recommended[24] as follows:

(i) A contract entered into between a company and another party (including a shareholder contracting otherwise than in his capacity as a shareholder) dealing with the company in good faith should not be held invalid as against the other party on the ground that it was beyond the powers of the company. He should not, however, be allowed to enforce the contract without submitting to perform his part of it so far as it is unperformed.

(ii) In entering into any such contract the other party should be entitled to assume, without investigation, that the company is in fact possessed of the necessary power; and should not, by reason of his omission so to investigate, be deemed not to have acted in good faith, nor be deprived of his right to enforce the contract on the ground that at the time of entering into it he had constructive notice of any limitations on the powers of the company, or on the powers of any director or other person to act on the company's behalf, imposed by its memorandum or articles of association.

(iii) The other party should not be deprived of his right to enforce the contract on the ground that he had actual knowledge of the contents of the memorandum and reasonably failed to appreciate that they had the effect of precluding the company (or any director or other person on its behalf) from entering into the contract in question.

(iv) There should be no change in the position of a company in relation to *ultra vires* contracts entered into by it. Unfortunately, the Jenkins Committee do not state what they regard to be the position of the company under such a contract. At the time of the report the assumption generally made was that the company could enforce such a contract, but the later decision of *Bell Houses v. City Wall* has cast a certain amount of doubt on the correctness of this assumption. As the rule is designed to protect shareholders by preventing expenditure on purposes unknown to them, and to enable creditors to assess the creditworthiness of the company, these are strong arguments in support of the view that an *ultra vires* contract should be wholly void, thus enabling the company to recover any money paid or property transferred under such an agreement.

22 Paragraph 41 of the *Report*.
23 (1855) 5 E & B 248; (1856) 6 E & B 327.
24 Paragraph 42 of the *Report*.

The Jenkins Committee noted that many objects clauses contain 'powers' rather than 'objects', such as the power to borrow money, and that this is partly responsible for the inordinate length of many objects clauses. They therefore recommended[25] that 'the Companies Act should be amended to provide that every company should have certain specified powers, except to the extent that they are excluded, expressly or by implication, by its memorandum; such powers being those which any company would normally need to pursue its objects'. (Several Commonwealth Companies Acts already set out these powers.) They also recommended[26] slight amendments to Sec. 5 of the 1948 Act (which deals with the alteration of objects) including the abolition of the list of purposes for which alterations are authorised, and allowing the alteration to extend to the inclusion of any new object which could lawfully have been included originally.

The *ultra vires* doctrine has been widely criticised. Professor R. R. Pennington in *Companies in the Common Market*[27] refers to 'the horrors of an *ultra vires* rule'. Professor Gower writes:[28] 'The *ultra vires* doctrine seems to have outlived its usefulness. Thanks to business practices and legislative changes it has ceased to be any real protection to either members or creditors; on the other hand it remains as great a trap as ever for the unwary third party.' It is applicable only to corporations. Other forms of business organisation, such as partnerships, can, by agreement amongst the members, engage in any transaction unconnected with the ordinary course of their activities. Moreover, even in the absence of advance agreement, the members may later ratify and adopt any activity outside the scope of the partnership's ordinary business[29]. The harshness of the *ultra vires* rule is perhaps highlighted in the case of small family businesses where it is entirely fortuitous whether the trade is carried on by a company or partnership. It seems rather anomalous that whether the family can carry out a particular transaction depends upon the chance circumstances of whether they are incorporated or not. In the case of a large company where the shareholders are divorced from the day-to-day management of the business, the problem has a different perspective unless the validity of the *ultra vires* contract is made to depend upon the prior approval or subsequent ratification of a general meeting. There is now considerable support for the proposal that a company should have all the powers of a natural person of full age. The Jenkins Committee appear to have rejected this proposal for two main reasons. The first was that directors would have too wide powers, and the second was that investors, shareholders and creditors would have too little knowledge of the existing and proposed activities of the company in which they were interested. However, the width of many existing objects clauses (which was emphasised by the Cohen Committee) at present gives to directors extremely wide powers. Moreover the 1967 Act[30] now provides that the directors' report shall state the principal

[25] Paragraph 54(a) of the *Report*.
[26] Paragraph 48 of the *Report*.
[27] At p. 12.
[28] *Modern Company Law*, 2nd ed., at p. 93.
[29] Compare *Ashbury Railway Carriage and Iron Co. v. Riche* (1875) L.R. 7 H.L. 653,
[30] Section 16.

activities of the company and its subsidiaries in the course of the year, and any significant change in those activities. However, this latter objection has in it something of 'bolting the stable door after the horse has gone'. The directors' report merely informs the reader of what was the position during the previous financial year after the changes have been made. It does not necessarily inform the potential investor and creditor of what is being done at present, nor of possible future alterations in the company's business.

Even if the precise form of the recommendation of the Cohen Committee is not acceptable, several other possibilities exist, some suggested by Civil Law systems. The position in such systems has been summarised by Rabel.[31] 'In modern civil law, capacity to have rights and powers pertains to juristic persons in the same full extent as to individuals, excepting natural abilities such as capacity to marry and to make a will, but including name, honor and credit. For the benefit of third persons dealing with corporation, the laws usually freeze this full capacity into a "formal", i.e. an absolutely fixed sum of faculties, independent of the purposes of incorporation and restriction imposed through charter or by-laws. Even though a juristic person ought not to make certain transactions according to the constitutional documents and resolutions of stockholder meetings, it can yet do them with legal effect. Any transaction with third parties, therefore, is valid at least if there is no fraudulent collusion between the agents and the third parties.'

It is often stated that companies have 'responsibilities' to their members, creditors, employees and customers, and to the country as a whole,[32] and a few proposals for reform are based on these responsibilities. Thus George Goyder, for example, has argued in his book *The Responsible Company* that companies should have a 'General Purposes Clauses' setting out, as fundamental objects, the obligations of the company to consumers, employees and the country as a whole, and requiring the directors to pay particular attention to the interests of these classes. Since the objects clause of a company defines its powers and not its duties, a 'General Purposes Clause' would not alter the existing duties of companies, although it might to some extent modify the rule that powers must be exercised for the benefit of the company alone and not for the benefit of any person or group. Several recent cases[33] have emphasised that it is not sufficient to render a contract *intra vires* and valid to show that it is a transaction within the scope of the objects clause. It must also be shown to be in the interests of the company, and it is an improper exercise of powers to enter into a transaction which is designed solely to benefit some other class of persons, such as employees.

A brief examination of the *legal* relationship between a company and its members, creditors, employees and customers, and of the position of a company in the country as a whole will indicate what the content (if any) of these 'responsibilities' is and whether it is either necessary or possible to state

[31] *The Conflict of Laws: A Comparative Survey*, Vol. 2, p. 158.

[32] See, for example, Sir Maurice Laing, *Responsibilities of the Industrialist in Modern Society*, London, Tavistock Institute, pamphlet No. 14, 1966.

[33] *Re Roith (W & M) Ltd* [1967] 1 All E.R. 427; *Parke v. Daily News Ltd* [1962] Ch. 927. A company may be altruistic provided that this altruism in some way materially benefits the company; see e.g. *Evans v. Brunner Mond* [1921] Ch. 359.

them in the form of legal duty. This examination also reveals the existence of a large number of statutory and other rules which affect the freedom of companies to pursue their objects. (See Chapter 2, pp. 99 ff below.)

In Britain great reliance is placed on the articles of association[34] as a limitation upon the powers of the directors of a company. The articles set out the powers of the directors, not the responsibilities of the company as a whole. They provide for the delegation of powers to various officers of the company for the day-to-day and long-term management of the company, and according to the Rule in *Royal British Bank v. Turquand*[35] any transaction entered into by an officer which is inconsistent with the terms of the articles of association is invalid unless it is approved by the company in general meeting beforehand or subsequently.

The articles of association also constitute a form of contract between the company as a legal entity and its members,[36] the shareholders, in their capacity as shareholders[37] and any reference to the 'responsibilities' of a company to its members may be taken to be limited to their rights as parties to the contract. Despite some remaining difficulties as to the precise legal nature of this contract, the rights of members are fairly clear, therefore no statement of so-called 'responsibilities' would appear to be necessary, particularly as, in theory, the members control the company. However, it is in this area of control that problems arise because of the Rule in *Foss v. Harbottle*.[38] The Rule provides that where a wrong is done to the company then only the company can sue unless the wrong cannot be ratified by a simple majority of the general meeting. The only exception to this Rule appears to be that an individual member can sue on behalf of the company only where the wrong-doers are using their voting control in the general meeting to restrain the company from suing them. The principle behind the Rule is basic common sense: it is designed to prevent multiplicity of actions. Unfortunately, it operates to cause hardship in a significant number of cases and there is increasing support for the suggestion that the whole problem of minority protection should be investigated with a view to reform.

There appears to be no body of opinion desirous of seeing the responsibilities of a company towards it employees made part of its articles of association, particularly as in recent years the growth of protective legislation, such as the Terms and Conditions of Employment Act 1959, the Contracts of Employment Act 1963 and the Redundancy Payments Act 1965, has increasingly defined the responsibility of all employers towards their employees.

There has been some discussion of the employee's 'property' in his job, but so far no attempt has been made to suggest that any such right should be incorporated in the legal objectives of the company. Indeed, as a generalisa-

---

[34] See the specimen set of articles of association in the Companies Act 1948 Table A. By Sec. 8(2) these articles apply to all companies registered under the Act, except in so far as they are not excluded or modified. In practice most large companies prefer to have their own articles specially drafted and to exclude Table A.

[35] (1855) 5 E & B 248; (1856) 6 E & B 327.

[36] Companies Act 1948 Sec. 20.

[37] See for example *Eley v. Positive Government Security Life Assurance Co.* (1876) 1 Ex D. 88; *Beattie v. E. F. Beattie Ltd* [1938] Ch. 708.

[38] (1843) 2 Hare 461.

tion, the responsibilities of a company to its employees do not appear to be regarded as an appropriate subject for legal codification. Both sides of industry, employers and trade unions, appear to agree that apart from a certain basic standard to be fixed by legislation, the relationship of employers and employees should remain free to be negotiated by the parties concerned. The law, in this area, can prescribe such narrow duties as the necessity to fence dangerous machinery, but it cannot meaningfully prescribe that the employee should be able, for example, 'to live a satisfactory balanced life' or 'to take a pride in his work, his achievements, and in the company or group to which he belongs', in the words of Sir Maurice Laing's Tavistock pamphlet, *Responsibilities of the Industrialist in Modern Society*. These matters are so closely connected to the individual's place of employment and the social facilities provided by the employer that it is better to leave them to negotiations at the local level on specific points and grievances.

FRANCE

In France, as in other countries, discussion on the definition of business objectives is confused. There is much theorising and insufficient regard for the facts as they really are. Even within groups representing particular interests, attitudes differ and are sometimes diametrically opposed. Three factors are to blame for this situation.

The period immediately following the war was difficult for employers. Their outlook was coloured by anxiety at the advance of communism and a certain feeling of guilt. The increased power of the communists had its roots in the Resistance and followed the strikes of 1936 and the Matignon agreement. Factors such as the presence of communist ministers in de Gaulle's first government, nationalisation of certain sectors and the setting up of works committees appeared to give substance to the employers' fears. Their feeling of guilt stemmed from criticism and reproaches levelled against them at the time of the Liberation. A certain 'profit-shame', which did not begin to abate until a few years ago, probably started at the same time. These psychological elements have inhibited a realistic approach to business objectives; there has been too much unreal talk.

The Catholic Church and Christian thought still play an important part in certain employer circles. Even when they are not directly conscious of being so, some people remain influenced by a certain generosity of outlook originating in what might be called 'Christian socialism'.

The trade unions are relatively weak, both because their membership is low compared with the total working population and because they are divided. Their respective positions are very much influenced by the communist CGT, which tends to block any reform which might allow the capitalist system to evolve and thus 'escape its downfall' and, on the other hand, encourages the other organisations to take a harder line in order not to lose their own membership to the CGT.

The result has been that 'Christian socialist' and employer circles, in an apparent attempt at self-justification, have given much thought to the objectives of business while the trade unions have given very little. 'It is curious', writes

Alain Cedel,[39] 'that definitions of business objectives have been rare and in-explicit, as if each side considered that they "went without saying". The odd allusion to them may be found here and there but it is regrettable that published works and debates have not placed more emphasis on the problem.'

The Church, while taking up quite progressive attitudes on social issues, has not gone further than stating broad principles. The episcopal note[40] said that 'at the level of the firm, ways must be found to allow the workers actively to participate in the elaboration, the supervision and the execution of decisions of special concern to them'.

The political left covers a wide spectrum. 'Marxist distrust of the association of capital and labour is well known', writes M. Waldeck-Rochet, Secretary-General of the French Communist Party. 'This association, and everything that resembles it, represents the opposite of the true progress of democratic principles in business life.' Nor have either M. Martinet (Deputy National Secretary of the Unified Socialist Party) or M. Guy Mollet (Secretary-General of the Socialist SFIO)[41] any greater confidence in the possibility of 'co-management' in the framework of capitalist business. Nevertheless, the fact remains that the non-communist Left, and especially the trade unions, have been generally in favour of workers sharing in the control and administration of firms. The modern attitude represented by the Club Jean Moulin aims at cutting away 'the dead wood of socialism': 'The time has come when higher wages, shorter hours and longer holidays will be better guaranteed by the dynamism of capitalism than by traditional socialist techniques.'[42]

A representative socialist view, voiced at a conference at Grenoble in 1966, was clearly more preoccupied with the means for achieving the objectives of the Plan than with the systematic extension of the public sector:[43] 'The French experience of nationalisation is significant . . . the results have not always measured up to expectations . . . the long-term aim of socialism is not necessarily nationalisation but rather the internal transformation of the management of firms.'

As for the Gaullists, a leading left-winger, René Capitant, wrote some time ago: 'The reform of the firm—conceived as the progressive association of employees with the firm—has for long been the goal and should remain in the future the fundamental idea of Gaullism on the company question.'[44] Most of the measures concerned with company reform over the last twenty years (nationalisation, works committees, the statue of 1959, the Capitant Amend-ment, the new law on commercial companies, the place of the unions in business and plans for sharing in self-financing) have been given momentum by General de Gaulle.

This trend is connected with both 'left-wing' and 'Christian' attitudes and is

[39] A. Cedel, *La réforme de l'entreprise devant l'opinion*, Cahiers du CREE, Fiche No. 1–3.
[40] The Note of the Episcopal Commission was published in *Cahiers d'action réligieuse e sociale*, No. 427, 15 March 1966.
[41] '12 hommes politiques repondent à 12 questions', *La NRF*, Nos. 24–25, October–December 1965.
[42] C. Bruclain, *Le socialisme et l'Europe*, Paris, Editions du Seuil, 1965.
[43] *La rencontre socialiste de Grenoble*, special number of *Citoyens*, May 1966.
[44] R. Capitant, 'Vers la réforme de l'entreprise . . . enfin trois premiers pas en avant', *Notre République*, 21 May 1965.

reflected in the ideas expressed by François Bloch-Laîné in his book *Pour une réforme de l'entreprise*, even if these do not imply any political allegiance on his part. It is striking that in the course of his press conference of 28 October 1966, General de Gaulle used words almost identical to those in the episcopal note in speaking of 'the active association of labour with economic activities, to the fulfilment of which it contributes'. After the Spring crisis of 1968, General de Gaulle made clear his intention of developing participation within the firm as a new middle way between socialism and capitalism. (See below, pp. 107 ff.)

The 'neo-liberal' point of view has been vigorously advocated by Pierre de Calan[45] and undoubtedly evokes a favourable response in employer circles, whether the CNPF, which chiefly represents big business and the 'managers', the Chambers of Commerce and Industry or the General Confederation of Small and Medium Businesses (CGPME), which represents individual and family businesses. In political circles, Valéry Giscard d'Estaing and his party support a liberalism slightly tinged with *dirigisme*. The Young Employers (CJP) try to achieve a synthesis between 'employers' liberalism' and 'Christian socialism'.

Thinking on business objectives can be summed up in three broad ideas, discussed briefly in the following paragraphs.

Profit is not the goal of business but rather a necessary tool and yardstick of efficient management. Such is the position of the Church, as set out in the statement of the Episcopal Commission of February 1966: 'At the level of the firm, profit may be considered a stimulant, a necessary constraint and the sign of healthy management; it should not be regarded as the decisive criterion of its social utility.' More subtle, but identical in the final analysis, is the position of Maurice Hannart, president of the Northern Employers' Association. 'Profit is not the true end of business . . . (but) every businessman *must* make a profit, for this is the sign that he is in good health, that is to say, fit enough to measure up to his final objectives both economic and social. The fact that, because of the inherent malignity of human nature, numerous capitalists see the possibility of profit *only* in their sharing in the capital of joint stock companies, without the faintest glimmer of awareness of the true goals of business, does not change these goals or the responsibilities of businessmen.'[46]

Business should set itself the objectives of growth, prosperity and the creation of jobs. This is an aim to which no one can take exception. It is also that most frequently quoted by official representatives of the employing class and its so-called 'liberal' wing. Paul Huvelin, as president of the CNPF, has often taken this line. 'Economic growth remains the major responsibility of business because this growth sets off a chain reaction of consequences which are extremely important from the human and social point of view and can be most efficiently achieved in a civilisation of free men and free action.'[47] It is also the point of view of Pierre de Calan, the spokesman of the 'liberal' wing of the

[45] P. de Calan, *Renaissance des libertés économiques et sociales*, Paris, Plon, 1964.
[46] M. Hannart, 'Mémoire sur les problèmes de l'entreprise', 1964, CREE Document No. 108.
[47] Address by M. Huvelin at the XIV Congress of the International Council for Scientific Organisation, Rotterdam, 1966, *Patronat Français*, No. 266, October 1966, p. 3.

employers:[48] 'As an economic entity, a business must at the same time ensure its own survival and play its part in the overall economic picture. . . .' In the first rank of the duties of business, he places 'not going bankrupt'. The Catholic hierarchy has singled out three duties incumbent upon those responsible for business: growth, 'entrepreneurship' and investment. The same goes for Fr Boyer, OP, Chaplain of the CFPC, for whom business exists just as much to produce goods and services as to provide a means of existence for its members.[49]

The company is a human community and, as such, should ensure the well-being of those who take part in its activities. This attitude is very much influenced by Christian thought but while it has often been stated it has rarely been spelled out in concrete propositions. It forms the basis of the reformist thinking of François Bloch-Laîné: 'Business pursues ends which concern the community.' He draws the conclusion that 'the head of the business cannot, in the last resort, be the sole judge of the rights and duties of the firm'.[50] According to Fr Boyer, this objective is even more definite: 'The company, as a place of work, should value a man as a worker. As men, by their labour, bring something of their life and individuality to the continuity and progress of the group which the company constitutes, fair exchange demands that the company contribute something to the betterment of the workers whom it has welcomed.'[51] Furthermore, the company is 'a place where men meet, which should unite men'. This theme of a human community is often taken up by the CJP and ACADI (Association of Senior Salaried Staff for Social and Economic Progress). 'A company is a community . . . a hierarchy of men and a complex of material means brought together in order to supply something of economic value.'[52] The consequence of this attitude is to recognise in a company a different personality from that of those who contributed its capital. 'Should not legislation', asks Jean Mersch, one of the founders of the CJP, 'recognise in an industrial or commercial business a different juridical personality from that of the contributors of capital, who have hitherto been considered the sole representatives of a company before the law?'

Some attitudes towards business objectives may be summarised from the point of view of the various parties involved in the activity of a company.

All shades of opinion appear to recognise a threefold responsibility towards employees. Firstly, the development of human personality through work. 'The company is for all its personnel a sphere of life', writes Fr Boyer. Pierre de Calan says that 'the status, the rights and the duties of the employees of a company exist on two totally distinct planes: the economic-juridical plane, on which employees are and remain exchangers of labour for wages; and the plane of human values, on which they should be members of the company'.[53] Secondly, the right to wages. Maurice Hannart writes: 'It is in the form of growing direct or indirect earnings that employees should enjoy their share in

[48] P. de Calan, op. cit.
[49] R. P. Boyer, OP, 'Recherches doctrinales sur la nature et les finalités de l'entreprise', *Cahiers Chrétiens de la Fonction Publique*, No. 54, 1963.
[50] F. Bloch-Laîné, *Pour une réforme de l'entreprise*, Paris, Editions du Seuil, 1963.
[51] Boyer, op. cit.
[52] *Bulletin de l'ACADI*, No. 212, May 1966.
[53] P. de Calan, op. cit.

economic progress.' In a somewhat devious and almost Malthusian fashion, the right to wages has been proclaimed by the General Confederation of Salaried Staff (CGC). Its president has called for a system guaranteeing staff a salary at least equal to that which they received from their previous employer if they are dismissed or redeployed as a result of a merger. Such an attitude was behind the formation of organisations like UNEDIC and ASSEDIC which represent both employers and employees and which guarantee unemployment pay out of contributions made by both sides. Thirdly, security of employment. This is at the moment a leading preoccupation in France, with the growing number of mergers, rationalisations and dismissals. UNEDIC and ASSEDIC have long been anxious on this score. In the long run security of employment should be the direct responsibility of business; but even the most 'liberal'—and notably the Perspectives et Réalités Club headed by the finance minister Valéry Giscard d'Estaing—admit that, in the last resort, the state should intervene when social problems of this sort arise.

It is also generally agreed that business has responsibilities towards the consumers. 'Things are produced for the consumer', writes Fr Boyer, 'and a double human duty is thereby introduced: to produce at the lowest cost and to produce things which people really need.' Pierre Massé, the former Commissioner-General of the Plan, has written: 'We should admit today that in an interdependent economy a company does not have a responsibility only towards its employees and its shareholders but also towards the consumers and, beyond that, towards the economy as a whole.' These responsibilities, however, have always figured fairly low among businessmen's priorities, perhaps because of a lack of 'commercial' spirit: it is only when a businessman really concerns himself with 'selling' that he gets down to studying the tastes and wishes of consumers and strives to satisfy them. Thinking on responsibilities towards suppliers and creditors has not advanced very far. Few companies have a real 'buying policy'. Big French firms make relatively little use of sub-contractors; they have scarcely realised their responsibilities as 'animators' and 'dominant firms', in the terminology of François Perroux. The new law for commercial companies provides creditors with a check, by *Commissaires aux Apports*, of valuation of contributions in kind. S. Boyer, a mining engineer, has approached the question from a different angle and has suggested the setting up of 'credit councils' within companies.'[54]

The definition of responsibilities towards shareholders has come up against the 'profit-shame' already mentioned. Moreover, a company's responsibility to pay dividends to its shareholders has been little developed. In France there is no dividend 'chopper' such as weighs so heavily on management in the United States. This phenomenon is very closely connected with the dearth of economic and financial information and to the lack of interest on the part of shareholders. The right of shareholders to manage a company has been far more widely debated. Pierre de Calan has written: 'If the owners of the capital have a legitimate claim to manage the company, it is not by reason of the nature of their contribution. (Bankers and debenture-holders also bring money to the company and have no right to manage it.) Rather they are exercising towards the company their proprietary right, with all the responsi-

[54] See J. Mersch, 'Sur une vision nouvelle de l'entreprise', CREE Document No. 62.

bilities and risks—for gain or loss—that this entails. A capitalist who risked his capital in a company without claiming the right and the responsibility of managing it—on his own or through an intermediary—would be a mere gambler'.[55] ACADI adopts a much more vigorous position: 'The shareholders of the capital company do not own the property of the business nor even a share of its assets and are not creditors, except in the case of liquidation, with respect to the assets and liabilities. Each shareholder is the owner of his own shares only, which give him a threefold right—of greater or less value—to dividends, to a vote and to sell.' François Bloch-Lainé believes that shareholders 'wish simultaneously to obtain maximum security and maximum return. When they are told that these two wishes are not altogether compatible and that they must emphasise the one or the other, it is seldom that they totally sacrifice one to the other.' It must be remembered that a great number of French companies, even large ones, remained family concerns for a very long time. Because the members of the family were very often paid as employees of the business—which avoided the payment of tax on profits— there was a tendency to give rather less attention to dividends paid out to the shareholders.

As for the public interest, the responsibility of the company as a creator of jobs has already been mentioned. There is still a tendency in France to keep alive by artificial means such as subsidies or public contracts companies which are condemned or running at a loss, solely to maintain employment and avoid social disturbances. Such methods often end by costing the state more than if immediate efforts had been made to carry out the changes that were necessary. French planning 'indicates' to the various sectors of industry a certain number of overall objectives. Even if the industries have generally participated in the working out of these objectives, they have no direct responsibility for achieving them. Planning, as conceived at present, provides for the state to make available the means necessary to accomplish the objectives and to alert industry to the changes which appear desirable and to encourage it to bring them about. The new type of contract drawn up between the state and the iron and steel industry is an important development in the sense that it involves all the parties concerned in the responsibility to make necessary changes in the public interest. The current formula of 'planning contracts' (*contrats de programme*) allows firms to remain free to fix their own prices on condition that they measure up to certain targets in employment, growth, exports and investment fixed by the government.

As long as advantages and help are given to companies which work in the public interest, one of the state's roles is encouragement. (This is the case for industrial decentralisation.) On the other hand if, as has been considered in the case of staggered holidays, companies which do not follow the recommendations of the state are penalised, they are made directly responsible for the satisfaction of the public interest.

ITALY

There have so far been no attempts to give a really precise definition of a

55 P. de Calan, op. cit.

company's responsibilities to employees, customers, suppliers, creditors or to the 'common good' in general. It is true that Art. 41 of the Constitution provides that private or public economic activity may be directed to and harmonised with social aims, but it is generally held that this possible intervention has nothing to do with a company's internal affairs and organisation. It rather concerns more general problems of company organisation and ways of public intervention such as nationalisation, state shareholding and national planning. It does not imply any reform of the existing structure of companies.

A privately sponsored company (a *società per azioni*), like any other form of *società* such as a *società di persone* (partnership), is set up to pursue its shareholders' interest. The *interesse della società* is the interest of the majority of the shareholders. Profit is therefore the criterion of a company's activity. This does not mean, of course, that in practice the needs of large companies have left this principle inviolate. Profit is regarded as long-term profit. Directors may therefore easily justify any course of action they follow, such as price reductions or other consumer benefits, pay or other employee benefits, or development expenditure within the firm.

Whether shareholders have an actual right to dividends (*diritto agli utili*) whenever profits are accrued is a matter of debate, and the debate itself may be regarded as an attempt to define the limits of such policies and the responsibilities of directors towards their shareholders. The prevailing theory seems to deny such an overall right to shareholders and to allow the ploughing-back of profits and to sanction the device of so-called 'hidden reserves' (*riserve occulte*).[56] Art. 13 of the draft on company reform, which provides a special remedy for shareholders,[57] tends in the same direction: shareholders can object to a majority decision concerning the approval of the balance sheet and the determination and distribution of dividends but only by proving that there has been abuse of power (*eccesso di potere*) on the part of directors or majority shareholders. The formula *eccesso di potere* (which broadly corresponds to the French *eccès de pouvoir*) has been criticised because it implies a judicial control on the merits of a decision of a shareholders' meeting. A further objection advanced is that it introduces into the field of civil law concepts created by and applied in administrative law. This could cause legal difficulties. But there has been no discussion about the basic ideas behind the proposed article—the strengthening of the shareholders' rights to dividends whenever the company makes a profit and a power to forbid directors to plough profits back when there is no specific need (i.e. when they abuse their powers).

The service a company renders to the community is not expressly acknowledged in Italian company law. It is up to each company to decide its own

[56] For various views on this matter, see: Rossi, *Utile de bilancio, riserve e dividendo*, Milan, 1957; Pettiti, *Contributo allo studio del diritto dell'azionista al dividendo*, Milan, 1957; Asquini, 'I battelli del Reno', *Rivista delle società*, 1959, p. 617.

[57] But it gives it only to shareholders representing one fifth of the total capital. The restriction applies also to the other instances of shareholders' rights to complain against majority decisions provided for by the current legislation (under Arts. 2377–2379 of the Civil Code), such as decisions which are formally irregular or which have an impossible or illicit content. This restriction has been widely criticised, among others by the National Economic and Labour Council (CNEL) in its opinion on the reform draft.

policies on, for instance, the release of staff for public purposes or on donations for education, research and charity. There are no provisions in the reform draft regarding plant or office location to meet national planning requirements, the protection of amenities or the acceptance of unremunerative or only partly remunerative public service responsibilities. It must, however, be remembered that the Italian state plays a very significant role in the economy by direct or indirect participation in various enterprises (see above, p. 64), and it is not uncommon for such state-run enterprises to have particular obligations laid on them. For example, all the companies held by IRI are required to locate a certain percentage of their investments in southern Italy, following the national policy for the development of that region.

Here, as elsewhere, the solution to the problems of the modern company is sought not in the field of company law but in the broader framework of *impresa*. Discussion on national planning does not seem to have changed this way of thinking. Apart from radical visions of a completely state-run economic system, the general feeling is that the government will have enough difficulty in trying to make public enterprises follow planning requirements to be able directly to affect and control the decisions of private companies as well.

Moreover, a legal definition of a company's obligation to the common good is still far from being reached. The reform draft restricts itself to problems concerning a company's relations with its shareholders. It introduces no change in the traditional idea that a company is not limited by its object clause and that the *ultra vires* act is valid, though directors responsible for such an act may be to liable the shareholders. 1 Art. of the draft, however, proposes a more detailed definition of a company's objectives in the memorandum of association and also seeks to limit the kind of activity that the objectives may cover by restricting them to the 'exercise of economic activities organised for the production and exchange of goods and services' (*esercizio di attività economiche organizzate al fine della produzione e dello scambio di beni e servizi*). These are the same words that Art. 2082 of the Civil Code uses to define *impresa*. They are restated here to confirm that a *società per azioni* must be used only to carry on an *impresa* and not as a useful device for other kinds of non-productive activity (such as estate administration in a company form in order to avoid personal taxation). If this occurs, the company will have to be dissolved, according to Art. 1 of the draft.

THE NETHERLANDS

In both law and fact the company in the Netherlands operates in a free enterprise system based on free competition. It is the government's responsibility to see to the country's general economic and social welfare, while companies, like all private persons, are basically free, within the terms of the system created by the government, to act as they think fit.

It is generally recognised that the primary objective of any company is economic, aimed among other things at ensuring its own profitable and productive continuity. This primary objective is the first and main criterion for fixing priorities in a company's policy. Secondary objectives, such as the maintenance of a sufficient level of employment, in fact enter into the policy of a company only in so far as they do not endanger the fulfilment of the primary objective.

The company, as an employer, is responsible to its employees under the terms of the labour agreements it has entered into and is also bound to observe the extensive statutory regulations laid down to protect the economic and social interests, as well as the health and safety, of employees. Quite apart from these obligations, however, employers have, particularly in recent years, taken on certain other responsibilities towards their employees. They have done so in some cases on their own initiative, in others under pressure from public opinion. This has led to the acceptance of certain rules which, though not laid down in writing, are in fact morally binding on every employer. In factory shut-downs, for example, which result in the dismissal of workers, employers who show an insufficient sense of responsibility towards their employees arouse sharp public reaction. Such reactions have forced them to modify their policies, and have led to new legislation providing for longer periods of notice of dismissal for older employees and a statutory prior claim for pension payments, when a company closes down or goes bankrupt. The Council of the Netherlands Employers' Federation has also responded by publishing directives which employers are recommended to observe when mass dismissals are unavoidable.

A few large companies have considered these secondary objectives to be so important that they have included some of them in the definition of their objects in their articles of association, in a provision more or less to the effect that the company shall, within the framework of its normal business, endeavour to promote the interests of all those connected with it by aiming at a long-term welfare policy and maximum useful employment.

There have been no formal proposals in the Netherlands that a company's obligations to the public interest should be legally defined, in spite of the fact that the existence of such obligations is now recognised. Some people think they should be stated in a firm's articles of association. A minority of the Verdam Committee (see p. 236) suggested the appointment to supervisory boards of persons representing the public interest but it is thought unlikely that this proposal will find its way into any amendment to company law.

SWEDEN

The Swedish companies act does lay down that the objective of a company's activity shall be stated in the articles of association and restricts the company's freedom to go beyond the limits laid down. The act, however, is far from adopting (for instance) the rigorous English doctrine of *ultra vires* and, in practice, a provision in the articles about the objectives of a company's activities is insignificant. According to the act which was in force before the current act of 1944, the objectives of a company's activities could be construed in extremely general terms—for example, 'industrial operations and activities associable therewith'. The act now in force requires a more exact definition of the field or fields of business that may be covered by a company's activities but the apparent strengthening has not had any real consequences in practice. The purpose of the provisions is to give protection to minority shareholders against a majority decision to extend activities beyond the range laid down in the articles. It has, however, proved to be exceptionally rare for minority shareholders to consider that there is any need to have recourse to this protection. (See also pp. 226-227.)

AMERICAN CONCEPTS OF THE CORPORATION

The formulation of public policy regarding corporations, and of corporate policy in the large company, depends upon the formulator's conception of the corporation. There are many possible conceptual approaches, some more useful than others. The historical approach, combined with a philosophical view of 'corporateness' as it has evolved over the centuries in Western legal and political thought, is not necessarily the best guide to future policy. Yet it is certainly one of the most interesting, especially when one goes deeply, following Gierke, Maitland and Pollock, into the idea of corporate personality as it has won its way from the Continent into English and American law. Protection of the corporate 'person', under the Fifth and Fourteenth Amendments of the US Constitution, against deprivation of their property by State and Federal governments without due process of law, is a basic doctrine of American public law; and that doctrine depends historically on received theories of corporateness and 'higher law' that are deeply rooted in Europe.[58]

Another—and intriguing—aspect of the historical approach is the tracing of the lineage of contemporary business companies back to such ancestral types as the great government supported trading companies of the early modern period of empire building such as the East India company. Attempts are sometimes made to establish the public responsibilities of modern business corporations on these shaky historical grounds. But while there are still a few companies that can claim a hoary age of centuries, the fact is that the business corporation of today is essentially *sui generis*. It does not fit into the old patterns.[59] It is a rapidly changing institution to be understood in terms of contemporary and projected social forces.

The corporation as an instrument

Nor is it at all satisfactory to let jurists or economists decide what the modern corporation is and what its powers and limitations should be. The corporation is an economic instrument and an instrument necessarily stated in legal terms;

[58] On the European heritage as on the source of these US constitutional doctrines, the best account is in Edward S. Corwin's classic papers on The *'Higher Law' Background of American Constitutional Law*, Ithaca, NY, Cornell University Press, 1955, reprinting articles from the *Harvard Law Review*, Vol. 42, pp. 149–185 and 365–409. The fascinating historical development of the American constitutional 'doctrine of vested rights' for the corporate 'person' is described in a chapter on 'The Property Right versus Legislative Power in a Democracy' in Corwin's *The Twilight of the Supreme Court*, New Haven, Yale University Press, 1934, Chapter II.

[59] See John P. Davis, *Corporations: A Study of the Origin and Development of Great Business Combinations and of their Relation to the Authority of the State*, originally published in 1905 and reissued as a paperback (New York, Capricorn Books Edition, 1961) with an introduction by Abram Chayes; also Oscar Handlin and Mary F. Handlin, 'Origins of the American Business Corporation', in Donald Grunewald and Henry L. Bass, *Public Policy and the Modern Corporation*, New York, Appleton-Century-Crofts, 1966, pp. 3–24.

but it is also an instrument of society broadly speaking. To say today that it is a legal instrument solely of stockholders for their own financial gain is to run into the difficulty that few people act on that principle, perhaps least of all the stockholders themselves.

On the contrary, the modern corporation has proved to be such an effective instrument of collective action that many others besides profit-seekers and entrepreneurs have laid claim to its use; indeed, one of the major issues is precisely whose instrument it in fact is and should be as a matter of public policy. The so-called managerial revolution in large publicly held companies has thrust upon directors and executive managers new problems about these claims and claimants that simply cannot be resolved by quick reference to the old clichés, the familiar rubrics of economic and juristic theory inherited from an earlier century. Corporate managers have to face contemporary conditions and not unconditional theory in their daily decision processes.

Managers who think deeply about this know that new theory has to be developed to fit the facts of today and the exigencies of the corporate world of tomorrow. They have difficulty in finding reliable doctrine for this purpose, partly because of paucity of knowledge, but more because there is lacking an adequate framework of ideas for organising the wealth of business data into a working conception of the corporation. As Professor Chayes has said, 'We are only beginning to grope toward a conceptual framework and a vocabulary which will permit us usefully to describe it.' He observes further that the associative elements have been refined out of it since, in law, it became 'a rubric for expressing a complicated network of relations of people to things rather than among persons' under which 'the aggregated material resources rather than the grouping of persons became the feature of the corporation'. Yet this abstract and formal conception can hardly hold its own at a time when—as in the middle ages—'a complex hierarchy of institutions mediates between the individual and the state, providing means by which men can aggregate their power and their voices against that of the state'.[60]

The corporation as an organisation

This conceptual problem is by no means unique to the corporation. It pervades the entire social structure in an age of rapid change, especially the structure resulting from what Professor Kenneth Boulding[61] has called the organisational revolution of our time. During the past eight decades there has been a phenomenal rise in the scale of organisations of all kinds. Huge business corporations are but one case. The organisational revolution is seen, too, in the concomitant rise of labour unions, professional, agricultural and trade organisations, scientific and professional associations and even churches, where it takes the form of the ecumenical movement. Most important of all is the great magnitude of rising governmental operations, civil and military.

The alleged diseconomies of scale do not seem to have halted the rise of

[60] Chayes, 'Introduction' to Davis, op. cit., p. xix.
[61] Kenneth E. Boulding *et al.*, *The Organizational Revolution: A Study in the Ethics of Economic Organization*, New York, Harper & Brothers, 1953, especially Chapters 1 and 2, on the nature and causes of the organisational revolution, and Chapter 8 on business organisations.

these great organisational structures, not, at least, at any predictable point. But the great proliferation of organisations does pose basic problems of political economy and at bottom serious ethical issues which become salient issues of public policy. To reverse the matter, issues of public policy concerning the regulation of organisations are at bottom issues of ethical theory. The necessarily hierarchical structure of government within a vast organisation, the bottlenecks that develop in the flow of information, the impersonal and bureaucratic tone of management, the dangers to the basic values of democracy, all of these and many other problems have come along with the organisational revolution. The rise of that remarkable instrument, the modern corporation, must be seen in the light of such issues posed by the entire array of collective-action instruments. The question can be raised whether the democratic ideal of individualism needs defence against the mass discipline of powerful organisations—and this question applies to all, not to the business corporation alone.

For countries in the Western tradition of human rights and the dignity of man this ethical question repeatedly recurs, and especially at the levels of corporate and public policy. In the case of the business corporation, the problem is accentuated due to great economic powers exercisable not only *vis-à-vis* outsiders but also against any recalcitrant 'organisation man'. In order to assure the survival of economic competition there is antitrust,[62] and to keep managerial action at an appropriate level of right conduct there is the protected and encouraged 'countervailing power' of other organisations, such as labour unions which in turn become potential oppressors.

The corporation and ethics

Some observers of the corporate scene profess to see a 'corporate conscience' at work in the great business companies, while others talk seriously about the obligations of the 'good corporate citizen'. The difficulty, however, is that the content of corporate citizenship often remains quite open-ended, while the 'corporate conscience' cannot possibly respond to any single known and immutable code. As Chester I. Barnard observed in *The Functions of the Executive*,[63] executive positions imply a complex morality that has to be

[62] Antitrust policy is a good example of the point about ethics and public policy on corporations. Reinhold Niebuhr in Boulding, op. cit., Part III, commenting on Boulding's thesis, says: 'A market economy is one in which there is a certain tolerable chaos, or a harmony distilled from the chaos of conflicting interests. But the harmony is tolerable only in so far as the conflicting interests are fairly evenly matched. When they are not, the contest of power results in injustice.' Arguing (at p. 238) that a community must avail itself of coercion to establish a minimal order, Niebuhr warned against the 'misleading distinction between a noncoercive economic society and a coercive political society' that has 'not been created by a factitious element of coercion' but is rather 'an inclusive involuntary society which cannot afford to deal with recalcitrance by the slow method of allowing it to destroy itself'. The state 'must suppress all harmful expressions of self-interest or particular interest which threaten the order of the community'. See also the chapter on 'Public Policy Toward the Competitive Sector: Antitrust Law and Policy' in Grunewald and Bass, cited in note 59 above, and Ellis W. Hawley, *The New Deal and the Problem of Monopoly—A Study in Economic Ambivalence*, Princeton, Princeton University Press, 1966.

[63] Chester I. Barnard, *The Functions of the Executive*, Cambridge, Mass., Harvard University Press, 1938, especially Chapters XI and XVII.

created out of the welter of private and organisational codes that contend with each other in a 'conflict of moralities'. It begs the question to ask the corporate executive to search *the* corporate conscience. Nor is it at all likely that he will turn, if he is an able and creative executive, to outsiders (including public officials) for guidance to that still, small voice. He will have to face 'the necessity of *creating* moral codes', as Barnard wisely put the matter, in his constant struggle to maintain co-operation among men in the organisation of a vast enterprise. This is more than a question of 'morale'. It is a question of constructing 'an economy of incentives', of developing methods of persuasion in the recruiting of organisation forces and preventing their dissipation, and of developing within an organisation appropriate mechanisms for adjudicating competing claims based on diverse codes.

If Barnard's argument for these methods of resolving the differences that arise within the corporation is sound, then it applies with equal force to the differences that arise in the external arenas[64] where the corporation is a major participant. In these arenas, both domestic and international, contenders for favourable power positions are constantly active. It is not only a question of economic power in a competitive market but also one of political power in an effort to effect changes in, or to avoid the impact of, unfavourable public policy. The modern corporation, in short, like all influential organisations, can be regarded as a quasi-political as well as an economic entity.

Realism requires this conceptual approach on the part of managers. They must be prepared to react to the forces in their environment simply in the pursuit of business policy, however narrowly defined (as for example in terms of profit-maximisation), and the necessity for anticipatory political action—as well as defensive reaction—is recognised by competent executives. When corporate purpose broadens, as it inevitably does because of the institutionalisation of big business, the quasi-political aspects of corporate management become even more obvious. Nor can one accept attempted rebuttals of this conceptual approach by those who take the untenable position that

[64] 'Arena', as used here, is a word of art from political science. H. D. Lasswell and Abraham Kaplan, *Power and Society: A Framework for Political Inquiry*, New Haven, Yale University Press, 1950, pp. 77 ff, have defined an 'arena of power' as 'any situation in which power is sought and persons are brought within the domain of power', 'power' being in turn a 'deference value' that refers specifically to participation in the making of decisions. The 'perfect market' of economics is not in this sense an arena of power (though some economists include this as a value sought) but rather a situation free from coercion, as Frank H. Knight pointed out in *Risk, Uncertainty and Profit*, Boston, Houghton-Mifflin Co., 1921, and Jevons described as one in which 'all traders have perfect knowledge of the conditions of supply and demand and the consequent ratio of exchange'. Lasswell and Kaplan (op. cit., pp. 250 ff) discussing the balancing of power as 'the power process among the participants in an arena', state that 'an arena is *military* when the expectation of violence is high; *civic*, when the expectation is low', and that the world as a whole constitutes a military arena while the internal life of a state ordinarily constitutes a civic arena. The present world arena, being 'pluripolar', is thus different in kind from the 'unipolar' civic arena of a national body politic organised around a single power. The distinction becomes important in Part III, Ch. 3 and Appendix G of this book when the world arena for the transnational business of multinational corporations is discussed. But it should be noted here in passing that there may be arenas within companies and other non-state organisations. These are organisations generally non-military or civic in character, but not always unipolar.

economics and politics are disparate spheres of human action; the corporation cannot be relegated by some theoretic sleight-of-hand to the completely non-coercive pure market of certain schools of economic thought.

The interdisciplinary approach

The more realistic concept of large corporations is therefore eclectic and inter-disciplinary. This approach is difficult since it demands the intellectual tools and techniques of economics, jurisprudence, sociology and political science, to say nothing of the new sciences of communication with mathematical and cosmological implications. Corporate managers often complain, and justly, of the tendency of some public officials to see the corporation solely in terms of simplistic, juristic and economic models, notably those of use in antitrust procedures. Reformers are sometimes inclined to see it only as a participant in the arena of power, and a malevolent and reactionary participant at that. There are other stereotypes. Hopeful applicants for corporate philanthropy may see the corporation as a great cornucopia to be tilted in the direction of 'worthy causes'. For many an Organisation Man it is simply a safe haven.

In all of these instances there is a germ of truth in the corporation stereo-type that forms the inarticulate major premise in one or another suspect, if not outright fallacious, argument. The zealous trust-buster who thinks of Big Business and the Modern Corporation as synonymous terms for threats of monopoly; the reformer who thinks only of the Private Interest of Corporations versus the Public Interest of the State; the charitable organisations that think only of the Big Contributor—all of these are apt to see this protean instrument in his particular light and to draw the desired conclusions.

But this intellectual process also applies to those more immediately connected with corporate operations. The stockholder, no longer a proprietor, sees it as an investment or a gamble, depending upon the fit of the company into the 'new capitalism' (discussed in Part I above). The employee sees it in terms of job security. The manager sees it as a problem of co-ordinating the activities of others for common purposes, including sheer survival as well as profitability and other aims. There are others near by, each with his own chosen stereotype: the suppliers and vendors of the goods and services the corporation requires and the customers who buy its products. Among the customers are the important categories of dealers and distributors, often big companies in their own right.[65] Among the suppliers must be reckoned certain key institutions in the financial community, including the security analysts and others who provide directly or indirectly the credit and other financial facilities for corporate operations. And finally there is a 'general public' in the corporate environment (an ill-defined term for purposes of formulating corporate policy, by the way) that must be kept informed and in a favourable state of mind, together with the public's representatives in governments at all levels, in host as well as home countries in the case of multinational companies, with whom direct relations must be maintained much as a state keeps its diplomatic relations in order throughout the world.

[65] In the civil suits brought under the antitrust laws against electrical manufacturers recently, suits for damage were brought by some of the largest utility companies as purchasers of generators and other power equipment at allegedly rigged prices.

A multifunctional institution

The point is that, for purposes of public policy-making in the field of company law, it is always necessary to bear in mind that this protean instrument—the modern corporation—is actually a *multifunctional major social institution* of our time, that is not static but rapidly evolving from old to new patterns of social action that are still indeterminate. Its managers are in business and primarily interested in a good record of earnings but they have to be interested in many other things as well. This span of interests is partly a function of size. Big organisations are expected to become involved in the affairs of their communities. The impact of such companies upon the lives of many people and the attendant publicity ensure that.

Business leadership is more than leadership in business; it entails community responsibilities, often of a higher order and potentially costly. Apart from any mixed motives in managers, some of whom are idealists and impelled by altruistic drives, their expenditure of time and energy on behalf of the company for external relationships, that may have only an indirect and sometimes a remote bearing upon earnings, can be justified as 'necessary business expense'. Who knows what is necessary? Business is itself an exercise in risk. Research and development, with costs that are sometimes astronomical, may lead to nought—or to a gold mine. But in the United States, at least, business judgment brings in other kinds of risked expenditures that would not have been admitted as a matter of good investment a few decades ago.

The growing volume and widening purpose of corporate giving is a case in point. The corporate executive faces a dilemma here. If gifts for health, education, welfare and the cultural development of the community are purely philanthropic—made, that is to say, merely on account of that love for mankind which alone moves the true philanthropist—they are vulnerable as an unwarranted dispersion of corporate assets. If, on the other hand, such gifts are regarded as a form of investment for indirect benefit, and often very long-range returns to the company, the problem of quantifying those anticipated returns is indeed formidable in many instances. There are also tax considerations, especially the deductibility of corporate contributions so as to reduce tax liabilities under statutes that some interpret—I think erroneously—as invitations only to purely philanthropic giving. This, with other dilemmas of corporate support payments, requires managements to review their giving, investment and accounting policies for a more creative rationale of corporate practice in these fields. One result has been the flood of business and legal literature on these questions during the past few decades.

The upshot of it all is that new conceptions of the corporation have appeared and are continuing to appear.[66] There is dynamic movement not only

[66] Some contemporary American conceptions of the corporation are examined at length in my study of *The Meaning of Modern Business*, New York, Columbia University Press, 1960. In the growing number of business journals published by graduate schools of business much attention is now being given to the concept of the modern corporation as well as to problems of corporate management at a less abstract level of thought. The law reviews, as cited in notes below, contain many penetrating commentaries on the nature of corporations. See further, A. A. Berle *et al.*, 'Symposium on the Impact of the Corporation on Classical Economic Theory', *Quarterly Journal of Economics*, Vol. 79, February 1965, pp. 1–51; Peter F. Drucker, *Concept of the Corporation* (New York, The John Day Co., 1946);

in the corporate institution itself but also in the intellectual environment in which the institution is conceptualised and assessed for many purposes. The legislative purpose is but one of these. Another, as indicated, is the review of investment policy in R & D as well as with respect to corporate giving. Still another is the investor's need to grasp the meaning of modern business. But perhaps the most important impetus to finding better and more viable conceptions of the corporation is scientific: the desire to know and understand the structure and dynamics of our society and the major institutions in it. No one doubts today that the modern corporation is such an institution, that its destiny is tied in with the destiny of society as a whole and that as a social instrument its constructive potentialities have not been fully tapped.

Major conditioning factors in the US political economy

To set the stage for a more detailed account of certain aspects of the corporation of the future in the United States, it is well to set forth briefly some of the more salient trends in recent history. One needs to look back roughly thirty years, to the period of the New Deal, in order properly to assess the evolving corporate institution of the next thirty.

First, the early 30s saw *a major shift in the centres of power* in the American political economy. National powers over the economy were strongly asserted under the New Deal and extended in more recent administrations. The older centres of power over finance, already to some extent brought under mild discipline by the Federal Reserve system, were further regulated by securities and exchange, holding company and other legislation. Washington began to exercise for the first time latent constitutional powers over the whole industrial system in measures designed to lift the output of the nation's productive plant; to maintain that output more evenly through business cycles that legislation also tried to reduce; to distribute the national income more widely both for human satisfaction and to make a greater mass market for more productive enterprise; and to provide for federal intervention when necessary, in order to enable such distribution of the national income through reasonably full employment and the use of taxation together with fiscal management, in order to counter depression, control inflation and reduce poverty. The net result of all these measures flowing mainly from Washington, though often with heightened state legislative action taken in concert, was

Edward S. Mason (ed.), *The Corporation in Modern Society*, Cambridge, Mass., Harvard University Press, 1959; Gerhard Colm and Theodore Geiger, *The Economy of the American People: Progress, Problems, Prospects*, Washington, DC, National Planning Association Pamphlet 115, 1958, and 2nd ed., October 1961; Marshall E. Dimock, *The New American Political Economy: A Synthesis of Politics and Economics*, New York, Harper & Row, 1962; Adolf A. Berle, *The American Economic Republic*, New York, Harcourt, Brace & World, Inc., revised paperback, Harvest Ed., 1965; and Robert L. Heilbroner, *The Limits of American Capitalism*, New York, Harper & Row, 1966. Corporate executives' conceptions of the modern corporation appear in the McKinsey Lectures at Columbia University, all published by McGraw-Hill Book Co. in New York; R. J. Cordiner, *New Frontiers for Professional Managers*, 1956; C. H. Greenewalt, *The Uncommon Man*, 1959; Roger Blough, *Free Man and the Corporation*, 1959; T. V. Houser, *Big Business and Human Values*, 1957; F. R. Kappel, *Vitality in a Business Enterprise*, 1960; T. Watson, *A Business and Its Beliefs*, 1963; M. B. Folsom, *Executive Decision Making*, 1962; David Rockefeller, *Creative Management in Banking*, 1964.

to bring public government into the economic structure to an unprecedented extent. Yet the private governments of industrial corporations were left with a large scope of authority while new centres of power were facilitated in labour unions through legislation protecting the right of collective bargaining. While many businessmen resisted the New Deal measures as dangerously centralising and socialistic, the net result of the reforms during the past thirty years has been a *redistribution* of the power to govern the economy and not a strongly centripetal movement that left anaemia at the periphery. So far as the distribution of powers in the federal system is concerned, the result has been the strengthening of national powers to attack nationwide problems while at the state level the power to govern local affairs without undue constitutional restraints has actually been fortified, particularly in the field of taxation. As to the distribution of powers between public governments and the private governments of the corporation and the labour union, the trend has been toward a decidedly pluralistic pattern in which it is recognised in legal and political theory that the existence of numerous decision centres throughout the social structure of the nation vitalises the economy, and is essential for the protection of basic liberties.

Secondly, with respect to the corporate sector in particular, while there has been much federal and some state legislation governing the economy, the general principle has been sustained that there must be *a high degree of decision-making autonomy for corporate managements*. The immediate implication of this is that both the powers and the responsibilities of business corporations have been broadened and not diminished. It is true that in certain fields of corporate policy-making federal and state legislation impose important new substantive and procedural requirements on corporate directors and executive managers that were unknown before the reform movements of the past thirty years. These requirements have affected corporate decision-making especially in corporation finance, labour relations and marketing. They have never gone to the core of corporate autonomy in principle. This can be seen in the corporation laws of the several states which are the repositories of most of the law governing corporate affairs. The federal law touches only exceptional matters, however significant these may be, both for national policy on the economy and for the day-to-day management of corporate affairs. The recognition of industrial corporations, however large, as legitimate centres of power in a pluralist society, just as trade unions and other aggregates are so recognised, means that in American social thought in general both the *laissez-faire* and socialist solutions of the central issues of political economy have been rejected. 'Bigness' in business, labour and public government is still suspect to many; yet it seems to have been accepted that some kind of 'organisation revolution' has made economies of size inevitable. On the other hand, the presence of legitimately big and powerful private organisations has led to the necessity for big public government to represent and guard the national interest, while leaving as much freedom as possible to autonomous and local organisations in the private sector to govern their own affairs.

Thirdly, however, *the need for restraint on the power of corporate managements* has received and continues to receive attention by lawyers, economists, political scientists and legislators. In both external and internal relations of corporations this problem arises and has led to self-imposed reforms in corporate governance as well as legislative action. The entire range of corporate policies is evolved. A basic financial issue, for example, concerns the scope of corporate powers to allocate risk, control and profit through the corporation's security structure. In marketing and mergers there is the recurrent problem of monopoly. In employee relations there are issues not only of collective bargaining but also of protecting other rights, such as freedom of expression and political action. In general, it is now recognised by a growing number of scholars that corporate government, like public government, needs to be subject to certain constitutional restraints, whether these be the limitations imposed by the public law of state and federal constitutions and statutes or the self-imposed restraints of corporate constituencies. Many of the issues raised in this connexion have close parallels in disciplines related to the study of national and local governments under constitutional regimes where the protection of the rights of the individual is a primary goal. There is a notable change in the climate of debate about corporate power since the old muckraking days. Along with recognition of the need for adequate corporate authority to govern matters of proper corporate concern there is today more emphasis on the channelling of power than reducing it. This leads naturally to the question: power for what ends?

Fourthly, *the substance of corporate goals* and the appropriate means of reaching these goals are becoming increasingly significant items on corporate agendas and in the public forum in the United States. The subject is closely related to the scope and channelling of corporate powers. Against the more traditional view that corporate directors have but one duty—to maximise profits for stockholders through legitimate business operations— there are now more complex formulations, ranging from cautious moves concerning the theory and practice of social responsibility to all-out acceptance of the company, with its multiple goals, as a smaller 'society' within the greater social order, a habitat for Organisation Man. It cannot be said that the basic issue in this confrontation of ideas about corporate purpose has yet been resolved nor is likely to be within the near future.

Fifth, the corporate system in its presently advanced stages of development has brought with it *changes in the nature and content of the property system* in the United States. There is a tenuous and increasingly insubstantial line that connects the holder of company stock with those who actually manage a company's plant, control the use of its capital assets and determine the allocation of its profits. In between these extremes—the owner of shares and the 'real' proprietors of the enterprise—there now enter great financial institutions, the standard-bearers of the 'paraproprietal society'.[67] Berle and Means, in their groundbreaking work, *The Modern Corporation and Private Property*, published in 1932, had documented the thesis that ownership had been separated from control of private property through the device of the corporation. In more recent studies, Fr Harbrecht and others have shown how a new kind of organic economy of three interlocking systems, of which the corporate structure is an integral part, has displaced property in the con-

[67] See below, p. 132.

ventional sense as the concept that regulates the relationships between men and things. It is a system that places control of much of the nation's wealth in corporations, makes claims on corporate income negotiable in the financial markets, and establishes financial institutions to collect and use those claims as a basis for new claims that they offer to the public. In this unified organic system many new kinds of financial institution have appeared, notably mutual and private pension funds. Berle and Means had argued that the separation of ownership from control in the large publicly held corporation had divided the originally unified property into two kinds: active property (control) and passive property (shares of stock and bonds); that the traditional logic of property provided no adequate rationale for the distribution of profits and benefits of power in the modern corporation; that neither the assignment of all corporate profits to the passive owners nor the unlimited power of those in control to dispose of income and assets was justifiable; and that the net result was a demand that the modern corporation must serve society and not the owners and controllers alone. Private ownership of property in a classically conceived economy thus literally disappears as the basis for allocating goods and services; a whole new range of institutions has entered the scene. From the standpoint of public policy, and in particular legislative proposals on corporation law, these developments are of the greatest significance. It cannot be said that they are developments that are well understood or that the analyses just indicated are generally accepted in the United States. But they are at least of germinal importance and will undoubtedly affect the evolution of corporate theory in the years ahead.

Finally, *the emergence of the multinational corporation*, not as an exceptional type of business organisation, but rather as a normal means of doing the combined domestic and transnational[68] business that permeates all economies with the rise of an international economy, is posing many issues still to be resolved in economic and political theory, in international law and diplomacy, and in the organisation and management of more and more companies. Transnational business, with corporations having subsidiaries in many countries, some of them 'underdeveloped', is different in kind from the older patterns of world trade. Companies based in the United States, now extending both their markets and their sources of supply to their own affiliates abroad, face new kinds of obligations as well as profitable opportunities. As they enter the world arena—a place of vying for power as well as venturing for profits— these multinational companies, in common with similar companies in other leading industrial countries, have to manœuvre under conditions radically different from those that prevail in the domestic marketplace. In the absence of a world order, corporate management then becomes quasi-political because of the need to use all the instruments of strategy that states use—or at least to rely upon the power of nation states far more than they would at home. The effect is to alter both the nature of the modern corporation and the play of forces in the world arena.

The New Industrial Revolution produced by the explosion in technology has two consequences that directly affect the multinational corporation:

[68] For the use of this word and a discussion of the multinational corporation, see Part III, Ch. 3 below.

first, an unprecedented capability of the contemporary world to produce the goods it needs and wants and, secondly, a rapidly growing capability in managerial knowledge which can turn scarcity into affluence whenever men and nations choose to do so. The modern corporation has had a major role to play on both scores, but it remains to be seen whether the managerial capability can and will be applied mainly in *corporate* form to attack the problems of scarcity at the danger points in the world of today and tomorrow. These danger points are visible within nations (poverty pockets, even in the most affluent) and in relations among nations, especially the rich and the poor, the developed and the underdeveloped, the satisfied and the dissatisfied. The modern corporation cannot attack these problems alone; but its role in the emerging international industrial system will not be minor. An important question that now confronts the multinational corporation is whether its promoters will merely seek out the most promising places in the under-developed world for maximum exploitation, or engage in systematic efforts to collaborate with national and international public authorities for an attack on the problems of food and fibre production and distribution and the provision of products and services that will raise the world to a common level of affluence.

Chapter 2

SOME POSSIBLE PRIORITIES

---

*Are there any valid criteria (enforced, available
or advocated) which firms can, or might, use to
settle the priority to be given to possible company objectives? What priority do firms give to
the following objectives?—and what priority
might they give in the future?*

*1. Price reductions, quality improvements and
other* consumer *benefits.*
2. Dividends and other current benefits to
shareholders.
3. Pay and other employee *benefits, including
directors' remuneration.*
4. Development expenditure *within the firm
(e.g. capital investment, R & D, training) and*
ploughed-back profits—*should the ownership
of the latter be shared with groups other than
the shareholders, such as employees or the
state?*
5. Expenditure arising out of relations with
other firms (*e.g. membership of employers'
organisations and the maintenance of good
relations with distributors and suppliers*).
6. Service to the community *and amenability
to its priorities.*

The numbered sections below (in country
sections) correspond to these numbered
topics.

The only constraint under Belgian law which falls under the headings of this
chapter concerns a company's 'legal reserve'. The companies act provides
that 5 per cent of annual net profits must be committed to the 'legal reserve'

98

until the latter reaches 10 per cent of the firm's statutory capital. There is nothing laid down about how this reserve is to be used.

BRITAIN

As mentioned above (see p. 71), in forming a company the parties are free to choose whatever objects and purposes they wish, provided only that such objects are not unlawful under the general law. There is no direct compulsion to have objects which are regarded as beneficial to the country as a whole, nor are there restrictions to prevent the carrying on of business even though this may result in a movement of economic resources away from vitally important sectors of the national economy. Incentives are offered to induce people to engage in certain types of activities or to set up businesses in certain parts of the country, such as the government's directives to bankers to make loans only to those businesses which have high export records or potential, but nothing compels a company to undertake such activities.

Once a company has chosen its objects there is no general set of controls or priorities to be borne in mind when making decisions as to the future conduct of the business. Subject to the general rule of *ultra vires* (see above, pp. 71 ff) that powers must be exercised and decisions must be made in the interests of the company—and it is an improper exercise of power to consider solely the interests of some other class—the company is free to make whatever decisions it wishes. Although there are no general lists of priorities of competing interests, within each category of such interests there have been specific interventions as to how the power may be exercised.

1. A measure of price control is now exercised in Britain through the National Board for Prices and Incomes which was established by Act of Parliament in 1966, to exercise some control in the public interest over increases in prices and wages. Notice of any proposed increases in prices must be given to the Secretary of State for Employment and Productivity and the increase may not take effect for thirty days thereafter unless the Secretary of State consents. During that time the Secretary may refer the proposed increase to the Board for investigation, and the increase may not be made until the Board has reported. The considerations to be borne in mind by the Board in making an investigation are set out in Schedule 2 of the Act which provides that, wherever possible, increased costs should be borne by the manufacturer through reduced profit margins or greater efficiency and productivity. However, the Board itself, even if of the opinion that the proposed price increase is not justified in the national interest, does not have power to prevent the increase from being made; this power is reserved to the government and the power itself must be renewed annually.

The Resale Prices Act 1964 prevents suppliers of goods from imposing restrictions upon the minimum resale price of their goods. There is now no general right to resale price maintenance. Henceforth prices can be maintained only with the sanction of the Restrictive Practices Court which may grant exemption[1] on the grounds that, on the abolition of resale price

[1] The Resale Prices Act 1964 Section 5(2).

maintenance, (a) the quality or variety of goods available would be substantially reduced to the detriment of the consumer; (b) the number of retail outlets would be substantially reduced to the detriment of the consumer; (c) in the long run the price of the goods would be increased; (d) retail sales would take place under conditions likely to cause danger to the health of the public; and (e) necessary services in connexion with the goods would be substantially reduced to the detriment of the public. There is also a general provision that even if a specified ground for exemption can be proved, it must also be shown that the detriment caused to the public would outweigh the detriments arising from the continuance of resale price maintenance. This Act is limited to the maintenance of minimum prices, there is no restriction upon the right of a supplier to specify the maximum price at which his goods may be sold.

Much current thinking appears to be based upon the assumption that monopoly and oligopoly are undesirable since lack of competition leads to high prices and inefficiency. To increase competition, the Registrar of Restrictive Practices[2] and the Monopolies Commission[3] have powers to investigate and control monopolies and restrictive practices amongst manufacturers and suppliers of goods. Where one third or more of the market is controlled by one person or group of persons the Board of Trade has power to call upon the Monopolies Commission to investigate restrictive practices in relation to the supply of goods or services and to report back. The Board may publish all or part of the report and take steps to terminate the practices. The Commission itself has no power to make orders as to the ending of practices of which it disapproves; this is left entirely to the government.[4] The Board also has power to refer any proposed merger to the Commission where this would lead to or strengthen a monopoly situation or where assets worth more than £5 million are involved. The Board can prohibit such a merger if the Commission's report is unfavourable.

The Registrar of Restrictive Practices and the Restrictive Practices Court were created to control agreements[5] restricting the prices of goods and services, the terms on which they are to be sold, the quantities to be manufactured and the persons to whom they are sold. Such an agreement must be registered and is void as being contrary to the public interest unless the Court sanctions it as complying with one of the 'seven gateways'.[6] These provide that an agreement is valid if (a) it is shown to be necessary to protect the public against injury; (b) its removal would deprive the public of some specific and substantial advantages or benefits; (c) it is necessary to counter steps taken by another person which have the effect of reducing competition; (d) it is necessary to negotiate fair terms with a person who controls a preponderate part of the market or trade; (e) its removal would increase unemployment or (f) would reduce exports; or (g) its retention is necessary to support

[2] The Monopolies and Restrictive Practices (Inquiry and Control) Act 1948 and the Restrictive Trade Practices Act 1956.

[3] The Monopolies and Restrictive Practices Commission Act 1953 and the Monopolies and Mergers Act 1965.

[4] See, for example, the Commission's report on Cigarettes and Tobacco (1961) on which no action was taken.

[5] The Restrictive Trade Practices Act 1956 Sec. 6.

[6] ibid. Sec. 21.

another agreement. Once again there is a balancing provision which requires the Court to compare the advantages to the public as revealed by proof of one of the 'gateways' with the detriment to the public in allowing the practice to continue. On the other hand, the arguments in favour of economies of scale have not gone unnoticed. The Industrial Reorganisation Corporation, set up in 1966, has been provided with money by the government to assist in the amalgamation of companies where this would be in the interests of efficiency.

As a consequence of the Report of the Committee on Consumer Protection (the Malony Committee) which reported in 1961, a Consumer Council was established to represent the interests of consumers and to deal with complaints of inferior quality goods. Recently, the Trade Descriptions Act 1968 has provided that it is a criminal offence to supply or to offer to supply goods under a false or misleading statement as to price reductions, quality, composition, durability and reliability. This Act, which is to be administered by local authorities through their Weights and Measures Departments, does not provide any additional civil remedies but is an attempt by the government to safeguard the consumer.

2. At present there is a measure of dividend limitation, as part of the policy of income restraints.[7] This appears to be aimed largely at securing the co-operation of the trade unions in carrying out a general incomes policy. In addition to this, the present structure of corporation tax and taxation of dividends in the case of larger companies is designed to encourage the retention of profits rather than allow the distribution of profits by way of dividend.

Apart from questions of national economic policy, there has been some debate as to the desirability of retaining profits in the company rather than distributing the whole amount as dividend. For example, Alex Rubner in his book *The Ensnared Shareholder* has argued that the whole amount of profits should be distributed. It should be for the individual shareholder, not the directors, to decide upon the application of the profits. The member should determine whether the profits should go to charity or to political institutions, as well as whether the money should be invested in further developments. Capital should be raised on the open market so that the investors can determine whether to put their money into these projects; such a decision should not be taken from the shareholders by the directors.

Certainly if money is retained within the company it should be put to a use the return on which compares favourably with other investment opportunities. Unfortunately this is not always done, and one of the reasons advanced for many recent take-over bids has been the fact that the company has reserves which are not being put to profitable use. Moreover, as a company becomes increasingly self-financing, power passes from the shareholders to the directors. However, a certain degree of flexibility in relation to dividend policy is essential to the long-term planning of the company's affairs, and in the last resort the shareholders can remove the directors if dissatisfied with their conduct.

[7] The Prices and Incomes Act 1966 Sections 12 and Schedule 2 Part IV.

3. The National Board for Prices and Incomes has made a study of executive incomes at the most senior level, but has so far not made a systematic analysis of managerial salaries. Many of these incomes now have to be disclosed in the profit and loss account. 'Fringe benefits' are widely used as a means of remunerating a company's executives, although taxation has gradually eroded the efficacy of this method of remuneration. Subject to the overriding qualification that such payments must be for the benefit of the company,[8] the only legal restriction upon them is contained in Sec. 25 of the 1967 Act which makes it an offence for a director to buy an option to call for shares or debentures in his company.

As regards wages, the newly established Department of Employment and Productivity has made a policy not to give way to national wage claims by trade unions if they exceed a certain percentage unless they are part of a productivity agreement. In addition the National Board for Prices and Incomes is frequently called upon to investigate national wage agreements.[9] In some cases productivity bargains have been disallowed on the ground that they were inflationary.

At the lowest end of the income scale there has been a certain amount of agitation for a statutory minimum wage. However, the system of Wage Councils is the nearest that the government has approached to this. The system, which is governed by the Wages Councils Act 1959, enables the Secretary of State for Employment and Productivity to establish a Wages Council if no adequate machinery exists for the effective regulation of wages amongst a group of workers; or on the recommendation of a body representing workers and employers; or on the recommendation of a commission of enquiry. The Council consists of representatives of workers and employers and independent members appointed by the Secretary of State. A Wages Council has power to submit to the Secretary proposals for fixing wages to be paid to the workers, holidays and conditions of employment. On receipt of any wage proposals the Secretary may make an order giving effect to the proposals and thus create a minimum wage level for the workers covered by the Council. (These now number over three and a half million.)

4. A number of schemes exist in Britain to guide the internal expenditure of companies. Perhaps the most direct is the Industrial Training Council's group of Training Boards for each industry. Under the Industrial Training Act 1964, the Secretary of State for Employment and Productivity is empowered to make orders establishing boards to improve training of persons over the statutory minimum school leaving age. The boards are to provide or secure courses and other training facilities for persons employed in particular industries, and give recommendations as to the nature and length of training. They may pay maintenance grants, fees and travelling expenses to or for students attending approved courses. To meet expenditure a levy is imposed upon employers according to the numbers of their employees.

The National Economic Development Office assists companies in various industries, for each of which there is an Economic Development Committee

[8] Re Roith (W & M) Ltd. [1967] 1 All E.R. 427.
[9] The Prices and Incomes Act 1966 Sections 13–18 and Schedule 2 Part IV.

('Little Neddy'—'Neddy' being the popular name for the NEDC), in business decision-making, by means of interfirm comparisons, though not in all industries nor among all companies, and other joint efforts. It also publishes material on investment decision-making and similar topics.

The British Productivity Council is intended to help firms with their cost reduction and production planning. The British National Export Council encourages companies with their export selling and the Export Credit Guarantee Department provides financial assistance to exporting firms by guaranteeing payment by foreign buyers. The Ministry of Technology, with its research associations, tries to help companies with collective research and development, and the National Research Development Corporation develops innovations and offers them to companies under licence for exploitation.

The extent of company investment is largely regulated by means of fiscal instruments. Thus companies are allowed to set off expenditure on certain capital items against corporation tax, as well as allowances for depreciation, and special tax concessions apply to companies which open up factories in 'development areas' in an effort to persuade them to take work to areas of high unemployment, where there are also subsidies for the employment of local labour and grants and loans for the establishment of new businesses. The Selective Employment Tax introduced in 1966 is designed to persuade employers to make the most efficient use of this labour force. It is a rather crude instrument to encourage a reduction in the number of persons employed in service industries and by means of a rebate or subsidy to cause the transfer of people shaken out of such employment into the manufacturing industries. Dividend limitation has inevitably caused the retention of profits within the company but there is little evidence that the general level of investment has increased in step with it.

5. There appears to be no general public policy regarding membership of trade associations, research associations or similar bodies, although the Confederation of British Industry has been working towards a policy of encouraging mergers of overlapping or identical associations with a view to reducing the cost to firms. It is itself the product of a merger of three employers' organisations.

6. Again there is no co-ordinated, clear-cut policy regarding the public or communal responsibilities of companies, and the *ultra vires* rule ensures that firms do not go far beyond the bounds of their legal objectives. Outside activities such as education may be supported by a company provided that it can be seen to be in the long-term interests of the shareholders. For example, a chemical company is permitted to donate money to encourage research into chemistry.[10] However, contributions to charity exceeding £50 per annum in aggregate must now be disclosed in the directors' report, as also must political contributions.[11] The interests of the company are paramount and if a transaction does not satisfy these interests it is invalid no matter how philanthropic

[10] See, for example, *Evans v. Brunner Mond & Co.* [1921] 1 Ch. 359.
[11] Companies Act 1967 Sec. 19.

or beneficial to the national interest it may be. Thus in the Savoy Hotel Case[12] the directors had engaged in various transactions in relation to a take-over bid which they thought would have consequences which would be injurious to the interests of employees, as it would lead to redundancies, and would be injurious to the national interest since the closure of the Berkeley Hotel might lead to a reduction in American visitors visiting this country and bringing in dollars. The inspector held that these were improper considerations. As Professor Gower states:[13] 'In the eyes of the law, directors must not have regard to these outside interests except in so far as they are relevant to the primary object of making profits for the shareholders.'

FRANCE

There has been so little hard thinking about the objectives and responsibilities of business in France that it is difficult to single out any dominant priorities. Indeed, industry bases its decisions on different and often contradictory priorities. Furthermore, certain obligations are imposed on companies more by day-to-day needs rather than by goals relevant to a long-term policy.

1. As far as prices are concerned, business objectives depend more on the needs of the economy as a whole than on the direct interest of the consumer. The prices of industrial products were, in theory, frozen in September 1963. In practice, however, there has been a 'thaw' and at the time of going to press rigid price control has practically disappeared. Following the events of the Spring of 1968, however, the government 'advised' firms not to raise prices by more than 3 per cent. Under the Fifth Plan there is a system under which a sector or firm may negotiate with the government for a contractual freedom whereby the notion of the average price, without being deliberately disregarded, is placed in a wider context. Price freedom is allowed for the duration of the Plan in exchange for undertakings which vary according to the problems facing the particular sector—gains in productivity and the sharing of these gains, renewal and development of fixed assets, export performance, research, production objectives, wages policy, etc.

No criteria have been imposed on firms as regards the price to the consumer. Nevertheless, the public authorities are committed to free competition. The 'Fontanet Circular' and the establishment of the 'Leclerc Centres' (mainly for the sale of foodstuffs) have put emphasis on forbidding 'refusal to sell'—a manufacturer cannot refuse to sell his products to a buyer if they are normally offered on the market to others. Furthermore, the practice of imposing a minimum resale price or margin on a retailer is forbidden. Consumer protection is not at all effective in France: consumers' associations (see p. 230) are not common and have little means at their disposal. The government has now set up a Consumers' Institute, financed (not very generously) from public funds, in order to try to strengthen the protection of consumers.

[12] See the *Report of the Investigation into the Savoy Hotel*, H.M.S.O. 1954; 68 Harv. L.R. 1176.
[13] *Modern Company Law* (2nd ed.), at p. 475.

2. Dividends and benefits to shareholders have been a controversial topic for some time, especially as part of the debate on profit-sharing. (Under the new *intéressement* arrangements (which are described below, pp. 113 ff), shareholders are granted a sort of contractual dividend, giving ordinary shares, as it were, the status of preferential shares; what remains after this distribution is shared between shareholders and employees.) Louis Vallon, former *rapporteur* of the Finance Commission of the National Assembly and a left-wing Gaullist, is one of those who have expressed regret that personal taxes have increased faster than the tax on company profits. On the other hand, Paul Huvelin, President of the CNPF, has written: 'If we have fears to voice, it would be on the subject of conditions created for the French economy at the fiscal level, where the charges imposed upon us are excessive in comparison with those which our [EEC] partners tolerate.'[14]

In 1965 the National Assembly voted on a government proposal to improve conditions for shareholders. The 24 per cent tax on distributed dividends was suppressed in the case of shares or anticipation rights paid to French residents. Shareholders were also granted a 'fiscal credit' which allowed them to deduct a sum representing half their dividend income from their individual tax payments. This amounted, in a rather devious fashion, to refunding to the shareholder part of the company tax relating to the yield distributed. The objective was to boost private investment and thus the stock market, and also to facilitate self-financing.

3. In fixing their wages companies are bound by the overall national incomes policy. The 'SMIG', or 'mininum guaranteed inter-professional wage', is increased by the government either on its own initiative or as a result of a rise in the cost of living index. The SMIG directly affects 300,000 employees and indirectly 700,000 others, making a total of about a million workers whose incomes do not depend on the free decisions of companies. The government has also seen fit in the past to 'advise' firms not to increase wages beyond a certain rate in order to restrain inflationary tendencies. Finally, companies' freedom of decision is diminished by the practice of collective agreements negotiated at industry level by the trades unions and employers' associations. Once signed, the government can give such agreements the force of law and thus make their application compulsory. Over the past few years, however, there has been a tendency for the industry level collective agreement to decline compared with agreements at company level between employees' unions and the head of the firm.[15] In nationalised industries wages are fixed every year in negotiations whose rules have been laid down in the 'Toutée procedures'. Because trade unions always place wages in the forefront of their demands, they tend to look coolly upon other possible benefits, for fear of allowing themselves to be deflected from their primary aim. This partly explains why they have been unenthusiastic towards the various schemes for profit-sharing and participation in the results of the growth of firms that have

[14] *Le Monde*, 4 November 1966.
[15] See R. Goetz-Girey, 'Problème des syndicalismes', Institut de Préparation aux Affaires de l'Université de Lille, Study Session of 20–21 January 1964, CREE Document No. 80.

been proposed. (These plans and their culmination in the *intéressement* decree of 17 August 1967 are described below, pp. 107–117.)

In recent years there has been a hardening of position with regard to directors' emoluments. Opinion has swung in favour of control through fiscal means and of internal shareholder control. The law of 12 July 1965 provides that companies must furnish the Ministry of Finance, together with the declaration of their results, with a detailed account of a certain number of general expenses. Among these are the direct and indirect emoluments of the highest-paid persons, including reimbursement of expenses. The contractual indemnities and expense allowances of company directors remain free of personal income tax and the contractual payment on wages, if they are used in conformity with their intention or if they correspond to expenses, inherent in the nature of the job, which are not covered by the contractual deduction of 10 per cent. The new law on companies of 24 July 1966 lays down that the emoluments of the general manager and assistant general manager—or of the members of the 'directory'—must be approved by the administrative board or the supervisory board, as the case may be. (See p. 152 below for the board structure of French companies.) The original bill had provided for approval by the shareholders' general meeting but this was suppressed after coming under heavy fire from the managerial side. However, shareholders can obtain the exact overall amount (certified by the auditors) of the emoluments paid to the highest-paid people, the number of these being ten or five depending on whether the company employs more or less than 200 workers. Thus, secrecy concerning directors' emoluments, a tradition in France, will be maintained. This may essentially be ascribed to lack of interest and curiosity on the part of shareholders, in so far as they do not seek to exercise their right of being informed.

4. The *issue of securities* on the public market is subject to the authorisation of the Finance Ministry when they exceed Fr. 250,000 in value. This has enabled the state to keep a 'calendar' of issues, notably of preference shares, to avoid private loans competing simultaneously with public loans. These measures, however, have become very flexible.

Business *investment* has been encouraged since 1967 by a 'fiscal credit' of 10 per cent. Companies buying certain specified plant delivered or ordered before a determined date, are authorised to deduct 10 per cent of the price of the plant from the amount of tax that they pay to the state. This amounts to an indirect reduction of 10 per cent on the cost of the investment. It was essentially a measure intended to boost investment at a time when it had been very hard hit by the stabilisation plan, on the eve of the total opening of the frontiers of the Common Market. The system had almost died out when it was re-established, slightly modified, after the May–June crisis of 1968.

Productivity has been encouraged chiefly by the setting up of various organisations intended to help firms. Some of these organisations, such as the technical centres for each industry, are partly financed by state aid, but mostly by a tax levied on companies in the relevant sector of industry. One of the indirect objectives of the price freeze of September 1963 was to stimulate productivity. Companies in some sectors have been forced to improve their productivity by the fact that while they have not been able to raise their prices, the prices of raw materials, labour and public and private services have continued to increase.

Vocational training plays a growing part in the activities of firms. Previously, companies were obliged to devote at least 0·4 per cent of wages paid out to this purpose and the rate has now been raised to 0·6 per cent. If training activities within the firm do not meet with the approval of the public authorities, these sums are paid in the form of an apprenticeship tax to specialised organisations, which can be chosen by the company if it wishes. Representatives of the trade unions and employers' organisations, as well as of the ministries concerned, sit on the general assembly of AFPA (Association pour la Formation Professionnelle des Adultes), formerly known as ANIFRMO, an organisation which runs centres for adult vocational training.

Profit-sharing and employee participation in the growth of firms

As already mentioned, there have been a number of experiments and proposals in France for involving employees in the financial affairs of the company in which they work beyond the exchange of labour for wages. This section describes (*a*) various schemes that have been put into effect, generally without much result; (*b*) plans and proposals stimulated by the 'Vallon Amendment' of 1965; and (*c*) the culmination of all these developments in the decree of 17 August 1967 which has made employee participation in the results of the growth of firms obligatory in all companies with a payroll of more than 100.

French experiments aimed at giving employees a share in self-financing go back for more than fifty years. Some of these schemes involved participation in a company's capital, others in its growth. 'Joint stock companies with workers' participation' were established as a legal form in 1917. In addition to the capital, properly speaking, a certain number of worker shares gave the employees the right to representation at shareholders' meetings and on the board. This formula has not been popular; there were less than a dozen companies of this sort at the end of 1964.

'Workers co-operative production companies' were also set up by a law of 1917, amended in 1919 and 1922. This law is characterised by limiting the rights of capital holders with regard to both profits and management by granting only one vote to each 'member of the company' (*sociétaire*), however many his shares, and a preponderance on the administrative board of *sociétaires* working in the company over those not doing so. The 'Work Communities', whose principal promoter was and is Marcel Barbu—better known for having been a candidate in the 1965 French presidential election—have this structure. They had no more than 1,300 members at the end of 1964. As for the workers' co-operative production companies, properly speaking, there were about 600 of these at the end of 1964, employing a total of 40,000 people. Their development has been hampered by their small size and insufficient finance. Most are small building, contracting and printing firms with an average payroll of about sixty-five employees. The formula has little appeal for investors who are in a minority *vis-à-vis* those who work in the co-operatives.

The conferment on employees of free or preference shares has been encouraged by the government for some years. The statute of 7 January 1959 provided, in particular, that when a firm signed a contract with its employees with the object of the latter sharing in the company's registered capital, the creation and distribution of shares for workers would be exempt from all taxes (i.e. the charge on capital gains, the flat charge on wages and personal income tax). This formula has enjoyed relatively very little success: only nine companies employing rather more than 23,000 workers have concluded capital-sharing contracts. The government tried to go further in what became Art. 33 of the law of 12 July 1965, the fourth paragraph of which is known as the 'Vallon Amendment' (see p. 109, below). The new law provided that firms distributing free shares or participating rights should benefit by a reduction in corporation tax proportionate to the percentage of capital distributed to their employees over the course of five years; furthermore, the exemption from taxes and charges at the time of the distribution of shares would no longer be dependent on a contract such as was provided for by the statute of 1959.

Of the various firms which have distributed shares some have done so on an annual basis related to dividends, profits or turnover. Others have chosen different methods. Péchiney, in 1959, distributed shares on an increase in capital realised by the incorporation of reserves. Ugine, in 1958, paid special bonuses on the subscription of 18,000 shares reserved for employees for the purpose of increasing capital. Ferodo concluded a five-year agreement in 1960 (and renewed it in 1965) providing for the free distribution of shares to employees every year, conditional on the payment of the statutory dividend. Finally, certain companies have allowed their workers to acquire shares on advantageous terms. Papeteries de Kaysersberg, for example, gives employees the opportunity every year to acquire one share in the company at half the quoted rate.

Even if the numbers involved are still too small to draw any wide conclusions, it does seem that employees have kept a greater proportion of the shares received than might have been expected. At Péchiney, the 35,000 shares distributed in 1959 were registered but could be converted and freely ceded by the bearer. In 1964 nearly half of these securities were still registered and represented about 0·2 per cent of the total capital composed of 8,600,000 shares. The Ugine employees who in 1958 received 18,000 shares had resold only 1,800 six month later and, in the following year, they subscribed 9,000 new shares which brought their contribution up to about 25,000 shares. Without precise details being available, it was known that the situation had not greatly changed by 1964, when there was a further increase in capital. In Forges de la Foulerie, where a similar scheme is in operation, the percentage of capital held by the employees stood at 11 per cent in 1965 compared with 13 per cent in 1959, when the distribution was made.

Many plans for worker participation in company growth were tried during the decade following the war, but none had much success. They included the Bacon project of 1946 for a capital and savings company (revived in 1952); the Temple proposal of 1951 for company reform and sharing in the growth of productivity; the Soustelle plan of 1951, taken up again the following year by Louis Vallon and the Gaullist RPF party, for contracts associating capital and labour; and the Boisde profit-sharing plan of December 1953.

Two later projects came to something. The decree of 20 May 1955, prepared under the direction of M. Bacon, the then Minister of Labour, aimed at encouraging firms to improve their productivity by offering their employees a share in profits. When profit-sharing led to an agreement between the company and the accredited representatives of the workers, the state granted an exemption from the 5 per cent payroll tax. The scheme evoked little enthusiasm, however, and at the end of 1958 only 60,000 employees were taking advantage of it. A statutory order of 7 January 1959 resulted from a report prepared by the same M. Bacon (again Minister of Labour) at the request of General de Gaulle. It provided that profit-sharing for workers could result from a contract having the effect of a collective agreement or from the application of a special type of contract on the proposal of the head of the firm, so long as it were ratified by a two-thirds majority of the employees. Three types of non-obligatory contract were envisaged: collective participation in the growth of the firm (turnover, profits); participation in capital or in self-financing (shares, securities, interest); and sharing in the results of increased productivity. Although more appreciable fiscal exemptions were allowed than those granted under the decree of 1955, not a great deal came of this scheme. At the beginning of 1962, there were in all 150 profit-sharing contracts in effect concerning 72,000 employees. Capital-sharing contracts involved seven firms employing 14,300 workers; profit-sharing contracts thirty-six firms employing 11,300 workers; and turnover-sharing contracts fifteen firms employing 2,800 workers. Profit-sharing based on higher productivity formed the basis of contracts in ninety firms employing 43,000 workers. (François Sommer has advocated this last system in a book showing how it was applied in his own company.[16]) Finally, two contracts offered composite arrangements. By the end of 1964, the provisions of the 1959 decree had been applied to 203 firms employing some 104,000 workers. In November 1961 the government appointed a commission presided over by M. Masselin, Chief Judge of Appeal at the Court of Accounts, to look into the reasons for the slow progress of these schemes. His report gave rise to a Bill in 1964 which never came to a parliamentary vote.

The Vallon amendment

In these recent years, the debate has become ever more concentrated on the question of self-financing. It is generally agreed that the rate of self-financing in French private business is quite inadequate and compares unfavourably with that in many other countries. The issue came to a head when Louis Vallon added a fourth paragraph to what became Art. 33 of the Law of 12 July 1965. The now famous Vallon amendment read: 'The government shall bring in a Bill before 1 May 1966 defining the manner in which employees will have recognised and guaranteed claims against the increase in the fixed assets of firms as a result of self-financing.' Towards the beginning of 1966 Vallon and René Capitant (both Gaullists of the left) relaunched the debate through their weekly *Notre République*.

[16] F. Sommer, *Au-delá du salaire*, Robert Laffont.

The Vallon amendment occupies an important place in the more general question of the *rapprochement* of capital and labour, a constant theme of Gaullist policy since 1945, and, during this decade, a feature of the social teaching of the Roman Catholic Church. John XXIII's encyclical *Mater et Magistra* contained the following sentence: 'It can be stated, we believe, that, having regard to their self-financing, companies should grant their workers a certain claim against it, especially if wages do not exceed the basic rate.' In February 1966 the note of the French Episcopal Commission, published with the approval of the permanent Council of the Episcopal Assembly, took up the same idea:[17] 'By its nature, its formation and its use, self-financing is a focus of multiple rights which must be recognised, assured and organised with the participation of the various interested parties.' Moreover, as early as 1965, Pierre Massé, then Commissioner General of the Plan, wrote in his report on incomes policy: 'One of the problems arising is that of the workers' right to acquire a share in the increase in assets brought about by self-financing.'

Vallon put his idea forward in very general terms. There was no lack of suggestions as to how it might be implemented. Marcel Loichot, President of SEMA (Société d'Economie et de Mathématiques Appliquées), made a proposal of what he calls 'pancapitalism', based on an association, or rather a merger, of capital and labour by a system of share distribution. Assuming that self-financing represents 6 per cent of the initial capital every year, a firm's employees would acquire, under the 'Loichot Plan', the majority of the capital in about twenty-five years, without any of the original shareholders having been dispossessed. Loichot suggested two ways of doing this. According to the first scheme, the company would pay at least 10 per cent of its direct profits into a tax-free self-financing account. The exchequer would make a grant equal to half the sum already credited to this account. Profits not paid into this self-financing account would be distributed to the shareholders. At the end of, or within six months of the end of, each financial year, the credited amount of the tax-free self-financing account would be incorporated into the firm's capital, one third being paid into a 'joint pancapitalist fund', which would belong to the employees, and the other two thirds being issued to shareholders. Under the second scheme, the company would not be required immediately to pay a part of its profits into the tax-free self-financing account. Instead, it would set aside 2·5 per cent of the capital directly employed for dividends, while all remaining profits would be paid into the self-financing account. In its turn, half of this account would be paid into the 'joint pancapitalist fund'. In this case also, the exchequer would increase the sum in the self-financing account by half by way of a grant. In both formulae, the monies paid into the 'joint pancapitalist fund' would be frozen for a period of ten years.[18]

The original 'Halff Plan' goes back to the time of the Masselin Commission in 1961. Its author, Maurice Halff, chairman of Houillères du Bassin de Lorraine and adviser to the Ministry of Social Affairs, later revised it. The

[17] The Note of the Episcopal Commission was published in *Cahiers d'action réligieuse et sociale*, No. 427, 15 March 1966.
[18] See 'Le Dossier de l'amendement Vallon', *Hommes et Commerce*, No. 92, September/October 1966.

proposed formula is moderate but obligatory.[19] 'Its spirit can be summed up thus: dividends that are deferred (by being incorporated into the capital of the firm) should be balanced by deferred wages. The former would finally lead to a distribution of shares; the latter to a supplementary payment. In order not to discourage present shareholders or savers, the state would, in the businesses concerned (all limited companies), have to compensate for a large part of the reduction in return to shareholders by lowering the rate of tax on industrial and commercial profits.' The mechanism proposed was the establishment of an 'Investment Bank for Employees' Self-financing' (CIPAS) to which would be paid, in the form of shares, a part of the net self-financing of companies (not including liquidations). The bank could in this way distribute to employees the amount of supplementary retirement pay corresponding to the shares thus accumulated. There would be a single bank for the whole of France and for all sectors of industry. Its administration would be the responsibility of employees' representatives, employers and the state.

Other proposals have been put forward, notably by Bernard Jousset, former president of the Christian Employers' organisation, who suggested adopting the formula of a 'Workers' Provident and Savings Society' (*Société Ouvrière de Prévoyance et d'Epargne*); and by Maurice Cliquet, a labour relations consultant, who advocated profit-sharing contracts with partial deferment of payment.[20]

Plans arising from the Vallon amendment aroused much lively hostility in 'neo-liberal' and employer circles. The left-wing Gaullists were obviously ardent partisans and made it something of a war-cry in the parliamentary elections that followed. The Perspectives and Réalités Club (of which Valéry Giscard d'Estaing is chairman and whose group in the National Assembly was responsible at the time for allowing the Vallon amendment to become law) was opposed to the proposed plans chiefly for technical reasons. Both in the name of 'liberalism' and the interests of employees, Jean-Louis Tixier-Vignancourt, a former presidential candidate, spoke for the traditional political Right when he said: 'The ... plans are designed to assure a share in profits, in the form of the distribution of shares, not to employees but to a national investment bank. Thus, in a few years' time, the technocratic state would be a majority shareholder in all French companies.' The official employers' organisations were strongly opposed to the plans. In an address in June 1966 to the General Assembly of the CNPF, its new president Paul Huvelin brought up four main objections, quite apart from his fear of seeing private property placed in question.[21] He maintained that sharing in self-financing would weaken economic growth in the face of international competition; would not ensure a fair redistribution of the fruits of expansion; would not help bring about better understanding between the two sides of industry; and would prevent the harmonisation of national laws within the EEC.

Some employers' representatives, however, were more in favour. Bernard Mallet, for instance, Chairman of Brissonneau et Lotz, considered that shares

---

[19] P. Drouin, 'Autofinancement et droits des salariés', *Le Monde*, 13 to 16 April 1966.

[20] M. Cliquet, 'Les contrats d'intéressement avec partie differée', *Le Quotidien Juridique*, No. 97, 3 September 1966.

[21] *Patronat Français*, No. 264, July 1966.

should be distributed to employees in relation to company growth confirmed over a fairly long period, say five years. Marcel Demonque, Chairman of Ciments Lafarge, wrote: 'There is no doubt that the problem of sharing in self-financing would be treated in a very superficial manner if only material investment were taken into account. The notion of non-material investment, the great riches of which should be tapped, suggests a striking confirmation of the largely collective nature of business ownership.'[22] Members of the Young Employers' Centre (CJP) were always favourably inclined towards sharing formulae, even if they have been sometimes more timid about putting them into effect. The Rouen branch of the CJP, for example, stated: 'Self-financing does not belong to a single sleeping partner; the workers can have a right to its administration. There should be participation of workers in self-financing, with the object of integrating the worker into his company to the maximum extent, without, however, chaining him to it.'[23]

Employees' organisations have consistently adopted a very cool attitude towards all participation formulae. The Mathey Commission report (see next paragraph) put it like this. 'All workers' groups think that they should intervene, but they differ about the levels at which organisations should be set up, and on possible formulae for implementing these ideas. Everything goes to show that the attitude of the trade unions would be lukewarm, and that the hope of sharing in self-financing would not cause them to abandon a single one of their claims.' The communist CGT continues to fight capitalism and has no wish to be associated with it. As early as 1958 it asserted that 'the association of capital and labour has no true end other than to make the workers share in their own exploitation'. The more[24] moderate CFDT does not want employees to become 'little capitalists' but would not be hostile to the establishment of a national development fund which would administer the workers' shares in self-financing and intervene on a national level to help realise the objectives of the Plan. The former CFTC, on the contrary, would accept agreements only at the level of the individual firm. 'We insist that this reform must be brought about by means of agreements negotiated between employers and employees. This is the only method which allows account to be taken of the factors which are involved in each firm.'[25]

In order to sort out the problem and to keep the undertakings included in the law of 12 July 1965, the government appointed the Mathey Commission which published its report on 1 July 1966. It is important to note that the government had at the outset fixed four conditions which any formula suggested should meet: (i) Workers' rights could come only from growth of a company's capital due to self-financing. (This ruled out the 'non-material' investments to which Marcel Demonque referred.) (ii) Funds representing the employees' share in the growth of capital should remain at the disposal of the firm for its investments. (iii) The administration of the funds representing the employees' share in capital growth could, at least in part, be exercised by

[22] M. Demonque, 'La firme et son rôle dans les systèmes économiques français', *Revue Economique Appliquée* (Archives de l'ISEA).

[23] CJP study paper, CREE Document No. 58.

[24] *Le Peuple*, 15 July 1958.

[25] *Syndicalisme 65*, No. 11, January/February 1966.

a body outside the company. (This excluded the national bank formula in the Halff and CFDT proposals.) (iv) Sharing by employees in self-financing should not affect firms' existing capacity for financing, their performance or administration, or jeopardise the maintenance of the level of investment.

The report of the Mathey Commission contributed abundant and valuable information on the amount of self-financing and on businesses running at a loss, sector by sector. It also reviewed all the various possible solutions. Its final conclusion was negative: 'These fundamental reasons lead all the members of the Commission, with the exception of one, to think that if the reform provided for by Art. 33 is not definitely decided on in principle, it would be right to abandon its application and to look for other solutions to the problem.' Nevertheless, the Commission made some proposals. It felt that the best solution would be to give employers and employees the opportunity of adopting an agreed system according to which they would decide what were the recognised rights of employees and how they should be catered for. The report concluded: 'The Commission does not try to hide the inconveniences and complexities of the provisions which it has studied. The proposals which it has not felt able to avoid formulating do not escape the objections developed above. They could hardly, to our eyes, be anything but a lesser evil.' The Gaullist left wing continued to back the project vigorously. Government circles, however, seemed reserved. The Minister for Economics and Finance himself was hostile and described the proposal as a 'diabolical myth'. The Prime Minister was, officially, less hostile as he was concerned to maintain the unity of the parliamentary majority. General de Gaulle, for the moment, kept his peace.

The new participation formula

The issue was, at least for the time being, settled by the decree of 17 August 1967, which made employee participation in the results of the growth of firms obligatory. The new system is familiarly known in France as the *intéressement des travailleurs*, i.e. the acquisition by workers of an 'interest' in their firm. (For convenience, the French word *intéressement* is retained in this account.) The details of the decree are complicated but a résumé of its broad outlines can be made.

The participation scheme involves four general principles. First, employee participation in economic expansion at the level of their own company has, for the first time, been recognised as a right. The procedure is now obligatory for all companies covered by the criteria laid down in the decree. Second, the benefits of this participation must be saved. The money laid aside for employees, calculated on the basis of the taxable profit of the firm and shared out according to wage rates, represents the wage-earners' part in capital formation within the enterprise. The sums due to employees are frozen for a period of five years, during which they may be neither sold nor claimed. Third, the *modus operandi* of participation entails an agreement between the parties concerned. The head of the company and the employees must between them determine, within the framework laid down by the decree, what is due, to what use it is to be put and how it is to be administered. The institutional forms and the content of these agreements may vary considerably; indeed,

113

the whole functioning of participation hinges on a spirit of 'contract' which must underlie its administration by the management and the official representatives of the workers. Finally, one of the basic aims of the scheme is the avoidance of any check to investment, of which there is a danger because of the reduction of resources available for re-investment. The provisions of the decree for this reason include incentives in the form of tax deductions from which firms may benefit when they devote to productive investment sums equal to those laid aside for their employees. In this sense, the decree offers firms a fiscal investment credit, of a general and permanent character, which is intended to encourage a desirable increase in capital expenditure.

The participation scheme does not apply to all French wage-earners; at least for the present, its application is limited to firms which regularly employ more than 100 wage-earners. Smaller companies are not obliged to put employee participation into effect since it could, in certain cases, be beyond their means. They may, however, voluntarily join the scheme and thus benefit from the tax advantages which come with it.

Just as the amounts due to shareholders which result from non-distributed profits are consolidated in various reserves figuring on the liability side of the balance sheet, the new participation rights of employees are also consolidated by means of a reserve. This reserve, however, is kept separate from the others and is designated the 'Participation Reserve'. (This holds good for both public and private companies.) The total annual sum of the *intéressement* is arrived at by means of the calculations described in the following paragraphs.

The originators of the scheme wished to link the value of employee participation to a figure which could be assessed as exactly as possible. Consequently, the chosen starting point is the company's taxable profit, which is calculated according to general rules fixed by law and administrative regulations and is also established by the company management. The notion of taxable profit has, however, been modified in two important respects by the decree. First, the amounts due to employees in respect of the previous financial year, and consolidated during that year in the special participation reserve, are deductible from the year's taxable profit. Second, a deduction may be made of an 'investment provision' equal to the sum paid into the participation reserve. In other words, firms can benefit from deductions equal to twice the amount of the *intéressement*.

Although the base for calculating the *intéressement* corresponds to a fiscal definition, the actual base sum is not exactly that of the pre-tax profit. In order to prevent the interests of employees being harmed by the 'investment provision' (which is aimed at furthering the economic ends of the enterprise), the decree lays down that the net profit serving as the base for the calculation of *intéressement* should be augmented by the sum made over to the investment provision. In other words, to calculate participation, the investment provision which is deducted for the establishment of tax is reintegrated into the taxable profit. Correspondingly, if this provision is carried forward to the taxable profit for the following financial year because it has not been used for its stated object and within the allotted time, its amount is then excluded from the net profit ascribable to the tax period during the course of which this carrying forward has been made.

The decree also provides that before the calculation of the *intéressement* a deduction should be made from the net profit (after tax) to remunerate the owners of the capital of the firm. This deduction (which is a matter of book-keeping independent of the dividend distribution policy of the firm) is equal to 5 per cent of the capital employed. (The capital to which this deduction relates consists of the following elements: registered capital; reserves; amounts carried forward; provisions which have borne tax; and special provisions.)

The basic idea of *intéressement* is that wage-earners should contribute, along with the other factors of production, to the growth of the enterprise. In labour-intensive firms, however, the part played by wage-earners in capital formation is very high, whereas in highly mechanised firms it is low. To take account of these differences, which are sometimes very large and which could otherwise have led to much unfairness, the decree lays down that the 'net profit' after tax should be adjusted by a coefficient of wages paid divided by value added. Such a 'key' seeks to reflect the share of labour in the creative activity of the firm. In labour-intensive industries this share could go as high as 65 per cent. In industry as a whole, the coefficient would most often be between 45 and 55 per cent. In advanced industries (oil refining, for example) the coefficient would be low; but as wage-earners would be few in number they would not suffer.

The total of the *intéressement* assigned to employees for the financial year is equal to half the sum obtained by the foregoing calculations. (The choice of this 50/50 split has no very precise logical foundation but in practical terms it seemed to be reasonable and fair.)

The *intéressement* is distributed to employees on a sliding scale according to wages. There are, however, two qualifications which stress the social character of the decree: (a) the wage taken into account for calculating an individual's share cannot exceed a sum equal to four times the ceiling set for the determination of the maximum amount of social security and family allowance contributions, i.e. Fr. $13,680 \times 4 =$ Fr. 54,720; (b) the sum which can be credited to an employee cannot, during one financial year, exceed a sum equal to half the annual sum of this same ceiling, i.e. Fr. $13,680 \div 2 =$ Fr. 6,840. In whatever form *intéressement* credits are granted to workers (see next paragraphs), they cannot in principle become available until a period of five years has elapsed. The amounts credited to employees are liable neither to income tax nor to the fiscal and other charges made on wages.

The employees' credits may be made over to them in three ways. Two of these entail a use of the sums paid into the participation reserve within the firm and are more especially concerned with the idea of associating employees with the company. The third seeks to meet another aim, that of diversifying the uses to which the *intéressement* may be put: the money may be devoted not only to shares in the worker's own firm but to those issued by other companies or institutions.

The first method, so long as the firm is a capital company, is to grant employees shares in their own enterprise. To do this, the company can augment its capital by incorporation of reserves or itself acquire its own shares. The second choice is to constitute the credits as debts of the firm. This may be done by, for instance, issuing debentures in principle frozen for five years or by opening a blocked account for the same period in the employee's name. In both cases, the sums involved must be re-invested in the company, this in a way forming the security for the debts. Whichever method is chosen, the debts on behalf of employees bear interest, the rate of which is fixed in a contractual manner between the head of the firm and the employees. Finally, the *intéressement* may be used on the financial market, either by paying the sums into an investment institution outside the company or by starting a company savings scheme.

The following is an example of a calculation of employee participation. It is ficticious but the data are close to those that would be met with in an average-sized limited company in manufacturing industry.

Bases

1.	Number of wage-earners	2,000
2.	Wage bill	Fr. 27,500,000
3.	Capital employed	Fr. 42,000,000
4.	Value added during financial year	Fr. 55,000,000
5.	*Intéressement* paid in respect of previous financial year	Fr. 800,000
6.	Investment provision (= 5)	Fr. 800,000
7.	Profit before deductions	Fr. 11,600,000

Calculation

8.	Profit of current financial year after deduction of *intéressement* paid in respect of previous financial year (7–5)	Fr. 10,800,000
9.	Taxable profit after setting aside of investment provision (8–6)	Fr. 10,000,000
10.	Corporation tax	Fr. 5,000,000
11.	Net profit (base of *intéressement*) (8–10)	Fr. 5,800,000
12.	Remuneration of capital (5 per cent of 3)	Fr. 2,100,000
13.	Disposable profit (11–12)	Fr. 3,700,000
14.	Application of coefficient (2÷4, i.e. 50 per cent) to disposable profit	Fr. 1,850,000
15.	Sum total of *intéressement* half of 14	Fr. 925,000
16.	*Intéressement* as a percentage of wage bill (15 as a percentage of 2)	3·36
17.	Average employee's share of *intéressement* (15÷1)	Fr. 462·50

It may be added that after the crisis of May–June 1968 and the 'Grenelle agreements', the government prepared several plans which fell in the area designated 'participation' by General de Gaulle. (This term extended to regional and university reform.) The main new trends in industry concern: (*a*) obligatory setting up of union plant branches; (*b*) better protection of employees' rights within the firm; (*c*) fuller information for employees on the situation of their company; and (*d*) obligatory consultation with employees before certain decisions are made by the management.

5. The problem of mergers and amalgamations remains a very lively issue in France. The law of 12 July 1965 appreciably modernised and reduced the tax burden attached to mergers, even if more progress can be made in this direction. One feature was that the public registration of a merger now involves a fixed duty of Fr. 50 and not a proportional duty. Mergers are exempted from the *publicité foncière* tax, and the take-over of liabilities which are a charge on the capital are freed of all transfer taxes and dues. Other benefits are allowed for the increase of capital resulting from a merger, and the profit on the revaluation of fixed assets by reason of the merger is not liable to company tax.

6. Directly and indirectly, companies are called upon in the public interest to undertake a certain number of tasks or to operate in a certain way.

Industrial decentralisation. Through the Territorial Planning Board, which is under the direct authority of the Prime Minister, the government is taking steps to steer industries at present installed in or around Paris to the provinces (the 'French desert' as it has been called). As far as possible the firms are re-located in the priority zones, especially in the western regions of the country. The authorities use various means to encourage firms to move, including grants of up to one third of the investment, loans, interest rebate, fiscal exemption and help in vocational training, etc.

Firms are bound to take note of a large number of administrative provisions affecting the *protection of local amenities*, particularly with regard to pollution from smoke and effluent. The fact remains that these regulations are not always scrupulously observed.

Housing comes within the area of company responsibility in France and firms are obliged to devote to building a sum equal to at least 1 per cent of their wage bill, usually made over to housing organisations. Big companies may allocate rented housing to their workers in developments blocks built with the aid of their payments.

The *resettlement* of certain categories of people has also, in part, been made the responsibility of private and public enterprises. 'Reserved jobs' are provided for war veterans, war wounded, etc. In more recent years, advantages have been given to firms employing repatriates from North Africa. These obligations are part of more general business responsibilities for maintaining the level of employment. If, in law, firms are quite free to dismiss workers whenever they consider it necessary, they are, in fact, very much subject to the agreement of the public authorities. Opinion is very sensitive on this matter and the authorities do their utmost to avoid any deterioration in the political climate.

Finally, it may be noted that the *Press* is considered to have a public function and therefore enjoys a certain number of advantages, generally of a fiscal or quasi-fiscal character.

THE NETHERLANDS

1. A Dutch company is in principle free to decide its own price policy. In practice, however, this freedom is limited by important external factors.

Under the Prices Act of 1961 the government has the power to fix maximum prices for goods or services, either in general or in respect of individual branches of trade or industry, if this should be in the general social and economic interests of the country. Companies can thus be compelled by ministerial price regulations, which remain in force for up to a year, to keep their prices stable or reduce them to the maximum level permitted by the minister. Government intervention of this kind seldom occurs, however, as a result of an *ad hoc* consultation system that has grown up between the government and industry and has come to be regarded as the cornerstone of prices policy; ministerial intervention is a last resort. This system has resulted in a number of rules of behavior which industry is expected to observe with regard to prices. Thus, intended price increases are reported to the government; in principle, no price increases are allowed on the grounds of wage increases, the government taking the view that the latter should be absorbed by higher productivity; prices, however, may be increased if costs rise as a result of external factors, such as higher raw materials costs, freight charges or the like.

2. There are no particular restrictions with regard to dividends and other benefits to shareholders.

3. Wages and other benefits are settled with the trade unions and laid down in collective labour agreements. Under the 1945 Act governing labour relations, the government has the power to intervene in collective agreements if the wage increase agreed upon threatens to conflict with general economic interests. Under this act all collective labour agreements have to be approved before they can enter into force. Holland has consistently pursued a national wages policy since 1945 and resolved upon a fundamental change in 1968. The period from 1945 to 1968 can be divided into three phases.

From 1945 to 1959 the government annually fixed a percentage wage increase ceiling which was binding upon all Dutch industry. A national system of job evaluation, strict rules governing incentive payments and a maximum level of incentive bonuses helped to maintain close control on the level of wages. This policy of stringent intervention was aimed chiefly at an equitable distribution of the limited national income and at avoiding inflation in the post-war period of economic and industrial recovery. Its success and the attendant industrial expansion enabled the country to improve its competitive position in world markets. Such a policy would not, however, have been possible without the willing co-operation of unions and employers. The fact that such co-operation was forthcoming was at least in part due to the work of the Labour Foundation formed in 1945. This body, in which employers' organisations and trade unions are equally represented, has enabled the two sides to get together to discuss their problems in an atmosphere of mutual trust and confidence.

The second phase, from 1959 to 1967, was one of rising prosperity and growing opposition, mainly on the part of the unions, to the rigid system of uniform wages rounds. In 1959 it was decided to allow exceptions from the national standard, provided the parties could demonstrate that the productivity of the enterprise or branch of industry justified a larger wage increase. This was not a success, mainly because the change coincided with a period of economic boom and very tight labour market conditions which themselves exerted strong upward pressure on wages. In 1962, therefore, the national rise in productivity was reinstated as the deciding factor, although this did not mean a return to the pre-1959 system of general wages rounds fixed by the government. The parties represented in the Labour Foundation were jointly to settle the percentage by which the national wage level could be allowed to rise without jeopardising economic stability. If the government approved the proposed percentage, both sides of industry had then to adhere to it, under the supervision of the Foundation. This meant that the latter bore the primary responsibility for wage trends at national level.

The effectiveness of this system was tested for the first time in 1964, in a climate of keen industrial expansion, growing exports and a shortage of labour. Wages were under severe pressure and in various sectors were widely paid in excess of the approved national level. As time went on the unions became less and less inclined to adhere strictly to the national level and began to regard the prescribed percentage as a minimum increase beyond which they sought to secure extra concessions in the bargaining process. There were only two alternatives: to continue with the prevailing system of a national guideline laid down by the Foundation in consultation with the government; or to change over to a system of freer wage negotiations.

The Netherlands opted for the second alternative at the beginning of 1968, chiefly because of a gradual change in the climate of industrial relations. The national wages policy had met with growing opposition from the unions, whose appeal to the worker had been adversely affected by the system: many workers were unable to identify themselves with the aims of a national socio-economic policy and a centralised wages policy subordinated to it. Some unions tried to solve this dilemma by demanding extra advantages exclusively for organised workers. This was strongly opposed by the employers who, for their part, felt that the wages policy of recent years had not made adequate allowance for what the individual industries and companies could afford. In effect, they agreed with the unions that, in the circumstances, there was a need for greater differentiation in wage levels than could be obtained under the system then in force.

January 1968 marked the most fundamental change that Dutch wages policy had undergone since 1945. For the first time joint wage agreements were to be concluded between unions and employers, either at industry or at company level, without national, fixed and binding percentage increases being laid down and without individual agreements having formally to be checked and approved against such a general guideline. This means that responsibility for wage trends again lies with the contracting parties although the liberalisation of wages has not ruled out every possibility of government intervention. Collective labour agreements have still to be registered and if there are signs that the general rise in the wage level presents a serious threat to economic stability, the Minister of Labour can still order a wage freeze whereby the existing joint agreements have to be extended for a certain period. Hence the new freedom is conditional but it certainly represents a considerable shift

119

away from the principles underlying Dutch wages policy since 1945. So long as the leadership on both sides fully recognise their responsibility to the national economy, the risks in the freer system are not excessive.

A Bill to replace the relevant parts of the Act of 1945 by new rules concerning wages was before parliament at the time of going to press. It provides, *inter alia*, that collective labour agreements may come into force only four weeks after the registration of the agreement with the Minister of Labour, who may prevent the agreement (or any part thereof) from entering into force if he considers this necessary in the public interest, from the social or economic point of view. The Bill also provides for the possibility of a wage freeze if such a measure is necessary to protect the national interest.

Policy with respect to the salaries of higher-grade employees is in principle unrestricted but is in practice tied in with developments in the lower grades. There is also freedom with regard to directors' remuneration. However, in certain cases the excessive remuneration of non-executive directors (i.e. members of a supervisory board) has come in for a fair amount of criticism in the press and there is now an increasing tendency to set maximum limits in the articles of association to the fees payable to supervisory directors.

4. Dutch companies are free under company law to determine the manner in which they wish to use retained profits (e.g. by ploughing them back or distributing them), with due regard, of course, to the provisions of the articles of association. The actual priority given to the use of profits in the company depends upon many internal and external factors.

One point that has been widely discussed in recent years is whether and, if so, to what extent employees are entitled to share in retained profits. The unions have repeatedly claimed that employees should be allowed to share in retained profits through the distribution of shares or through a money payment, neither to be distributed immediately to the employees but to be paid for investment purposes into an account blocked for a period of five years. The unions would like to see this done through their own investment institutions.

The three employers' associations examined the profit-sharing proposals put forward by the three national federations of trade unions and stated certain objections (in a report entitled *Ways towards Property Formation*) which may be summarised as follows.

Profit-sharing in companies which have ploughed back profits tends to have an inflationary effect on the share capital, resulting in a steadily increasing dividend charge and thus reducing the stability of operating results. The result of this may be a downward pressure on share prices on the stock market and less interest on the part of investors, thus making it more difficult to attract fresh capital. Moreover, profit-sharing through the trade unions' own investment institutions would lead to a concentration of share ownership with the trade unions and could have adverse consequences on relations within the enterprise and on the management's essential freedom to make financial decisions. In any event, very few firms have excess profits to the degree implied by the trade unions, claims the report, and for the great majority of employees profit-sharing would therefore have little or no significance. Finally, from the point of view of the national economy as a whole, profit-sharing would tend to slow down economic growth, make the economic system less attractive and entail a slower rise of real incomes—profit-sharing being seen in terms of rising wage costs.

The report suggests other ways by which employees might be better enabled to acquire property, such as wage-saving schemes and making use of state facilities to encourage saving (savings premiums, for instance, or exemption from taxes and social premiums). Companies could stimulate wage saving by granting extra premiums to employees on the amounts deducted as savings from their wages.

Generally speaking, employers in the Netherlands are not opposed to making extra annual payments to their employees if business has gone well, since it is felt to be right and proper that employees should have some share in the results. Many companies therefore do, in fact, have profit-sharing arrangements and privileged savings schemes for their employees. In many cases employees are allowed to invest part of their income or profit share towards the purchase of securities or a house (for instance), which is again a method of encouraging property formation. The use of these savings for the formation of assets receives further encouragement from the state in that they are exempt from taxation and from the payment of social insurance premiums, provided they remain for a specified number of years in a blocked account. In existing profit-sharing schemes and suchlike there is usually no question of employees sharing in the total profit, but simply in the distributed profit. (See also 6, below.)

5. There are no problems as far as company law is concerned with regard to expenditure arising out of relations with other firms, provided it is in the long-term interests of the company. Several organisations have been set up for co-operation in certain fields of common interest such as wages, prices and trading policies and research. In general, these inter-firm relations are established in areas where the companies concerned consider them to be useful and necessary for the well-being, continuity and progress of their business. The necessary funds are raised by subscriptions, donations and contributions.

6. Under the heading of 'service to the community' there is again no problem of company law, so long as the basic interests of the firm are not compromised. In general it can be said that large and expanding companies have contributed since the second world war, on a voluntary basis, to the spread of industry to those parts of the country where its establishment was desirable for structural reasons and as such was encouraged by the government. Many firms—usually large ones—considering it important for their continuity and prosperity to promote healthy staff relations and good working conditions, provide various other services in the general social field. These include amenities in the field of public health and industrial medicine, recreational facilities, local activities and donations to education, research and charity. Companies also serve the community by releasing senior staff for educational work outside the firm, by setting up company educational and training

schemes and by giving additional encouragement to the growth of asset formation among employees, as outlined above. Other benefits include: financial assistance towards the building of a house, financial support for the further education of employees or of their children and the promotion of cultural activities in the local community. Recently some companies have also begun to subsidise trade union activities in connexion with the education or recreation of their members, this being thought to be of general importance from the social as well as the company's point of view. It cannot be said that there is at present any particular pressure to have these and similar activities regulated by law. In some instances, however, services or amenities such as a swimming pool or playing grounds are provided with the object of inducing government authorities to grant certain permits. The dangers of such practices have been pointed out by several authors.

SWEDEN[26]

1. There are, of course, numerous laws and regulations in Sweden which protect the consumer by prescribing the limits of action within which a firm must operate; but Swedish law has nothing directly to say about how a company—or any other type of business—should act in order to promote benefits for the consumer. On the other hand, legislation on the freedom of trade (which has been gradually extended) is based on the idea that the greatest possible freedom of competition works in favour of consumers. In a competitive market consumers choose between various alternatives offered for sale and price relations between goods and service reflect their marginal preferences.

It would clearly need much detailed research to give an accurate assessment of the precise place which the promotion of consumer benefits occupies on the scale of priorities of Swedish companies. From a general point of view, the Swedish attitude would be that the pursuit of these benefits as such cannot be an objective for the activities of a firm, but that because of the mechanism of competition they will, albeit indirectly, play a central role. A firm cannot and should not itself decide what is best for consumers; this is something consumers must do themselves. What a firm does will ultimately depend on its 'strategic' judgment of the interaction of price, quality and demand.

2. The legal restrictions on the right to distribute dividends have been mentioned in a preceding chapter (p. 50). As far as public companies are concerned (private companies have their own special motives), a dividend in

---

[26] The Swedish section of this Chapter is based on the current Swedish Companies Act and on the attempt now being undertaken to draft a companies act common to all three Scandinavian countries and Finland (see p. 50 above). Reference is also made to the debate now going on in Sweden and which is to a certain extent influenced by thinking in other countries. Particular use has been made in this section of a study published by Studieförbundet Näringsliv och Samhälle (SNS) in 1966 under the title (translated) *Who runs the company?* This book summarises the opinions of Swedish directors on the Swedish company. It deals especially with the division of responsibility and power between the four company institutions mentioned in the Companies Act—the annual meeting of shareholders, the board, the managing director and the auditors. (See also pp. 226–227.)

practice is probably very much thought of as residual—something to be paid out after all allocations and other consolidation measures have been made. A company management whose expansion plans are limited by its liquidity position certainly does not give priority to the distribution of profits to shareholders but rather considers it—with some pointedness—as a 'necessary nuisance'. The objective of professional management is the company's long-range development and competitiveness. A dividend increase would take place only if it were thought to be necessary because of a future issue of new shares or in order to prevent share prices from declining. (This assumes, of course, that the board of directors and the managing director are, in fact, those who decide the amount of dividend, not, as in theory and form, the shareholders' meeting.)

3. The setting of wage rates and other payments to employees in Sweden has been more and more 'delegated' to the contracting parties on the labour market. The upward wage adjustment trend is to be regarded as a function of manpower supply and demand. At higher levels in a company it is true that a management has more control over the trend but even here rates of pay are largely dependent on the supply of qualified manpower.

4. Development expenditure is much less governed by market mechanisms. In this case priorities are far more a matter of choice, encouraged by the big depreciation allowances provided for by Swedish fiscal legislation. (On the other hand, the total tax burden in Sweden is very high.) The possibility of distributing a share of ploughed-back profits to groups other than shareholders has not been much discussed, partly because heavy taxation already absorbs such a considerable part of a company's income.

5. Trade associations, research institutes and other trade organisations are to be regarded as 'special functions' to which a firm has, for economic reasons, delegated certain tasks including, in certain cases, research and development work. Relations with customers and suppliers are determined by economic market factors.

6. When a firm thinks it necessary to pay special regard to the interests of the community, it is generally directly to improve or, alternatively, to prevent damage to, the environment in which the firm operates. Directors are asked to take a greater part in communal activities and not to delegate such tasks to others. No one has maintained that the promotion of the good of the community should in itself be the objective of a firm. On the other hand it is quite common for a firm to put down roots in an area in which it has been working for a long time. It is then in practice obliged to take the community interest into account in a way which could quite seriously conflict with its objective of maximising its earnings.

There is, indeed, a strong feeling in Swedish industry, and particularly in big companies, of a responsibility to co-operate with the government and other state and local authorities to the benefit of the community as a whole. There are frequent contacts between the state and industrial organisations regarding, for instance, the framing of economic policy. Many questions have been resolved through voluntary agreements or through recommendations which have been effectively followed up, although firms have not been legally obliged to implement them. Indeed, 'voluntary' agreements between the state and industry are not always entirely voluntary, since the state can always threaten to impose its will by legislation. However, the climate of relations between government and industry is favourable enough to make compulsory measures and threats of such measures of relatively limited importance. Many social problems have been solved by industry reforming itself, the necessary measures being supported by industrial organisations and often being directly administered by them. An example of a voluntary agreement between the community and industry is the PRYO (practical occupational guidance) scheme under which industry maintains about 300,000 vacancies at the disposal of pupils in the higher classes of secondary schools.

CORPORATE SOCIAL RESPONSIBILITY IN THE USA

There has probably been more discussion of corporate social responsibility in the United States than anywhere else. This discussion goes all the way from empty generalities to specifics named in responsible corporate statements. It runs the gamut from the idea that corporations are accountable to unlimited numbers of outsiders for limitless beneficent actions to the most egocentric views of corporate privilege. The subject is not a purely academic one reserved only for abstract debate. It is of immediate concern to directors and executive managers in the largest and the most powerful companies in the country.

From this point of view, the matter was well expressed by W. T. Gossett when he was vice-president and general counsel for the Ford Motor Company. Modern management must 'consider how the facts and realities in a corporation's affairs will square with the public philosophy, with the values of the total national community and its sense of where it is headed'; nor was this 'just a matter of what is legal or illegal or doubtful today—it is at the very root of the problem of what area of freedom the corporation will have tomorrow'. This is a pragmatic view of the question, stated by a lawyer who was keenly aware of the necessity for corporate assumption of social responsibilities as the price of reasonable corporate autonomy.

In a statement concerning the role of the corporation in public affairs, Gossett went even further. 'The modern large corporation is in some respects a public institution and is one of the key economic units in our society; it holds power in trust for the whole community; its actions and often its statements have a determining effect upon the interests of customers, shareholders, suppliers and employees. But the measure of its effectiveness in public affairs is the degree to which its policy reflects the values, objectives, aspirations and reservations of society as a whole. If a corporation's policies are at odds with these or seem to be, then no amount of money, techniques or noise is likely to have the slightest public influence.'[27]

[27] William T. Gossett (then General Counsel, The Ford Motor Co.), 'The Role of the Corporation in Public Affairs', an address before the Committee on Corporate Law Departments, American Bar Association, 25 August 1959. In *The Meaning of Modern Business*, cited in note 66 to the previous chapter, some notable contemporary positions on corporate responsibility are discussed at length at pp. 69–94 and 209–338.

What does 'social responsibility' mean?

Social responsibility, whether regarded in terms of enlightened corporate self-interest or otherwise, can be interpreted in many different ways. A popular view of corporate social responsibility is focused on corporate giving. This is a decidedly narrow view, but it is interesting to note the managerial philosophy underlying corporate 'philanthropy' (as it is sometimes inappropriately called).

The response of the business sector to requests for support of educational, charitable and other non-profit organisations has been generous but it has not always been backed by a sound rationale. When Ralph J. Cordiner was president of the General Electric Company he took a guardedly prudent position on corporate contributions to education and other community activities, declaring that 'regardless of how generous their motives may be, managers or directors have no legal right to distribute the shareowner's money with a lavish and irresponsible hand in order to satisfy some vaguely conceived public obligation'. General Electric, he said, 'collects money from its customers, at competitive prices, in return for products and services. All this money is in turn redistributed to employees, shareowners, suppliers and others in proportion to their respective contribution to the company's results, and also to the government's tax collectors. To the degree that education and other community activities contribute to the success of the company and the society in which it operates, they should and do receive a share of the proceeds.' The contributions of General Electric to education as well as to health and welfare activities in its plant communities and for the nation generally have been substantial. And so have the contributions of thousands of business corporations in the United States. (See Appendix F.)

Corporate giving is not, of course, the only or even the most important facet of social responsibility. What do we mean by 'responsibility' in this context? Are corporate directors responsible to society in any sense? If so, to whom specifically, and for what? What are the means of enforcing such 'social' responsibility? Is not the corporate support of, say, a college, for the good of society as well as the eventual good of the donor company through indirect benefits, simply a case of creative unilateral action by the company, not demanded as of right by any educational institution? If there is such a thing as corporate social responsibility, does the terminology imply some form of contract? This goes too far; yet it is patently inconsistent to talk of obligations unless one has some notion of the identity of obliger and obligee as well as of the substantive matter: what the corporation is supposed to do or not to do. It is generally agreed in the contemporary discussion of corporate social responsibilities that the subject lies well outside the realm of contractual obligation in the legal sense. It is elementary that a corporation should obey the law and live up to its contracts. The social responsibilities of business involve more complex issues.

On the other hand, it is erroneous to identify corporate social responsibility with business ethics, which points more directly to personal rules of conduct for the businessman. The focus is rather on the corporation as a business unit. Corporate responsibility refers to the collectivity. It is true that corporations act only through natural persons, but there is value in focusing upon the

125

organisation as such, upon the collective economic power it represents, and upon its role as an institution in local, national and international communities, regardless of the succession of men and women who work for it and act on its behalf.

While it is true that there is a need today for the reaffirmation of homely virtues for men in office anywhere, Barnard's observations on the conflict of moralities in organisations are in order here. The business executive in charge of a large organisation cannot be guided simply by such virtues learned at Sunday School. He has to create a morality suited to the role of his organisation in society; and this role cannot be understood by reference to the Golden Rule alone. The relevant issues take one deeply into the entire social structure as part of the corporate environment.

Corporate responsibility and private property

The best example of the need for a 'creative morality' as the basis for corporate social responsibility is to be found in the interplay of the corporate system and contemporary institutions of private property. A schematic view of directors' responsibilities—both legal and non-legal—would comprise at least the following obligees: stockholders, employees (including managers), customers, suppliers and governments. Of these obligees it has been traditional doctrine to yield primacy to the stockholders as property-owners. Directors presumably have the use of their property but, more accurately, the stockholders' money has been translated into corporate property held by the directors who are expected to make returns from earnings in accordance with principles established by law and custom. The property relationship is nevertheless a primary one, to which all others are subsidiary in considering directorial responsibility. And while it is sometimes the practice to display a code of company responsibilities that covers a long list of dependents and beneficiaries, managerial responsibilities in practice centre upon the traditional values of property and profits.

It does not follow, on the other hand, that directors always act on the principle that the corporation is 'the instrument of private property and completely responsible to private property', as demanded by Kelso and Adler[28] in their call for 'a radical reformation of the relation of the owners of capital to operating management'. Their complaint is that the effective ownership of capital has been transferred out of the hands of the stockholders, where it belongs, and that the modern corporation has become 'an instrument for a distribution of wealth that is primarily laboristic'.

Property rights in capital, Kelso and Adler assert, have been so attenuated that the corporation can be regarded as a device 'for almost alienating' property from its owners. In our mixed economy there has been 'an erosion of private property in concentrated holdings of capital through the diversion of the wealth such capital produces, from the stockholders who own it to the mass of workers who need it and whose use of it provides a mass market'. This is perhaps an extreme view, for it attacks the 'involuntary investment by stockholders' in the form of large reinvestment of corporate

[28] L. D. Kelso and M. J. Adler, *The Capitalist Manifesto*, New York, Random House, 1958.

earnings and demands more than the present 'trickle' that finds its way into stockholders' dividends. The managerial revolution, so often underlined in contemporary comment on the modern corporation, is for Kelso and Adler a reversible reaction that is urgently necessary for the fulfilment of the basic managerial obligation. Managers are 'responsible to their principals, the owners, as the officers of government are responsible to their masters, the citizens'.

Lengthy quotation from this book seems justifiable, not because it is well known and widely referred to in the United States (for it is not) but because it falls about as near the traditionalist end of the scale of theories of corporate responsibilities as any. Indeed, it falls far beyond the position that most of the conservative section of the financial community would take. And the financial community contains most of the stockholders in terms of stock values, because of the high degree of concentration of stockholding in institutions such as pension funds, investment funds and insurance companies. One does not hear them complaining about managerial irresponsibility.

Corporate endocracy

The extreme position just indicated is, in the United States, a maverick's position. There is certainly no major move, or even a minor embroilment, to have 'the stockholder's hand returned to the economic throttle of the corporation', as Kelso and Adler demand that it should be, and as certain romantic characters, who haunt the annual stockholders' meetings of 'endocratic' corporations to harry the management, hope for in the form of 'corporate democracy'.

'Corporate endocracy'—a term introduced by Eugene V. Rostow[29] to emphasise the realities of managerial power—is the normal and accepted form of government in the large publicly held company. Its directors are endowed with immense discretion. Where no stockholder owns more than a small fraction of the stock the directors normally control, or come close to controlling, the electoral process from which their powers derive. But, as Rostow goes on to say, the corporation is nevertheless the chosen instrument of the law for carrying on a large part of the economic life of society. The endocratic corporation is 'an autonomous body politic in a legal order of decentralised power'. Its directors have to comply with legislation and they are under the influence of their own sense of fiduciary duty. But the board of directors may consist largely of corporate employees who are dependent upon the president for their future in the company. In Rostow's words, the board is then 'simply a fictional projection of the president himself, whose power is diluted only by the possible presence on his board of bankers, representing creditors' interests, or directors representing important customers, or of an occasional so-called "public" director'.[30]

If it be said that this picture is overdrawn, as indeed it probably is for many companies, it still puts succinctly the state of affairs in many others and

[29] Eugene V. Rostow, 'To Whom and for What Ends are Corporate Managements Responsible?' in Edward S. Mason (ed.), *The Corporation in Modern Society*, pp. 46–71.
[30] ibid., at p. 51.

confirms the venerable thesis of Berle and Means[31] concerning the separation of ownership and control in large publicly held companies. This separation raises fundamental questions about corporate responsibility, but more particularly managerial responsibility to stockholders. At first glance this does not seem to touch the issue of corporate *social* responsibility, that is to say, the responsibility of the corporation as a whole to its social environment. Yet that is too quick a judgment, and for this reason: today it is widely assumed that social responsibility includes managerial responsibility to a span of obligees that includes the vast numbers of dispersed shareholders who have no effective means of asserting their authority within the internal structure of corporate governance.

For practical purposes, then, it is fictional to talk of the stockholders as though they were internal to the corporation, even though on traditional principles it is they who form the basic constituency of corporate government. Realism, of course, requires us to pass over this formalism to the facts of corporate life. It is neither possible nor desirable to run a large publicly held company on the principles of town-meeting government. The 'endocracy' that Rostow speaks of is one of the political facts of life that we have to live with in a pluralistic society where many organisations in the private sector may choose to depart from principles of representative government adaptable to the public sector.

The endocratic trend, however, has had profound implications for the private property system in the United States, particularly in view of the appearance on the scene of huge institutional investors in the form of pension funds, mutual funds and other financial devices that introduce the 'para-proprietal society' discussed later in this section.

To whom are corporate directors responsible?

We must first consider the now famous Berle–Dodd debate in the early 1930s on the difficult legal question: 'To whom are directors responsible?'

[31] A. A. Berle, Jr and Gardiner C. Means, *The Modern Corporation and Private Property*, New York, Commerce Clearing House, 1932; see also Berle's preface, 'Property, Production and Revolution', in the revised edition of this work, New York, The Macmillan Co., 1968. In 'Modern Functions of the Corporate System', *Columbia Law Review*, Vol. 62, March 1962, pp. 433–449, Berle recalls that in 1932 *The Modern Corporation and Private Property* was 'thought so dangerous as to be almost worth suppressing' and though 'first brought out by a law publishing house then affiliated with the Corporation Trust Company', 'publication was promptly suspended after a few copies had been sold' upon the discovery of 'the viper they had nourished in their corporate bosom'. Macmillan then reissued the book in successive editions. For a recent view of the Berle–Means thesis, see R. J. Lanier, 'Ownership and Control in the 200 Largest Nonfinancial Corporations', *American Economic Review*, Vol. 56, September 1966, pp. 777–787. He examines the evidence to sustain, as of today, the thesis that 'ownership of wealth without appreciable control and control of wealth without appreciable ownership appear to be the logical outcome of corporate development' (Berle and Means, op. cit., p. 69). He concludes that the 'managerial revolution' Berle and Means were observing in process thirty years ago seems today to be nearly complete. Cf. Frank D. Emerson, 'The Role of Management and Shareholders in Corporate Government', in *Law and Contemporary Problems*, School of Law, Duke University, Spring 1958, pp. 231–238; David B. Weaver, 'The Corporation and the Shareholder', in *The Annals of the American Academy of Political and Social Science*, September 1962, pp. 84–94. See also Joseph L. Wiener, 'The Berle–Dodd Dialogue on the Concept of the Corporation', *Columbia Law Review*, Vol. 64, No. 8, December 1964, pp. 1458–1467.

This debate has in fact continued ever since and was expertly summed up by Professor J. L. Wiener in the December 1964 issue of the *Columbia Law Review*[32] in honour of Adolf A. Berle. Berle and his colleague, Professor E. Merrick Dodd, Jr, began the debate in a famous exchange in the *Harvard Law Review* in 1931–32.[33] Berle's position was that corporate powers were powers in trust and 'exercisable at all times only for the rateable benefit of all shareholders as their interest appears'. He examined five corporate powers (such as the power to issue additional stock and the power to declare or withhold dividends) and, although he held that corporation law becomes 'in substance a branch of the law of trusts', he added that the rules of application 'are less rigorous, since the business situation demands greater flexibility than the trust situation'.[34]

Berle's thesis, be it noted, did not focus on the problem of corporate social responsibility as such. His essay, as Wiener points out, represented the culmination of a series of earlier studies in corporation law and was the result of his conviction that there was a 'need for some synthesis to harmonise the many apparently individual rules in the law of corporations', as well as his dissatisfaction with the trend of corporation law practice in the 1920s. A few years earlier, in 1927, Professor W. Z. Ripley of Harvard had castigated corporate financial practices in his epochal book, *Main Street and Wall Street*.

Against the Berle trusteeship concept Professor Dodd, while completely agreeing with Berle that legal control was needed to prevent the diversion of corporate profits into managers' pockets instead of the stockholders', questioned the emphasis on 'the view that business corporations exist for the sole purpose of making profits for their stockholders'. Dodd's position was rather that 'public opinion ultimately makes law, has made and is today making substantial strides in the direction of a view of the business corporation as an economic institution which has a social service as well as a profit-making function, that this view has already had some effect upon legal theory, and that it is likely to have an increased effect upon the latter in the near future'.[35]

Berle, in reply, agreed that those in control of great enterprises often function more as princes and ministers of industrial government than as promoters or merchants. But it was 'only theory, not practice' to conclude that this would justify their assumption of social responsibility. He warned against weakening their responsibility to stockholders except for 'a clear and reasonably enforceable scheme of responsibility to someone else'. How, otherwise, could managements be held properly responsible and accountable for the exercise of their power? He noted the spread of stock ownership and indirect interest in corporate securities through life insurance companies and

---

[32] The relevant articles are Joseph L. Wiener, cited above, and Carlos L. Israels, 'Are Corporate Powers Still Held in Trust?', *Columbia Law Review*, Vol. 64, No. 8, December 1964, pp. 1458–1467.

[33] Berle, 'Corporate Powers as Powers in Trust', *Harvard Law Review*, Vol. 44, 1931, p. 1049; Dodd, 'For Whom Are Corporate Managers Trustees?', *Harvard Law Review*, Vol. 45, 1932, p. 1145; Berle, 'For Whom Corporate Managers *are* Trustees: A Note', *Harvard Law Review*, Vol. 45, 1932, p. 1365.

[34] Berle, *Harvard Law Review*, Vol. 44, p. 1074.

[35] Dodd, *Harvard Law Review*, Vol. 45, p. 1154.

E

savings banks, and wondered what would happen when half the population was to be affected if 'the fund and income stream upon which this group rely are irresponsibly dealt with'.[36] The law might eventually treat the stockholder in still indeterminate ways; he might ultimately be considered as having an equal participation with a number of other claimants, or he might emerge with a primary right to residual income but subordinated to other claims of society.

Yet Berle had already stated, in the preface to *The Modern Corporation and Private Property* (1932), that the corporation had 'ceased to be a private business device and had become an institution'. He and Professor Means, in their analysis of corporation finance, had concluded that with the separation of ownership and control the passive stockholders had 'surrendered the right that the corporation should be operated in their sole interest'. Managers had become 'a purely neutral technocracy' whose task was to balance 'a variety of claims by various groups in the community' and assign to each 'a portion of the income stream on the basis of public policy rather than private cupidity'.

Professor Wiener concludes that the differences between Dodd and Berle appear to come down to the absence of machinery for enforcing a legitimate community demand upon the corporation as a social institution. In a later statement, made in 1942,[37] Dodd noted that business obligations toward labour had been implemented by means other than treating business managers as in some measure fiduciaries for their employees; it had been accomplished, he said, in part by granting labour certain specific statutory rights which business corporations and their managers were now bound to respect, and in part by encouraging labour to organise so that it might bargain with management on something like equal terms. Dodd was referring, of course, to such legislation as the Railway Labor Act and the National Labor Relations Act of the New Deal period. But he distinguished between the fiduciary obligation owed by a trustee to a beneficiary, on the one hand, and the obligation owed by a modern corporation to labour. In the first instance, there is the obligation to administer the trust fund so as to secure for the beneficiary the largest possible return consistent with safety; in the latter instance, the obligation to give recognition to certain specific claims is accorded to labour by modern legislation.

Corporate managers, Dodd went on to say, might assume that a certain suggested course of action would increase both the short-term and the long-term earnings available to shareholders, that such a course of action would possibly have no tendency to produce the sort of unfavourable public reaction which might injure the corporation as a profitable enterprise, and that the pursuit of that course of action in the interest of the stockholders would violate neither any rule of law nor the contract rights of any person, including those of the managers themselves. Given these conditions, they ought to pursue that course of action according to orthodox trusteeship principles. But he saw no similar legal duty to pursue a course of action that would enable the corporation to benefit its employees by raising wages.

[36] Berle, *Harvard Law Review*, Vol. 45, p. 1368.
[37] Dodd, *University of Chicago Law Review*, Vol. 9, 1942, p. 538.

Turning to consumer interests and claims upon the corporate institution, Dodd observed that trusteeship for these was no less a misnomer than trusteeship for employees. Consumers had, to be sure, acquired during the later 1930s a number of new rights by statute. Labour and the consuming public had thus strengthened their legal position as against business enterprises. To call this relationship a trust, however, was, to lawyers, as discredited a thesis as that which held that corporate capital is a trust fund for creditors. These observations throw light not only on the locus of corporate social responsibilities but also the nature of their content and the so-called obligees. The idea of trusteeship has not been much relied upon in recent years, since the Dodd–Berle debate. But other ways of specifying the relationship have been enunciated. It is true that in 1954 Berle made a much quoted statement that his debate with Dodd as to whether corporate powers were powers in trust for shareholders or for the community had been 'settled (at least for the time being) squarely in favour of Professor Dodd's contention'.[38] But he has since denied that this meant that Dodd was right all along. 'It is one thing to agree that this is how social fact and judicial decisions turned out. It is another to admit that this was the "right" disposition; I am not convinced that it was.'[39] What he had conceded in 1954 was simply that modern directors 'are not limited to running business enterprises for maximum profit, but are in fact and recognised in law as administrators of a community system'.[40]

There remains, however, the big question of implementation, the problem of machinery for accountability, even if one concedes this idea of the corporation as an integral part of the community system. How can one be sure that corporate managers will act in accord with this responsibility? Berle's writings seem to indicate the value of a 'corporate conscience' and the dependence of managers on 'public consensus'. Others challenge this view. 'It is not going to happen; if it did happen it would not work; and if it did work it would be intolerable to free men.' This was the acid comment of Professor Ben W. Lewis.[41] To Dean Rostow it was merely the 'rhetoric of managerialism' to talk of such a consensus and disturbing in its legal and political implications. It would be hard to find in the United States any substantial support for the idea that the government might purchase shares in companies to achieve accountability through socialism. The German practice of *Mitbestimmungsrecht*, with workers' representatives on the board, would not be acceptable. More effective provisions for visitation and control have been proposed by Professor Bayless Manning, a kind of 'second chamber' distinct from the board of directors and with more limited powers but acting somewhat as a voting trust for stockholders.[42] The government of corporations

---

[38] Berle, *The 20th Century Capitalist Revolution*, New York, Harper & Brothers, 1954, p. 169.

[39] Berle, in the Foreword to Mason (ed.), cited.

[40] ibid.

[41] Ben W. Lewis, 'Economics by Admonition', *American Economic Review*, Vol. 49, Supplement, 1959, p. 395.

[42] Bayless Manning, 'Corporate Power and Individual Freedom: Some General Analysis and Particular Reservations', *Northwestern Law Review*, Vol. 55, March–April 1960, pp. 38–53. I have examined this article and other ideas for implementing corporate accountability at length in *The Government of Corporations*.

is still a little-explored territory and the *theory* of such governance is only in its elementary stages.

The 'paraproprietal society'

Turning to the effect of the great institutional investors on the corporate system, on concepts of private property, and consequently on views of corporate social responsibility, one must note the writings of Father Harbrecht[43] on the 'paraproprietal society'. He states that we are today witnessing a change 'from an economic system of possessory property into an economic system of administered power'. He thinks the 'paraproprietal organisation' may become the dominant mode in our society. The new centres of power are the managers, not of manufacturing and industrial but of *financial* institutions; and this has come about not through guile and intrigue but simply because 'the control of property gravitates to those who can, by the use of property, perform a function valuable to society'—in this case the function of distributing 'among the generality of people the wealth which the corporations are creating'. The banks, the insurance companies, the mutual funds, the pension funds distribute *income-producing* wealth; and this goes a step beyond the function of the industrial corporation as a distributor of products and of earnings in the form of wages and dividends.

But this step towards making people sharers in capital wealth required the development of financial institutions in which power and control is increasingly being relocated. This 'migration of power' further and further away from the stockholder and the contributor to a pension fund, towards the trustees of such funds, results in the virtual disappearance of the property rights of the so-called 'ultimate owners' of these funds and a vast accretion of power in those who manage the funds and in the unions and corporate employers. 'Power is following property into all of the financial institutions which purchase shares of capital for their clients', and 'the economic power that is growing in the institutions is being drawn, or shunted away, from the generality of the people'.

The effect of this migration of power, according to Father Harbrecht, is to leave behind 'a society organised by individual property ownership and diffused power'. For the organising principle is no longer *property* but *power*; and thus we see the transition to the 'paraproprietal' society. This seems appropriate to Father Harbrecht as signifying 'beyond property' because in the paraproprietal society 'the connexion between man and things, which is another way of saying property, is so attenuated that the fundamental function of property is not dominant, though it still serves a purpose'. Certain things had begun to be called property in Western society, writes Harbrecht, because they were said to have 'belonged' to a man, pertained to him in a special way, were 'proper' to him. They could be thought of as an extension

---

[43] See Paul P. Harbrecht, SJ, *Pension Funds and Economic Power*, New York, The Twentieth Century Fund, 1959, and (with A. A. Berle, Jr.) *Toward the Paraproprietal Society: An Essay on the Nature of Property in Twentieth Century America*, New York, The Twentieth Century Fund, 1960; also 'The Modern Corporation Revisited', *Columbia Law Review*, Vol. 64, No. 8, December 1964, pp. 1410–1426. The passages quoted from Harbrecht will be found in *Toward a Paraproprietal Society*, pp. 28 ff.

of his personality. The fundamental notion of property thus was intimately connected with the ideas of 'own' and 'ownership'. But, Harbrecht continues, 'there is nothing personal about General Motors or the Metropolitan Life Insurance Company in this sense. "Mine" and "thine" have very little meaning when applied to them. Something that is owned by everyone is truly owned by no one. Ownership in connexion with the modern institutional organisation of wealth has very little of its former meaning.'

The concepts of the property system have certain functions that persist, however, in Harbrecht's view as devices for transferring control over property. 'Where once the concepts of property served the function of attaching things to men, they now serve the function of assigning powers over things. The thing itself is not given to a man, power over it is. The objects exchanged in such a system are not the things themselves but powers over things. This is why we can say that our society has passed from a property system to a power system.'

Corporate social responsibility in a 'paraproprietal' society poses new problems of corporate and public government. Berle has taken the position that corporation managers in mid-twentieth-century America have become administrators of a vast and crucial sector in an era where dominant economic achievement lies precisely within the manufacturing and industrial area operated by these managers. This is a universal phenomenon. The result is that power devolves upon administrators, whether they be Soviet or capitalist. But whereas Soviet administrators operate under a doctrinaire dictatorship, it is different in democracies. There are oligarchies in both; but Berle believes that in a democracy the economic governors are ultimately capable of being directed, limited or otherwise dealt with by a political government which in turn is capable of being influenced or changed by a public accustomed to the democratic process. 'As an instrument, our system is obviously capable of doing anything the American public consensus really wishes it to do.'[44]

Is the structure of representative government in the Western democracies adequate for the purpose of holding accountable the administrators of the paraproprietal society? The question has no present answer, and is indeed a major one that will have to be debated at length before there can be an answer in terms of public policy. The problem of corporate social responsibility really centres here, even though other obligees of the corporation— suppliers, customers and employees—have important and unsatisfied claims upon management.

The traditionalists go too far; yet their main point about the private property base of a free society has never been challenged except by the socialists and the communists. The erosion of property from its initial phase of personal ownership and control through the corporation form and now into the extremely attenuated claims that individuals hold in such things as common stock, rights in pension trusts, participation in mutual funds and the like, would seem to strike at this private property base as we have known it and as most received doctrine treats it. The received doctrine is strangely out of date. 'Property', as Berle has said, is 'one of the most abused words in the English language', covering 'a surprising range of possible meanings

---

[44] Berle, *The American Economic Republic*, cited note 66 to previous chapter, p. 7.

and implications, few of which seem to have bothered twentieth-century theorists.'[45]

Before one can speak authoritatively about accountability for the use of property (certainly a first responsibility of corporate managements), one must note the significant shift of decision-making in the economic world during the past few decades. Ownership in the traditional sense plays little or no part in decision-making, according to Berle's most recent analysis, 'in from two thirds to three fourths (and perhaps more) of the American economic republic'. That power lies instead in 'corporation managements, in administrators of savings-gathering institutions and pension trusts, in the offices of the larger commercial banks, in government agencies, and in an inchoate emerging group which may be called the "scientific community" '.[46] He has added the latter category as decision-makers over a new and growing margin of 'incorporeal capital' comprising 'the vast stratum from a mathematical formula in the mind of a university scientist to the engineer's calculation that an artificial satellite in space may transmit messages more cheaply than a transoceanic cable'.[47]

It might sound strange, Berle observes, to think of a scientific institute of scholars as primary decision-makers in capital allocation; yet in the end they have a controlling influence through their insights, perceptions and intuitions. Here is a new layer of decision-making which 'more nearly resembles the action of princes than of proprietors', proceeding in an 'upper house' of capital control. The potential of this upper house has never been analysed, but it should be. Huge amounts of 'savings' of private property go and will go into experimental work and vast projects that the scientific community will decide upon. Government departments and the R & D departments of the largest corporations will make decisions about these matters, but not without the wholehearted support of scientists and technicians.

Philosophies of state corporation laws

The speed of this shift of locus in decision-making with respect to the uses of property has been so rapid during the past fifty years that it has been impossible for public policy to keep up with it. The United States had, during the 1930s, extensive new legislation on securities and security exchanges in the interest of the investing public, mainly stockholders in industrial corporations. Today there is need for new approaches based on knowledge of the new institutional developments. That knowledge has not yet reached definitive form. When that happens it must still be brought to the attention of public policy-makers in operational form.

Major developments of this kind must be looked for at the state level rather than the level of federal legislation. This is because of the primary responsibility of the states for legislation in the field of corporation law.[48] State

---

[45] ibid., p. 219.   [46] ibid., p. 75.   [47] ibid., p. 73.

[48] But see: 'Panel Discussion, The Emergence of "Federal Corporation Law", and Federal Control of Inside Information', *University of Missouri at Kansas City Law Review*, Vol. 34, Summer 1966, p. 228; M. Eisenberg and D. J. Lehr, 'An Aspect of the Emerging "Federal Corporation Law": Directorial Responsibility Under the Investment Company Act of 1940', *Rutgers Law Review*, Vol. 20, Winter 1961, p. 181; W. H. Painter, 'Inside Information: Growing Pains for the Development of Federal Corporation Law Under Rule 10b–5',

legislation has in general proceeded on the basis of traditional doctrine about the nature and government of corporations and the conception of private property. There have been four main points of view expressed by the state legislatures in their incorporation statutes, and each of the four carries certain implications as to corporate governments.

These four points of view, as summarised by Professor W. G. Katz,[49] are: (i) that a corporation statute should be merely an 'enabling act' making limited liability freely available, leaving the promoters relatively free to define the scope of the enterprise and to allocate risk, control and profit through the corporation's security structure; (ii) that this allocative authority, while still very broad, should be modified in certain respects because the common-law doctrines of contracts, torts and agency are not enough to assure responsible individual decision in the corporate setting as compared with unincorporated business organisations; (iii) that the legislature needs to prescribe definite restrictions on the freedom of the parties to allocate risk, control and profit by contract (e.g. such restrictions as the outlawing of non-voting stock, the prescription of a specified margin of safety for creditors, the requirement of a simple majority vote for various corporate adjustments); and (iv) that corporate managers have a 'social responsibility' to exercise corporate powers not only—or even mainly—in the interest of stockholders, but also in the interest of employees, customers and the 'general public'.

The second and third of these theories were regarded as protective primarily

Columbia Law Review, Vol. 65, December 1965, p. 1361; A. Fleischer, Jr., ' "Federal Corporation Law": An Assessment', *Harvard Law Review*, Vol. 78, April 1965, p. 1146; W. B. Barton, 'Corporations in Politics: How Far Can They Go Under the Law?', *American Bar Association Journal*, Vol. 50, March 1964, p. 228.

[49] Wilber G. Katz, 'The Philosophy of Midcentury Corporation Statutes', *Law and Contemporary Problems*, Vol. 23, No. 2, Spring 1958, pp. 177–192. This entire issue of the journal was devoted to 'The New Look in Corporation Law', with articles on the role of the States in corporate regulation and investor protection, the roles of management and shareholders in corporate government, capital and surplus under the new state corporation statute, the question of fixed rights of the class shareholder, minority and dissenting shareholders' rights in fundamental changes, indemnification of insiders' litigation expenses, legislation affecting close corporations, and 'miscellaneous novelties' in the new corporation statutes. For more recent changes in State legislation, see 'Symposium on South Carolina Corporation Law', *South Carolina Law Review*, Vol. 15, No. 2, 1963 Symposium Issue; 'Symposium on New York Business Corporation Law', *Buffalo Law Review*, Vol. 11, Spring 1962; E. L. Folk III and C. D. Clark, 'South Dakota's General Incorporation Law: Need for Revision', *South Dakota Law Review*, Vol. 9, Spring 1964, p. 172; E. L. Folk III, 'Revisiting the North Carolina Corporation Law', *North Carolina Law Review*, Vol. 43, June 1965, p. 768; R. S. Stevens, 'New York Business Corporation Law of 1961', *Cornell Law Quarterly*, Vol. 47, Winter 1961, p. 141; 'Report on New York Business Corporation Law', *New York State Bar Journal*, Vol. 33, December 1961, p. 435; 'The Model Business Corporation Act: An Appropriate Starting Place', *Washington Law Review*, Vol. 38, Autumn 1963, p. 538; 'Institute on Arkansas Corporation Law', *Arkansas Law Review*, Vol. 17, Winter 1964, p. 347; 'Institute on Corporation Law: The Nebraska Business Corporation Act', *Nebraska Law Review*, Vol. 43, February 1964, p. 296; E. M. Casey, 'New Business Corporation Law', *Massachusetts Law Quarterly*, Vol. 50, September 1965, p. 201; E. R. Latty, 'Why Are Business Corporation Laws Largely "Enabling"?', *Cornell Law Quarterly*, Vol 50, Summer 1965, p. 579, and 'Transition to the Model Business Corporation Act in Utah', *Utah Law Review*, Vol. 9, Summer 1965, p. 689; 'Symposium on Corporation Law', *Colorado Law Review*, Vol. 36, Fall 1963, p. 9; 'Company Law Revision: A Synthesis of Opinion', *Detroit Law Journal*, Vol. 40, April 1963, p. 439.

of the interests of investors and creditors, but the proponents of these theories also wanted 'to reduce the likelihood of financial catastrophes which might destroy the climate of reasonable confidence which business enterprise requires'. Katz thought the third theory was one of 'paternal responsibility' because it sought to protect the interests of investors and creditors by limiting the area of permissible arrangements made by corporate managers. The first theory, by contrast, 'calls for no limitations of size, duration, purposes, or general powers [of the incorporated business]', and would make the enabling act sufficiently detailed to leave no doubt about these matters.

Professor Katz was describing, in the main, the theories that underlie current statutory rules and not theories that might be found in the general literature on corporations, but he does say that the fourth theory, though much discussed by philosophers of corporation law (e.g. Berle and Dodd), 'has almost no reflection in the actual statutes'. He thought the recent statutes reflected an 'enabling act' theory—the first one mentioned above—'more or less modified by the theory that corporation statutes, while assuring freedom of contract, should reinforce in various ways the responsibility of individual decisions; and that the freedom of the parties should be limited in order that the results of responsible freedom may more nearly be approximated'. Had he elaborated upon the more general literature, he might have mentioned writers like Friedman, Kelso and Adler, whose views are comparable with the third theory listed by Katz. He regarded Peter F. Drucker as a proponent of the fourth theory, since Drucker had advocated the abolition of share-holder voting rights and the vesting of voting power in perpetuity to the board of directors, who would elect to their number 'representatives' of investors, management and the 'plant community'.

The 'enabling act' theory stands in contrast to the second, third and fourth, since all of these latter theories insist upon varying degrees of managerial responsibility enforceable by statute. The latter theories are, in a sense, all 'social responsibility' theories, but the second and the third are concerned almost exclusively with investors and creditors of the corporation, whereas the fourth theory extends the list to other social segments.

The debate on corporate social responsibilities proceeds apace and there is a vast literature on it.[50] There is no one definitive answer to the question: 'Who in the corporation is responsible to whom for what?' It depends in part upon what kind of company one is talking about, as indicated in the previous chapter on a 'spectrum of companies'. (See p. 51 ff.) It depends, further, upon

---

[50] For a recent survey, see Clarence C. Walton, *Corporate Social Responsibilities*, Belmont, California, Wadsworth Publishing Co., 1967. See also Donald K. David, 'The New Relationship of Business to Society', in Dan H. Fenn, Jr. (ed.), *Management's Mission in a New Society*, New York, McGraw-Hill Book Co., 1959, pp. 66–73, and Erwin D. Canham, 'For a Revised Sense of Values', in the same volume, pp. 75–88; also Andrew Hacker (ed.), *The Corporation Take-Over*, Garden City, N.Y., Anchor Books, Doubleday & Co., Inc., 1965, especially the papers by Scott Buchanan, W. H. Ferry, Arthur Miller and A. Hacker. In 'The Johnson Treatment', *Harvard Business Review*, January–February 1967, pp. 114–128, Theodore Levitt explained how President Johnson had won a substantial part of the business community over to a philosophy of vigorous government efforts to improve social and economic conditions, thus indicating changed attitudes of management on the locus of social responsibility.

whose instrument a company is expected to be, and in the case of a very large 'endocratic' company there seems little doubt that society as a whole lays a great and justifiable claim to the values provided by that instrument. Yet to rule out the stockholder claim as subordinate to society's claim is obviously at odds with the principle of private property in a free society. The great difficulty, however, is that the institution of private property is undergoing profound change, especially in the corporate system of our 'paraproprietal society'. The traditionalist may inveigh against this trend of affairs, but at length both public and corporate policy must come to terms with it.

Part III

COMPANY ORGANISATION AND CONTROL

This Part is especially concerned with those aspects of company organisation and control which are or may be regulated by law. Two basic questions are pursued: (*a*) who, within the company, settles the company's objectives? and (*b*) which interests directly or indirectly exert pressure on or supervise those who make the choice of objectives? *Note*. Discussion of the structure and functions of German company boards is, for reasons there apparent, placed not in Chapter 1 but in Chapter 2, Section C, of this Part. See also pp. 42 and 240.

Chapter 1

CHIEF EXECUTIVES: POWERS AND ACCOUNTABILITY

Is the 'chief executive' an individual or a collective? How is the chief executive's freedom to decide on company objectives and the means to carry them out to be reconciled with accountability to interests directly involved in the firm and those external interests that have a relationship with it? What is a board of directors? How are chief executives appointed and dismissed? What are their powers with regard to third parties? How far are they responsible for the actions of their subordinates?

BELGIUM

(a) *Some academic views*

Professor de Barsy (see p. 69 above) maintains that the source of authority in the company is not to be found in the property relationship. (The generally accepted idea that authority does rest on property is a relic of the positivist individualistic attitudes of the nineteenth century.) Authority, according to de Barsy, originates from the will of the founders to establish an economic institution, that is, to fulfil a social function. This authority is shared by all those who intend to exercise and continue this social function. It is subsequently passed on to all those who become members of the institution in the same spirit. De Barsy draws two conclusions. First, the theoretical sovereignty of the general meeting of limited liability companies consisting of anonymous shareholders appears to be based upon a faulty conception. Second, this sovereignty should be restored to those who consider themselves the legal successors of the founders, to those who support the institution by their professional activity, and also to the financiers who are prepared to commit and 'bind' their money to the company.[1] The authority of the company (as

[1] E. de Barsy, *Raisonnement sur l'entreprise*, Société d'Economie Politique de Belgique, No. 312, December 1965, pp. 27 and 28.

141

Professor Vandeputte points out) has to prove itself strong, and capable of fulfilling its task—otherwise complete failure is inevitable—but it should not be arbitrary.[2]

Unity in authority must go hand in hand with internal differentiation. The company and its authority will be all the stronger if the men in power are conscious of the inevitable process of differentiation in internal management. This differentiation is a necessary process of adaptation to the scale of the company, to its rate of growth and to the development of the environment in which the company works. Awareness of the need for differentiation will enable those in power to organise and to control the spread of authority.[3]

Authority in the company has to be supervised. From the new attitude towards company objectives it appears that, apart from the acknowledged interests of capital, the interests of employees and the community must also be defended. To this end existing company law should be adapted to the notions of 'company institution' and 'company community'. (See p. 69 above.) On the one hand, entrepreneurs with managerial authority and control are the embodiment of necessary and acknowledged executive power and, on the other, a supervisory and authorising body should be the embodiment of the will of the three interests that confront one another in the company—labour, capital and the common good.

It would be desirable, in the view of R. Henrion, for such supervision to bear only upon the general policy of the management, but provision could be made for a form of prior authorisation in a limited number of cases which could be considered as turning-points in the life of the company. The relationship between the management and the supervising function should be that of an institutionalised dialogue.[4] (The involvement of employees in real and comprehensive co-management is regarded by the trade unions, for all practical purposes, as an unattainable goal. See below, p. 202, and Appendix A, pp. 339–342.) In cases of deadlock between the managerial authority and the general supervisory and authorising functions, R. Vandeputte has suggested an 'economic magistracy'.[5] He asks why it should be inconceivable for a really basic conflict between capital (represented by the management) and labour to be resolved by an 'economic court'. If accurate and objective criteria could be established, why should not the employee representatives on the works council have the right to bring certain problems, of fundamental importance to the company's future, before such a court? R. Henrion rejects this suggestion because it would lead, he thinks, to the coercion of those ultimately responsible for company decisions and would, moreover, cause uncertainty as to where responsibility really lay. As he sees it, an institutionalised dialogue would be a sufficient safeguard against arbitrary authority. He would leave the ultimate decisions to heads of firms, but oblige them to justify themselves before their employees and shareholders and before an authority that represented the public good.[6]

[2] R. Vandeputte, *Le statut de l'entreprise*, Brussels, Bruylant, 1965, p. 110.

[3] De Barsy, op. cit., p. 28.

[4] R. Henrion, 'Système économique et statut de l'entreprise', *Annales de sciences économiques appliquées*, August 1965, pp. 337–365.

[5] Vandeputte, op. cit., p. 102.

[6] Henrion, op. cit., p. 361.

(b) *Present Belgian law*

1. The current provisions of the Code on Commercial Companies (Art. 53 ff) regarding the management of a *société anonyme*, and the respective powers of directors (*administrateurs*), managers (*directeurs*) and the general meeting of shareholders, have already been set out in Part I, Chapter 1 of this book. (See p. 35 above.) The actual state of affairs is, however, quite different from the statutory balance of powers there outlined. In *sociétés anonymes* (unless they are family owned) the shareholders' meeting has become a purely formal occasion, the only real function of which is the appointment of directors and the approval of accounts. In larger companies even the board of directors has in practice very limited authority, the real power being exercised by a small group of 'managing directors' assisted by senior executives.

The official committee on company law reform has advocated bringing the law into line with reality by withdrawing residuary powers from the shareholders' meeting and entrusting them to a 'management board' (*conseil de gestion*) which would be authorised to perform all acts necessary or useful for the fulfilment of the company's objectives. For certain acts relating to the general welfare of the company, prior approval from a 'supervisory board' (*conseil de surveillance*) would be required by law.[7]

2. Under the present Code, directors and statutory auditor(s) are appointed by the shareholders' meeting and may be dismissed by that meeting at any time. If authorised to do so by the articles of association, the board of directors may appoint and dismiss its chairman, the managing directors and all other agents or employees and may fix their powers and remuneration. According to the proposals of the company law reform committee, the members of the 'management board' would be elected by the supervisory board, while the latter would be elected by the shareholders' meeting.

The legal status of chief executives is not essentially different from that of 'intellectual' employees in general.[8] They are considered as such if their contractual obligations are executed in a relationship of 'subordination' towards the employer. In other words, their legal status is expressed in an individual labour contract for intellectual employees. As such, the various provisions concerning the position of all employees, including social security benefits, are applicable to them, except, in certain instances, when their annual salary exceeds Fr. 180,000 (approximately £1,440).[9] Terms of appointment are usually set out in a written contract[10] in which salary and conditions are freely fixed. (Wage regulations and working conditions contained in collective agreements are not applicable to chief executives if their annual salary exceeds Fr. 180,000.)

Chief executives complain bitterly about their status. Their ill-defined

---

[7] For further details, see P. van Ommeslaghe, *La réforme des sociétés anonymes*, Epargner et investir, 1965, pp. 13 ff.

[8] The distinction between 'intellectual' and manual workers is still very important in Belgium, although an effort is being made to abolish it and to introduce a single legal category of workers.

[9] The present tendency is towards the abolition of this financial ceiling.

[10] In a strictly legal sense this is not necessary.

position between the employer on one side and employees on the other, together with lack of mobility, leaves them (rightly) with the impression that they are more or less dependent upon the goodwill of their employer. There is, however, a growing recognition of this problem. It has recently been argued that the juridical construction put upon the relationship between chief executive and company can no longer be that of a contract of employment, in the sense of 'hiring' of services, but rather a form of partnership. In this way the idea of a permanent collaboration would be stressed.

Chief executives may be dismissed at any time and without any stated reasons provided the employer gives notice. The period of notice in the case of chief executives is lengthy and may be two years or more. It is calculated according to duration of service in the company, the importance of the job, salary, the difficulty of finding a similar job and age.

3. As a general rule a company is not bound by acts performed by its legal representatives outside the scope of its objectives (*ultra vires*) or of the powers granted to the representative in question. This also holds good if the limitation on the representative's power results from a provision of the articles of association, so long as it has been published in the manner prescribed by law. However, the effect of this rule has been mitigated by court decisions invoking the 'apparent authority' doctrine. According to this doctrine a company is liable to third parties who have done all which could reasonably be expected to ascertain the precise scope of the company's objectives or its representative's powers and who, relying on external evidence such as, for instance, the normality of the act, have been deceived.

Under the EEC Directive elsewhere mentioned (pp. 49, 158, 162, 165, 174), Belgian law, as outlined above, will have to be modified. Art. 11 of the Directive provides that a company will not be bound by acts exceeding its objectives nor by those exceeding the powers given by law to a company's representative. Restrictions on legal powers laid down in articles of association will no longer be a defence against grievances of third parties, even though they have been published, with the exception, however, of a 'joint signature' provision.

4. According to Art. 1584, para. 3 of the Belgian Civil Code, any principal is responsible for damages caused by his employees and subordinates in the course of their employment. This article also applies to the case of a company acting as employer and the responsibility is a direct liability of the company itself and not of its chief executive.[11]

BRITAIN

Most articles of association provide for the delegation of the management of the firm to the board of directors. For example, Art. 80 of Table A of the 1948 Act provides in part: 'The business of the company shall be managed by the

---

[11] For the responsibility of the company for wrongful acts committed by its directors, see G. van Hecke, 'La responsabilité des sociétés pour faits de leurs administrateurs en droit belge', *Rivista delle società*, 1956, p. 1010.

directors, who may pay all expenses incurred in promoting and registering the company, and may exercise all such powers of the company as are not, by the Act or by these regulations, required to be exercised by the company in general meeting. . . .' Thus, apart from such matters as the declaration of dividends, consideration of the accounts, balance sheets, and reports of directors and auditors, the election of auditors, and the election and removal of directors which are the basic matters which must be exercised in the general meeting, as must any powers to alter the company's articles and memorandum of association or capital structure, all powers are conferred on the directors.

Such an arrangement raises many problems as to the relationship between the board of directors and the company in general meeting. It is not certain how far any residual power remains in the general meeting to control the actions of directors. It appears that when there is deadlock on the board the general meeting has power to resolve the deadlock;[12] also the general meeting may initiate litigation.[13] However, there are decisions which suggest that if a power is delegated to the directors under the terms of the articles, the general meeting cannot direct the board how to exercise that power, nor overrule any decision made by the directors,[14] at least provided the board are acting in good faith and in the interests of the company. It appears that this extends as far as powers not expressly reserved to the general meeting by the Act or the articles. Thus it would seem that ultimately the control of the general meeting rests solely in its power to remove directors and to alter the articles of association. On the other hand, each individual member has a right to have the affairs of the company carried out in accordance with the provisions of the articles of association and to restrain the company from acting in an illegal or *ultra vires* manner.[15] Although this gives a limited degree of control to the shareholders, it is an area where reform and codification seem necessary.

The articles of association normally provide for the appointment, retirement and disqualification of directors.[16] It is necessary for a public company to have at least two directors, although one director is sufficient for a private company. The articles normally provide for the appointment of directors by an ordinary resolution of the members in general meeting, and in the case of public companies each director must be appointed individually on a separate resolution[17] to prevent the combination of directors whom the members wish to appoint with those whom they do not want. In this context there has been a limited amount of support for cumulative voting rights to prevent the majority from securing the appointment of their candidates, and to enable the minority shareholders by exercising all their votes in favour of a few candidates to have some representation on the board. This appears to be limited to shareholders in smaller companies where the majority consists of a few people who occasionally abuse their power. On the whole people appear

[12] See for example *Barron v. Potter* [1914] 1 Ch. 895, *Foster v. Foster* [1916] 1 Ch. 532.

[13] *Marshall's Valve Gear Co. v. Manning, Wardle and Co.* [1909] 1 Ch. 267.

[14] *Shaw and Sons (Salford) Ltd. v. Shaw* [1935] 2 K.B. 113; *Scott v. Scott* [1943] 1 All E.R. 582.

[15] *Quin and Axtens Ltd. v. Salmon* [1909] A.C. 442; *Russell v. Wakefield Waterworks Co.* (1875) 20 Eq. 474.

[16] See for example Table A, Art. 92.

[17] Companies Act 1948 Sec. 183.

to be satisfied with the present position in public companies where it is more difficult to secure voting control and the presence of institutional investors and the financial press acts as a restraint upon abuses. The main complaint in connexion with members' rights in public companies is concerned with the issue of non-voting shares. Many people are dissatisfied with the position which requires shareholders to part with their money and not to receive any control over its fate in return. The arguments in favour of voteless shares appear to be that they are useful on occasions as a means of raising fresh capital without losing control and any prohibition on the issuing of voteless shares could be easily evaded. The first of these arguments begs the whole question of whether a company should be entitled to raise share capital and not lose control as other means are available; and the second argument is not entirely convincing. Nevertheless a majority of the Jenkins Committee[18] came to the conclusion that the case for the abolition of voteless shares had not been made out.

Under the 1948 Act[19] a company may by ordinary resolution remove a director before the expiration of his period of office notwithstanding anything in its articles or in any agreement between him and the company. However, the usefulness of this power is severely restricted in that subsection (6) of Sec. 184 provides that 'Nothing in this section shall be taken as depriving a person removed thereunder of compensation or damages payable to him in respect of the termination of his appointment as director or of any appointment terminating with that as director.' Since the 1967 Act requires disclosure of directors' remuneration[20] and copies of any service contract to be available for inspection,[21] shareholders may now form some estimate of what it may cost them to remove a director, but some dissatisfaction exists with the necessity for paying heavy damages to inadequate directors who have taken long-term contracts appointing them as managing directors.

In the case of a public company a person who is seventy years of age or older may not be appointed unless 'special notice'[22] is given and his age mentioned, and the appointment approved by the members in general meeting.[23]

The articles of association usually provide for meetings of directors and the election of a chairman and managing directors.[24] Boards of directors are in practice often divided into executive and non-executive members. The nature of the legal relationship between a director and the company of which he is a director is not defined in the Companies Acts and only appears from an analysis of the authorities. Directors are, in the first place, agents of the company with power to bind it. They cannot, however, validly perform acts which are *ultra vires* the company, although they may be personally liable to the outsider with whom they deal under such circumstances.[25] If they perform acts which are *intra vires* the company but which exceed the powers conferred upon them by the articles of association, such acts can be ratified by an ordinary

---

[18] *Report* paragraphs 123–140. [19] Sec. 184. [20] Sec. 6.
[21] Sec. 26. [22] The Companies Act 1948 Sec. 142.
[23] ibid. Sec. 183. [24] ibid. Table A, Arts. 98–109.
[25] *Firbank's Executors v. Humphries* (1886) 18 Q.B.D. 54, cf. *Rashdall v. Ford* (1866) L.R. 2 Eq. 750.

resolution of the company. Where the company does not ratify such actions, its liability for the unauthorised acts of directors is governed by the rule in *Royal British Bank v. Turquand*[26] which provides that a company will be bound by a contract entered into by a director even though an irregularity in the internal management of the company has taken place—such as that an ordinary resolution authorising the contract has not been passed as required by the articles—and so long as the exercise of power by a director is consistent with the terms of the articles.

It is sometimes incorrectly stated that directors are also in the position of trustees in relation to the property of the company. But as Mr Justice Romer stated in *Re City Equitable Fire Insurance Co.,*[27] 'It has sometimes been said that directors are trustees; if this means no more than that directors in the performance of their duties stand in a fiduciary relationship to the company the statement is true enough. But if the statement is meant to be an indication by way of analogy of what those duties are, it appears to me to be wholly misleading. I can see but little resemblance between the duties of a director and the duties of a trustee of a will or of a marriage settlement.' As Professor Gower points out,[28] 'The duties of the trustees of a will or settlement is to be cautious and to avoid all risks to the trust fund. The managers of a business concern must, perforce, take risks; one of their primary duties is to carry on a more or less speculative business in an attempt to earn profits for the company and its members.'

The true position appears to be that the directors are agents of the company and, as agents, are under certain fiduciary duties to the company. It has been established that the duties are owed to the company, which does not mean the individual shareholders,[29] but, it has been suggested,[30] 'the present and future members of the company'. The effect of these duties is that directors cannot, for example, retain secret profits made as a result of knowledge acquired in their position as directors.[31] However, the absence of any duty towards shareholders means that a director may speculate in the shares of his own company making use of confidential information unknown to other shareholders, and no case has so far held a director accountable even to the company for profits made on such speculation. The restraint imposed on such insider trading is in Sec. 25 of the 1967 Act which prohibits directors from buying options in shares of their company or of any associated company.

As agents, the directors owe duties of care and skill to their company. However, as the cases have explained these duties, the director need exhibit only a fairly low level of skill to escape liability.[32] Directors need not exhibit the care and skill of an objectively reasonable director; they are merely required to exhibit only the degree of skill that may reasonably be expected from persons of their knowledge and experience. A director is not bound to

[26] (1855) 5 E & B 248, (1856) 6 E & B 327.
[27] [1925] Ch. 407 at p. 426.
[28] *Modern Company Law* (2nd ed.), at p. 472.
[29] See for example *Percival v. Wright* [1902] 2 Ch. 421.
[30] *Report of the Investigation into the Savoy Hotel* (HMSO 1954).
[31] *Regal (Hastings) Ltd. v. Gulliver* [1942] 1 All E.R. 378; *Phipps v. Boardman* [1967] 2 A.C. 46.
[32] *Re City Equitable Fire Insurance Co.* [1925] Ch. 407.

give continuous attention to the affairs of the company; his duties are of an intermittent nature to be carried out at board meetings. However, he is not bound to attend all board meetings and it appears that he is not liable for anything done at a meeting which he did not attend. In the absence of grounds for suspicion, he is justified in trusting officials to perform their duties honestly and is not bound to investigate their reports. On the other hand, it appears that this does not apply to directors and, in particular, managing directors who have contracts of service with the company. These people are expected to display an objective standard of care and skill.

The Jenkins Committee stated that the provisions of the 1948 Act on the appointment and tenure of office of directors 'appear to be generally satisfactory'[33] but recommended[34] that Sec. 185 of the 1948 Act (on the retirement of directors under age limit) should be amended to provide for the retirement of a director at the annual general meeting next after his seventieth birthday, and not at the end of his current term of office, though he should be eligible for re-election without the need for the special notice procedure; and that Sec. 188 (on the power of the Court to restrain certain fraudulent persons from managing companies) should be extended to cover any person who was convicted on indictment of any offence involving fraud, not limited to fraud on a company; who was a persistent defaulter in complying with the provisions of the Companies Acts; or who had shown himself reckless or incompetent in relation to the management of company affairs.

Although the Report of the Jenkins Committee rejected any attempt at the codification of 'responsibilities' of companies in the form of legal duties,[35] those 'responsibilities' can also be examined from the point of view of the directors' powers. Thus the 'General Purposes Clause' proposed by George Goyder in The Responsible Company would have the effect of empowering directors to have regard to the interests of employees and the country as a whole. It is intended that such a clause would, for example, empower directors to make gratuitous payments to employees although at present such payments may be held to be ultra vires, as in the circumstances found to exist in Parke v. The Daily News Ltd.[36] It has been suggested that such an extension of the powers of directors would not affect their duties to 'the company' which, however construed, does not include the employees, with the result that directors would not be protected from actions for breach of duty if they acted in a way beneficial to the employees but detrimental to 'the company'. However, it is difficult to see that if directors were ordered to consider other interests it could still be maintained that they owed their duty solely to 'the company'. But if such is the case, any such amendment would presumably redefine directors' duties in this area so that they were not owed solely to 'the company'. A further difficulty, which is frequently voiced, is that any extension of directors' powers would make control more difficult since there would be fewer matters left to the control of the general meeting. (See beginning of this section.) In connexion with this, it has been argued that it should be for the members themselves to decide whether such matters should

[33] Report paragraph 79.　　[34] Report paragraph 85.　　[35] Report paragraph 87.
[36] [1962] Ch. 927. The particular difficulty in that case has, to some extent, been overcome by the Redundancy Payments Act 1965.

be relevant considerations and not for the board of directors to be generous at the expense of the shareholders.

It is generally accepted that the present powers of directors, as set out in normal articles of association, are, in general, as wide as is commercially necessary, and there have been no proposals for the further extension of those powers except in so far as they would be extended by the abolition of the rules of *ultra vires* and that a person is treated as knowing the contents of a company's objects clause even though he has not read it.

When examining the duties of directors the Jenkins Committee accepted the opinion of the General Council of the Bar[37] that codification of the existing duties of directors would be impossible and leave lacunae which would make it more difficult to determine what those duties were in particular circumstances. The Jenkins Committee considered, however, that a statement of the basic principles underlying this relationship would be useful and recommended[38] that the Act should provide that 'a director of a company should observe the utmost good faith towards the company in any transaction with it or on its behalf, and should act honestly in the exercise of his powers and the discharge of the duties of his office'.

The Committee considered that it was wrong that a director could make use of confidential information to make a profit at the expense of individual members to whom at present he owes no duties and recommended[39] that, in addition to the present law requiring registration of directors' sharedealings,[40] if the information might be expected materially to affect the value of those securities, the director should be liable to compensate a person who suffered from his action unless that information was known to that person.

The Report includes recommendations that wider duties of disclosure should be imposed on directors in relation to their interests in contracts to which the company of which they are directors is or may be a party. At present the position of directors is that, in the absence of provisions in the articles of association, a director may not contract with his company no matter how fair the contract may be, since this involves a conflict of duty and interest.[41] However, the articles of association usually contain some provision relaxing this strict rule.[42] This right to waive the basic rule is not unlimited. Sec. 199 of the 1948 Act requires a director to disclose to the board any interest, direct or indirect, which he may have in any proposed contract. Failure to disclose renders him liable to a fine of £100 and liability to account to the company for any profit. A certain amount of criticism cynically doubted the effectiveness of disclosure to fellow directors to restrain abuse, although the Jenkins Committee,[43] did not support a proposal for disclosure to the general meeting but recommended[44] that he should disclose to the board any material interest in any contract and that copies should

[37] *Report* paragraph 87; Minutes of Evidence Vol. 13, p. 985.
[38] *Report* paragraph 99(a).　　　　　　　　　　　　[39] *Report* paragraph 99(b).
[40] Companies Act 1967 Sec. 29 replacing Sec. 195 of the 1948 Act.
[41] *Aberdeen Railway v. Blaikie* (1854) 1 Macq. 461; *Parker v. McKenna* (1874) 10 Ch. App. 96.
[42] See for example Table A, Art. 84; but compare *Rules of the Stock Exchange*, Schedule VII Part A, D(2) paragraph 112.
[43] *Report* paragraph 96.　　　　　　　　　　　　[44] *Report* paragraph 99(i)–(n).

be sent to the Registrar and be available for inspection by the members. Sec. 16 of the 1967 Act requires material interest of directors in significant contracts with the company to be disclosed in the directors' report. In addition, the Committee also recommended[45] that Sec. 190 of the 1948 Act (which prohibits loans to directors) should be widened.

It has been argued that the duties of care and skill are too low and that directors should be liable for inefficiency. On the other hand, it has been suggested that it would be inappropriate for the Court to have to determine the correctness of purely commercial decisions, and that the solution lies rather in the direction of more extensive management training and a more professional attitude towards management.

The chief executive, as contrasted with the other directors, is seen by the Jenkins Committee (and other authorities) as having general responsibility for achieving the whole of a firm's objectives, and it is thought by them that he should have 'a reasonably free hand' in order to do so effectively. In all these matters care should be taken that, in attempting to save shareholders from the occasional rogue or incompetent, too many fetters are not placed on the ordinary reliable directors preventing them from performing their functions effectively. At the same time, British investigators have held that the chief executive must remain under the control of the shareholders and respond to their pressure.[46] Yet the fact remains that in many companies such control is difficult to exercise, if not impossible.

In practice, the chief executive may also be instrumental in shaping policy, although increasingly, nowadays, within the framework of a management committee responsible to the board. In the larger British companies it is increasingly found that the chairman of the board and his fellow directors, especially if they are non-executive, constitute a long-range policy-making committee with responsibilities for the company's financial situation, while the day-to-day running of the company within an agreed policy framework falls to the chief executive and his staff of managers or to a management committee composed of their senior executives, usually with divisional responsibilities, and with the managing director or chief executive in the chair. He then becomes the sole link between board and management, which allows him extremely wide powers.

FRANCE

1. The current French debate on the organisation and control of firms goes back to the publication in 1963 of François Bloch-Lainé's book *Pour une réforme de l'entreprise*, which alerted his countrymen to the problem of the 'government of the company' and, in particular, to the dilemma of reconciling freedom and responsibility. The new law on commercial companies of July 1966, new proposals and discussions on works councils and the role of the unions and the whole question of 'participation', brought to a head by the crisis of May–June 1968, have all in turn carried the debate a successive stage further.

[45] *Report* paragraph 99(p).
[46] Cf. M. Fogarty, *A Companies Act 1970?*, PEP, pp. 123 ff.

The root of the matter is the question of authority. There seems to be agreement on all sides that authority must lie with the head of the business. The 'Employers' Charter' of the CNPF, issued in January 1965, is, naturally enough, particularly clear on this point. 'In matters of business administration, authority cannot be shared. All the evidence shows that every other formula leads to impotence. And it is the presence of a responsible man at the head of a firm which best allows for authority to be exercised in a humane fashion and ensures the necessary dialogue with the employees.' On their side, the employees' organisations also recognise the authority of management. Nor are they at all keen that employees should be involved in the making of decisions, since they wish to be able to challenge them later. Georges Levard, at the time President of the CFTC (now the CFDT), has said: 'Even the militant admit the necessity for authority. . . . You cannot run an enterprise, small or large, economic, civic or social, without one responsible person taking upon himself the responsibility for decisions and, when necessary, all their consequences.'[47]

The need to distinguish between owner and manager has gained ground. Bloch-Laîné has introduced a double distinction: 'Those whose function is to oversee and advise should not be confused with those whose function is to manage. And among the latter, it would be well to distinguish more clearly between the "governors" and the "governed".'[48] The main employers' organisation, the CNPF, has accepted these distinctions all the more easily because it is chiefly composed of representatives of big companies, that is to say the 'managers'. Maurice Hannart, of the Northern Employers, wrote in 1964: 'It seems desirable that the supervisory role of the present administrative board should be strengthened; it might even be necessary to change its name. The board would still have the right to appoint the representative of the entrepreneur, that is, the general manager (*directeur général*), who could, as now, be dismissed "on the nod". But he would have full powers of management, and, of course, be free to avail himself of all the help necessary to carry out his very heavy responsibility.'[49] Bloch-Laîné proposed the institution of a 'college of (administrative) directors' alongside a 'supervisory committee' on the German model. The Capitant Amendment introduced this idea into the 1966 Companies Act: firms may now, if they wish, adopt a new structure including a board of management or 'directory' (*directoire*) and a supervisory board. (The term 'directory' is used here in order to distinguish it clearly from the administrative board of 'traditional' single-board companies.)

Some people wanted to go further. J. Dubois[50] suggested that membership of the administrative board was incompatible with senior management positions. Art. 93 of the new Companies Act is more timid. It lays down that the number of members of the administrative board under contract of employment with the company may not exceed one third of the board's

---

[47] 'Débat sur la réforme de l'entreprise', in *Revue de l'Action Populaire*, No. 175, February 1964.

[48] F. Bloch-Laîné, *Pour une réforme de l'entreprise*, Paris, Editions du Seuil, 1963.

[49] M. Hannart, *Mémoire sur les problèmes de l'entreprise*, 1964, CREE Document No. 108.

[50] J. Dubois, *Recherche d'une plate-forme de politique économique de synthèse pour la France pendant les 15 années à venir*, 1963, CREE Document No. 125.

membership at any one time. A chairman/managing director (*président-directeur général*) or member of the board may not obtain a salaried position in the firm after appointment to the board.

Different opinions have been expressed on the 'control'[51] to be exercised over management. 'Many juridical formulae to settle this question are conceivable', says Bloch-Laîné, 'from simple "controlled co-option", with a right of challenge open to all the "governed", to a kind of "driving licence", a "permit to manage", which only a magistracy outside the firm, but invoked by the interested parties, could take away.' The extension of control to the employees is advocated in many circles. For Jacques Duhamel, Deputy for the Jura and a member of the Rassemblement Démocratique, 'every search for a formula reconciling unity of management and plurality of control must be through the unions'.[52] ACADI has made a subtle distinction between 'control' and 'advice'. Its proposal aims at 'collegiate management, that is, a Board of Managers appointed by the shareholders' general meeting and a Joint Committee, called the Examination Committee, set up with the direct intention of forming a desirable link between capital and labour and having the specific object of being a source of advice and not of control'.[53] Pierre de Calan, the representative of the 'liberal' employers, is against all widening of 'control'. He maintains that the proposed reforms would remove the exercise of proprietary rights from the shareholders and would endow employees and their representatives with a power which would be wrongful (because unsanctioned by responsibilities) and/or an equivocal moral responsibility which would weaken their true powers of challenge *vis-à-vis* the management. Similarly, the representatives of the state would gain a wrongful power of intervention unsupported by direct responsibilities. In the place of the present powers of managements, which are very broad but clearly sanctioned by their dependent relationship to the owners of the capital, there would be substituted either absolute power or paralysis—or a mixture of both together.[54] No legislative proposals aimed at extending control over managements have as yet been put forward.

2. The present law (the Act of 1966) provides that in the 'traditional' (i.e., single-board) *société anonyme* the chairman/managing director (*président-directeur général*) is appointed by the administrative board, and by it alone, from among its number. The general manager (*directeur général*) is also appointed by the board, on the nomination of the chairman, and may be neither a member of the board nor a shareholder. The new (and optional)

[51] The French word *contrôle* presents serious difficulties of translation. It does not mean 'control' in the usual English sense but rather 'supervision' or 'checking' with, as it were, a concomitant power of applying sanctions. The idea of 'control' is latent in the word but only as a result of an act or faculty of 'supervision'. Its implications may perhaps best be illustrated by recalling that the ticket-collector on a French train is called *le contrôleur*. Thus its central meaning could be paraphrased as 'making sure that things are as they should be'. In this section, but not always elsewhere in this book, the word is translated, in both its substantive and verbal forms, as 'control', with the reservations of the foregoing remarks.

[52] '12 hommes politiques répondent à 12 questions', in *La NRF*, No. 24/25, October/December 1965.

[53] J. Mersch, *Sur une vision nouvelle de l'entreprise*, CREE Document No. 62.

[54] P. de Calan, *Renaissance des libertés économiques et sociales*, Paris, Plon, 1964.

'directory' is composed of from two to five members, except in companies with a capital of less than Fr. 250,000 which may be run by a single general manager. These directors need not necessarily be shareholders and may not at the same time be either members of the supervisory board or the firm's auditors. They and their chairman are appointed by the supervisory board. Under the former law, jurisprudence had upheld the validity of the clause in the statutes allowing the possibility of co-option on to the administrative board. It may be supposed that, *mutatis mutandis*, co-option on to the new type of board is possible so long as the statutes expressly provide for it and so long as the director's co-option is ratified by the supervisory board.

Two widely contrasted alternative systems have been proposed for the appointment of directors: 'controlled co-option' (see footnote 51, above, for the meaning of 'controlled'); and election by employees. Concerning the first suggestion, Bloch-Laîné has put the question whether any formal ratification would really be necessary. 'Employees may not be eager to take part in any way in the "consecration" of management; but they deplore the fact that other people, who are called upon to do so, have this theoretical superiority over them. It would be no very novel departure, then, if the same system were applied to all the parties involved, in order to achieve equality of treatment. Choices made by co-option would be announced, and at the same time explained, and would be considered valid unless they were challenged.' Bloch-Laîné's co-option proposal has been strongly criticised, on the grounds that it would set up aristocratic castes within industry. Jean de Menthon[55] has written in favour of the second proposal. 'Co-option would not legitimise power in the eyes of the employees. Moreover, it is doubtful whether it would ensure good management. . . . In the long-run, with higher levels of education, could not the election of directors by the employees be envisaged?' Bloch-Laîné is against this proposal. 'The electors would either be docile—in which case they would, by voting, limit their future freedom of dispute without having benefited from a true freedom of choice—or they would make such demands that would force the candidates to outbid each other with promises which would diminish their authority and independence in advance.' J. Dubois has proposed a solution midway between the arrangements actually in force and co-option, ratification and election. In all 'commercial companies' employing more than 200 people, every directorship nomination made by the administrative board would be submitted to the approval of the works council. The secretary of the works council would preside over a vote by secret ballot and all proposed appointments would require approval by two thirds of all council members and not merely of those voting.[56]

Family companies pose a particular problem. Dubois thinks it would be necessary to 'forbid the inheritance of functions in commercial companies employing more than 100 people (and in agricultural concerns of more than 200 hectares) by anyone not holding a diploma from one of the *grandes écoles* under the age of thirty, so as to eliminate family parasites . . . and to dismiss the relatives and descendants of members of the administrative board or of

[55] J. de Menthon, *Cahiers chrétiens de la fonction publique*, No. 54, August 1963, CREE Document No. 34
[56] Dubois, op. cit.

managers from all responsible posts'. Bloch-Laîné considers that reform in this area could be limited to providing the head of the firm with a 'family council', which would not only reflect links of blood or property but would also include the most highly qualified 'wise men' among the salaried staff and the friends of the family. This proposal aroused violent hostility in certain employer circles and particularly in the General Confederation of Small and Medium Businesses (CGPME) led by Léon Gingembre.

Under present French law as far as 'traditional' single-board companies are concerned, the duration of the chairman's mandate, fixed by the statutes or the administrative board, cannot exceed six years at the most, the length of his term as a member of the administrative board. He may be re-elected. His dismissal can be decided on at any time by the administrative board, any clause to the contrary being regarded as null and void. As in the case of other members of the board, jurisprudence allows that wrongful dismissal gives a right to payment for damages. The same goes for the general manager who can be dismissed 'on the nod' by the administrative board, but only on the proposal of the chairman.

In the new 'directory', directors have been given more independence. While the appointment of the members of the 'directory' is within the competence of the supervisory board, their dismissal may be decided only by the shareholders' general meeting, on the proposal of the supervisory board. This change, say Roger and Jacques Lefebvre, 'is justified by the fact that the shareholders' meeting can thus play the role of arbiter in cases of conflict between the 'directory' and the supervisory board. Furthermore, as it seems very undesirable that a director should keep his job despite the hostility of the supervisory board and the shareholders' meeting, his dismissal, even if arbitrary, must follow. The law still provides that a director dismissed without due cause can demand damages'.[57] The mandate of members of the 'directory' is fixed at four years. In the absence of contrary legal provisions, it appears that members of the 'directory' may be re-elected, unless the statutes provide otherwise. (Other matters related to the choice now possible in France between the single- and two-board formulae are examined below, pp. 189-191.)

Ideas concerning the dismissal of senior management are developing under the influence of certain proposals of Octave Gélinier, the management consultant and deputy managing director of CEGOS. His two books *Morale de l'entreprise et destin de la nation* and *Le secret des structures compétitives* have made a deep impression in French employer circles. For Gélinier, efficiency implies sanctions. 'Those who wield power should be subjected to very powerful positive and negative sanctions, which should have a double effect (of motivation and selection). The granting of power to an incompetent damages the organisation as a whole. In order that such mistakes should be as rare as possible, it is right that bad management should cost the bad manager dearly, and even more dearly those who chose him.'[58] Gélinier has made two proposals, the first for official recognition of the 'take-over bid',

[57] R. and J. Lefebvre, 'La réforme des sociétés commerciales', *Tableaux Pratiques*, Editions Juridiques Lefebvre.
[58] O. Gélinier, *Morale de l'entreprise et destin de la nation*, Paris, Plon, 1964.

the second for the easier dismissal of senior management. Concerning the first, he says: 'Shareholders and directors guilty of a faulty choice are deprived of profit, suffer losses on their capital and frequently, as the result of a "take-over bid", have to give up their power to another group which considers itself more suitable.' Consequently, 'competition between management teams' should be stimulated by 'the promulgation of a law formally authorising the "take-over bid" and laying down proper measures to protect minorities'. On the second proposal, Gélinier has written: 'French law stipulates, in a very pertinent manner, that a chairman/managing director can be dismissed "on the nod" and without indemnity, notwithstanding any clause to the contrary. Would it not be desirable if this wise provision were extended, at least partially, to the senior management directly responsible to the chairman? Is it not shocking that when a badly managed company comes to be liquidated, the directors who contributed to its downfall receive copious dismissal compensation, while the staff who carried out their orders are treated less favourably? Let us repeat the maxim of Auguste Deteuf: "Management has no right to security." '

3. Concerning the powers of management towards third parties, Maurice Hannart[59] considers that a general manager (*directeur général*) (who, under the 1966 Act—see above—may not be a member of the administrative board) should be responsible to third parties only if the latter could never find themselves faced with any *ultra vires* act on his part. In this way, they would feel absolutely secure in their transactions. (The long-drawn-out efforts to define a 'European Company' formula include a provision of this sort.) Such an arrangement would go with an obligation on the part of the general manager to 'consult' the administrative board as a matter of course and to seek its 'authorisation' before making decisions in certain important areas which would be precisely defined in the statutes. The 1966 act goes some way in this direction. The statutes or the administrative board can limit the power of the chairman, but it is expressly provided that these limitations cannot apply to dealing with third parties. The same goes for the general manager and the 'directory'. However, the authorisation of the supervisory board is obligatory if the 'directory' wishes to involve the company in bail-bonds, endorsements or other financial guarantees, except in banking or finance companies. Roger and Jacques Lefebvre think[60] that 'the limitation of power in this case, since it originates in law and not in the statutes of the company, should be applicable to dealings with third parties. Consequently, a guarantee accorded without the prior authorisation of the supervisory board should be null and void.'

4. The responsibility of directors for the acts of their subordinates is not clearly defined in law. In cases of industrial injury, the head of the firm is without doubt penally responsible. Attitudes on this question seem to be hardening. In a legal action following a catastrophe at the Feyzin refinery, for example, the court laid the blame not only on the manager of the refinery but also on the general manager (not, be it noted, the chairman) of the owners.

[59] Hannart, op. cit.   [60] Lefebvre, op. cit.

ITALY

Under the Italian system, it is the directors, acting under the influence and subject to the supervision of the shareholders, and in the latter's exclusive interest, who determine the objectives a company is to pursue. The legal organisation of a company reflects this conception but in practice things are sometimes rather different. Directors of big companies in fact enjoy considerable freedom of manœuvre and there is a tendency to use a company on behalf of the vested interests of its controlling groups. Moreover, there has been no discussion in Italy about the source of the powers of chief executives. These are held to derive from shareholders who are the sole judges of their use. Creditors may take action against abuses only in cases where the shareholders do not do so; under Art. 2398 of the Civil Code (CC) they may bring an action *utendo juribus*, i.e. in the place of shareholders. The control of *sindaci* and the judicial control that may be demanded by a tenth of the shareholders (CC Art. 2490) are also safeguards for the shareholders' interests.

1. The Italian board system is similar to the British and American. In practice, one or more directors may be given powers to act on their own and the rest of the board assumes a supervisory role. (Art. 2381 of the Civil Code provides for a *comitato esecutivo ed amministratori delegati*.) This distinction, however, is not used to introduce the concept of a permanent and necessary division of functions within the board. Each director is liable to the shareholders, even if he did not actually participate in a particular act. A director may be exempted from such liability only if his dissent is written into the minutes of the board meetings (CC Art. 2392) and notified to the *sindaci*.

2. Directors are first appointed by the memorandum of association for a term of three years. They are subsequently elected by shareholders every three years (CC Art. 2383). They may also be co-opted by the elected directors (CC Art. 2386), conditional upon confirmation by vote at the next shareholders' meeting.

3. Directors' powers are limited by the object clause, but only as regards shareholders. There is no doctrine of *ultra vires*. Art. 1 of the company law reform draft expressly states: 'A company cannot raise the objection against third parties that a transaction made by them is unrelated to its object.' The draft proposes no changes in board organisation and function and does not discuss the system now in force. It merely seeks a more precise definition of some of the duties of directors with regard to the balance sheet and other information about company activities. (See below, p. 172.)

THE NETHERLANDS

The management of a Dutch company has a large measure of freedom to act in what it believes to be the company's best interests. The legal definition of its duties is very wide: it is responsible for managing the business of a company, for administering its assets and for representing it both at law and otherwise (Art. 47 of the Commercial Code (CC)). The final word on these duties lies with the general meeting of shareholders, as the providers of the company's risk capital. The law (CC Art. 50) allows, however, the setting up within the framework of the company of a supervisory board which can keep a closer watch on the management's running of the firm. Most Dutch companies have made use of this option and have stipulated in their articles of association that there shall be a supervisory board. In many articles of association it is laid down that the supervisory board's duties are to advise the management and to supervise its conduct of the business. As a result, therefore, of these provisions in a company's articles the management is also accountable, in some measure, to the supervisory board.

This system and the conditions in which it operates make it possible for any company to establish a proper balance between the management's necessary freedom of manœuvre and its accountability to those who have provided the company's risk capital. The considerable flexibility inherent in the Dutch system of company law has also proved its value from the economic point of view. For this reason it is generally agreed that the present accountability of management under the law and the articles of association should be basically maintained. This, however, does not mean that it is felt that management, apart from its accountability to the general meeting of shareholders and the supervisory board, should otherwise have complete freedom of action. Indeed, it is increasingly held that managements, particularly those of large enterprises, should take into account the interests of all those who are more or less directly concerned with the company, such as employees, bankers, suppliers, customers and, last but not least, the government, as the protector of the public interest.

A bare majority of the Verdam Committee, however, advocated the placing of further limitations on the managerial freedom at present afforded by the law of a company whose shares or depository receipts are quoted on the stock exchange. These restrictions would consist in: (a) making the appointment of a supervisory board compulsory by law; and (b) laying down by law that certain important and specified decisions could be taken only with the approval of the supervisory board.

Chief executives (i.e. the board of management), as well as supervisory directors, are appointed by the general meeting of shareholders, which may also remove them from office (see CC Arts. 48, 48b, 50c and 50d). The law does not specify that appointments should be for a particular period. A bare majority of the Verdam Committee, however, recommended the following changes as far as quoted companies are concerned: (a) the supervisory board should be the only organ of the company empowered to appoint the members of the board of management; (b) the supervisory directors should be appointed by the general meeting of shareholders for a period not exceeding four years, though the articles of association could state that they are eligible for re-election; and (c) the dismissal of supervisory directors in the interim should be permissible only for reasons of sufficient gravity.

The suggestions of the bare majority of the Verdam Committee have met with considerable opposition from the employers' organisations. The position of the supervisory board and its powers are still under discussion in the Social and Economic Council. (See pp. 225-226 and also 195-7.)

The powers of chief executives in relation to third parties are regulated by law (CC Arts. 47 ff) and by the articles of association, and go no further than is laid down therein. In particular, an executive director of a company can contract for the company only in transactions that are covered by the company's objects as defined in the articles of association; transactions that do not come within the defined objectives are null and void. There is little chance, however, of actions being void as a result of this stipulation since, in most articles of association, objectives are defined very widely. Actions of particular importance are, in some articles of association, made subject to the approval or agreement of another organ of the company, such as the supervisory board. If any act of this kind is performed without the required approval or agreement, the company is not contractually bound to the third party concerned, unless the organ that should have granted its approval or agreement has given that third party the definite impression, as a result of its behaviour, that the required approval or agreement had been granted. (Whether or not this was so would be judged according to case law.) A company is, however, contractually bound by an unauthorised act if that act is subsequently confirmed by the company (provided it comes within the objectives as defined in the articles of association) or if the interests of the company are served by that act. An executive director who has acted *ultra vires* is deemed to have entered into the contract on his own behalf, unless the third party chooses to claim damages against the director concerned (CC Art. 47b).

Changes in the powers of representation of executive directors are not immediately foreseen in Holland at the present time. It should be noted, however, that the first Directive of the EEC Commission under Art. 54(3)(g) of the Treaty of Rome (see p. 49 above) contains certain provisions that differ somewhat from those now applicable in the Netherlands. In the present context this means that Dutch law will at some moment have to be amended in such a manner as considerably to restrict a company's ability to avoid being bound by the decisions of its representatives. (See Arts. 8 and 9 of the Directive.)

There are no special rules in the Netherlands concerning the accountability of chief executives for the actions of their subordinates, nor have any been proposed.

SWEDEN

Any comparison of the laws of various countries on company organisation is hampered by the fact that the provisions of the law do not always reflect the actual state of affairs. Parliament may have given a certain body the right and duty to make important decisions but this does not necessarily mean that these decisions are in fact made by this body. It is quite likely that the decision-making function has been delegated to a subordinate body, while the higher, in spite of the letter of the law, fulfils a merely supervisory role.

To take a Swedish example, according to the Swedish Companies Act the board of directors administers the company's affairs, while the managing director is in charge of 'current management'. Similarly, the authority to sign on behalf of a company belongs to the board as a whole, while the managing director is entitled to sign in respect only of 'current management'. As for matters outside 'current management' (and all acts involving legal consequences and for which written forms are prescribed), the managing director has to call in a board member and together with him sign for the company.

However, in big Swedish companies the management of affairs is usually transferred to the managing director, and the entire board of directors do not need to sign for the company. The board has in fact become an advisory and supervisory body, while the managing director is the real controller. This seems to have come about because the managing director is an expert who devotes all his working time to the company and accordingly gets to grips with the company's problems. The board members, on the other hand, are not employed by the company; indeed, their main activities are elsewhere and they give their time to the company only at intervals.

If, therefore, we wish to compare conditions in various countries it seems pointless to start from what the law says about who shall take what decisions and who shall be responsible. It is better to begin by recognising the fact that the management of a company, normally, is in the hands of one or more 'insiders' who devote all their working time to the company and to whom this work is a living. Besides the manager (or managers), there is usually also a group of 'outsiders' who do not devote all their working time to the company but meet now and again to be brought up to date about the company's affairs and to make certain decisions.

In the larger Swedish companies, therefore, the board of directors consists of a group of 'outsiders', usually with the 'inside' managing director as a member of the board. Swedish law recognises the managing director as the only person inside the company responsible for its management. It is common practice, however, for the managing director and those immediately responsible to him to form a joint working team, often called a 'management committee'. The Companies Act, however, contains no provisions for such a team but prescribes categorically that the managing director shall be the only decision-making person. The management committee thus cannot legally be anything but a group for the discussion of questions upon which the managing director afterwards and by himself makes decisions.

Furthermore, a managing director is not allowed under Swedish law to be chairman of the board of directors. It is therefore necessary to have an outsider in a key position 'above' the leading insider. The chairman is merely the leader of the board's deliberations; he has no authority to give orders to the managing director. In the last few years some large companies have introduced a 'working chairman' on the Anglo-American pattern who devotes all his working time to the company. Such an arrangement, however, is difficult to reconcile with the provisions of the Swedish Companies Act, and it works well only if the chairman and the managing director are temperamentally suited to working together.

The arrangements in a large Swedish co-operative (the Co-operative Union and Wholesale Society) show how necessary it is to be careful about terminology when comparing different organisational systems. In this case the board of directors is composed of insiders, one of whom is chairman although he is not entitled, on his own, to make decisions of the sort which a managing director has a right to. On the other hand, the group of outsiders in this co-operative is called the administrative council. Through this choice of terminology it has proved possible, without seeking parliamentary approval, to set up an organisational system in which there are a number of insiders acting together in a collegiate manner. According to the Companies Act such a thing is not possible and it presumably does not correspond to parliament's original intentions with regard to co-operatives. While the group of outsiders in big companies is called the board of directors and has, according to law, to 'manage the company's affairs', as well as being authorised to sign for the company, the administrative council in a big co-operative has only a supervisory function, laid down more precisely in the by-laws of the co-operative. In practice, however, a big company's board of directors carries out much the same function as the administrative council of a large co-operative.

Some comparisons with foreign—and especially West German—law put the problem in a clearer perspective. In Germany there are two 'top' bodies—the *Aufsichtsrat* and the *Vorstand*. According to the law, the *Vorstand* conducts the company's affairs while the *Aufsichtsrat* has a supervisory function. The *Vorstand* is composed of one, or several, senior executives of the company, while the *Aufsichtsrat* is made up of other persons who do not usually devote all their working time to the company and in any event are not key senior executives. The *Vorstand* may thus be most closely compared to the managing director of a Swedish company or the board of directors of a Swedish co-operative.

The *Vorstand* may be composed of one or several persons. In the latter case the members have to make decisions *gemeinschaftlich*, that is to say, in a collegiate fashion. However, the by-laws or special regulations may prescribe otherwise—but not to the effect that one or more board members may take a decision *against* the view represented by a majority of the *Vorstand*. The upshot of this seems to be that if the power to take decisions is concentrated in *one* person, the *Vorstand* must consist of him alone, while his closest collaborators are to be classed as senior executives outside the *Vorstand*. (The same person can be a member both of *Aufsichtsrat* and *Vorstand* only in exceptional circumstances.)

Under French law (before the choice between single- and two-board companies was introduced by the new Act of 1966) the right to take decisions was concentrated in one person, the *président directeur général,* who at the same time was the chairman of the group of 'outsiders', the *conseil d'administration.* The *président-directeur général* was normally not an employee of the company in a legal sense. He could be an employee, and if he were the fact was demonstrated by his being also a *directeur technique.* However, even if he were not a *directeur technique,* he probably as a rule devoted all his working time to the company for remuneration.

The characteristic features of the top organisation of a single-board French company, therefore, are that there is only one 'insider' with a sole right to make decisions and that this insider has also to be chairman of the group of 'outsiders'. By contrast, according to Swedish law the managing director is *not* allowed to be chairman of the board of directors and under German law no inside member of the management at all is allowed to sit on the *Aufsichtsrat*.

From this it may be concluded that a constructive discussion of these questions cannot be based on a theoretical distinction between bodies which, according to the law, have a managing function and those which, according to the law, have a supervisory function. Big companies have developed in such a way that it is quite impossible for them to be managed by outsiders. If outsiders are appointed to a body which, according to the law, has an administrative function, that body will then change its character and acquire a supervisory function. The heart of the matter, therefore, in any discussion of different organisational alternatives, is the method adopted for the combination of outsiders and insiders. If there is to be a group of outsiders in an organisational relationship with one or more insiders, there is still the question whether the insiders' right to make decisions is to be entrusted to one individual or to a collegiate body in which the leader shares his responsibility with his closest assistants and may possibly be obliged to comply with their decisions. It has also to be settled whether one or more insiders are to be allowed to be members of the outside group and, if so, whether an insider may be permitted to be chairman of this group or whether possibly he may be obliged to be so, as required by the French law regarding single-board companies. It appears, therefore, that the terminology of the German Act accords better with reality than that of the Swedish.

It cannot be said that there has been much interesting political discussion in Sweden on this subject. Moreover, it should be remembered that parliament, as already mentioned, has very little scope to influence the real state of affairs. The experience of the last fifty years shows that on the whole events have run ahead of legislation and that parliament, at every successive revision of the Companies Act, has contented itself with catching up with the developments that have occurred. For instance, legal provisions regarding managing directors were introduced only in the Act of 1944, although big companies had already been in the habit of appointing managing directors for many decades.

Although political debate on these questions has been somewhat tepid, there has been more and more discussion in legal and business circles. Enquiries set in train by the Studieforbündet Näringsliv och Samhälle offer some evidence that Swedish business leaders are beginning to debate issues such as the increasing powers of managing directors and the opportunities for revitalising the work of boards in much the same way as some of their foreign counterparts. (See also pp. 226–227.)

To return to the specific points covered by this chapter, it is the board of directors that has the right under Swedish law to appoint and dismiss managing directors. Many representatives of Swedish industry seem to think this to be the board's most significant and even, perhaps, its only function apart from its general supervisory role. No real discussion on the appointment of managing directors by more broadly based 'election committees' can be said to have taken place, though some thinking along these lines does seem to be emerging from the political left.

Board members are appointed for a maximum period of three years by the shareholders' meeting which is always at any time, and without explaining its reasons, entitled to dismiss a board member. It has never been suggested that this right of the shareholders' meeting should be limited. A managing director is appointed, within or outside the board of directors, by the board.

As far as relations with third parties are concerned, it has already been mentioned that Swedish law maintains the old-fashioned requirement that it is the entire board of directors that signs jointly for the company. It is also the board, thereafter, that decides which other persons, solely or jointly, are to be authorised to exercise this function. However, the managing director is always entitled to sign alone for the company in matters pertaining to 'current management' and he has entire authority to sign with any *one* of the board members.

If a person authorised to sign for a company is in fact acting contrary to the by-laws, or to the decision of a shareholders' meeting, or any other superior body, his action will not be valid, whether the third party realised, or merely ought to have realised, that the action was irregular. A third party should be familiar with the legal limitations of the authority of companies and with such provisions of the by-laws as are entered in the Register of Joint Stock Companies, e.g. those concerning the objectives of a company's activity. He may, however, protect his interests by objecting that he did not, nor had grounds to, realise that a particular agreement was, for instance, inconsistent with the objectives of the company.

In practice, this much weakened principle of *ultra vires* is seldom pleaded. The Swedish principle that a third party is protected only if he has acted in good faith differs both from the requirements of German law and from the first EEC directive on the harmonisation of company law (which is mentioned on several occasions elsewhere in this book; see pp. 49, 144, 158, 165 and 174) under which limiting regulations or bylaws cannot be pleaded against a third party, even though he acted in bad faith.

As far as interested parties are concerned, Swedish law has nothing to say about the matters commonly discussed in the literature of business organisations. The Companies Act recognises only one interested party (in the sense here used), namely the shareholders. Nevertheless, a Swedish managing director outwardly appears to be his company's responsible leader to a greater extent than in Britain or the USA. Consequently, it can be said that in the eyes of public opinion he is 'responsible' to a considerably wider circle than the company's owners.

Swedish law subjects a managing director to a heavy burden of responsibility for the actions of his subordinates. He is also often held responsible under criminal law for purely technical irregularities of book-keeping, tax returns, etc. It has often been suggested that this responsibility should be more widely spread. This is a complicated problem and one which relates more to criminal than commercial law. Many regulations in company law and elsewhere start from the assumption that the head of the company should be punished for infractions of the law committed by anyone in the firm. However, the contemporary trend towards greater and greater delegation of responsibility to subordinates has robbed the head of the firm of his ability to exercise real and immediate influence all the way down the line. In practice, however, convictions have resulted mainly in fines and have for this reason possibly been regarded more as nuisances than as matters of serious importance.

Chapter 2

THE REPRESENTATION AND PROTECTION OF INTERESTS WITHIN THE COMPANY

Section A: Disclosure

*How much disclosure does the law require?
Should it demand more? Whom or what is
disclosure chiefly meant to benefit or protect?*

(a) *Some academic views*

As will have been apparent from earlier sections of this book, the opinion is widespread among Belgian academics that the purpose of the company is to fulfil the fundamental aspirations of those who devote their efforts to it. Such persons should be able to go beyond the narrow field of their own specialities by 'understanding' the company and by sharing in its responsibilities. De Barsy calls this a right of participation based on natural law, necessarily linked with the right to found a company, as it is of the same order.[1] The ability to 'supervise' is governed by the availability of sufficient information on the activities of the company. This means, in particular, that the system of company accounting should be rationalised and that the *Institut des Reviseurs d'Entreprises* (the auditors' organisation) should be reformed. While it is true that legislation stipulates what information is to be given to works councils (under the law of 20 September 1948 and the Royal Decree of 27 October 1950), the basis on which the information rests has not yet been strictly defined. Lack of uniformity in book-keeping practice makes it difficult for people who are not thoroughly familiar with the firm's own system to draw meaningful conclusions from the documents.[2] Among those who have put forward proposals for the reform of the *Institut des Reviseurs d'Entreprises* and of the competence of the *reviseurs*, R. Vandeputte has suggested that the auditors should be controlled by a public body. The auditors should

[1] E. de Barsy, *Raisonnement sur l'entreprise*, Société d'Economie Politique de Belgique, No. 312, December 1965.
[2] R. Vandeputte, *Le statut de l'entreprise*, Brussels, Bruylant, 1965, p. 110.

164

be independent persons chosen for their intellectual and moral worth, authorised to give information and to answer questions in connexion with submitted documents and reports. They should also have more time to prepare their audit.[3]

In connexion with the new ideas on the purpose of the firm, these proposed reforms are necessary conditions for the achievement of the 'company-community'. Complete and objective information is an absolute prerequisite to the 'institutionalised dialogue' between management on the one hand and 'supervisors' representing the workers and the general public on the other. (See pp. 69 and 141 for an exposition of these ideas.) As far as profit-sharing by workers is concerned, R. Henrion observes that such a share in the profits, and especially the grant of a special title of property, can be achieved only if the books of the company are able to stand up to professional criticism. Professor Vandeputte agrees with this view.[4]

(b) Present Belgian law

The Belgian Code on Commercial Companies contains various disclosure requirements. The charter of a *société anonyme*, and any amendments, must be published in the supplements of the Official Gazette (Art. 9). So also must be the election and resignation of directors, auditors and liquidators and, in the last case, the instruments stating the manner of liquidation (Art. 12). The annual balance sheet and profit and loss account, as approved by the shareholders, must also be published in these supplements, together with a list of directors and auditors in office and the allocation of the annual profits (Art. 80), as well as any transfer of the location of the company's head office (Art. 81, para. 3). All documents emanating from the company must bear the name of the company, its legal form and head office address (Art. 81). Special disclosure requirements apply in the case of public issues of shares or bonds (Arts. 32, 33, 84 and 85). In addition to publication in the supplements of the Official Gazette, registration of the company in the Trade Register is required.

Various demands have been made for an extension of disclosure requirements, both in the interests of shareholders and third parties such as creditors and also for the benefit of company employees. These demands are directed mainly to accounting documents. The official committee on company law reform has proposed specific rules for the various particulars which must figure in the annual balance sheet and the profit and loss account, and also for methods of valuation. Special attention has been paid to the 'comparability' of successive annual accounts.[5] The EEC Directive referred to elsewhere (pp. 49, 144, 158, 162 and 174) will entail some emendations of Belgian law.

BRITAIN

The underlying philosophy of British company law is that the disclosure of

---

[3] ibid., p. 64.

[4] R. Henrion, 'L'entreprise et les apporteurs de capitaux,' *Cahiers économiques de Bruxelles*, No. 22, 1964, pp. 227–235; Vandeputte, op. cit. p. 109.

[5] Vandeputte, op. cit., pp. 30 ff.

all matters will prevent abuse, and it has already been noted in Chapter 1 of Part I of this book that disclosure by British companies has been much extended by the 1967 Act. The Cohen Committee stated:[6] 'Much of our report is based on the principle, of the validity of which we are convinced, that the fullest information practicable about the affairs of companies should be available to the shareholders and the public.'

The arguments on disclosure were set out by Professor Harold Rose in *Disclosure in Company Accounts,* published by the Institute of Economic Affairs in 1963, in which he argues that disclosure should not be limited to the prevention of abuse and to the exercise of shareholders' control. 'The wider economic interest of society demands disclosure because a free economy operates through the spontaneous attraction of resources to points of highest productivity, using the mechanism of the markets and prices; and to this process the provision of finances is crucial.'

The other arguments in favour of disclosure usually advanced are that it provides for traders the information which they require in deciding whether to grant credit to a company and for trade unions the information which they need to enable them to assess the justice of wage rates offered by employers. The usual argument advanced against disclosure is that it gives competitors an unfair advantage: it informs competitors of favourable areas for exploitation if the other company's accounts reveals a high rate of return on its local operations or on certain types of goods. However the Cohen Committee stated:[7] 'We do not believe that publication would have so completely one-sided consequences. In any event, in the public interest, stimulation or elimination of the inefficient, whether small or large, is desirable. Moreover, if the disclosure be made general by making it obligatory, the objection is overcome.'

Professor Rose further criticises the traditional method of setting out company accounts as being unhelpful to investment analysts and the financial press. The balance sheet as an historical record and little else is a concept that has been weakened by rising prices caused by full employment and the consequently increasing problem of asset valuation. He contends that the insurance value of assets should be published as well as their nominal book value. Current legislation[8] has now made it compulsory for firms to reveal when assets have been revalued, by whom, and in what manner. Professor Rose approves of the American disclosure rules and concludes that 'there is not much doubt that disclosure plays a material part in keeping American management at full stretch'.

In connexion with publicity one can mention the valuable role played by the financial press in acting as a watch-dog over companies. However, in dealing with these matters journalists feel inhibited by the law, in particular the law of defamation, which is such that any error, however slight, can lead to heavy liability regardless of the good faith of the publisher.[9] It has been

---

[6] *Report of the Committee on Company Law Amendment,* 1945, Cmd 6659, at paragraph 50.

[7] ibid. at paragraph 57.

[8] Companies Act 1967 Sec. 16 and Schedule 2 Part I.

[9] See for example *Lewis v. Daily Telegraph* [1964] 2 Q.B. 401.

suggested that a possible reform or classification of the law could provide that a publisher who acted in good faith and without malice or negligence should not be liable, and, in view of the services rendered by newspapers, this is a matter that could be investigated.

The 1967 Act[10] greatly extended the information which must be disclosed in the accounts and the directors' report. (See above, p. 38.) It is now necessary to disclose details of shareholdings in other companies, the turnover, the relative profitability of each part of the company's business where more than one trade is carried on, details of any significant changes in the company's undertaking and fixed assets during the year. Greater details of the remuneration of directors and highly paid employees are required as are details of political and charitable contributions exceeding in aggregate £50. Where more than 100 people are employed, the directors' report must state the average number employed each week during the year and their aggregate emoluments. These rules provide for more information for shareholders and the general public, and the Board of Trade is empowered[11] to investigate where it appears that the members are not receiving all the information which they might reasonably expect. As company accounts are difficult for a layman to understand, this additional disclosure is perhaps useful in that it provides more information for the press to use as the basis for comment.

FRANCE

Information on the situation and activities of firms is of general interest to the overall national economy and of more particular interest to shareholders, creditors, customers and suppliers, on the one hand, and, on the other, to employees. Such information is still scanty in France, for the reasons discussed in the following paragraphs.

(a) *General disclosure*

The business secret is a notion which has remained dear to French businessmen, who do not feel that information needs to be passed on and tend to consider even quite ordinary pieces of information as confidential—even if everyone knows about them from another source. The fact that there is little delegation of directors' responsibilities helps to reinforce the wall of silence.

The economic and financial press remains weak in France compared with that in other countries; it is less read and consequently has insufficient means at its disposal. It is symptomatic that when a group of big industrial and banking firms gained control a few years ago of a considerable financial press group no reaction was apparent. Furthermore, the ordinary daily press gives little business news. Taking the figures quoted by Robert Salmon,[12] André Plagnol, chairman of the Institute for Research and Financial Studies, noted in 1966 that the number of pages devoted to company news in the important French dailies was only a quarter of those in the British *Daily Telegraph*.[13] (It

[10] Sections 3–24.
[11] 1948 Act Sec. 165(b) (iii).
[12] R. Salmon, *L'information économique, clé de la prosperité*, Hachette-Entreprise.
[13] *Entreprise*, 21 July 1966.

must be admitted that this state of affairs is now rapidly changing. Much remains to be done, but financial and economic coverage has considerably expanded in the past year or two.)

The number of companies quoted on the stock exchange is small and they are the only ones to get any publicity or to be interested in it. According to André Vêne,[14] 'only a minority of companies is quoted in official lists, 971 in Paris and 568 in the provinces. There are, in addition, 639 securities from the Franc Zone which are dealt in more or less regularly in the Paris unlisted market, and about 1,000 dealt in the unlisted provincial markets. The shares of a great majority of companies—about 60,000—are dealt in neither in the official nor in the unlisted market.' (Since he wrote, however, the proportion of companies with a Paris quotation has increased.)

The use of consolidated balance sheets in the case of subsidiaries varies from one business to the other. François-Maurice Richard noted in his report to the Economic and Social Council:[15] 'From the shareholders' point of view, the growth of subsidiaries and of holdings in other companies has been accompanied in a great number of firms by lack of information as to the financial situation and results of the concerns in which the parent company is interested. ... The balance sheet of a company holding important interests is drawn up like a riddle or a smokescreen. ... The technique [of the consolidated balance sheet] is not unknown in France but it is little practised.' Most important of all, the method of consolidating the balance sheet differs from one firm to another. In addition, the 'financial professions' have remained comparatively weak. Financial analysts are ill-organised; studies made by banks are insufficiently publicised; stockbrokers are only beginning to provide administrative and advisory services.

Companies whose stocks are quoted on the stock exchange and their subsidiaries are, however, obliged to disclose certain information to shareholders and to the public. The decree of 29 November 1965 brought in a number of innovations which remain valid in the framework of the new company law of 1966.

Quoted companies whose capital exceeds Fr. 10 million must publish the following documents in the *Bulletin of Obligatory Legal Announcements*:

    (i) Within the month following the annual general meeting: balance sheet, information relative to extra-balance sheet liabilities, distribution and allocation of profits, information on subsidiaries and holdings in other companies, general accounts, profit and loss account, inventory of movable securities.

    (ii) Within the month following each financial quarter-day: the amount of turnover, with the figure for the preceding quarter and the corresponding quarter of the previous year for comparison. (In the case of companies which are involved in different sectors of industry the turnover must be broken down sector by sector.)

    (iii) Within three months following each quarter of the financial year: the provisional balance sheet taken at the end of the previous quarter.

[14] 'Mais où sont les actionnaires d'antan?', *Le Monde*, 9 September 1966.

[15] 'Consolidation des bilans', a study by the Section des Finances, du Crédit et de la Fiscalité on the report of F.-M. Richard, Conseil Economique et Social, 21 December 1965.

Quoted companies whose capital does not exceed Fr. 10 million are not subject to these requirements but they are obliged to send certain items of information to any shareholder who asks for them, within fifteen days of the request. (See next section.) The subsidiaries of quoted companies are equally obliged to disclose various facts.

(b) *Disclosure for shareholders and creditors*

At the time of its formation a company is bound by certain disclosure obligations which vary according to its juridical form. In addition, certain items of information are required for the benefit of third parties when the company appeals to the public for investment capital or when assets of a particular kind accrue to the company (commercial funds, patents, real estate, etc.). Most important of all, every company must be registered at the Registry of Commerce. This is the final disclosure measure and the most significant because commercial companies have neither the status of a corporate body nor legal existence until their date of registration.

In order to ensure that every company is regularly constituted, the government had envisaged instituting a system of judicial checking (*contrôle*; see footnote 51, p. 152 above) that would precede registration. This proposal met with strong criticism, particularly from the National Association of Share Companies[16] (of which Maurice Polti is chairman) and was replaced by an *a posteriori* checking system. The government, however, seems to have a long-term intention of introducing a 'previous investigation' procedure.

The dissolution of a company also requires various disclosure formalities. It does not take effect as far as third parties are concerned until the date it is published in the Registry of Commerce. The same goes for the nomination, dismissal or resignation of persons charged with carrying on, administering and directing the company, who cannot be declared by the company to be acting *ultra vires* in dealings with third parties until facts concerning them have been duly published.

Apart from the disclosure requirements intended for the benefit of partners or third parties, shareholders have certain rights of access to a number of documents, either at any time or at the time of the general meeting or of an extraordinary meeting. These rights are summarised in the following paragraphs.

At any time in the year, shareholders have a right of access to certain company documents concerning the last three financial years and also the minutes and attendance rosters of the meetings held in the course of the three previous financial years. The documents are: the inventory, the general business account, the profit and loss account, the balance sheet and the reports of the administrative board (or of the 'directory' and the supervisory board) and of the auditors. It seems that this information can be given only at the head office or administration department of the company. The existing legal texts do not specify whether this right may be exercised by a non-shareholding proxy. The government has undertaken to withdraw the right to take a copy of the inventory. The question of copying has not been specified for the other documents.

[16] ANSA, *Rapport du Conseil d'Administration à l'Assemblée Générale du 27 avril 1966.*

Any shareholder of a quoted company whose capital does not exceed Fr. 10 million may receive within fifteen days, on request, the balance sheet and its appendices, the general business account, the profit and loss account and the inventory of moveable assets held in portfolio.

Within the fifteen days which precede the annual general meeting, shareholders have right of access (at the head office or administration department) to the following documents (in addition to those available at any time): a list of all directors; the text and the summarised objectives of resolutions to be proposed; information concerning candidates for the administrative or supervisory boards; and the total sum, certified by the auditors, of the emoluments paid to the highest paid persons, the number of these being five or ten according to whether or not the payroll exceeds 200 employees.

Within the fifteen days which precede an extraordinary meeting, shareholders must be provided with the text of the proposed resolutions, the report of the board, and, if relevant, the auditors' report and any merger plan.

Within the fifteen days before the general meeting, the list of shareholders (taken on the sixteenth day which precedes the meeting) must be put at shareholders' disposal. The list must show the surname, first name and address of registered securities entered on that date in the company register and of every holder of bearer stocks who has at that date made a permanent deposit at the head office, together with the number of shares which each holds. Failure to honour these disclosure obligations can incur a fine varying from Fr. 2,000 to Fr. 40,000. (It may be noted that André Plagnol[17] has drawn attention to the 'screen' that banks can erect between boards and shareholders. 'It is practically impossible for a company, without paying quite a heavy commission, to get from its bankers a complete list of its own shareholders. How, then, can it effectively pass on the information intended for the shareholders?')

A *Commission des Opérations de Bourse*, modelled on the American SEC, has recently been set up, primarily to check the truth and completeness of information provided. It has still, however, only limited means at its disposal.

(c) *Disclosure for employees*

The law on works councils has specified a company's disclosure obligations towards its employees, represented by the council. In joint stock companies (*sociétés anonymes*), the management is obliged to send to the works council (before their presentation to the shareholders' general meeting) the profit and loss account, the balance sheet, the auditors' report and the other documents submitted to the meeting. The council members enjoy the same rights of communication and copying as shareholders.

In all companies, whatever their form, the head of the firm must give the works council information on (i) future plans likely to affect manpower structure, hours of work, conditions of employment and redundancy; (ii) quarterly production and order levels and operating and plant projects; (iii) a general report, at least once a year, on the activities of the firm and the development of wage structures and levels over the past financial year and plans for the coming year. As a counterpart to these wider rights of information, the law has bound works council members to secrecy in matters concerning informa-

[17] *Entreprise*, loc. cit.

tion given as confidential by the head of the firm and, as in the past, in all questions relating to manufacturing processes.

The government is now in the course of making new arrangements for the provision of information for employees, in the context of greater 'participation'. (See Part II, Chapter 2, p. 116 above.)

GERMANY

The disclosure of the affairs of the company for the protection of present and future shareholders should, in place of state supervision, make it possible for individual shareholders to protect themselves from deception and fraud. The history of company law has certainly shown how difficult it is to prevent the public being misled and, especially, creditors being deceived as to the state of the company's assets. The development of company law has therefore always been marked by a sharpening and refinement of provisions for disclosure, especially with regard to creditors.

The crucial point of the legal duty of disclosure lies, in addition to the annual report, in the principle of clarity in the annual accounts, the value of which the Act of 1965 has increased by making more stringent demands of them. The disclosure requirements of the 1965 Act are set out in Sections 177 and 178, which correspond to Sections 143 and 144 of the former Act of 1937. The new wording of Sec. 177 is intended to make it even more certain that the annual statement of accounts (i.e. the balance sheet and profit and loss account) as entered in the *Handelsregister* corresponds truly with the certified accounts. Furthermore, the *Registergericht* (court of register) now has a formal and material duty of verification with regard to the annual statement. Such a duty was not included in the Act of 1937. The most important difference between Sec. 178 of the 1965 Act and Sec. 144 of the old Act is the distinction now made between obligatory and optional disclosure. Many companies used to publish their annual statement of accounts in abbreviated form and accompanied by the auditor's certification notice in publications (such as newspapers) other than those laid down by law and thus may have given the impression that this was the full statement of accounts. Para. 2 of Sec. 178 deals with this possible misunderstanding by requiring that if the statement of accounts is not reproduced in full this fact must be explicitly declared in a heading, an auditor's certificate must not be attached and the number of the *Bundesanzeiger* (the official gazette) in which the full statement is published must be given. Certain new provisions on the annual report, on the other hand, are likely to have only a small effect in practice, since publication of the report is not required in any way by the Act and only in rare cases by articles of association. The new Sec. 178 does not include the requirements of Sec. 144, para. 2, of the 1937 Act that the sum totals of assets, liabilities, expenditure and income be set out as separate items in each case, since this is self-evident and follows from the principles of proper accounting procedure. Para 1(3) of Sec. 178 prescribes that the resolution of the annual general meeting concerning the application of the profit, because of its significance for the economic position of the company, is to be disclosed. Before the Act of 1965 it was possible to bring down the profit by undervaluing the assets, and by building up hidden reserves to conceal the true yield. The new law has sought a more accurate reflection of real assets in the balance sheet by strict provisions for valuation (Sec. 153 ff) aimed especially at the prevention of undisclosed reserves; furthermore, the methods of valuation and any essential alterations in them are to be stated in the report.

As increased disclosure makes possible a more accurate judgment of share values, the new provisions are welcome because they can make saving by investment in shares more popular—a development which should open up new sources of capital to companies. On the other hand, numerous investigations indicate that AG which do not offer shares on the market are trying to avoid disclosure obligations. This has revived the main company law controversy. Although it has been assumed hitherto that disclosure was primarily to inform shareholders and creditors, on whom the joint stock company depends, there is now a tendency to regard 'the publication of the state of the assets from the point of view of public control of great capital complexes and the economic power associated with it' (Würdinger). Such a statement, however, indicates a superimposition on company law of considerations which belong rather to the general sphere of political economy which would bring about considerable changes in the legal situation if they were put into effect. A disclosure obligation connected with the idea of control of economic power could not be limited to the AG but would have to embrace all big businesses. It seems questionable, however, whether such an extensive interest in disclosure exists among the public. The intended reform of GmbH law will throw some light on this.

ITALY

Under the present law the balance sheet, prepared by the board, must be certified by the *sindaci* and approved by the annual shareholders' meeting and thereafter filed in the registry of companies. Its contents and the valuation criteria for individual items are strictly laid down in Arts. 2424 ff of the Civil Code but as the law seems mainly concerned with the dangers of overvaluation directors are given much room for manœuvre.

The draft project for the reform of Italian company law calls for greater disclosure. The measures suggested (which have received wide support) include: more detailed specification of individual items in the balance sheet (Art. 29 of the draft) or in the directors' report (Art. 30); a separate directors' report for any proposal for a merger, the issue of bonds or shares or changes in the articles; the publication of a special bulletin for quoted companies, where all the most important decisions would have to be published (Art. 49); and the communication of certain information on companies' operations to a special public authority (Art. 46) which would control quoted companies. (See below, page 278.)

There is much discussion in Italy about the place to be accorded to disclosure in the general movement for the reform of company law. To some, its function is to give the market in general enough information to enable it to react meaningfully to company policies. Most observers, however, consider this to be only an indirect result of disclosure, the chief purpose of which is the information of shareholders. Furthermore, the external control of the proposed new authority over quoted companies has been linked with the need to keep shareholders informed about their company. But why should shareholders be informed? To enable them to vote more intelligently at company meetings, or to allow them to act in the market? The first theory (the 'shareholders' democracy' doctrine) still has many followers in Italy, but the reform draft seems rather to take the opposite view and to rely on general meetings for the protection of small investors.

THE NETHERLANDS

The traditional view was that only shareholders had a right to be informed of the contents of a company's annual accounts. In 1928, however, a provision was included in the Dutch Commercial Code (Art. 42c) which made it obligatory for the management of companies within the meaning of Art. 42c ('open' limited companies; see p. 49) to publish the contents of the annual accounts by depositing them at the *Handelsregister* (Registry of Commerce). Other forms of limited company (generally referred to as 'close' limited companies) are under no such obligation. Also in 1928 a number of provisions were added to Art. 42 of the Commercial Code specifying what the annual accounts had to contain. These provisions, however, are very brief. The opinion is growing that annual accounts should give a real and reasonable insight into the economic and financial affairs of a company. The accounts of most firms therefore contain more information than is required by law, and, partly because they are usually audited by external auditors (particularly in large companies), they achieve a high standard of reliability. In recent years there have been proposals from many quarters (for example, from the Council of the Dutch Employers' Federation in 1954 and 1962) that what has become established practice should be laid down by law, thus considerably strengthening existing legal requirements governing reporting by companies. On the basis of established practice, and elaborating on proposals already put forward, the Verdam Committee has produced a draft Bill, which proposes: (a) that much more rigorous provisions should be laid down in a new Act with regard to the information which annual accounts should provide; and (b) that every interested party should be enabled by law, through a special divisional court (an *Ondernemingskamer*) to be set up within the Court of Appeal at Amsterdam to compel managements to make their annual accounts comply with the provisions of the new Act if they should fail to do so.

Under the draft Bill the managements of open limited companies would be bound within eight days after the adoption of the annual accounts to deposit them with the *Handelsregister*. (In the draft Bill open limited companies are basically defined as limited companies with more than Fl. 250,000 issued in bearer shares or in bearer certificates in circulation. Under Art. 42c of the Commercial Code, as it now stands, the lower limit is Fl. 50,000.) The accounts would have to be drawn up in the manner specified in the Act and be accompanied by a statement from an independent auditor showing that the accounts had been audited and that they complied with the new Act. The draft Bill leaves the 'close' company free from the obligation to publish annual accounts.

The Social and Economic Council, which has submitted a report on this draft Bill to the government, is for the most part in favour of it. It differs from the Verdam Committee, however, in the following proposals: (*a*) Companies should be compelled to include in their annual accounts the names of those enterprises in which they own, directly or indirectly, more than half the issued capital, provided that important interests of the company are not prejudiced by doing so. Whether important interests bar such a disclosure should be decided by the Attorney-General at the Court of Appeal at Amsterdam. (*b*) Close companies with an issued capital of at least Fl. 500,000 should also be compelled to publish annual accounts and an auditor's statement by depositing them at the *Handelsregister*.

These proposals of the Social and Economic Council have been criticised in a report published by the executive committees of the two major accountants' associations in the Netherlands, NIVA and VAGA. With respect to proposal (*a*), the report argues that the disclosure of majority participations is desirable only if it is necessary in order to provide the genuine information required by Art. 2 of the Verdam Committee draft. As for (*b*), the accountants' organisations refrain from expressing any opinion, but believe that if it should become compulsory to publish such information it would always be desirable to exempt close *subsidiary* companies from compulsory disclosure. The report's general criticism of the Verdam Committee's draft Bill is that it is not flexible enough. For example, the draft Bill requires that a large number of specified items should always be mentioned in the balance sheet. The report suggests that compulsory disclosure should be limited to cases where the inclusion of such items is necessary in order to provide the genuine information required under Art. 2 of the draft.

A government Bill concerning annual accounts, to a large extent following the proposals of the Verdam Committee, was submitted to parliament in May 1968. With regard to the first suggestion of the Social and Economic Council, the Bill provides for the obligatory publication of the names of majority-owned subsidiaries, with the exception, however, of subsidiaries whose combined assets represent not more than 15 per cent of the total assets of the parent company and its subsidiaries. The Bill says nothing about the Council's second suggestion. The government has, however, announced its intention of bringing in another Bill which would oblige close companies with a balance total of Fl. 8 million or more to publish a (simplified) balance sheet. A majority-owned subsidiary would be exempt from this obligation, provided that its parent company (*a*) published consolidated accounts (which covered the operations of the subsidiary) and (*b*) assumed liability for the debts of the subsidiary. This new Bill is announced as an interim regulation, because an EEC Directive on annual accounts under Art. 54(3)(g) of the Treaty of Rome (see pp. 49, 144, 158, 162 and 165) will, before March 1970, be laying down which types of companies are to publish their accounts. The Directive will, moreover, specify the requirements as to the contents of the annual accounts. This means that the Dutch Bill which was submitted to parliament in May 1968 will probably have to be amended, in due course, to bring it into line with Community regulations.

Apart from the obligation to publish annual accounts under Art. 42c, the Dutch Commercial Code (Arts. 36f and 45e) also requires managements to publish articles of association and amendments thereto in the official gazette (*Nederlandse Staatscourant*). The Code also obliges managements to keep a register (open to general inspection at the offices of the company) containing the names of all owners of shares that have not been fully paid up. The *Handelsregisterwet* of 1918 (Register of Commerce Act), furthermore, lays down that managements must publish certain specified data relating to the company and its executive and supervisory directors. Publication is technically effected by making the data available for inspection at the *Handelsregister*. (The EEC Directive mentioned in the previous paragraph also covers this field and may entail further amendments to Dutch law.)

Finally, it should be mentioned that the (private) Stock Exchange Committee requires its members, in the case of an issue of shares, to publish a company prospectus giving specified data concerning the issuing company and particulars of the issue if the shares are to be traded on the stock exchange.

SWEDEN

Requirements on disclosure are laid down in detail by the Swedish Companies Act which, at the time it was passed, was rather radical compared with similar legislation in other European countries. Parliament considered disclosure primarily as an instrument for the protection of shareholders and creditors; the experiences of the Kreuger crash of 1932 greatly influenced this legislation. At the end of the 1940s, however, the issue became a matter of political debate, with greater emphasis on the rights to information of employees and society. One result of this debate was that the Act's disclosure provisions were made more stringent in 1950.

The work on a new West German company law during the last decade seems to have drawn attention to the Swedish provisions on disclosure and the German legislation on the subject appears to a certain extent to have been inspired by them. However, the new German law, in practice, takes disclosure requirements further (if anything) than current Swedish legislation.

However, here again, the law has not caught up with the conditions actually prevailing. In the last ten years or so, more and more big companies influenced by accountants and their own desire to win a good reputation on the capital market, have begun to give more detailed information in their annual reports than the minimum required by the Act. These developments have been closely watched and commented on by the press, which has called attention to the companies which have lagged behind and remained content with the legal minimum. One problem arousing much interest in the 1960s was whether inventory reserves and changes should or should not be shown officially. (Swedish law still permits hidden reserves to an extent not accepted by, for instance, British and American law.) Other matters discussed have been asset depreciation principles and the presentation of consolidated accounts.

175

Section B: The Shareholder

Should shareholders participate directly in the control of a company? If not, can they be assured of adequate protection by market forces, disclosure, general publicity and/or institutions exercising external control?

What are the powers of shareholders' meetings? Should they be strengthened? If so, how?

What is the situation regarding intermediaries such as banks and institutional investors? Should it be changed? Should there be distinctions between different classes of shareholder? Are minorities given enough protection against actual or potential controlling groups?

BELGIUM

(a) *Some academic views*

Questions concerning the ownership of the capital of a company have arisen because of the increasing volume of reinvested surpluses and retained profits. The management in this way controls an important part of the capital, much of which, in many companies, is represented by investment financed by undistributed profits. The amount of this compulsory saving has been, to all intents and purposes, determined and imposed on the shareholders by the management. It appears to the shareholders as if they have lost all control over the destiny of their firm and of its profits.[18]

The extension of internal financing puts ever greater resources at the disposal of the firm, which increasingly becomes an institution whose assets are certainly not exclusively and even not always mainly provided by external sources of finance, the so-called legal owners. Moreover, the objectives and the conduct of this institution will be determined by its management largely as it thinks fit. Self-financing has its own purpose—independence of the capital market rather than the enlargement of the property rights of the shareholders. It is a manifestation more of the idea of the 'company-institution' (see above, p. 69) than of the original goal of a capital association, founded on the will of the company to provide for itself the necessary capital for its independence, continuity and progress.[19] Being the symbol of the institutionalisation of the firm, self-financing is regarded as the most important reason for the vicious circle of the decline of offers on the capital market. The high level of internal financing leads to a lower distribution of dividends and thus to a discouraging trend in stock market prices. The result is a lack of interest on the part of investors for new public issues and this in turn necessitates a higher degree of self-financing.

[18] Vandeputte, op. cit. (see footnote 2, p. 164), pp. 16–17.
[19] R. Henrion, 'Autofinancement et structure de l'entreprise', *Cahiers économiques de Bruxelles*, No. 17, 1963, pp. 3–11.

The balance of power within the firm has become very different from that envisaged by company law, according to which power over the firm is supposed to be wielded by the shareholders. In fact, the latter's general meetings have become mere formalities. The 'majority group' in these meetings, which often does not hold a real majority of shares, gets its own way, the actual control of many companies being concentrated in the hands of a few persons. The average shareholder has no interest in the general meeting, since the important decisions have already been made by the managing committee with the permission of the board of directors, which has itself been nominated by the same pressure group. The right of property which belongs to the common shareholders has, so to speak, become a juridical fiction. The real policy-makers do not own the company; they act as if they had been given a mandate by the shareholders which is not, in reality, the case. Shareholder influence is further weakened by the increasing significance of internal financing, born of relatively low dividends, comparatively high depreciation rates or tax avoidance. Resources acquired in this way, Vandeputte points out, 'do not correspond to the normal conception of ownership [and] illustrate the fictitious character of the mandate that has been assigned to management by general meetings'.[20]

(b) Present Belgian law

1. The powers of the Banking Commission (*Commission Bancaire*) with respect to commercial companies are described in Art. 26 ff of the Royal Decree of 9 July 1935, as amended. The Commission's function is to co-ordinate the approach of commercial companies to the capital market and to protect prospective investors against false information. Thus, any Belgian or foreign company wishing to raise funds on the Belgian capital market, either by (i) issuing shares or bonds to the public, (ii) offering such commercial paper for sale, (iii) requesting the quotation of its shares or bonds on the stock exchange or (iv) (since the law of 10 June 1964) making a public offer for the purchase of shares or bonds (i.e. take-over bids), must inform the Commission of its intention to do so at least fifteen days in advance. If the Commission does not approve the proposed transaction, it can make recommendations for the modification of the terms and, if its objections are not met, can postpone the proposed transaction for a period of not more than three months, and, if it so chooses, may make public its decision to postpone. Apart from these general powers, the Commission has other extensive powers of supervision over deposit banks and investment funds. It should be emphasised that although the powers of the Commission with regard to commercial companies are limited, it enjoys a very high reputation which has enabled it to introduce in the financial world many new practices and customs which it thought desirable.

2. As was pointed out in Chapter 1 of this Part, the main powers of the shareholders' meeting consist in the election (and dismissal) of directors and auditors, and in the approval of the annual accounts. Amendments of the articles of association must also be approved by an extraordinary meeting of

[20] Vandeputte, op. cit., pp. 69–80.

shareholders subject to special requirements as to convocation, attendance and voting quorums. In practice, however, except in some family-owned companies, the powers of shareholders' meetings are often purely formal.

As to proposals for reform, two trends of legal thinking may be distinguished. First, there are those who, like the company law reform committee, are of the opinion that the *status quo* should be maintained, although they admit that the actual role of shareholders is minimal. This group believes that nothing should be done to strengthen the position of shareholders (or, rather, of some groups of shareholders) and that the powers granted to shareholders by law should be maintained. Others want to distinguish between shareholders who wish to exercise their voting power and who show a real interest in corporate matters and those who regard their shares simply and solely as investments; and to widen the powers of the former and curtail those of the latter.[21] (See also (3) and (4) below.)

3. Present Belgian legislation does not contain general provisions with respect to the representation of shareholders at a meeting. The courts have interpreted this to the effect that powers of attorney for the exercise of voting rights are valid even if made irrevocable, provided, however, that they are granted for a definite period of time.[22] One special provision relating to institutional investors is to be found in Art. 2, *in fine*, of the law of 27 March 1957 on investment funds. According to this article, powers of attorney authorising the company managing the mutual fund permanently to represent the holders of mutual fund certificates at the shareholders' meetings of Belgian and Congolese companies, part of the stock of which is held by the mutual fund, are null and void.

The reform committee advocates the regulation of the exercise of proxy voting rights, in order to avoid proxy disputes (which are almost unknown in Belgium) and to prevent the granting of irrevocable proxies which might result in intolerable restraints on the freedom of a shareholder to vote at his own will and discretion. The committee suggests that the period of validity of a proxy to vote at one or more shareholders' meetings should be limited to eighteen months, and that bank proxies granted to the company or to one of its directors or employees, or to a subsidiary of the company or to a director or employee of such a subsidiary, should be revocable at any time.

4. Distinctions between committed and uncommitted investors has been referred to under (2) above. The use of trusts or *administratiekantoren* to entrench the position of controlling groups is unknown in Belgium.[23] The reform committee, however, has proposed that voting agreements should be valid[24] within certain limits. The so-called *clauses de représentation proportionnelle* are valid under present legislation but are not commonly used. Under

[21] Vandeputte, op. cit., pp. 69 ff.

[22] Cours de Cassation, 13 January 1938. See *Pasicrisie*, 1938, I, p. 6.

[23] Van Ryn, *Principes de droit commercial*, I, p. 442. See also, for further details, P. Roose and L. Maeyens, 'La représentation proportionnelle pour la nomination des administrateurs', *Revue pratique des sociétés*, 1963, p. 141.

[24] Van Ommeslaghe, *La réforme des sociétés anonymes*, Epargner et investir, 1965, p. 26.

these clauses a group (e.g. a minority group of shareholders) is permitted to propose to the shareholders' meeting a list of directors from which the meeting must then elect one or more, the number to be proposed by each group being proportionate to their voting rights. As long as the principle of equal voting rights for shareholders owning the same amount of stock is respected such a clause is considered valid. In the case of a *société anonyme* (as opposed to a *société de personnes à responsabilité limitée*), the group of shareholders may even be given the right to designate 'their' directors directly at the meeting of shareholders itself, instead of proposing a list to the meeting.[25]

Special attention should be paid to a legal provision which is peculiar to Belgium, namely, Art. 76 of the Code on Commercial Companies. According to this provision no one shareholder may vote at a meeting more than one fifth of all the outstanding shares *or* more than two fifths of all shares present or represented at the meeting. This provision, intended to limit the voting power of controlling shareholders, has not served its purpose, chiefly because it may all too easily be set aside in a country where bearer shares are common. The reform committee has proposed its abolition. It should also be mentioned in this connexion that the committee, in an effort to strengthen the position of committed investors, has proposed that the issue of non-voting preferential equity shares (which is not permissible under the present legislation) should be allowed under certain conditions.

BRITAIN

It is generally agreed that the functions of the law governing the relationship between directors and shareholders should be to balance the need to protect shareholding members with the need to give the directors sufficient power and freedom to manage the company effectively. Principally for historical reasons, the protection of shareholders has been based on the reservation to them of certain powers and the requirement of disclosure of certain material information.

The rights of such members are set out in the memorandum and articles of association of the company and the Companies Acts. The memorandum and articles of association may provide that certain shares shall have restricted voting rights or none at all. They may also include provisions that special rights are to be attached to certain classes of shares. Thus they may confer extra votes on certain shares provided that this is not done as part of a deliberate policy to deprive the majority of voting control.[26] They may confer preferential rights as to the payment of dividends or the repayment of capital. Despite the fact that the articles of association may be fairly freely altered by special resolution,[27] where such an alteration involves the variation of class rights or the special rights attached to a particular class of shares, the 1948 Act[28] contains additional restrictions to protect holders of those shares. An

[25] See Roose and Maeyens, art. cit.
[26] *Rights and Issues Investment Trust Ltd. v. Stylo Shoes Ltd.* [1965] Ch. 250; *Hogg v. Cramphorn Ltd.* [1966] 3 All E.R. 420.
[27] Companies Act 1948 Sec. 10.
[28] Sec. 72, Table A, Art. 4.

application may be made by holders of not less than 15 per cent of the issued shares at that class to the Court within twenty-one days after the resolution was passed. As an additional safeguard of special class rights, Sec. 23 of the 1948 Act permits the rights to be set out in the memorandum of association and contains severe restrictions upon the power to vary such a clause in the memorandum. The Jenkins Committee recommended[29] that there should be a general power to alter class rights on the lines of Table A Art. 4 incorporated into all articles, but that dissentients should be allowed twenty-eight days within which to apply to the Court and that the minimum number of shareholders concerned should be reduced from 15 to 10 per cent.

Under the 1948 Act certain powers can only be exercised by the members in general meeting and cannot be delegated to the board of directors. (See p. 145 above.) These include the power to change the company's memorandum[30] and articles of association,[31] especially the objects clause[32] and variations in the company's capital;[33] and the powers of declaring that the affairs of the company ought to be investigated by an Inspector appointed by the Board of Trade[34] and of resolving that the company be wound up by the Court[35] or voluntarily.[36] In addition certain powers are given to members to be exercised outside the general meeting such as the power of members holding not less than one tenth of the paid up capital of the company entitled to vote to requisition a general meeting;[37] and of requiring the circulation of members' resolutions and a statement of not more than one thousand words prepared by them.[38] The Jenkins Committee recommended[39] that where the members requisitioned a meeting the directors must convene a meeting within twenty-eight days of sending out the notice calling the meeting, otherwise the requisitionists should be entitled to convene the meeting.

Criticism has been made of the Jenkins Committee recommendations concerning Sections 132 and 140 as not being sufficiently radical, in view of the fact that they recognised the difficulty of rallying enough support in the time available to take such steps, particularly in the case of large companies with widespread membership. In some cases it is physically difficult to contact the number of persons representing even 10 per cent within twenty-eight days, to receive replies and to formulate conduct. It is arguable that the requirements should be made less strict, particularly in the case of Sec. 140, which requires that a sum reasonably sufficient to meet the company's expenses must be deposited.

The powers of members are normally exercised in general meeting and an annual general meeting must be held once in each year and not more than fifteen months after the previous meeting.[40] Where there is any difficulty in calling a meeting there is a power for any director or member to apply to the

---

[29] *Report*, paragraph 198(a) and (e).
[30] Companies Act 1948 Sec. 4; see, on the alteration of various parts of the memorandum, Sections 5, 17–19, 22, 23, 61–70 and 1967 Act Sec. 46.
[31] Companies Act. 1948 Sec. 10.
[32] ibid. Sec. 5.
[33] ibid. Sections 61–70.
[34] ibid. Sec. 165.
[35] ibid. Sec. 222(a).
[36] ibid. Sec. 278(i)(b)
[37] ibid. Sec. 132.
[38] ibid. Sec. 140.
[39] *Report* paragraphs 458 and 468(b).
[40] ibid. Sec. 131.

Court for a meeting to be called.[41] The resolutions that may be proposed at a meeting may be either 'ordinary', 'special' or 'extraordinary'[42] and each of these has its own procedure and majority required. It can be said that, roughly, the more serious the matter to be discussed the more likely it is to require a special or extraordinary resolution to achieve it.

Generally, voting at a meeting is on a show of hands, on the basis of one man one vote regardless of the number of shares held. However, Sec. 137 of the 1948 Act provides that a poll may be demanded by either not less than five persons having the right to vote at the meeting, or members representing not less than one tenth of the voting rights or paid-up capital entitled to vote at the meeting. On a poll the voting is on the basis of shares held and the votes conferred on those shares by the articles of association.

Any member entitled to attend and vote at meetings may appoint a proxy to act for him.[43] However, in the absence of anything to the contrary in the articles a proxy can vote only on a poll, not on a show of hands, and, in the case of a public company, he is not allowed to speak at the meeting. The Jenkins Committee recommended[44] that proxies should be entitled to speak at meetings.

The Jenkins Committee stated[45] that these powers would appear to leave members with a reasonable degree of control. The Report, however, does contain two main recommendations[46] for the extension of the powers of members which have been widely accepted as desirable. The first is that the directors should not have the power to dispose of the whole or substantially the whole of the undertaking or assets of the company without the approval of the company in general meeting. At present, subject to the restrictions of the company's objects clause, the directors may do this and embark on a completely new enterprise, provided that they subsequently notify the shareholders in the directors' report. It appears that any shareholders who object to the change may apply to the Court for the company to be wound up because of the disappearance of the whole substratum[47] provided the directors have not started upon the new enterprise. However, the shareholders have to act quickly, and it is not certain whether the petition would be successful in view of the multiplicity of most companies' objects. Moreover, winding up is rather a drastic step to force a member to take to protect his investment.

The second recommendation is that directors should not have the power to issue any shares without the prior approval of the company in general meeting. Recently, the power to issue shares has been abused in several take-over battles, normally being issued to defeat the take-over bidder by giving control to supporters of the existing directors.[48] The shares may, of course, be issued to force a take-over bid upon an unwilling majority. These abuses have been criticised severely by the financial press.[49]

---

[41] ibid. Sec. 135.   [42] ibid. Sec. 141.
[43] ibid. Sec. 136.   [44] *Report* paragraphs 462–464 and 468(g).
[45] ibid. paragraph 102.   [46] Paragraph 122(e) and (g).
[47] *Re German Date Coffee Co.* (1882) 20 Ch.D 169 but cf. *Re Kitson and Co. Ltd* [1946] 1 All E.R. 435.
[48] See for example *Hogg v. Cramphorn Ltd.* [1966] 3 All E.R. 420; *Bamfords v. Bamfords Ltd.* [1969],
[49] E.g., *The Economist*, 22 July 1967 'Back to the Jungle'. The new City Take-Over Panel may exercise a restraining influence over such abuses.

The Report contains several recommendations on meetings[50] including recommendations that 'extraordinary' resolutions should be abolished and that there should be an express provision that a resolution in writing signed by all those who would have been entitled to vote upon it at a general meeting shall be equivalent to a special or ordinary resolution (as the case may require or as the resolution may state) passed by the appropriate majority at a general meeting convened by the appropriate notice.

It is often stated that shareholders are apathetic and that the management of companies is, in practice, becoming further and further divorced from the control of the members.[51] If all the recommendations of the Jenkins Committee were implemented the members would have control over many of the important steps in the life of the company such as the issue of shares. Yet, if the articles of association are based on Table A of the 1948 Act the basic powers of management of the business of the company will have been delegated to the directors. It is clear that such delegation is commercially necessary and it is fair to say that the main problem is to protect the members in relation to the abuse or improper exercise of powers by the management of the company, rather than to give them control, particularly if the powers of control which do exist are becoming less effective as a result of the apathy of the members. It is preferable to aim at greater training for management and to make directors more aware of their responsibilities to their shareholders, and to provide adequate safeguards against abuse, rather than to give powers to the shareholders who must frequently exercise them on the basis of an imperfect understanding of the situation, in a forum which is not suited to arriving at the most reasonable solution, because a simple answer of 'yes' or 'no' is required rather than a consideration of alternative policies. Moreover, giving power to the general meeting inevitably involves delay and a loss of secrecy when in some cases speed may be of the essence of the transaction.

Minorities are protected in several ways. The majority must not use their voting power so as to commit 'a fraud on the minority'. This has rather a limited definition at the moment and appears to extend only to those cases where the majority are attempting to expropriate the minority or to deprive them of property which belongs to them, or the majority are wrongdoers vis-à-vis the company and are using their votes to restrain the company from bringing an action against them.[52] Additional protection is afforded by Sec. 210 of the 1948 Act which provides that a member of the company may apply to the Court for any order, as an alternative to an order for winding up, if the affairs of the company are being conducted in a manner 'oppressive' to some part of the members, including himself. This section has been criticised as being too limited. The member must be oppressed in his capacity as a member not in the capacity of a director or employee.[53] The meaning of 'oppression' is somewhat restricted in that the court requires evidence of fraud, unfair

---

[50] Paragraph 468.
[51] See for example Berle and Means, *The Modern Corporation and Private Property*; *The Report of the Committee on Company Law Amendment* (1945) Cmd 6659, paragraphs 7(e) and 124.
[52] See for example *Greenhalgh v. Arderne Cinemas Ltd.* [1951] Ch. 286.
[53] *Re H. R. Harmer Ltd.* [1958] 3 All E.R. 689.

treatment or breaches of duty extending over a period of time. Moreover, the Court will only grant relief where it could grant a winding up order on the 'just and equitable' ground.[54] The Court has been conservative in the exercise of its power to 'make such order as it thinks fit'. Only in *Re H. R. Harmer Limited* has it made an order other than for the purchase of the complainants' shares. The Jenkins Committee recommended,[55] *inter alia*, that the section should be amended to cover isolated acts as well as a course of conduct, 'oppressive' acts should be extended to conduct which was 'unfairly prejudicial', and the power to grant relief should be freed from the requirement that the facts would justify a winding up order on the 'just and equitable' ground. They also recommended that the Court should be empowered to authorise, on such terms as it thought fit, the bringing of proceedings in the name of the company against third parties; and that the personal representatives of a deceased shareholder should be entitled to demand written reasons from the directors setting out why they refused registration of the executors as members.

Minorities are further protected by the power[56] of the Board of Trade to appoint an inspector on the application of 200 members or members holding at least one tenth of the company's issued share capital, but the Board may, and usually does, require the production of evidence to show that there is reason for an investigation; or if there is a special resolution requesting investigation. The Board may also appoint an inspector if it appears that the company's business is being or has been conducted with intent to defraud creditors, or in a manner oppressive of the members, or the management have been guilty of misconduct towards the company or its members, or if it appears that members of the company have not been given all the information with respect to its affairs which they might reasonably expect. There is some dissatisfaction with these powers. They are normally exercised only after there has been misconduct and it has come to light. The Board are reluctant to interfere except in cases where strong evidence of misconduct is produced since the appointment of an inspector can have a disastrous effect on a company's business, even where there are no grounds for the complaint.

The members as a whole are protected by the duties of disclosure which are imposed on the company and the directors by the Companies Acts. The matters which must be contained in the annual report, profit and loss account, balance sheet and directors' report were outlined above. (See p. 167.) An additional safeguard to disclosure is the requirement of the appointment of an auditor,[57] who has security of tenure and can be removed only by the company in general meeting. His duties are to investigate the company's accounts and records and to see that the profit and loss account and balance sheet present a true and fair view of the company's financial position. If he is not satisfied he must specifically state so to the company and refuse to sign a report. Recently, in *Re Thomas Gerrard and Son Ltd.*[58] it has been suggested

---

[54] See for example *Re Bellador Silk* [1965] 1 All E.R. 667.

[55] *Report* paragraph 212.

[56] Companies Act 1948 Sections 164 and 165 and Companies Act 1967 Sections 38 and 109.

[57] Companies Act 1948 Sec. 159.　　　　　　　　　　　[58] [1967] 2 All E.R. 525.

that the duties imposed upon an auditor to investigate matters where there is anything suspicious may be higher than the older case would indicate.[59] There has been a certain amount of criticism of the position of auditors. Conducting an audit is not a very lucrative business, and there is far more money to be made through acting as consultant and financial adviser to a company. Many auditors occupy both positions and there is a suspicion that this may involve a conflict of interest and duty and that they are not as thorough in the audit as their duties require, through fear of the loss of the more rewarding consultancy work.

Disclosure makes it possible for the financial press to analyse the performance of companies and this gives further indirect protection to members. The financial press has criticised, in particular, the procedure adopted in recent take-over battles.[60]

Rules on take-overs were drawn up by the Issuing Houses (a small group of firms specialising in the flotation of companies) soon after the bid of Mr Charles Clore for Watneys Limited. These have proved to be unsatisfactory in preventing abuses and are being re-examined. These rules do not have the force of law and it is widely accepted, even in some sectors of the City of London, that legally binding rules are necessary.

The Jenkins Committee recommended[61] that the Board of Trade should have power to make rules, by statutory instrument, applicable to every take-over offer and to every circular containing a take-over offer, or a recommendation to the members of the offeree company by their directors to accept such an offer, no matter by whom such offer or circular is made or distributed, but that the Board should have power to exempt any particular take-over offer from compliance where to comply would be inappropriate. The Report also contains detailed recommendations on take-over procedure: any circulars making offers or recommending acceptance must be sent to the Registrar of Companies before circulation and he should be empowered to refuse registration if the circular does not set out the information required; if the offeror subsequently increases the price offered, this price should be payable to all who accept the offer, including those who accepted before the increase was announced. If the take-over offer is declared unconditional the offeror must disclose the number of shares which he controls, and he must reveal details of payments made to directors of the company taken over. Sec. 209 of the 1948 Act which provides for the compulsory purchase or sale of shares of a dissenting minority in a take-over situation should be amended to provide greater powers for a minority shareholder where the majority of shares are held by one person or a holding company so that the minority have no power to influence company policy.

The Jenkins Committee also stated that 'there is inadequate co-ordination of the experience and views of the Board of Trade and of other bodies concerned with the protection of the investor'. They, therefore, recommended[62] that the Companies Act Consultative Committee should meet regularly to

[59] *Re Kingston Cotton Mills* (No. 2) [1896] 2 Ch. 279; *Re London and General Bank* (No. 2) [1895] 2 Ch. 673.
[60] See for example *The Times* 20 July 1967, 'Why the new take-over code must have teeth'.
[61] *Report* paragraph 294(a).   [62] *Report* paragraph 234(a).

co-ordinate the experience of the various bodies concerned with the protection of investors and that it should advise the Board of Trade on changes in the law (including the Board of Trade's rule-making powers) which they consider desirable. Unfortunately, this body appears to be in cold-storage.

The main alternative proposal, which has received some support in the financial press and elsewhere, is the formation of an independent body similar to the United States' Securities and Exchange Commission. The Jenkins Committee conceded[63] that there was a good deal to be said for such a body, in theory. However, they took the view that the number of stock markets and the size of the country distinguished the United States from Britain and concluded, 'We are not persuaded that a system of control on the US model would work as well in this country as the more flexible, though perhaps theoretically less perfect, system which has grown up here over the years.'

There are clear advantages in using an existing body rather than creating a new one, provided that the existing body operates satisfactorily and is capable of exercising any powers which it may have effectively. The Board of Trade has been criticised for containing too few trained lawyers and accountants in particular and too small a staff in general. This is, however, a matter of administration rather than law. But it is perhaps more accurate to describe the British system as haphazard rather than flexible. There is no one body which exercises control or supervisory powers over the whole of the company field. The Registrar of Companies has no power to investigate the economic feasibility or desirability of a proposed company's objects. On the other hand he has in the last resort power to strike off a company where through persistent failure to file annual statements he believes that it is no longer carrying on business, and the Jenkins Committee recommended[64] that he should have powers to interfere in certain take-over bids. The Stock Exchange exercises some control over the constitution of a company, its flotation and subsequent business life, provided that it seeks a quotation. Its attempts to restrain abuses are, however, not particularly efficient. The main sanction available to it—the suspension of dealings in the company's securities—is a severe step and may cause more harm to the innocent shareholders whom it is seeking to protect. It has not yet successfully tackled the problem of take-over bids and the associated problem of 'insider trading'. (This term refers to officers of the company speculating in the company's shares on the basis of confidential information in the performance of their duties as officers or on advance knowledge of accounts or proposals for dividends.) Abuses such as these may discourage the investor from going into the market, and the feeling that ordinary shareholders are bound to lose to the insiders must eventually lead to a loss of confidence in its fairness. The Board of Trade has more varied powers, but it deals only with certain aspects of a company's life. It exercises some control over flotations through the Licensed Dealer (Conduct of Business) Rules 1960. The other main powers of the Board are connected with the investigation of a company's affairs. Thus there are areas where various bodies overlap and, more importantly, there are more areas where no body has power to intervene.

If Britain is not to have an SEC, then, there is certainly an argument in

[63] *Report* paragraph 228.   [64] *Report* paragraph 227.

favour of combining or co-ordinating the work of these various bodies to prevent confusion and hardship through unnecessary duplication. The recommendation of the Jenkins Committee that greater use should be made of the Consultative Committee might go some way to deal with this problem. The argument that the integrity of City institutions is the best possible safeguard appears somewhat weak in view of the blatant disregard of the recent take-over code within a few weeks of its publication, and there is increasing support for a 'watch-dog' with stronger powers than present institutions.

On the whole, however, it seems that if the recommendations of the Jenkins Committee are implemented, particularly those in favour of greater use of the Co-ordinating Committees, they may achieve a balance between the need to provide freedom for the directors to manage the company effectively and the need to protect the members of the company.

FRANCE

1. Market forces, alone, are hardly strong enough to give shareholders adequate protection. The weakness of the French financial press, and the consequent difficulties of seeing that adequate information is provided, have already been mentioned in Section A of this Chapter. The question of the actual exercise of 'control' (see footnote 51, p. 152 above) appears more straightforward in so far as large shareholders have a considerable importance. 'The influence of large shareholders in the general run of companies is decisive. Two investigations in 1957 (on private portfolios held in banks and on capital gains) disclosed that at that time the [numerical] proportion of small portfolios (which did not then exceed one million old francs) was of the order of 77 per cent of the total, whereas their share in the total value of securities was only 13 per cent. It is probable that the situation indicated by these figures has been maintained or accentuated since then.'[65] This predominance of large shareholders is not always found at company level, in that big portfolios are very widely spread. A spokesman for the Ugine company, for example, stated some years ago[66] that 'the biggest shareholder in Ugine has 3 per cent of the capital. . . . Since no other group of shareholders or financial interests has as large a proportionate importance, voting capital, as such, does not exert any influence on the conduct of the firm nor on the choice of its managers. . . . In a case of this sort (and if it is not typical neither is it an isolated example), power does not flow from a positive act of will on the part of the owners.'

French law provides for various measures to safeguard the interests of shareholders who are, as we have seen, ill-protected by market forces. The *a posteriori* procedures that have to be gone through at the time of a company's formation have already been mentioned (see p. 169 above). The government has not abandoned the idea of prior 'control' which would be an additional safeguard although it might result in lengthy legal proceedings which could hinder firms at the 'take-off' stage.

[65] *Le Monde*, loc. cit. (see footnote 14, p. 168), 9 September 1966.
[66] At a private meeting at Clamart on 24 February 1964, following a talk given by F. Bloch-Laîné. CREE Document No. 101.

The position of auditors has been much strengthened by the 1966 law, 'above all by the organisation of the accountancy profession; this is one of the most ambitious objectives of the plan, and also one which has been only outlined in the bill'.[67] From now on, only persons or corporate bodies entered on a special list may act as auditors. Rules forbidding certain links between the company and its directors and its auditors have been made more stringent. Public companies must have at least two auditors, appointed by the ordinary general meeting for a term of six years instead of three as before. Auditors' fees, paid by the company, are now fixed according to scales laid down by decree and are no longer left to be settled by the general meeting. Finally, the auditors must now be called to all shareholders' meetings; their absence renders the chairman and directors liable to heavy penalties.

All these measures were intended to reinforce the independence of auditors and complement a widening of their duties. As before, they must verify the books and assets of the company and check the regularity and truthfulness of the company accounts and of the information given in the annual report and the financial documents sent to shareholders. They may not involve themselves in management; but they have been given the important new tasks of certifying the regularity and truthfulness of the inventory, the general business account, the profit and loss account and the balance sheet. They are also responsible for seeing to the equality of all shareholders and for verifying that all shares of the same category have truly benefited from the same rights with regard to votes, dividends, etc. As a counterbalance, the civil and criminal responsibility of auditors has been increased. If the auditors welcome an extension of their role, they would like to see their responsibility made lighter. ANACACI (the National Association of Accountants) is studying a plan under which its members would be able to insure themselves in cases where their responsibility as auditors would be involved. It seems, at first sight, dangerous that auditors could by this expedient evade some of the responsibility inherent in their job.

Other proposals for the improvement of the protection of shareholders include the suggestion of Octave Gélinier with regard to take-over bids which has already been mentioned. (See pp. 154–155.) His proposal would guarantee the efficiency of management as well as protecting shareholders and ensuring the regularity of operations. Such, indeed, were Gélinier's intentions. Maître Maurice Letulle considers that the whole question of investment by shareholders who know little about business 'can only be resolved by legal supervision or by setting up a body similar to the American Securities and Exchange Commission'.[68] Some people argue that making good the lack of such an organisation could be part of a general reorganisation of the stockbroking profession.

2. In recent years shareholders' meetings have been vigorously criticised for their neglect by almost all shareholders and for their frequently being regarded

---

[67] F. Le Douarec, *rapporteur* of the new company law before the National Assembly, at a meeting organised on 12 May 1966 by ANACACI—Association Nationale des Commissaires aux Comptes Indépendants du Ressort des Cours d'Appel de France.

[68] *Le Monde*, loc. cit.

as mere 'chambers of registration'. Efforts have recently been made simultaneously to improve the work done at these meetings and to make them more 'democratic'. The following paragraphs discuss the general meeting in the light of the new Act of 1966.

As before, the articles of association may limit *access* to ordinary general meetings to shareholders holding a minimum number of shares; this minimum may now not be more than ten. Shareholders have the right to pool their shares in order to achieve the minimum number provided for in the articles and to send one of their number (or a husband or wife) to represent them. Any shareholder, however, whatever his number of shares, always has right of access to any extraordinary general meeting.

The grant of acting powers (*pouvoirs en blanc*) was a matter of much debate at the time of the vote on the new Company Act. Under the Act, the articles of association can no longer freely fix the conditions of the *representation* of shareholders at meetings. The right to vote can be exercised only by the owner or his proxy. Of course, the means by which a shareholder can have himself represented have been, in practice, seriously limited because he (or she) may be represented only by another shareholder or by his (or her) spouse. The articles may, however, fix the maximum number of votes of which the same person can dispose, whether in his own name or as a proxy. Representation by a non-shareholder has thus been excluded on the grounds that there was a danger that anyone could be present at the meeting in the guise of a proxy. The idea of 'professional delegates' charged with representing shareholders at meetings has found no favour. The original text of the Bill for the new Company Law would have allowed a shareholder to 'have himself represented by any person of his own choice', but this formula was dropped. The National Association of Share Companies (ANSA) was among those who opposed it, but some employers' organisations seemed less hostile, in spite of a somewhat cautious approach. 'The granting of powers by small shareholders to delegates representing them at general meetings should be regulated in order to avoid abuse (as in the case of professional delegates) or make-believe (as in cases where delegates would represent banking establishments having cross-shareholdings in companies).'[69]

François Bloch-Laîné has proposed 'giving a Government Commissioner acting powers . . . to represent in the capital assemblies of all firms of any importance those shareholders who had not taken up the role of "active partner". [See below, page 191, for an explanation of this term.] An alternative would be to allow a magistrate rather than a civil servant to play the role of spokesman for silent shareholders. He would ensure that controlling minorities, now allowed by law, did not abuse their powers; he would also have the particular task of consulting the managers of investment institutions (who have no right of access to meetings), in order to ask questions in their name and represent the points of view that they suggested to him, or which he judged appropriate in the interests both of the shareholders and of the public.' Employers were extremely hostile to this proposal and even the CJP dismissed it curtly.[70] Pierre de Calan has sought to restrict the use of acting powers. 'It is

[69] M. Brissier, *Réflexions et propositions sur le livre de M. Bloch-Laîné Pour une réforme de l'entreprise*, CJP October 1963.　　　　　　　　　　　　　　　　　[70] ibid.

possible to envisage some modest means of involving shareholders in the life of the company. One method would be to pay shareholders for attending general meetings, and to allow these payments only to shareholders physically present, or represented by a named proxy, with a differential rate in favour of those actually attending in person. This could reduce the practice of granting acting powers.'[71]

The *calling* of a meeting falls in the first place to the administrative board (or the 'directory'), which is bound by law to convene the shareholders within six months of the end of the financial year in order to submit the balance sheet and accounts to them. However, the right of convocation can also be exercised by: (*a*) the auditor(s), without (under the new law) having to prove urgency; (*b*) a proxy legally designated either at the request of any interested party in a case of urgency, or of several shareholders who together hold at least one tenth of the capital (or one tenth of the interested shareholders if a special meeting is in question); (*c*) the supervisory board, in companies which have adopted the new formula; and (*d*) (if relevant) the liquidators.

The *agenda* is laid down by the convener of the meeting. However, one or more shareholders representing at least 5 per cent of the capital may table resolutions to the agenda, except for proposals concerning candidates for the administrative or supervisory boards. (It is probable that this minimum of 5 per cent will be reduced in the near future for companies whose capital is more than a certain amount.) The shareholders' meeting can deliberate only on the items on the agenda. It can, however, always dismiss and replace one or more members of the administrative or supervisory boards. This measure is the legal recognition of what are generally called 'incidents at sessions'. When, for lack of a quorum, the meeting has not been able to deliberate at the first session, the agenda cannot be changed for the second. For deliberations to be valid, the attendance at ordinary meetings must total one quarter at the first session, but no quorum is required at the second. In calculating the quorum, account is, of course, taken only of shareholders having a right to vote. The general meeting then reaches its decisions by majority vote, unmarked voting papers being invalid. Rules are stricter for extraordinary meetings. A quorum of a half is required at the first session and one of a quarter at the second. The extraordinary meeting works on a two-thirds majority, unmarked voting papers being invalid. The shares of contributors in kind, or the beneficiaries of other special advantages, are not taken into account when calculating the majority.

The administrative or supervisory boards, according to whichever formula a company has adopted (see p. 152), are the bodies permanently responsible for representing the shareholders. Administrative directors (referred to simply as 'directors' in this and the following paragraph), at least three in number and twelve at most, must be chosen by the shareholders. Except at the start of a new company, they are appointed by the ordinary general meeting for renewable terms of not more than six years. The co-option of directors has, however, recently been allowed by law. The articles may provide

---

[71] De Calan, op. cit. (see footnote 54, p. 152).

that in cases of one or several vacancies, the administrative board may make provisional appointments between two general meetings, to be ratified at the next ordinary general meeting. ACADI has expressed its regret[72] that 'the fairly general system of co-opting directors does not give them enough independence with regard to the chairman.'

A director can no longer be represented at meetings of the board and quorum and majority conditions are calculated with regard only to those members of the board actually attending. This was a very controversial question during the debates on the new law in the National Assembly and the Senate and the strictest interpretation, ensuring the best protection of the shareholder, was finally adopted. The conditions concerning the quorum and the necessary majority have also been tightened up: the deliberations of the administrative board are now valid only if at least half of its members are present, any clause to the contrary being null and void. Similarly, decisions are taken by a majority of members present, though the articles may provide for more stringent majority rules. French courts have clearly been hostile to voting agreements and to all advance engagements by directors to vote in any set way during an unlimited period. 'The directors of a joint stock company should be able, at all times, to make up their own minds in the company's interest and to express their opinion in a free vote.'[73]

The supervisory board, under the new (optional) formula, has the same role as the administrative board under the old, although its duty is now exclusively to represent the shareholders, thus ending the confusion of the tasks of the chairman (*président-directeur général*) in the old formula. Composed of at least three members and twelve at most, its appointment and procedure rules are practically identical with those for the administrative board.

Present legislation provides that two members of the works council (where one exists) should attend all meetings of the administrative or supervisory board (as the case may be), but without a right to vote. This rule has been much abused. In many cases, there is a previous 'private' meeting of the board to discuss the matters in hand without the presence of the works council members. It frequently happens, therefore, that the latter only attend board meetings which serve merely to confirm what has already been decided in private. During the parliamentary debates on the new company law, the provisions concerning the new formula of supervisory board plus 'directory' included a clause known as the 'Capitant Amendment'. (This term generally covers the whole of the new formula.) The amendment read as follows: 'The supervisory board and the works council may establish equal joint committees to examine all questions relative to the progress of the firm. They may, if needed, hold joint meetings.' In the minds of the movers of this clause (M. Capitant and M. Le Douarec), and probably in that of M. Bloch-Laîné too, the authorisation of such joint meetings would help to ease the transition until such time as legislation could effectively include employee

---

[72] 'De quelques problèmes relatifs à l'entreprise', *Bulletin de l'ACADI*, No. 191, June 1964.

[73] R. and J. Lefebvre, 'La réforme des sociétés commerciales', *Tableaux Pratiques*, Editions Juridiques Lefebvre.

representatives on the supervisory board. The proposal met with great hostility, especially in the Senate, and was not included in the law finally passed. (Various proposals concerning the presence of employee representatives within the administrative board are examined in Section F of this Chapter, pp. 239–240. On works councils, see pp. 208 ff.)

3. *The representation of shareholders by intermediaries.* Investment institutions have a growing share of the movable security market. The Caisse des Dépôts et Consignations plays an important role and insurance companies are increasing their portfolios. The 'SICAV' (investment companies with variable capital) have spread rapidly and one for savings banks is now being set up. 'The multiplication and expansion of these institutions', writes François Bloch-Lainé,[74] 'is inevitable and in many ways may be considered healthy. But they bring a very formidable third force, besides owners and managers, into play.' Among others, Bloch-Lainé has proposed two solutions to ensure that these intermediaries do not abuse their 'disturbing power'. According to the first, they would be regarded as ordinary capitalists, either as true 'active partners' (*veritables 'commanditaires'*) or as 'ordinary savers' with no particular rights. (For this distinction, see (4) below.) 'The institutional saving organisations would thus be led to include two kinds of stocks in their portfolios: those which they could negotiate freely and secretly and which would give them no so-called right of management; and those which they would convert into true investments, thus participating in a deliberate and visible way in economic power.' His second proposal is that such intermediaries should receive a special mandate, renewable each year, from the general meeting, actively to represent third parties in the company. The result would be that intermediaries would ultimately have only fairly small voting rights in their hands. The same idea is found in the studies of J. Dubois.[75] (Bloch-Lainé's idea of giving 'acting powers' to a government commissioner or to a magistrate has already been mentioned. It could be adapted to the problem of institutional investors.) It should be noted that the law forbids a deposit bank to own more than 20 per cent (the previous limit was 10 per cent) of the capital of a firm and a SICAV to hold more than 10 per cent of the stock of any one company.

4. *The different categories of shareholder.* Several proposals for distinguishing between the rights attached to shares have been made. Bloch-Lainé has suggested limiting the general meeting by granting the right to vote and appoint proxies only to shareholders who would accept the position of 'active partners' (*commanditaires*). The others would be treated the same as debenture-holders and employees (information, written questions, appeal to an 'economic magistracy' (see p. 188), etc.). 'To qualify as an "active partner" it would be necessary permanently to abandon a position of anonymity, to possess voting stock and not to dispose of this stock except with the agreement of the majority of one's fellows, or without sufficient previous warning being given to them.' The aim of this proposal is to associate with the running

[74] Bloch-Lainé, op. cit. (see footnote 48, p. 151).
[75] Dubois, op. cit. (see footnote 50, p. 151).

191

of the firm only those shareholders who genuinely accept a binding link between their own interests and those of the company. Professor Jean Schmidt has also suggested that only those shareholders who wish to be 'active' in company affairs should be admitted to general meetings. The mere 'savers' would receive certified accounts by post.

Other proposals are intended to prevent situations in which the majority might be defeated (especially in cases of firms in which American companies have interests and in which the latter might profit) by introducing distinctions in voting rights. Shares without voting rights have been suggested by Senators Armengaud and Coudé du Foresto. An amendment accepted by the Senate stipulated that 'any company may, as a result of debate in an extraordinary general meeting . . . , create shares without voting rights enjoying the other rights of ordinary shares. The proportion of shares with voting rights may not exceed 25 per cent of the capital nor be less than 10 per cent thereof. In companies creating shares without voting rights and shares with voting rights, the latter must be registered and reserved for shareholders of French nationality or citizens of a member state of the European Economic Community.' This amendment would thus have made it possible for 10 per cent of the shares to lay down the law to the other 90 per cent and was finally thrown out by the National Assembly. A draft Bill had, in the same spirit, taken up the idea of non-voting shares which could not represent more than one third of a company's registered capital.

Under the 1966 Act, a right to a double vote may be granted by the articles or an extraordinary general meeting to all fully paid-up shares registered in the name of the same holder for at least two years. (This provision is clearly inspired by the idea of the 'active partner' advanced by Bloch-Laîné.) As before, the articles may reserve the right of double vote to shareholders of French nationality or citizens of any member state of the EEC. A right of triple or quintuple vote was proposed by the government for shares held as registered for five or ten years. This proposal was rejected at the time of the vote on the Bill.

Some provisions tend rather to protect minority shareholdings. For instance, a company cannot validly vote with its own shares which it has bought back. Further, in matters to do with the company articles or changes conferring special advantages, the number of votes which one shareholder can dispose of remains fixed at a maximum of ten. The articles may also limit the number of votes which a shareholder may have at ordinary and extraordinary meetings, on condition that such a limitation is imposed on all shares without distinction of category. The new law has also, since 1 February 1967, prohibited the issue of participating or founders' shares and, moreover, provides for their stage-by-stage abolition.

Following certain proposals of the Pleven Commission, the new law stipulates that one or more shareholders representing at least a tenth of the registered capital of the company may demand the appointment of an expert to submit a report on any business operation. The report of the expert is then sent both to those who requested it and to the administrative board and is annexed to the auditors' report presented at the following general meeting. The same procedure allows for the dismissal and replacement of the auditor(s).

Stützel differentiates between four types of shareholder in a way which usefully clarifies their various interests. These types are: (*a*) the exclusive shareholder holding all the shares of a company; (*b*) the small shareholder, who has only a small investment in the basic capital as an individual; (*c*) the portfolio holder whose income is limited to what the portfolio yields ('portfolio holder without side interests'); and (*d*) the portfolio holder who has other sources of income, from his own business, for example, or from other commercial companies ('portfolio holder with side interests').

'The interest of the exclusive shareholder in the possession of shares', says Stützel, 'is determined by his own judgment of the level of the future yield of his company.' This means that the interest of the exclusive shareholder is equivalent to the worth of the company capital. There is no room here for any conflict of interest. The individual shareholder, on the other hand, can have several reasons for participating in an AG. Like the others (especially the 'portfolio holder without side interests'), he can seek a permanent investment yielding a regular profit or may hope, as a speculator to whom the future fate of the company does not matter, to get a quick profit through a price rise on the stock exchange. In general, however, the interest of the individual shareholder, relying on company law, is to obtain a share in the yield of the company proportionate to his investment. He will therefore put a premium on wide—and even complete—disclosure, which may for many reasons be contrary to the interests of those large shareholders who might, for instance, be aiming to gain control of the firm, or gain special advantages as customers or suppliers.

As for the portfolio shareholder, German arrangements give him an essentially greater interest (reckoned in DM per share) than the individual shareholder. This is because holding a portfolio brings with it an opportunity to influence the fortunes of the company. Such a power, however, is worthwhile to the 'portfolio holder without side interests' only if it would bring in money which could not be attainable without the exercise of his corresponding voting rights. In the final analysis this can only be the case if the portfolio holder succeeds in becoming a member of the supervisory board and thus taking a share of the profits. The situation is different for the 'portfolio holder with side interests.' If he seeks actively to influence the company (and particularly its administrative board), he may expect to increase his income (as a large shareholder 'with side interests') and gain other financial advantages—by offering contracts, for instance, which could benefit both him and the company in which he holds an important stake.

It is easy to appreciate, even from this brief description, that serious conflicts of interest may arise between the various types of shareholder. Strains of rather the same sort may disturb the relationship between shareholders and the administrative board, though shareholders, because they differ so much among themselves, can never present a 'united front'. Nevertheless, the closeness of interests between the AG and its shareholders is usually such that the danger of conflict between shareholders and the board should not be overestimated. Serious difficulties can, of course, arise if the company comes to be dominated by groups of shareholders, if the latter's interests do not coincide with those of the firm. Problems of this sort are likely to be more troublesome than any attributable to so-called 'board domination'.

For these reasons special importance is attached to the protection of minorities and this is reflected in German company legislation. The law has taken the interests of minority shareholders into account in many ways and has put them into a position to block a legal majority decision or, conversely, to enforce their will against an objecting majority. It was one of the essential concerns of the recent company law reform to make the recognition of the rights of minorities easier. This was done by lowering the necessary capital participation and by reducing the cost risks for minority proposals. The new Act differentiates between three types of minority rights. First, there are rights which already existed under the previous legislation—for example, the validity of claims for indemnity against founders, administrative directors or the supervisory board (Sec. 147). For this purpose (as hitherto) a 10 per cent stake in the basic capital is necessary. Second, those rights which the courts have been charged to enforce—for example, a request for a special audit under Sec. 142 of the Act. Lastly, there are rights which may be exercised without court enforcement—e.g., when separate voting takes place to clear a member of the administrative or supervisory board of some charge brought against him. (Sec. 120.) In these last two cases a set nominal minimum amount (of DM 2 million) or 10 per cent of share capital allows the exercise of these minority rights. These provisions have appreciably strengthened a minority's power to protect its interests, especially in big public companies.

ITALY

The basic principle in Italian company law is shareholders' sovereignty. The need for protection therefore arises only when a minority interest is in danger. In such circumstances a variety of powers and remedies is extended to individuals and minorities under the Civil Code (Arts. 2330, 2367, 2408). The draft project for company law reform puts the main burden of the protection of small investors on the shareholders' meeting and suggests (Art. 41) that quoted companies should be allowed to issue a kind of voteless equity share, known as *azioni di risparmio*, up to 50 per cent of total capital. These shares would carry no right to vote in any decision, however important, and in this would differ from the existing *azioni di godimento* (Art. 2353 of the Civil Code), which give voting rights with regard to mergers, share issues and other major decisions. The *azioni di risparmio* would be preferred stock; they would have a right to at least 5 per cent of dividends and if a lesser amount were distributed they would have an entitlement to recover the difference in the following three years. In this way, the reform draft has sought to introduce a distinction between committed and uncommitted investors in order to make the shareholders' meetings a place where only people with a specific interest in the company's management go and vote.

With this purpose in mind the draft has also proposed certain changes in the rules of meetings. Art. 11 confirms the legality of the *sindacato di voto* (a kind of voting trust), doubtful according to existing precedents and comments, but sets some limits to it. Art. 6 expressly forbids the *clausola di gradimento* (right of first approval) in stock transactions, with the exception of banks and insurance companies. Art. 8 limits to a maximum of ten the proxies a single individual can hold for a meeting.

The danger of these proposals—that more power would be given to the existing management—was stressed in the discussion on the *azioni di godimento*. To many people (including Professor Santoro Passarelli, a member of the Commission which drafted the reform proposals), the introduction of such a class of shares necessitates the establishment of a public authority externally to provide the control which shareholders can no longer exercise. To others (among them Professor Ferri, Professor Visentini, vice-chairman of IRI, and Professor Nicolò) external control is justified by deeper considerations than the need to protect uncommitted investors; it should also cover companies which do not issue *azioni di godimento*. This class of share is regarded merely as another useful means for stimulating investment in productive activities. In this sense, opinion is generally favourable to their introduction. It has received authoritative support from Sig. Carli (Governor of the Bank of Italy) in a speech at the Giornata Mondiale del Risparmio in November 1968 and from Sig. Lombardi, chairman of the Associazione Italiana tra le Società per Azioni.[76] Sig. Carli has also urged the setting up of investment trusts and legislation to this end is expected.

THE NETHERLANDS

1. Supervision of the management's conduct of a company's affairs by the general meeting of shareholders is felt, in the Netherlands, to be indispensable. The Verdam Committee also recognises in its draft Bill that it is desirable to leave certain essential powers to the general meeting. Some members of the Committee, however, wish to see the powers of shareholders' meetings curtailed by transferring some of them to the supervisory board (see Part III, Chapter 1, p. 157 and (2) below). Under Art. 43 of the Commercial Code all powers that have not been reserved for the management or for others are vested in the general meeting. This article specifies the law and the articles of association as the general limits of these powers. The powers possessed by a general meeting depend very often on whether the firm is an open or a close limited company. In the case of an open company with dispersed capital, the principal powers are usually: (*a*) the right to appoint and dismiss members of the management and of the supervisory board; (*b*) the right to adopt the annual accounts and to discharge the management and supervisory board from liability; and (*c*) the right to alter the articles of association. In the case of a close company the general meeting often has greater powers.

2. A bare majority of the Verdam Committee proposed that in the case of open companies the powers of the shareholders' meeting mentioned under

---

[76] *Problemi e prospettive delle società commerciali*, Atti del convegno indetto dall' ISLE (Rome, 16 November 1965), Milan, 1965, p. 116,

(*a*) and (*b*) above should be transferred to the supervisory board. This proposal, however, has met with considerable opposition. It has been claimed that it would endanger the flexibility of the legal form of the company, which at the moment allows it to adapt to organisational, technical and social developments; and would disturb the present balance of power between management, supervisory board and shareholders, which is the result of this flexibility. Critics have also maintained that the transfer to the supervisory board of the general meeting's power to approve the annual accounts would greatly impair the open nature of the company, which is otherwise so strongly supported by the Verdam Committee.

The extent to which supervision is exercised by the shareholders' meeting depends largely on the type of company concerned and on whether or not— if it is an open company—the shares are widely dispersed. In a close company the shareholders are usually intimately in touch with the company's business operations. Because they are few in number, continuous consultation between the shareholders is easily arranged and they are thus enabled to exercise constant and effective supervision over the management. In an open company with widely dispersed capital the shareholders are much less directly involved in the company's operations. The names of the shareholders are not usually known (shares are generally made out to bearer) and the shareholders are so dispersed as to rule out the possibility of consultation and supervision. In uneventful periods the general meeting is therefore attended by a very small proportion of the shareholders. At these times its greatest influence is negative: in its conduct of the company's business the management has to keep constantly in mind the existence of the general meeting and of the criticism that may be expected there. At moments of crisis, however, shareholders are often sufficiently alarmed (by press reports, for example) to take the trouble to attend the general meeting or to deliver a proxy to a representative. Shareholders may also convene an extraordinary general meeting under Art. 43c of the Commercial Code. In such cases the power exercised by the shareholders' meeting often comes clearly to the fore. Individual owners of large blocks of shares in an open company can, of course, exercise much more effective supervision.

3. Proposals for combined meetings of shareholders, employees and representatives of other interests have been put forward by the *Christelijk National Vakverbond*, one of the large trade unions, but have not been taken up. The Verdam Committee has suggested, however, that holders of depositary receipts should be admitted to the general meeting, without being granted voting rights.

It is not the normal practice in the Netherlands for shareholders to be represented by proxy at general meetings, although such a procedure is permitted by law (CC Art. 44a, paragraph 1). This is one of the reasons why the proportion of the company's capital represented at a general meeting is often so small. Proposals concerning representation through banks or other agencies are not under consideration.

4. No distinction is made in the Netherlands between committed and uncom-

mitted investors. Nearly all Dutch limited companies have an oligarchic structure, which is designed to promote the greatest possible continuity in the company. Many firms try to establish this oligarchic structure by one or more of the following measures.

(i) The management and/or the supervisory board may be empowered in the articles of association to put forward to the general meeting a binding list of nominations for appointments to the management and/or to the supervisory board. (The effect of such 'binding nominations' is that votes cannot be validly cast for persons not included in the list.)

(ii) Special powers, including the right to put forward a binding list of nominations for appointments, may be vested by the articles of association in the holders of priority shares. The nomination lists mentioned under (i) and (ii) may, however, be deprived of their binding nature by a resolution carried at a general meeting by at least two thirds of the votes cast and representing more than half the issued share capital. (CC Art. 48a, paragraph 2.)

(iii) The public may be enabled to acquire, instead of shares, depositary receipts which give the holders of these receipts the right to dividend and other distributions but not the right to vote. The shares themselves, and the voting rights attaching to them, remain in the hands of depositaries or administrative agencies (*administratiekantoren*). The Verdam Committee recommended that the position of holders of depositary receipts be somewhat improved by: (*a*) admitting them to the general meeting, without, however, giving them the right to vote; (*b*) giving them the right to institute an enquiry into the management's conduct of the company's affairs (see below, p. 279); (*c*) allowing them the right to appeal to the proposed *Ondernemingskamer* (see above, p. 173) against the adopted annual accounts.

(iv) A holding company may be formed to hold a large block of shares.

SWEDEN

1. As a broad generalisation it may be said that shareholders in big quoted companies are unable to protect themselves by control through the general meeting. Their protection, in fact, depends chiefly on the general provisions for disclosure and, more simply, on a company's desire to maintain a good reputation on the capital market. There is no control corresponding to the United States Securities and Exchange Commission. However, some discussion has begun on the question of whether disclosure provisions might not be further strengthened by legislation relating to the Stock Exchange, which at present may be said to act as a 'critic' and a corrective. A fall in prices, for instance, may easily be interpreted as a symptom of lack of confidence which can be fatal next time the company needs to increase its capital stock. Whether this 'market control' may be thought sufficient is, of course, dependent on the type of company, possibilities of other sources of finance, etc. It may also be mentioned that all companies are obliged to send their annual reports to the Patent and Registration Office, where anyone may consult them, and that

company tax assessments are public. (Whether shareholders should keep their present exclusive right of control and decision-making is a question frequently discussed by the political Left.)

2. The shareholders' meeting is, according to Swedish law, the highest company organ. As in other countries, however, it has, in big companies, usually surrendered most of its power to the directors. The board has thus become the highest organ and is, moreover, self-perpetuating. Managements were for a long time in general satisfied with this situation but it now seems that younger progressive managers strongly believe that shareholders' meetings should regain at least something of their importance. Some companies therefore intentionally try to make their shareholders' meetings more efficient, but it is doubtful whether it is possible to achieve any meaningful results in this way. Moreover, the motive behind such attempts to revive the general meeting may perhaps often be a fear that, if nothing is done, parliament will step in and put other limitations on the power of management.

Representation of interests other than shareholders in shareholders' meetings (or other company organs) has been discussed from time to time and from various viewpoints. These questions may become live political issues in the next few years, particularly because of government studies of the structure and ownership of industry and commerce which are expected to be completed soon.

In one special field the Swedish parliament has taken an initiative to do something about the powerlessness of shareholders' meetings. This is in the case of the mutual insurance companies, which are, in fact, associations with memberships consisting of all their policy-holders. The government grants a charter, given the setting up of a truly 'democratic' organisation, the form of which is left to the companies themselves. One method has been to divide the country into a large number of small voting districts; every year a small number of voting districts, chosen by lot, is permitted to send representatives to the shareholders' meeting.

3. It has for a long time been common in Sweden for representatives of banks and other large suppliers of credit to be appointed to boards of directors. (The banks' powerful indirect influence on industry and commerce, through holding and investment companies, has often been pointed out in political debate.) On the other hand, it has never been proposed that creditors should have a formal right to be represented in the decision-making or executive organs of firms.

4. The general question of distinctions between different classes of shareholders has not been widely debated in Sweden. The issue of non-voting shares is not permitted and the difference in voting rights between different shares is not allowed to be greater than ten to one. On the other hand, there are provisions for the proportional election of auditors, and for a minority representing one tenth of the share capital to have a right to demand from an authority the appointment of an 'extraordinary minority auditor'. These provisions, however, do not mean much as far as big companies are concerned.

Section C: The Employee

How is the employee's voice heard within the company? Should employees serve or be represented on company organs? If not, can their interests be adequately protected by (for instance) works councils, unions and labour legislation? What pressures are there for greater employee representation and control?

BELGIUM

(a) *Some academic views*

In Professor Vandeputte's opinion general discontent arises from dissatisfaction with the legal framework of company organisation. Neither chief executives nor management personnel are satisfied with their position. In particular, they do not think that their salaries are commensurate with the riches they help to create. They therefore make two demands: for association with and more information about the company; and for profit-sharing of both distributed and undistributed profits and also of capital resources won by self-financing.[77] Greater understanding of the purposes of the company has shed new light upon the soundness of these claims.

Professor de Barsy thinks that the demand for participation in the running of the firm may be characterised as a natural right, inseparably linked with a right of the same order, that of foundation. The human purposes of the firm can be attained only if those who 'support' it participate in the company which would have no 'life' but for them. Participation means knowledge and understanding of the company. The right of participation generates the right to intelligible and reliable information, hence the demands for the reform of the accounting system and for the extension of the competence of auditors, who should be allowed to explain and to comment upon the documents submitted as information. Participation also means a sharing of responsibilities, which will differ in degree according to circumstances. It is not denied that a strong centre of authority is necessary for the success of economic activity but this should not exclude some form of plural control.[78]

Professor Henrion writes that 'co-management' is still premature and that, instead of a division of authority in the firm, it would be wiser to develop an 'institutionalised dialogue'. This would have the advantage of leaving final decisions to the general management appointed by the shareholders, to whom they would have to justify their activities.[79] One of the conditions for achieving such a dialogue is a flow of accurate information. If both sides—the management and the employees—should come into open conflict or distrust (despite the fact that the new structure encourages such a dialogue), it is

[77] Vandeputte, op. cit. (see footnote 2, p. 164), p. 60.

[78] De Barsy, op. cit. (see footnote 1, p. 164), p. 17.

[79] R. Henrion, 'L'entreprise et les apporteurs de capitaux,' *Cahiers Economiques*, No. 22, 1964, p. 232; 'Système économique et statut de l'entreprise', *Annales de Sciences Economiques Appliquées*, August 1965, p. 360.

desirable, according to Vandeputte,[80] to provide, outside the framework of the new company-institution, a kind of 'Economic Jurisdiction' or 'Economic Court of Arbitration'. Henrion opposes this view.[81] (For an exposition of concepts referred to here, see pp. 69–71.)

Vandeputte considers that the conception of 'company-community' cannot be fully achieved.[82] 'The workers want to institutionalise the firm. They want to be part of it. This partnership would give them the right to more accurate information on results, to demand stronger and more durable ties between themselves and the company, to lay claim to a certain proportion of profits and to be more respected as members of a working community.' (These aims might be achieved by nationalisation but this solution has been but rarely resorted to in Belgium in recent years.) Vandeputte believes that to enable employees to become joint owners of the company—and thus entitle them to representation at the general meeting—would be a leap in the dark. It could, moreover, mean lower income for employees, when business slackened, and could weaken the power of the trade unions to make claims on their members' behalf. Nor does he favour 'co-determination' on the German model, because he remains unconvinced of its success so far; he believes that it has undermined the right of the trade unions to challenge and make claims and has endangered the position of a strong and undivided labour leadership.

Employee representatives, however, continue to pursue some kind of working community within the firm. If, asks Vandeputte, this working community cannot be achieved by a genuine contract of partnership and, if a contractual tie between the company and each employee is desirable, 'are we not obliged to recognise that this contract will necessarily be one for the hiring of services corresponding to the idea of a labour contract or a contract of employment?' Little basic change is needed, from the legal point of view, in the relation between labour and the firm. If labour wants to continue playing a fully independent opposition role, he argues, the workers will juridically remain 'outside the firm', a situation which suits them best.

The right of participation also obliges employees to share in the product of their activity. This is the financial aspect of the right of participation in a 'company-community'.[83] (See p. 70 above.) Within the concept of 'company capital association' and on the basis of the labour contract, the employer has no obligation other than to pay the contracted wages, in accordance with social laws and regulations. If he pays more, it is assumed he does so for reasons of his own and certainly not because the employees have any right to higher wages.[84] But the employees are unwilling to accept that the firm they belong to, and to which they devote all their activity, should constantly expand without their being able, in one way or another, to benefit from the wealth they help to produce. Not only do they demand a share of distributed profits but also the grant of some title to share in the results of the self-financing process.[85]

[80] Vandeputte, op. cit., p. 100.
[81] Henrion, 'Système économique', op. cit., p. 361.
[82] Vandeputte, op. cit., p. 89.
[83] Henrion, 'Système économique', op. cit., p. 363.
[84] De Barsy, op. cit., p. 31.
[85] Vandeputte, op. cit., pp. 41–44.

All 'new thinking' on company objectives accepts the principle that workers should share in distributed profits. F. A. Smets thinks that if a 'profit surplus' remains after the payment of the exact return on invested capital (taking monetary depreciation into account), a distribution of this 'surplus' should be made.[86] De Barsy and Henrion agree, maintaining that employee participation should lie in the successive distribution of company income on the same level as the distribution of a second dividend.[87] Vandeputte wonders why the trade unions, backed by such unanimous academic opinion, have not put in a stronger claim for profit distribution. The unions have, of course, sought extra payments based on production quotas and have also pressed for an end-of-year bonus. But these extras are merely additional wage payments and do not represent participation in annual profits. The unions appear to have held back so far chiefly because the necessary financial information has been both scanty and insufficiently clear.[88] Henrion remarks that this is yet another proof that clear and honest accounts are essential for the realisation of the concept of the 'company-community'.[89]

No concrete suggestions have been made in Belgium about employee participation in undistributed profits. The authors who accept the principle of participation in distributed profits seem to agree that some title to share in the growth achieved by self-financing should be granted to workers[90] but they have yet to suggest any practical way of putting this into effect.

As for employee participation in company management, Professor Vandeputte considers the works council to be the appropriate locus. Works councils can also improve the 'social atmosphere' in the firm and increase a company's chances of success 'by going beyond the contract of employment or service, but not so far as to make the workers the associates of the shareholders'. He believes the works council should have a wider right to give advice on its own initiative and recommends obligatory consultation between the council and management on certain decisions. He also suggests the setting up of an economic court that would offer workers a place of recourse when an 'absolutely fundamental conflict' arose between capital (as represented by the head of the firm) and labour. Vandeputte further proposes that employee representatives should have the right 'to bring before an economic court certain problems of primordial importance to the company's future', especially in situations when the competence of the head of a firm to continue in his post is seriously in question.[91]

Henrion comes to the conclusion that a greater degree of employee participation in company management would best be achieved by an 'institutionalised dialogue' within the firm. He supports a trade union movement that 'checks' the operations rather than participates in the management of firms. 'The opportunities for challenge must always remain open.'[92]

---

[86] F. A. Smets, *Refléxions sur le gouvernement des entreprises*, quoted by Vandeputte, op. cit., p. 108.

[87] E. de Barsy, *De Onderneming en de sociale vooruitgang*, Brussels, 1963, pp. 49–50.

[88] Vandeputte, op. cit., p. 109.

[89] Henrion, 'L'entreprise et les apporteurs de capitaux', op. cit., p. 235.

[90] Henrion, 'Système économique', op. cit., p. 363.

[91] Vandeputte, op. cit., pp. 91–93 and 102.

[92] Henrion, 'L'évolution du droit de l'entreprise', *Bulletin social des industries*, August/September 1965, pp. 400–407.

(b) *Works councils*

Strictly speaking, employees are not represented within the organs of Belgian companies. The idea of active economic and financial co-determination has been abandoned by union leaders. (See Appendix A, pp. 339 ff.) Employees are represented within the firm through the works councils (*conseils d'entreprise*) instituted by the law of 20 September 1948 and first elected in 1950. All firms regularly employing more than 150 people are obliged to set up a works council. The chief aim of the councils, which are composed of an employer's delegation and elected representatives of the employees, is to foster a spirit of collaboration between employer and employees. The councils have a right to information on the company's economic and financial situation and an advisory function concerning organisation, labour conditions and productivity. They are also involved in 'co-determination' with regard to the management of company welfare services, the organisation of holidays and the definition of shop-floor regulations (*règlements d'atelier*) in which general working conditions are laid down.

Works councils have been much criticised, chiefly on the following grounds. (*a*) They are in many cases not representative of the firm as a whole. In the first place, executive employees (*personnel de cadre*) are not represented as such. Second, the results of the elections, from lists presented by the unions, have in many cases meant that some sections of the firm are not represented at all. (*b*) Their remit is too limited and too vague. The unions claim that their social 'co-determination' rights should cover labour conditions in the widest sense and that consultation on technical matters should take place before, not after, decisions are taken. The complaint about the lack of full and detailed information is also relevant here. There is, moreover, growing distrust between council members and other employees, because all information given in the council is 'commercially secret' and may not be passed on.

Under the law of 1948, the employee council members have the right to ask an auditor to check the financial and economic information given by the employer. In practice, this provision has meant little or nothing. The task of the auditor is limited to declaring whether or not the information is complete and correct; he cannot give any further information to the council's employee members without the consent of the employer. Furthermore, the employer is the auditor's client, so that the latter will be generally unwilling to do more than confirm the employer's information. A complete revision of the law on company auditors has been demanded.

(c) *Representation of employees at shareholders' meetings*

It is generally accepted, by both sides of industry (at least at the institutional level), that the structure and function of the firm can no longer be determined by the 'liberal' individualist philosophy of the nineteenth century. 'Ownership' cannot justify the authority of the employer over the firm, which is more seen as a community of interests—capital, labour, management and the community. If the present legal structure of firms no longer corresponds to things as they are, a new structure, wherein these diverse components would be represented, must be found to close the gap between law and reality. It

202

remains true, however, that no one has yet got to grips with this problem in the sense of formulating concrete proposals for the practical realisation of this concept of the firm. No one has yet made the fundamental choices that are necessary for reaching this goal.

The trade unions, and the socialist movement as a whole, no longer believe in the nationalisation of private firms, although the Fédération Générale des Travailleurs Belges (FGTB) proposed the nationalisation of some basic industries, such as power, in 1956. There are various reasons for this attitude: the chief is a realisation that the fact of private ownership is of secondary importance only; management, the actual running of the company, is the heart of the matter. Union leaders no longer hanker after the idea of active co-determination (the involvement of their representatives in the decision-making process) in financial and economic matters and would be satisfied, at least in the short run, with full information. They do, however, seek greater co-determination in social affairs. (See (b) above.)

The representation of employees at shareholders' meetings has never been proposed as such. A somewhat vague move in this direction was made by the Christian trade union movement at its 1964 Congress which advocated that the management of a firm should justify its policy and decisions to a general council in which capital, labour and the public interest would be represented. Recently the Christian trade union organisation (the CSC) made detailed proposals for such a council.

To sum up, Belgian unions pin their faith for a better deal for the workers on more detailed information on all aspects of company activity; genuine consultation in cases where financial and economic decisions affect employees' conditions; and full co-determination in social affairs. (A general account of Belgian trade unions' attitudes to company reform is given in Appendix A, pp. 339 ff.)

BRITAIN

The Jenkins Committee considered the position of employees only in connexion with take-overs. The Report states[93] that the Trades Union Congress suggested that any bidder should be placed under a duty to disclose his intentions as regards the future of the company bid for and its employees, but the Committee rejected this recommendation on the ground that it would frequently be ineffective since the bidder would in many cases not know what changes might be necessary if the offer succeeded.

At present, the directors may act for the benefit of employees only where this would also be for the benefit of the company,[94] although recent legislation such as the Factories Acts and Contracts of Employment Act 1963, the Terms and Conditions of the Employment Act 1959, the Redundancy Payments Act 1965 and the Industrial Training Act 1964 have to a limited extent provided safeguards for the interests of employees. However, recently there

[93] Paragraph 267.
[94] See for example *Parke v. The Daily News Ltd* [1962] Ch. 927. Cf. Companies Act 1948 Sec. 54(i)(b) which enables directors to create profit-sharing schemes for the benefit of employees.

have been proposals for giving employees greater protection. Some of these proposals have favoured protection through wider disclosure. Thus Professor K. W. Wedderburn has asserted[95] the 'right of employees and of their representatives who conduct collective bargaining on their behalf to information about the company'. Similar claims were put before the Cohen Committee.[96] The Labour Party Report *Industrial Democracy*[97] states: 'The union or unions organising the workers in a company must be assured of access to the information they require for effective bargaining and participation.' *Labour's Economic Strategy* (a Party report issued in August 1969) calls for greater management accountability to employees, possibly underpinned by specific legal obligations, company reports for employees and 'provision for a ministerial investigation where a representative body of employees considered the company was defaulting on its obligations'.

Professor Wedderburn also proposed that the next Companies Act should provide that one of the modern conditions for incorporation with limited liability be a willingness to conduct collective bargaining wherever a company employs a substantial number of workers. Sanctions might include compulsory winding up or striking off the register of companies. There have been proposals for the compulsory representation of employees on either the existing board or a supervisory board based on the Federal German *Aufsichtsrat*.[98]

The views of the various sectors of the community, together with the main arguments on the alternative schemes, can be summarised. Of the two schemes, the government appears to be considering representation on the existing board more seriously.[99] The trade unions in their memorandum of evidence to the Royal Commission on Trade Unions and Employers' Organisations[100] stated that 'legislation of a discretionary character would be widely welcomed'. The memorandum saw considerable drafting difficulties in the way of compulsory representation. The Labour Party Report, *Industrial Democracy*,[101] stated: 'The question of worker representatives [on the board] in the private sector gives rise to a number of difficult problems and we cannot see it as a suitable starting point for the extension of industrial democracy. We think it likely to arise after the further extension of the scope of collective bargaining and of statutory protection.' Needless to say, the City of London and employers in general are opposed to the participation of employees in management.

Arguments raised in favour of the representation of employees on the existing board include the argument that industrial relations would improve and that productivity would increase as a result. At present it is believed that much industrial unrest is caused by the lack of communication between em-

[95] *Company Law Reform*, Fabian Society, Tract No. 363.

[96] *Report of the Committee on Company Law Amendment*, Cmd 6659 (1945), paragraph 50.

[97] June 1967, p. 9.

[98] See, however, Douglas Jay, *Socialism in the New Society*, p. 331.

[99] See for example the Lord Chancellor in *Parliamentary Debates* (House of Lords), Vol. 278, No. 72.

[100] 1966, Chapter 10, paragraph 290.

[101] At p. 10.

ployees and management. Decisions are arrived at without consultation of employees' representatives, and are frequently announced without any attempt to explain what were the considerations which led to those decisions. Once a decision has been reached it is difficult for trade unions to persuade employers to reconsider in the light of the workers' interests, unless there is a work to rule, a strike or similar industrial action to produce a direct confrontation. It has been suggested that there might be a greater willingness by workers to co-operate with management if they knew that their interests had been put before the board at the time when the decisions were made. However, this argument is very hard to substantiate and, in the absence of experiment, it is also difficult to refute. Clear support for it cannot be derived from the Federal German Republic in which different conditions exist, as Professor M. Fogarty has explained in *Company and Corporation—One Law?*

A second main argument is that employees are entitled to representation as a matter of social justice. The fact that their contribution to the well-being of the company takes the form of labour rather than of capital is not sufficient justification for their exclusion from the consideration of policy matters. Unlike shareholders who can spread their capital through several companies and reduce their risks, an employee cannot easily divide his labour between several employers, so that his welfare may be more closely linked to the success of the company than is the case with the average shareholder, yet the interests of the latter are paramount. This argument is very shaky. Some form of hierarchy and division of responsibility is inevitable if companies are to operate effectively, and to allow workers to participate in management may lead to a slowing down of the decision-making process, and cause confusion by adding a whole new perspective of interests that must be considered. Moreover, social justice will not be achieved solely by giving employees representation on the board of directors; it may be satisfied if future generations have equal opportunities, particularly educational, to become directors or manual workers.

There is a number of arguments which have been raised against the representation of employees. The first is primarily a legal argument. The duties of the directors as at present defined are owed to 'the company as a whole' and it is improper for a director to act solely in the interests of a particular member or group of members,[102] and therefore it is wrongful for a director to act solely for the benefit of employees. Thus an employee representative on the board would not be able to support the persons whom he was appointed to represent. He would also be subject to the rules which inhibit the use of confidential information and these might cause difficulty and embarrassment in any negotiations between workers and management on pay and conditions. A second argument against the direct representation of employees is that it would merely cause bitterness between the representative and his electors since the representative who attempted to be objective in his assessment of the situation would be treated as a 'Quisling'. Moreover, there could be strained relations on the board where the employees' representative was also one of the leading negotiators for the employees. His fellow directors might regard his conduct as

[102] *Scottish Co-operative Wholesale Society Ltd. v. Meyer* [1959] A.C. 324; *Selangor United Rubber Estates v. Craddock* (No. 3) 1968 2 All E.R. 1073.

akin to treason. Thirdly, workers are not, in general, qualified to be directors. The President of the Board of Trade has accepted this difficulty,[103] and even the trade unions pointed out the increase in management specialisation in their memorandum of evidence to the Royal Commission.[104] Even though a distinction is drawn between directors chosen from the employees and directors chosen by the employees, it may be difficult to find sufficient qualified people who are prepared to act for the employees. Fourthly, the trade unions have been examined by the Royal Commission, and although the Trades Union Congress made proposals for a three-tier system of worker representation—at plant level, at regional or some intermediate level, and on the board of directors—the Royal Commission did not feel able to recommend the appointment of 'worker-directors'. Such representational schemes as co-partnership and profit-sharing should be settled by negotiation.[105]

The Liberal 'Yellow Book' of 1928 proposed a supervisory council based on the German *Aufsichtsrat*, while N. S. Ross published a study of the *Democratic Firm* in 1964 for the Fabian Society in which he proposed a 'representative council' containing representatives of both shareholders and employees. There would appear to be little general support for either of these proposals and the last two arguments against representation on the existing board can also be raised against a supervisory or representative council. Sir Reay Geddes, of the Dunlop Company, has suggested a further argument against a supervisory board in an address on 'An Approach to the Philosophy of Company Law':[106] 'Either there is duplication or executive board members are denied the criticism and stimulus which independents can provide when they take part in the formulation of policy decisions and really understand the problems, prospects and programmes of the company.' The employee element in the Federal German *Aufsichtsrat* has, in general, not had great influence on the management of the *Aktiengesellschaft* (to which *Aufsichtsräte* are restricted),[107] and it is questionable whether the existence of the *Aufsichtsrat* has led to a marked improvement in industrial relations.

The Labour Party Report, *Industrial Democracy*, states that workers must 'have the right to determine their economic environment by participating in a widening range of decisions within management'. But, on the whole, there is only slight general pressure for the representation of employees in either voluntary or compulsory form, and, on balance, it seems that the case in the UK for such representation in a truly democratic system has not yet been satisfactorily made out. (See also Introduction, pp. 27–28.)

The Industrial Relations Commission recently established by the government[108] is designed to promote procedural improvements in the machinery of collective bargaining, to improve the position of shop stewards and to investigate working conditions. However, it does not have power to compel

---

[103] See Anthony Crosland, *The Future of Socialism* and *The Conservative Enemy*.
[104] Paragraph 275.
[105] *Report*, Cmnd 3623, paragraph 1105. For the general discussion, see Chapter XV.
[106] Delivered to the Institute of Bankers on 20 March 1967.
[107] See Professor M. Fogarty, *Company and Corporation—One Law?* at p. 120.
[108] See Royal Commission on Trade Unions and Employers' Organisations *Report* (Cmnd 3623) and the White Paper *In Place of Strife*.

employers to recognise trade unions nor has it any powers to punish for failure to observe negotiating machinery when established.

FRANCE

The representation within the company of the interests of employees lies at the very heart of the wider French debate. But here, as elsewhere, the attitudes of the various parties concerned are often ambiguous.

The employers have always been intransigent, either flatly opposing reforms or endeavouring to put off the moment of discussion or decision. Pierre Drouin has written: 'Does the CNPF, which has loudly proclaimed the rights and duties of free enterprise, know how the tide is flowing? It does not give the impression that it does. Its attitude on questions that are much less controversial than the Vallon Amendment has become progressively harder. Witness its refusal to recognise the union plant branch, to allow the revision of outdated collective agreements or to discuss with the CGT a strengthening of the position of works councils.'[109] Pierre de Calan has given a clear answer: 'If what is in question is a real sharing of power between the owners of capital and the employees, we consider it a total error—or, to be more precise, either a trick or an aberration.' Professor Georges Lasserre regards the workers as 'indifferent to the fate, success and future of the business except when they fear dismissals'.[110]

Christian circles have been more favourable towards employee participation. The Episcopal Note already quoted on several occasions in previous chapters speaks of a more active association. However, the influence of these ideas does not extend beyond the rather narrow Christian employer circles and the CJP.

The unions themselves have not been at all forthcoming on the subject. Georges Levard, chairman of the CFDT in 1964, declared openly: 'It is certainly necessary that the firm should be more of an arena for co-operation but the personality of the worker must not be submerged in the firm. It is right to be restrained about the objectives assigned to the company or to its reform. The association of employees in it can be only of a very special nature.'[111] The fact is that union leaders want no more than a 'modest' increase in the powers of works councils, and consider that the union plant branch is the best means of consolidating their influence. Furthermore, the unions seem to fear that worker representatives would, through lack of experience, support decisions which would ultimately be against their own interests.

Any slight improvement in the representation of employees over the past twenty years or so may be ascribed—apart from a few 'extreme' attitudes adopted, for example, by the Lasserre report to the Economic Council and the work of Francois Bloch-Laîné—to influence of pressure from two sources:

[109] P. Drouin, 'Et la réforme de l'entreprise?', *Le Monde*, 16 April 1966.

[110] *La réforme de l'entreprise*, Colloques de l'Institut des Etudes Coopératives, Royaumont, 2–3 May 1964.

[111] E. Maire, 'Rapport d'orientation' to Comité fédéral national of the Fédération des Industries Chimiques CFDT.

the Gaullists, for whom employee participation has always been a battle-cry, and salaried staff seeking better representation for themselves. Opinions differ, however, on the organisation of salaried staff representation: the CGC (General Confederation of Salaried Staff) wants the problem separated from that of other employees, while the salaried staff sections of the big union confederations are concerned that they should not be cut off from employees in general.

(a) *Employee delegates*

As defined by the law of 16 April 1946, the function of 'employee delegates' is to put forward to their employers all unsettled individual or collective claims concerning the application of wage rates and job classifications, the Labour Code and of the other laws and regulations dealing with the protection of workers, health, safety and social security. In addition, it is the task of employee delegates to inform the Factory Inspectors of all complaints or observations relating to the application of legal requirements or regulations, the oversight of which is their responsibility, and to accompany the Inspectors on their visits. The delegates are elected by the employees of the firm as a whole and their job is essentially to put forward claims. 'One of the difficulties generally encountered by a delegate within the organisation of a firm', notes Jacques Dumont, general delegate of CADIPPE,[112] 'is that his is a part-time job: each delegate has fifteen hours a month at his disposal, not counting the time devoted to meetings with the management.'

(b) *Works councils*

Works councils were legally established, in the excitement following the liberation, by the law of 22 February 1945, subsequently and variously amended—most recently by the law of 18 June 1966. As M. Capitant stated before the National Assembly on 8 June 1965, the final objective is that the works council 'should oversee the management in the name of labour, as the supervisory board will do in the name of capital'. (See p. 190.)

The works council has always had a triple role, social, environmental and economic. It undertakes or oversees the administration of all the welfare services established in the company for the benefit of employees and their families. It co-operates with the management in the improvement of working and living conditions, against the background of the regulations in force. It has a consultative right to be kept informed about the plans and the situation of the company. (See Section A of this Chapter, p. 170 above.) The council may propose rewards for workers who have made a particularly useful contribution to the firm by their initiative or suggestions. Thus, unlike the employee delegates who have a 'claim-making' role, the council should normally play a 'co-operative' role. However, in the spirit of the legislation, the council's job is also to press claims, at least by implication. As a result, there is often confusion between the task of the delegates and that of the council.

The establishment of a works council is normally obligatory in firms employing fifty or more workers. If there are several separate establishments,

[112] CADIPPE *Bulletin*, No. 18, December 1963.

a council must be formed in those with more than fifty workers, with a central council at the head office of the company. In certain nationalised industries (electricity and gas, for example) the works councils are replaced by joint production councils and health councils. During the debate on the 1966 Act, the government defeated an amendment that would have made works councils obligatory in the public sector.

The works council consists of the head of the firm (or his substitute), who is *ex officio* a member and chairman of the council, and of between two and eleven titular or substitute delegates, elected for two years by the employees. Every recognised union in the firm may designate a representative employee to attend the council in a consultative capacity. The salaried staff have the right to elect at least one special delegate when the number of employees exceeds 500. Some companies, especially in northern France, have for some time taken the development of works councils into their own hands.[113] Some have, for instance, jumped the gun and recognised the union plant branch, while others have arranged for the representation of employees under the age of eighteen (or twenty-one) or have organised a 'college of technicians and salaried staff', where the firm employs more than ten of these grades. CADIPPE has organised meetings which reproduced the actual composition of a council. It has done this in an attempt to make the true role of works councils understood and, above all, to teach both sides how to work together within the framework provided by the councils.

So far, however, the works councils have been a failure. The number in existence is far below the level required by the latest law. The then Minister of Labour, Gilbert Grandval, told the National Assembly in June 1965 that councils had been set up in barely 30 per cent of the eligible firms with less than 150 employees and in rather more than 50 per cent of those with more than 500. It would seem that the level is about 10 per cent in establishments with 50 to 100 employees but that it rises to 100 per cent in those with more than 2,000 employees. The UNR-UDT *rapporteur* to the National Assembly, René Caillé, has estimated that while some 25,000 French establishments employ more than 50 workers, only about 9,000 have a works council; and that of these councils no more than a third can be considered to be functioning satisfactorily. (More recent figures are not available.)

François Bloch-Lainé explains the 'crisis' of the council in the following way. The hostility of employers has hardened, as the climate of 1945 has evaporated over the years. Meetings have been called less frequently, little information has been given, scant interest has been shown in their suggestions, while the attitude of certain unions (which have used the councils as weapons of class war) has confirmed the adverse reactions of businessmen. Finally, low standards of education among employee representatives makes them ill-equipped to examine economic problems. The chairman of one important French company thinks that one of the most disappointing aspects is illustrated by the auditor whom the council may appoint.[114] The latter's report seems to be, in practice, drawn up for the use of the 'dominant' trade union. Others

[113] See *Revue Française du Travail*, October/November 1965.
[114] 'Note sur le fonctionnement d'un Comité d'Entreprise', December 1965, CREE Document No. 120.

have pointed out that the unions have become hostile to the councils because they see in them a threat to their own power.

The law of 18 June 1966 was enacted to give the works councils a new lease of life. It stiffened the penalties against heads of firms who deliberately impede the function of a council or the appointment of its members. It widens the responsibilities of councils, especially with regard to vocational training, and makes it obligatory that they should be informed in good time of redundancy plans and that they should give their views on such plans and the ways in which they are to be carried out. Their right to information is also broadened in exchange for an 'obligation to secrecy' on questions relating to production processes. (See also p. 170 above.)

Salaried staff had a longstanding claim satisfied by the new Act. Their delegate (in companies with a payroll of more than 500) had hitherto generally been elected by a college of electors comprising, apart from technicians and salaried staff properly speaking, foremen and also clerks and technicians who ranked with foremen by reason of their position in the company structure. Salaried staff may now constitute a special college to elect their own representative in firms in which their number is at least twenty-five and accounts, in companies employing more than 500 people, for at least 5 per cent of all employees at the time of the council re-election.

Various proposals had been made in the past for the improvement of the representation of salaried staff, on the grounds that they are the category of employees whose function it is to form a link between the management and the employees in general. As early as 1963 the CJP suggested that[115] 'the head of the firm should provide himself with a management committee which would include the most senior members of the salaried staff. This committee would prepare the major decisions submitted to the administrative board and settle objectives, policies and programmes. It would not be set up by legislation. . . . A formula for including salaried staff on the administrative board does not strike us as very effective, in view of the board's structure and function. In fact, since the head of the firm is responsible to the board, it can hardly be expected that members of the salaried staff, chosen by him and under his orders in the company "hierarchy", would argue in the administrative board against the proposals or decisions submitted by him to the board's opinion.' (The same line of thought runs through the new legislation's distinction between the supervisory board and the 'directory'. See p. 152.)

The new law also went some way towards strengthening the position of the union representative on the works council, who now has the same advantages as elected members—twenty hours a month (in firms with more than 500 employees) for the exercise of his duties and the same safeguards against dismissal. The union representative may be dismissed only with the agreement of the council; in cases of disagreement, the decision lies with the Labour Inspector. An employer, however, retains the right summarily to suspend a representative elected or designated by the union, in cases of grave misdemeanour, pending a definitive decision. If the decision goes against dismissal, the new provisions stipulate that the suspension be annulled and its

[115] Brissier, op. cit. (see footnote 69, p. 188).

effects fully quashed. This would seem to imply the reinstatement of the person in question.

Among the suggestions put forward to improve the performance and recruitment of works councils, the Christian employers' organisation has proposed, *inter alia*, that in establishments of fifty to 300 employees (in which it is often difficult to find a sufficient number of employees willing to be either an employee delegate or a council member) the law should allow, on conditions to be fixed in agreement with the firm, the formation of a single comprehensive body for employee representation.

During the debate on the new works council law, three points caused lively reactions, especially from the employers:[116] time allowed for the union delegate, the extension of the legislation to agricultural concerns and the establishment (in companies with more than 300 employees) of a special economic committee within the works council. The first point was incorporated in the Bill finally passed, as was the second in a rather restricted form— 'when the conditions of employment and work of the employees are comparable with those in industrial and commercial firms'. As for the special economic committee, its remit is limited to training and further education and to the employment and working conditions of women and young persons.

Since the crisis of the Spring of 1968, René Capitant has put forward the idea that there might be, on an equal footing within the firm, 'co-operatives' of capital and labour which, between them, would oversee the management of the company.

(c) *The union at plant level*

The recognition of the union plant branch and the definition of the status of the shop steward (*délégué syndical*) have long been demanded by the unions but have met with strong reservations on the part of employers. The unions know that success here would have a beneficial effect on their present poor levels of recruitment and would help them to resist the real harassment of union leaders and the war of attrition that some firms wage on them. An official recognition of the obligatory status of union plant branches was included in General de Gaulle's 'package deal' of June 1968. The details of putting this into effect are now being worked out between the government and the parties concerned.

The 1966 law on works councils was a move towards the definition of the status of shop stewards—but no more than a first step as far as the unions were concerned. In February 1963 the CGT issued a statement placing the recognition of the union plant branch at the head of its demands. Such recognition would, in particular, include the right of union representatives (who would not necessarily be employees of the firm) to have free access to and movement within firms on union business. The CFDT and later the CFTC have been more moderate in their demands, their chief aims being that the plant branch should be able to meet, as of right and with proper facilities, to issue notices and publications and to collect dues.

[116] 'La réforme des comités d'entreprise' (extracts from the periodical *Perspectives* published in CREE Fiche No. 4–1).

The employers are bitterly opposed to the union plant branch. Marcel Macaux, Chairman of the Compagnie des Aciéries et Forges de la Loire, stated clearly in 1963:[117] 'One of the objections most often made to the union plant branch is the danger of foreign elements being parachuted into the company.' Maurice Hannart[118] has written: 'The idea must be regarded as fundamentally bad, if it means allowing the unions, with all their apparatus, to operate at company level, at which they have neither competence nor responsibility. On the other hand, it might be salutary if "liaison agents" between the unions and their rank and file were effectively recognised and respected, on condition that they were nominated by the rank and file and confirmed by their organisation.' This hostility is also found in 'neo-liberal' political circles; the Perspectives et Réalités Club sees no point in recognising a union plant branch since the representational role has already been granted to the works council.

The unions' reply to the anxieties of employers is that they are not asking for the plant branch to be given rights to intervene in the management of a firm but merely that it should be recognised. Georges Levard, estimating that perhaps 300,000 firms might be concerned with this question, has said: 'I do not see the union organisations sending out delegates chosen outside the company to intervene in the functioning of the plant branch or in the various consultative procedures.'

The question of union finances is also controversial. The CJP magazine *Jeune Patron* replied as follows[119] to the proposals of François Bloch-Laîné: 'We are in agreement with François Bloch-Laîné in favouring means towards a strong union movement, yet the idea of compelling each worker, and, in proportion to the number of his employees, every head of a firm, to make a monthly contribution in the same way as social security payments, appears to us to go very far beyond the stage of development we have reached.' C. J. Gignoux wrote in 1964: 'M. Capitant's proposal, taking up the same idea [of Bloch-Laîné], specifically fixes a deduction from wages at a rate of 0·2 per cent. It should be noted that, according to calculations made by the Group of Parisian Metallurgical Industries, the unions would thus benefit from a contribution equivalent to 30 or 40 milliard old francs, a sum higher than that paid out for vocational training in the form of apprenticeship tax, and double the present amount of employers' contributions to unemployment insurance. It can be foreseen, on this basis, that the communist CGT would have at its disposal some 15 to 20 milliard old francs and would find itself subsidised by business—a somewhat piquant situation.'[120]

Some firms have signed agreements defining the status of plant branch shop stewards. Almost all the agreements specify that the shop steward must be on the company's payroll. Some state that the 'collection of union dues is authorised in the firm when it does not involve argument and disruption. It can be carried out only in rest periods and outside offices and workshops.'

[117] *Revue de l'Action Populaire,* loc. cit. (see footnote 47, p. 151).

[118] Hannart, op. cit. (see footnote 49, p. 151).

[119] See M. Millot, in *Revue Jeune Patron,* May 1963.

[120] C. J. Gignoux, 'Un singulier projet', *Journal des Finances,* 14 February 1964, CREE Document No. 98.

The main criticism that can be levelled at the present time against the representation of employees in the firm is the duplication of responsibilities. 'Except in very large firms employing more than 1,500 people there is very often duplication of functions among the members of the works council, the employee delegates and even union leaders within the firm. The reason for this is the inadequate number of trained workers. The unions are fighting this shortage by organising education courses.'[121]

(d) *Factory legislation*

Many laws and agreements (collective and at company level) provide for the protection of workers' interests with regard to working conditions, health, rest days, etc., and in cases of possible dismissal. Special measures protect women and children. As for dismissals, joint councils of 'wise men' see to the proper respect for the regulations. The application of the rules governing working conditions is the concern of the Factory Inspectors, but the legal provisions, organisation and means of inspection do not always ensure that they can fulfil their task. The small number of works councils shows that the Factory Inspectors are incapable of seeing that the law is applied.

GERMANY

(a) *Historical background and legal basis of co-determination*

The history of employee participation and the idea that workers should have a say in the making of decisions in all matters which closely concern them in their place of work goes back for well over a century in Germany. The movement has its origins in the social problems of the industrial revolution. Factory workers saw their very existence threatened not only by long working hours that drove them to the limits of human endurance but also by extremely low wages and the lack of any system of social security. During this period of intensive industrialisation, accompanied by the collapse of traditional social structures and other profound changes in all walks of life, there were, of course, a few outstanding entrepreneurs who attempted to improve the conditions of their workers. By and large, however, the lot of the wage-earner was undoubtedly one of poverty and misery. The demand for participation in the management of the firm was one of the first attempts made towards achieving some security in the new conditions of industrial life. These efforts culminated in the 1890s in laws providing for protection against accident, illness, unemployment and old age. The first moves towards the concept of co-determination were for many decades centred on the improvement of living and working conditions in industry. It has now reached the stage of a call (already voiced in the 1920s) for comprehensive economic democracy, with its implications of far-reaching changes in the political, economic, legal and social spheres.

The idea of co-determination was first legally expressed in the establishment of workers' committees under the Workers' Protection Law of 1891. (The

---

[121] 'Enquête sur le fonctionnement des comités d'entreprise', *Droit Social*, April, 1964, CREE Document No. 1014.

constituent national assembly held in the Paulskirche at Frankfurt in 1848 had considered a draft enactment for the election of so-called factory committees in the framework of an anticipated regulation of industry, but this never became law.) The arrangement of 1891, however, had little effect. Its administration was entirely in the hands of the employers, and two extensions of the legislation at the beginning of this century scarcely increased its significance. Some progress was apparent as a result of the law promulgated during the first world war on 'auxiliary service to the fatherland'. Under this law, workers' committees, which were to be set up in all firms employing more than fifty people, were bound to act in a manner calculated to maintain industrial peace. A decree of 23 December 1918, which applied to all firms with a payroll of more than twenty, brought in additional measures concerning industrial safety and health and introduced a certain degree of participation in the fixing of wage agreements. Even by this stage, however, it was still a matter only of advisory and welfare functions; the nettle of true co-determination in social, personnel and, even more, economic affairs had not yet been grasped.

A decisive step forward was Art. 165 of the Weimar Constitution. It may indeed be true that the practical significance of this 'committee article' was limited and that the industrial committees whose competence was spelt out by the provisions of the Industrial Council Law of 4 February 1920 occupied the lowest place in the envisaged system. Nevertheless, this article deserves to be quoted in full both for what it says and because it remains to this day one of the main sources of the ideas which influence the debate on co-determination at 'supra-factory' level. The Article reads as follows:

'Workers and employees are called upon to co-operate in equal association with employers in the regulation of wage and work conditions, as well as in the overall economic development of the means of production. Organised bodies on both sides are recognised.

'Workers and employees, for the safeguarding of their social and economic interests, shall have legal representation on industrial committees, as well as on regional committees for industrial sectors under a National Workers' Council.

'The regional committees and the National Council shall unite for the fulfilment of stated economic objectives, and shall co-operate in the execution of social laws with the representatives of employers and other parties concerned in regional economic councils and a National Economic Council. The regional economic councils and the National Economic Council shall be constituted in such a way that all important interests shall be represented according to their economic and social significance. Bills and important matters of social and economic policy shall be submitted for the approval of the National Economic Council before they are tabled in the Reichstag. The National Economic Council shall itself have the right to draw up proposed legislative measures. If the government does not approve the proposals, the latter may nevertheless be submitted to the Reichstag with an explanation of their objectives. The National Economic Council may delegate one of its members to present its proposals to the Reichstag.

'Agreed areas of supervisory and administrative authority may be transferred to the workers' and economic councils. The control of the membership and functions of the workers' and economic councils as well as their relationship to other self-governing social bodies is exclusively the concern of the nation.'

The demands here laid down in constitutional form, which go far beyond the ideas of co-operation and participation originating in the early days of industrialisation, had for a long time been connected with other lines of development and in particular with the thinking that emerged from the German revolutionary councils of 1918–19 and with the basic idea that a social democracy should operate not only on a political but also on an economic plane. However, apart from a temporary National Economic Council, the only concrete result of the programme laid down in Art. 165 of the Weimar Constitution was the Industrial Council Law of 1920 which provided for the setting up of industrial councils in all firms which regularly employed more than twenty people. This law gave the industrial councils not only a quite new advisory function but also a measure of true co-determination which was especially apparent in the procedures laid down for fixing working conditions. In 1934 the Industrial Council Law, which had been successfully implemented up to that time, was repealed. After 1945 the independent development of a new Industrial Constitution Law was begun on the basis of the outline Supervisory Council Law No. 22 in the occupation zones, and later in the *Länder*, and culminated in the unified Industrial Constitution Law of 11 October 1952 applying to the whole Federal Republic. This had been anticipated in the coal and iron and steel industries on 21 May 1951 by the 'Law on the participation of employees in the supervisory and administrative boards in the mining and iron and steel producing industries', which was later supplemented by the so-called Holding Law for companies which, on the basis of a parent/subsidiary relationship, controlled a company subject to the law of 1951.

These three measures—the Industrial Constitution Law (referred to in the following pages as the BVG), the Co-determination Law (MG) for firms in the mining and iron and steel industries and the Co-determination Supplementary Law (MEG)—form the current legal basis for the varying forms and degrees of co-determination.

(b) *The scope of co-determination*

The application of co-determination as laid down by law extends not only to the factory or establishment (i.e. any dependent economic unit which, according to the usual definition, pursues a commercial purpose through organised labour co-operation) but also to the firm which, as a legal and economic unit, makes the decisions on which business activity depends. Attempts to go beyond this to a so-called 'supra-factory participation' in such organisations as Chambers of Commerce and Industry, in which the unions, in particular, think there should be representation of both sides of industry, have not reached the statute book. A Weimar-style National Economic Council could not be established now, since its function would be regarded as the representation of the sectional interests of the economy as against those of the state in general.

Co-determination, defined as partnership and participation rights, embraces a range of social, personnel and economic matters and has its basis, irrespective of the legal form of the company, in the relevant provisions of the BVG. Thus, the BVG is basically valid for all firms under civil law, and also for companies in the mining and iron and steel industries and their parent companies, in so far as the stipulations of the Co-determination Supplementary Law (MEG), which will be mentioned later, do not apply in their case.

Co-determination in social (i.e. non-commercial) affairs (BVG Sec. 56 ff) is obligatory in all firms which have an industrial council (the membership of which will include at least five full-time elected employees) and, in personnel affairs (BVG Sec. 60 ff), in all firms employing more than twenty people. These forms of co-determination apply directly in the social sphere, in the production process and, in general, in relations between workers and management within the firm. They do not extend to what is here called 'economic co-determination', under which employees influence and participate in *business* decisions. 'The place for social and personnel decisions is the individual plant; economic decisions, on the other hand, are the business of the management of the firm.' (Dietz.)

'Economic co-determination' as exercised in industrial councils (BVG Sec. 72, paras. a, b and c) may still be regarded chiefly as the protection of social interests. Any direct influence on the economic decisions of a firm will derive from the appointment, obligatory in capital companies (as explained in (c) below, para. 3), of employee representatives to the supervisory board (*Aufsichsrat*) or, in the case of firms in the mining and iron and steel industries, to the administrative board (*Vorstand*) as well. Co-determination in social and personnel affairs aims at preserving the balance of interests within the firm, and is expressed in actions which influence the working conditions and the composition of the staff in the widest sense and only indirectly the organisation of the firm. Economic co-determination, on the other hand, involving the representation of employees on supervisory and administrative boards, can directly affect the organisation of the firm and thereby the legal structure of the company. So while there may be greater opportunities for co-determination to exercise its influence in individual instances in social and personnel affairs, it is in the economic sphere that its application is most significant and most hotly debated.

(c) *'Economic co-determination' under the Industrial Constitution Law and the Co-determination Laws*

It has already been mentioned that industrial councils, which are obligatory in all firms employing more than twenty people, have a co-determination competence in matters involving changes in company organisation. In addition, the introduction of new working methods are subject to the approval of the councils, in so far as these are not obviously relevant to national economic progress, as Sec. 72 of the BVG expresses it. There is provision for official arbitration in cases of dispute. Beyond this, the industrial councils have no direct rights of economic co-determination. Their competence lies predominantly in social and personnel affairs—something which is no longer a matter for argument. The BVG does, on the other hand, provide for other forms of economic co-determination—the economic committees which, according to Sec. 67, must be set up in all firms regularly employing more than 100 people and the appointment of employees to supervisory boards under rules which vary according to the type of firm, as outlined in the following paragraphs.

The economic committee consists of equal numbers of employee and employer representatives. It is set up for firms, not individual plants; all its members work in the firm. The industrial council appoints the employee representatives, the law providing that there must be at least one industrial council member for every four to eight committee members. This form of co-determination is designed to 'promote co-operation and full confidence between the industrial council and the firm and ensure an exchange of information in economic matters.' (BVG Sec. 67.) It is purely an expression of co-operation, not of real economic co-determination, since the economic committee is advisory only. Within this framework, production and work methods, rest periods and all operations 'which essentially touch upon the interests of the workers in the company' are discussed, so that the representatives of the employees may be given basic information. Here also an official arbitrator may be called in if conflict should arise on the committee's right to information on matters such as, for instance, the annual balance sheet. (BVG Sec. 70.)

More far-reaching in its effects (at least in principle) is the appointment of employee representatives to the supervisory boards of joint stock companies (AG), limited partnership companies issuing shares (KGaA), limited liability companies (GmbH) and mining law unions with independent legal personality. The last two types of company, and commercial and economic co-operative societies, are affected only if they employ more than 500 people. In addition, Sec. 77, para. 2 of the BVG specifies how the co-determination provisions of Sec. 76 apply to mutual insurance companies employing more than 500 people if they have a supervisory board. Joint stock companies (AG) which are family businesses, with all the shares held by one person or his close relatives, are not covered by these provisions if they employ fewer than 500 people.

Whenever employees are appointed to supervisory boards they account for one third of the total membership of the board. They are chosen by the universal, secret, equal and direct vote of all qualified employees of all units of the firm. (BVG Sec. 6.) The maximum number of supervisory board members which the articles may stipulate, under the new company law, may be nine, fifteen or twenty-one at most, according to the firm's basic capital; the minimum membership is three. An important provision is that, apart from at least two employees from the firm, two other persons, unconnected with the company and usually union members, may be elected to serve on the larger supervisory boards. Nevertheless, the minority position of the labour representatives on supervisory boards shows that there has been no true transfer of power in the companies subject to the BVG. The significance of the arrangement lies in the fact that a long-term claim to management co-determination has been staked at the supervisory level, with the prospect of winning mutual trust and co-operation between labour and capital and the opportunity of putting forward the legitimate wishes and demands of employees more directly and more effectively through their own representatives.

The influence of employees is much stronger under the co-determination laws applying to companies in the mining and iron and steel industries. In contrast to the so-called 'simple co-determination' of the BVG, these firms operate under 'equal co-determination', with labour representatives on the supervisory board being elected from the nominees of industrial councils and unions, in the same way as the representatives of the shareholders are elected by the general meeting. The supervisory board usually consists of eleven members but the membership rises to fifteen in larger firms with a basic capital of between DM 20 and 50 million and to twenty-one beyond that. The number of members representing labour and shareholders is always equal.

Two labour representatives are nominated by the industrial council after consultation with the unions, while the others are candidates of the senior union officials. It is laid down that one of the members elected by each side, labour and shareholders, should be non-partisan, but this requirement has little meaning in practice. It is obvious, however, that the choice of the eleventh member, with whom the other ten have to reach agreement, can be of decisive importance as it is usual for supervisory boards to reach their decisions by simple majority. The Co-determination Supplementary Law (MEG) lays down similar regulations for holding companies of the mining industry, including a complicated system of election.

It is obligatory in companies subject to the MG and MEG for a labour director to be appointed to the administrative board. His election must result not only, as with the other members of the board, from a simple majority in the supervisory board but from a majority of its labour members. (This rule does not apply to dominant companies in combines, where (under Sec. 13 of the MEG) the labour director is appointed by a simple majority of the supervisory board.) The labour director is not in principle legally responsible for the social and personnel matters that come before the board, but in practice this will often be his minimum sphere of influence. Taken all in all, the labour director, needing as he does the confidence of his staff, the industrial council and the unions, both for his appointment and for his work as an employer, has a delicate position. He must be a man of strong personality with a flair for negotiation.

The nature of supervisory and administrative boards into which the law has introduced employee representation has appreciably changed, especially in the case of mining companies. In the advisory economic committee, representatives of employees and management sit together, without affecting the legal constitution of the firm. A change, however, in the function of the bodies charged with supervision and administration under company law can cause changes in the law itself. This happens because the pattern of the law is essentially altered by the transfer of determinative rights to a group which, writes Dietz, 'lies outside the corporation and corporation matters ... (whose) activities will be determined by the will of its members'. Almost more significant is the fact, further indicated by Dietz, that the balance of decision

218

does not lie so much with 'the employees' as with 'labour'—the trade unions and their senior officials. 'The supervisory board has ceased to be the supervisory instrument of the owners and has become a parliament built into the AG, an organ which preserves the balance of opposing politico-economic interests.' (Würdinger.) However, the appointment of employee representatives is not seen by everyone as a break in the organisational pattern of company law. Vallenthin, for example, stresses that the supervisory boards should not be regarded merely as a shareholders' committee, and that even before the introduction of co-determination company law had already demanded of the directors that they should administer the firm in the way required by 'the well-being of the firm and those who belong to it'. The supervisory board is certainly the organ of the joint stock company in which co-determination fulfils its function; but the question doubtless arises whether 'economic co-determination' is not alien to the system, an objection often expressed in principle. Böhm has described it as 'a foreign element which explodes the bases of our constitutional order, within all branches of our law'. This, however, is only one point of view in a wide-ranging debate, summarised in the following section. (See also Appendix E.)

(d) *The debate on 'economic co-determination'*

'Equal co-determination' aims at enabling workers to extend their influence over the management of a firm. It is hardly surprising that argument on a matter of such basic social and political importance has not been limited to the parties immediately concerned. It is obvious that the extension of co-determination rights from the social and personnel field into the economic will trigger off a debate in which all those who have strong ideas on what represents a just social and economic policy and on the rights of property will take part.

The Institute of Trade Unions, commissioned by the Co-determination Foundation, has carried out an extremely interesting and useful study into the wealth of arguments deployed on either side. The findings of this very balanced and remarkably accurate survey are summarised in the following paragraphs.

Neo-marxists have little influence in the Federal Republic in the present economic and political circumstances. Their thinking is narrow and, as far as co-determination is concerned, they must 'either reject it because it camouflages the class struggle or welcome it as, at least, a step in the direction of socialism, if not towards the dictatorship of the proletariat'. (This line of argument will always attract a certain amount of support in any theoretical discussion on the 'better and more just ordering of society'.)

Social democratic thinking is much more important and now overwhelmingly supports the concept of economic co-determination, so long as ideas on the nature of property and the market continue to develop. There are, of course, varying shades of opinion in socialist circles, with the trade union attitudes towards the further development of economic co-determination being a predominant influence.

The churches have played an important part in the debate. During the discussions which preceded the Co-determination Law of 1951, which almost led to a government crisis, the Roman Catholics (at Bochum in 1949) and the Evangelicals (at Essen in the following year) came out strongly in favour. The evangelical attitude generally supports economic co-determination, although its first concern until recently has been with the relationship of the individual to his immediate work surroundings, without taking a stand on the actual problems of economic co-determination in the firm. Catholic social ideas are somewhat divergent. In some cases economic co-determination is rejected 'because it cannot be reconciled with the concept of the natural rights of property', in others it is plainly welcomed. Some Catholic writers limit their objections to the participation of union representatives. Suggestions made by the Federation of Catholic Businessmen (BKU) at its annual conference in the autumn of 1966, for the 'ordering of economic and social life', tend in another direction. While the chairman of a BKU study group emphatically rejected the wider union demands, he spoke at the same time of the opportunity which the BVG offers, in the opinion of the BKU, for an extension of co-determination within the firm or factory. He favoured a supplementary preamble to the BVG which would be chiefly concerned with the definition of the basic rights of factory workers and a widening of the obligation of management to provide economic information. He also proposed that the law should allow for the appointment of a personnel and social director in all firms of a certain size.

Similarly, many representatives of contemporary 'neo-liberalism', if they do not completely reject economic co-determination, make a sharp distinction between co-determination (in the sense of Sections 76 and 77 of the BVG) in the factory or plant and 'equal co-determination' in the firm. This school of thought regards the BVG type of co-determination as being compatible with the idea of two bodies equal and autonomous in civil law, undoubtedly 'an essential element conforming to the system of the market economy, of the company in civil law and of democracy'. (Böhm.) 'Equal co-determination', on the other hand, is seen as 'intervention without responsibility' and is forcibly condemned as being 'alien to the system'. Such objections must be taken seriously but Vallenthin is surely correct when he writes that 'the attempted use of formal systematic considerations to undermine co-determination in the supervisory board, which is a legal fact' means using 'theoretical speculation against political reality'.

The objections of the neo-liberal school will play an important part if the debate centres (as it has increasingly of late) on the more extreme demands of the unions. These are based on two propositions: that political equality, which is an essential principle of democracy, is not possible without economic equality; and that economic concentration, as a typical contemporary phenomenon, leads to concentrations of political power, in which the employees should share. The unions therefore demand the extension of economic co-determination by the establishment of 'equal' supervisory boards in all big companies and changes in the laws applying to Chambers of Commerce and Industry to provide for the formation of joint economic boards for 'supra-firm co-determination'. They also propose the setting up of a Federal Economic Council in which delegates of employers and of the unions would be represented, without any limitation of the autonomy of either side.

The debate on the reform of company law has been one of the main factors in stimulating discussion of union demands. More recently, however, two other important issues have led to fierce dispute on the unions' proposals for 'overall order', and particularly on the extension of economic co-determination. The political climate for a gradual extension of economic co-determination now seems rather more favourable; and the wage restraint policy now expected of the unions will need to be paid for, perhaps, in part, by wider rights of co-determination and also by improved disclosure.

Developments over the whole range of co-determination will also be affected by the long-drawn-out efforts to formulate a system of European company law.[122] The legal basis for employee participation varies considerably from one member state of the EEC to another, and it remains to be seen which of the concepts now being discussed (the harmonisation of national laws or the establishment of European companies under national or supranational laws) will finally be put into effect. It is clear, however, that the harmonisation of co-determination rights, and their incorporation in the administrative and supervisory organs of firms, will be extraordinarily difficult at Community level. Demands for co-determination and participation play a greater part in the Federal Republic than in the other EEC countries. Current negotiations under Art. 220, para. 3 of the EEC Treaty for an agreement which would make possible the merger of companies subject to the legal provisions of different countries (the so-called international merger) have already shown that the other member states, which do not, like Germany, have co-determination laws, find it impossible to take the German legislation into account. It appears that a solution on German lines is ruled out, and there is therefore a fear that, if and when international mergers do occur, German companies will be absorbed into foreign companies but not vice versa. A similar problem may be expected when it comes to the formation of a European company, since reincorporation would inevitably be necessary in other member states. The disadvantages for the Federal Republic are obvious, not least the danger that non-European firms would prefer to form subsidiaries elsewhere in the EEC. It is therefore to be hoped that the unions will see the whole question of co-determination in the light of these undeniable international problems and that they will make proposals calculated to ease progress towards this particular aspect of European unification.

ITALY

Employees have never been represented on the organs of Italian companies and no proposals for such representation have been made. It is true that Art. 46 of the Constitution lays down that 'to the end of the economic and social progress of labour and according to the needs of production, the Republic recognises the right of workers to co-operate, in the manner and within the limits fixed by law, in the management of firms'. Nevertheless, because of the

[122] It should be noted that this text was written before the publication of the Sanders proposals for a European company statute. (These are discussed in a paper in the joint Chatham House/PEP European Series, written by D. Thompson and published in 1969.)

fascist flavour that this clause still retains, it has been ignored by all the employees' organisations (apart from the neo-fascist CISNAL), which prefer to seek indirect solutions to their representation problems through the new national planning institutions. L. Mossa has been the only influential person to speak in favour of *impresa socializzata*.[123]

The general approach to problems of employee participation is to consider them as matters sharply distinguished from problems of company law. Company law regulates the position of shareholders as regards their participation in and control over the management of a company; but the activity of a company (or that of any other economic entity) is regulated according to the broader context of the *impresa*. This is where the problems of the employees' active participation in the economic process come in, but only as part of their contract of employment. Because of the distinction between company and enterprise organisation, it is easy to understand why Art. 46 of the Constitution is commonly held not to contemplate a right on the part of workers to co-determination of an activity but merely a contractual right to determine with their employers the conditions of work in the enterprise. If, therefore, there is no case in Italy for employee participation in a company's organisation, there has been a remarkable improvement in the workers' position in the enterprise. This has come about mainly through collective bargaining, especially since 1959 when an act of parliament laid down that individual collective agreements between employers' associations and unions could be made binding on all, even on non-members of the associations or unions, by government decree. By collective agreements for industry and commerce (in 1953 and 1958, respectively), it was established that in every enterprise having forty or more employees, the latter should elect a *Commissione Interna* to represent them before the management. (In enterprises with less than forty but at least six employees, there is a single employee representative.)

The main purpose of the *Commissioni Interne* is to 'co-operate in maintaining normal relations between employees and management . . . in a spirit of collaboration and reciprocal understanding for the normal exercise of the productive activity'. The management has therefore a duty to heed the proposals and suggestions of a committee in matters concerning such questions as the improvement of working conditions, internal regulations, holiday arrangements and shift variations. The introduction of the committees was strongly supported by the unions which are still firmly in control of them. The future trend, however, is likely to be for the unions to lose control over the election of committee members and for the more local interests of employees in any particular enterprise to become predominant. Such a trend would be encouraged by managements which (in state as well as private enterprises) would welcome a lessening of the unions' influence. Management in large enterprises is generally in favour of the committees but those of the smaller often try to persuade their employees not to set one up. The situation, however, differs widely from one sector to another; the steel industry, for instance, which is mostly in the hands of the state through IRI holdings, has

[123] See L. Mossa, *Trattato del nuovo diritto commerciale*, 4 vols., Milan, 1951–57.
NOTE. Since this text was written, a new debate on employee participation has begun, in great measure set off by a conjunction of workers and students.

very progressive attitudes, while the building contractors have so far succeeded in preventing the formation of committees.

The story of the *Commissione Interna* confirms how employee participation is seen in Italy as only one aspect of the broader contractual relations between employer and employee—a relationship more, as it were, of *Mitsprache* than *Mitbestimmung*. Reciprocal agreement, rather than legislation, is thought the best way to a solution. From a legal point of view, this means that employee participation is a particular aspect of the employment contract which (along with some of its other peculiarities) gives it perhaps the character of a *contratto d'organizzazione* (an *Organisationsvertrag*)—that is to say, a contract in which there is not only an obligation to do something, and receive money in exchange, but also for the employee to find a place within an organisation (the *impresa*). Also from the legal point of view, this implies, as already stated, that the problems of employee participation in an *impresa* must not be confused with those of employee participation in the structure of a company.[124]

Only one large corporation, Olivetti, has experimented with employee participation on the basis of democratic ideas. The Olivetti *consiglio di gestione* (management council) is composed of fifteen members: three are elected by blue-collar and three by white-collar employees, one by senior executives and one by all three together. The chairman of the company is also a member and six other members are chosen by him from employees or management. The council has full powers over the distribution of social welfare funds and must be consulted on a large number of questions, including production and plant planning; general policies on raw materials and the cost of services; measures to improve labour productivity; welfare organisation; and personnel policy and training. This experiment in limited co-determination is only one aspect of the general policy followed by the firm, inspired by the writings and thinking of its founder, Adriano Olivetti. Other achievements include the establishment of a publishing house; the publication of the magazine *Comunità*; the formation of a political party, the *Partito di comunità*, which returned a member to parliament at the 1958 elections; and the remarkable development of economic and social activities in the areas where Olivetti plants operate, particularly in the Ivrea region and northern Piedmont. The Olivetti experiment is the product of a very special way of looking at things. Although it may be considered a survivor of the many *consigli di gestione* set up soon after the war, it can hardly be seen as a forerunner of further developments in this direction. Indeed, since Olivetti's stock is now held by IRI, its

[124] For problems of employee participation as an aspect of contracts of employment, see: Santoro-Passarelli, *Nozioni di diritto del lavoro*, Naples, 1967 (especially pp. 30 ff concerning the *commissione interna*); Corrado, *Trattato di diritto del lavoro*, Vol. I, Turin, 1965; Persiani, *Contratto di lavoro e organizzazione*, Padua, 1966; Neufeld, *Labor Unions and National Politics in Italian Industrial Plants*, Cornell international industrial and labor relations report, Ithaca, NY, 1954; Ardau, 'Commissione interna di impresa', in *Noviss. dig. it.*, Vol. III, Turin, 1959, p. 642; Mancini, sub 'Commissione interna' in *Enciclopedia del diritto*, Vol. VII, Milan, 1960, p. 881; Mengoni, 'La rappresentanza dei lavoratori sul piano dell' impresa nel diritto italiano', in *La rappresentanza dei lavoratori sul piano dell' impresa nel diritto dei paesi membri della CECA*, Luxembourg, European Coal and Steel Community (Italian version), 1959, p. 255; Mengoni, 'Recenti mutamenti nella struttura e nella gerarchia dell' impresa', *Rivista delle società*, 1958, p. 689.

own policies will lose some of their influence as they become harmonised with the broader framework of the state holding company.

The practice which had grown up within companies of forming consultative bodies consisting of representatives of management and employees was finally given legal form in the Works Councils Act of 1950. The purpose of a works council is to contribute towards the best possible functioning of the company while recognising the independent entrepreneurial task of the employer. It has the following powers: to consider requests, complaints and observations from employees; to discuss holidays, working timetables, shift work, etc.; to ensure compliance with the terms of employment applicable within the company; to supervise the observation of legal safety regulations; and to advise on and make proposals for the technical and economic improvement of the operations of the company.

The head of the firm is bound to co-operate fully with the works council in the exercise of these powers and to provide it with all the information it may need. He is also obliged periodically to inform the council about the financial condition of the company. The Works Councils Act does not give employees a share in the taking of managerial decisions; the council's rights in this respect are limited to being kept informed about the affairs of the company and to discussing them.

A firm with twenty-five or more employees is bound under the Act to appoint a works council. The chief executive of the company is a member of the council and presides over its meetings. He may appoint another person to act in his place as chairman. The members of the council, with the exception of the chairman, are elected by those employees of the company who are entitled to vote. They are elected from one or more lists of candidates drawn up by whatever organisations of employees have been authorised for that purpose, which may include trade unions. In large firms it is often the practice, within the terms of reference of the works council, to appoint departmental advisory committees in consultation with department managers. These advisory committees are entrusted with specific questions relating to the departments concerned. Like the members of the works council, the committee members are elected from candidates nominated by the trade unions and also from uncommitted candidates. The members of the works council are in such circumstances drawn from representatives of these committees.

There are no regulations providing for the representation of employees as a group on the supervisory board, nor as yet any for giving the trade unions the right to represent their members within the company in matters of personnel policy. There are at present no shop stewards or trade union representatives within the company. (See below.)

The question of how employees as a group might be given more influence in the management of the company is now under discussion. This question divides into two topics: influence on the higher levels of management and a greater influence on the daily running of the firm. The debate has led to the appearance of numerous reports, articles and studies—from the trade unions, political parties, the employers and academics. It was this that prompted the government to set up the Verdam Committee to work out proposals for changes in the law.

The Verdam Committee has advised the government to introduce three new statutory provisions in this context. First, the Works Council Act should be supplemented to provide, *inter alia*, for the co-ordination of works councils and for obligatory consultation between councils and managements on the consequences for employees if firms move, are wound up or carry out mergers, or if production is substantially restricted or changed. Second, employees of quoted companies should (in the opinion of a bare majority of the Committee) be given power by law to appoint one or two representatives to the supervisory board. (The unions are not in favour of labour representatives on supervisory boards but have made other proposals which are outlined below.) Third, trade unions should have the same entitlement as shareholders to institute a legal enquiry if they suspect mismanagement.

Meanwhile, the trade unions are trying to get their own appointed delegates inside the company, to liaise with the employees' representatives on the works council (thus improving their own knowledge of conditions in the firm) and to be better able to represent their members' interests in connexion with internal personnel problems. Dutch industry is not familiar with the shop steward or trade union representative who, in the employ of the company, enjoys certain facilities, such as the right to visit departments and make use of meeting rooms and notice boards. Firms are hesitant on this question and have so far gone no further than giving union members in their employ paid leave of absence in order to attend a limited number of union meetings.

Dutch employers consider the first and third of the Verdam Committee's proposals to be acceptable in principle. They reject the second, partly because they feel the proposal would result in the supervisory board becoming an arena in which conflicts of interests between employees and shareholders would be fought out. Because the proposal would give the supervisory board considerably greater power over the management, the employers believe that such a conflict would hamper the conduct of the company's affairs.

The third proposal of the Verdam Committee, having been examined by the Social and Economic Council, formed the basis of a government Bill laid before parliament in May 1968. This Bill provides that central organisations of trade unions may, like shareholders under the present law, institute proceedings for the Court to order an enquiry into the affairs of a company by investigators appointed by the Court. (The Court would be the proposed *Ondernemingskamer* already mentioned on p. 173 above.) The Bill also provides for similar rights to be granted to holders of depositary receipts (see p. 196 above). Applicants for a Court order would have to prove there was reason for serious doubt as to the soundness of the management. If an investigation led to the conclusion that there had been mismanagement, the Court would be able to take far-reaching action, such as dismissing administrative or supervisory directors or quashing management decisions. The first proposal has been discussed in the Social and Economic Council, which, in a report in November 1968, proposed a strengthening of the role of the works council, especially in connexion with the points mentioned by the Verdam Committee.

The Social and Economic Council is still not yet in sight of agreement on the proposal for employee representation on the supervisory board. Two trade unions (the NVV and the NKV) first made public some new ideas submitted by labour representatives to the Council, showing that they were not in favour of employee representatives sitting on supervisory boards. They proposed instead that the decisive function of making binding nominations[125] for the appointment of supervisory board members should be given to the Social and Economic Council. On the basis of such a binding nomination, the actual appointment would be made by a committee on which employees and shareholders would be equally represented. This system was suggested for all companies with a works council. Another union (the CNV) then advocated employee representation on supervisory boards, with equal representation of capital and labour. (This, of course, was going further than the Verdam Committee.) In 1969, however, the three unions agreed upon a new proposal, envisaging (a) nomination of all members of the supervisory board by a special committee of shareholders and workers, equally represented, and (b) the appointment of all members by all shareholders and workers (the two groups having equal voting power). In respect of large companies the unions further propose that one or more members of the supervisory board be appointed on the basis of binding nominations made by the Economic and Social Council.

Employers' organisations have shown strong opposition to these new labour proposals, in part because they believe it would be extremely undesirable to give the power to make binding nominations to an advisory government body. Their counterproposal is that it should be made legally obligatory for nominations for appointments to the supervisory board to be discussed beforehand by the works council.

SWEDEN

Employee representation on the board or within other company organs has been a matter of debate in Sweden for a long time but until quite recently the desire to do anything about it did not seem much stronger than it was during the discussions on industrial democracy in the 1920s. Employers have always taken a negative attitude, on principle, while employees appear to be wary, particularly about the 'double loyalty' which representation on the board, for instance, might possibly involve. During 1968 and 1969, however, the debate has become keener and of greater overall political importance than perhaps ever before. The remarkable result has been a new willingness, in state-owned enterprises, co-operative companies and private firms, to put in hand practical experiments in various forms of industrial democracy (including employee representation at board level) without waiting for changes in the law. Support for the new ideas has been surprisingly wide; not only the Social Democrats but also leading members of the Liberal opposition have, for instance, advocated employee representation on company boards. The

[125] On 'binding nominations' see p. 197 above.

government, although naturally wishing the whole matter to be thoroughly discussed before it takes far-reaching steps, has already put forward a proposal for state representation on the boards of commercial banks. Perhaps most importantly, while the starting-point has been the question of the representation of employees, the debate has now widened into one on future company law and organisation in general and, in particular, on the roles of the different interests involved in a company and on whether these should be recognised by legislation. The attitude of the unions is still uncertain; on the other hand, it is clear that the debate has been invigorated and opinion widely affected by radical groups, including the students.

Section D: The Consumer

Are consumers adequately protected by market
forces and legislation? If not, in what ways do
(or could) consumers ensure that their interests
are safeguarded?

In recent years a great deal has been done in *Britain* to ensure the protection of consumers. None of this intervention is specifically limited to companies but applies to all manufacturers, wholesalers and retailers.

Following the report of the Molony Committee on Consumer Protection in 1963[126] the Consumer Council was set up, sponsored by the Board of Trade, to supplement the work of voluntary organisations such as the Consumers' Association founded in 1957. The Consumer Council describes itself as 'an independent national body financed by government grant'. Its job is to inform itself about consumer problems and matters affecting consumer interests, to promote action to deal with such problems and provide advice for the customer. The Council may not carry out comparative testing, take up complaints on behalf of individuals or engage in legal action; it concerns itself with what the consumer wants in his purchases of all types of goods and services. It publishes a monthly magazine, *Focus*, setting out reports on its investigations into various complaints and advising the public against various types of unscrupulous dealers and shoddy goods.

The Consumers' Association is a private organisation intended basically to protect the public against the supply of inferior quality goods. It, too, publishes a monthly magazine, *Which?*; this is sent to subscribers and reports on tests made on various types of goods and recommends particular goods as being reliable and value for money.

Legislative intervention in the area of consumer protection is increasing. The Sale of Goods Act 1893 was designed to codify the law relating to sale and sets out the basic obligations owed by a seller of goods for the buyer as to title, quality and fitness for the purpose. However, this Act does not represent an obligatory code of duties. It is entirely voluntary and the parties are free to amend or exclude the duties as they see fit. This aspect of the statute has been severely criticised since the rise of mass production and monopolistic organisations. The buyer is no longer free to negotiate his terms, he is faced with a standard form contract which deprives him of all or many of his rights under the Act, and he must accept these terms if he wishes to purchase the goods. This area of consumer protection is at present being reviewed by the Law Commission with a view to strengthening the position of the consumer.

Hire purchase legislation, being later than the Sale of Goods Act, deals with these problems a little more specifically.[127] The obligations of the seller of goods cannot always be excluded, and where exclusion is permitted this is on condition that it is shown to the prospective hirer and its effect explained to him. The Board of Trade have made regulations as to the printing of hire-purchase forms. In an attempt to protect the public against the high-pressure

---

[126] Cmnd 1781. [127] See the Hire Purchase Act 1965.

door-to-door salesman, a hirer of goods is allowed a four-day period within which he may repudiate the transaction, provided that it did not take place on trade premises.

In December 1968 the Trade Descriptions Act came into force. This makes it a criminal offence to offer goods for sale under a false or misleading trade description. This replaces and extends the provisions of the Merchandise Marks Acts and imposes a penalty upon any supplier of goods who describes the goods, their constituents, the process of manufacture, or the price in such a way as to deceive the public. In addition to this, the Weights and Measures Act 1963 controls the accuracy of instruments of measurement, and the Food and Drugs Act 1955 establishes certain standards of quality of food to prevent adulteration and mislabelling of food. An inspectorate has been established to ensure that these Acts are observed and is a branch of local government. Although these Acts provide only criminal sanctions the Sale of Goods Act and the Hire Purchase Act provide a fairly wide area of civil remedies for the buyer and the Misrepresentation Act 1967 now enables a purchaser to repudiate a contract and to claim damages in cases of negligent misstatements by a seller of goods.

One point about the civil remedies is that generally they are available only against the seller of goods who may not be the manufacturer. However, the Common Law in *Donoghue v. Stevenson*[128] provides the consumer with a remedy against the negligent manufacturer of defective goods. This duty on the manufacturer differs from that imposed upon the seller of goods. The latter is absolutely liable for selling defective goods, that is he is bound to compensate the buyer even though he did not know and could not reasonably be expected to know the defects, whereas the buyer can claim against the manufacturer if he can show that the manufacturer did not take reasonable care to see that the goods were sound. However, the duty of the manufacturer extends to persons other than the purchaser, and covers people such as members of the buyer's family who are injured by the goods and, under certain circumstances, to the general public, whereas the seller of goods is liable only to the purchaser.

Apart from hire purchase,[129] advertisers are free from legal restraint, although the Trade Descriptions Act 1968[130] applies to persons who publish misleading advertisements in the ordinary course of their business. The government has prohibited the advertising of cigarettes on television, but other matters at present are under the control of the Independent Television Authority which sets certain standards for television advertising. However, the Advertising Association is a professional body which has been established to maintain standards in the public interest.

The nationalised industries all have, as part of their constitutions, consumer consultative committees to receive and investigate complaints made by consumers of the products or services of these industries. They have been criticised as being captive bodies in that they are not elected but are appointed either by the appropriate Minister or the Chairman of the Committee who is himself

[128] [1932] A.C. 562.
[129] Advertisements (Hire Purchase) Act 1957.
[130] Sec. 25.

appointed. Moreover, they do not have the expert assistance that is sometimes necessary for a complaint to be investigated adequately. They receive a very small number of consumer complaints. For example, it was stated in the 1967–8 annual report of the Domestic Coal Consumers' Council that only forty-six complaints had been received, as compared with fifty-six in the previous year. This reduction was attributed to the introduction of an Approved Coal Merchants Scheme. In the context of the National Coal Board's millions of customers these figures could be interpreted as representing a high level of consumer satisfaction. Less optimistically it suggests that the public is not only unaware of the function of these committees, but also ignorant of their existence.

Loosely connected with the area of consumer protection where there has been intervention by Parliament are the fields of monopolies and restrictive practices. To some extent these have been outlawed by the Restrictive Trade Practices Act, the Monopolies and Mergers Acts, and the Resale Prices Act, in an attempt to keep a competitive element to increase the quality of goods and services.

The poor organisation of consumers in *France* has already been mentioned (see p. 104) and so far very little has come of the consumer movement. A small group of employers, the Union of Heads of Business—Action for Human Organisations (UCE-ACT), seems to have given the matter some thought. 'A fruitful idea would appear to be to make "associated consumers" bear a part of the risks of the firm (under some such title as a consumers' co-operative) by giving them the responsibility of settling the economic policy to be followed (how much to produce and buy), while a "labour company" (which might be called a workers' partnership), under the responsibility of capable workers, would have the task of deciding the means of action (how to do the work). The "associated consumers" would have to guarantee the workers a fair remuneration and a degree of continuity.'[131]

There have been only two achievements of any importance in this area. First, the consumers' co-operatives, which nevertheless represented no more than 2·5 per cent of the turnover of French commerce in 1960. These are tending more and more to become complete distribution networks and even manufacturers. Second, there is the case of the nationalised industries. René Capitant has written: 'Parliament has established the principle that the nationalised industries should not be run purely by the state but that their management should involve the double participation of workers and users. Hence the tripartite composition of the administrative boards of public enterprises, composed of equal numbers of representatives of the state, the employees and the users. However, the ideal has not been realised. In fact, the prerogatives of the administrative board have been continually whittled away and executive powers more and more concentrated in the hands of a single general manager, who is a representative of the state. In this way, the very type of state management that people flattered themselves they had done away with has been reintroduced.' (It should be added that the state has often

[131] UCE-ACT, *Structures humaines dans l'entreprise et dans l'économie*, CREE Document No. 1021.

seized the opportunity of having its 'own' men nominated as consumer representatives.) Professor Georges Lasserre has proposed another solution for involving consumers, by forming joint companies with capital participation by both the state and the users. He notes that the Compagnie Nationale du Rhône had something like this form when it was first set up.

At the political level, both main groups (the present government and the 'socialist' opposition) are at one in supporting the better organisation of consumers. From the government's point of view, this would be a way of keeping a check on prices. Speaking for the other side, Claude Bruclain, in his book *Le Socialisme et l'Europe*, says: 'In the modern socialist conception, a whole range of democratic groups should lie between the state and the market—co-operatives, consumer groups, cultural organisations, trade unions, etc.'[132]

The main French consumer organisations are comparatively new and have little power. The UFC (Federal Consumers' Union) was formed in 1951 and has no more than 5,000 individual members, while 20,000 others have gone to it for information without becoming members. ORGECO (General Consumers' Organisation) was founded in 1959; its magazine *Information-Consommation* has a circulation of 35,000. As far as national planning is concerned, consumers are represented by the National Consumers' Committee but this began to function regularly only a very few years ago. The government has now set up a National Consumers' Institute (see p. 104) which will have the threefold task of providing general information through the media of television, radio and the press on the problems of advertising, consumer credit, labelling, etc.; supervising advertising and public relations; and conducting comparative tests of products on the market. This institute, aided by a state subsidy, should be able to give the consumers' organisations the information and resources that they require.

Three types of legislation exist for the protection of the consumer in France. First, regulations about advertising. These concern the marking of products, the display of the price of the products or services offered and the truthfulness of various forms of 'advertising', with regard to (for instance) 'net price', reductions, rebates and 'sales'. Second, constraints imposed on retailers to protect the consumer where the latter is not in a position to protect himself. These measures include the suppression of restrictions on free competition (e.g. a prohibition of refusal to sell), the setting of obligatory prices or margins, and the prohibition of price maintenance. Third, regulations to protect the consumer against his own foolishness or inexperience or the sharp practice of others. Examples are the regulation of credit, the prohibition of gift coupon sales or reselling at a loss and the limitation of sales by unrequested postal delivery. There is even talk of limiting door-to-door sales.[133]

In *Italy*, although consumer co-operatives are allowed by legislation, under the general terms of Art. 45 of the Constitution, the question of consumer representation within the company has never been considered.

[132] C. Bruclain, *Le socialisme et l'Europe*, Paris, Editions du Seuil, 1965.
[133] 'Les consommateurs, peuvent-ils se défendre ?', *Information-Consommation* ORGECO, April 1966.

Nor have there been any proposals for consumer representation within the company in the *Netherlands*. Outside the company, however, various consumer organisations have a fairly considerable and still growing influence, partly as a result of their publications on the quality of manufactured products.

Consumer protection, by the exercise of influence within the organisation of the company, is regarded in *Sweden* as mainly of academic interest. It is generally assumed that it should be taken care of by 'outside' influences and by various kinds of consultation between consumer representatives and business. The organisation of consumer information in Sweden is mainly undertaken by the government and business organisations, with the main stress on long-range 'education'. There has so far been no evidence of any wish on the part of consumers to become involved in management decisions. There are no legal forms for the representation of consumers in manufacturing companies. It may be mentioned, however, that in insurance companies the government appoints two board members whose special responsibility is to attend to the interests of the policy-holders. (See p. 237.)

Section E: The Public Interest

*Should the public interest be represented with-
in private enterprises? If so, how?*

BELGIUM

The belief held by many Belgian scholars that the 'company community institution' (see pp. 69–71) is a plural reality has led to the conclusion that this plurality must be expressed in one general purpose. All these authors attribute a 'public' purpose to the company because the company influences the community: decisions are made and results obtained that leave their mark upon society. Society therefore has counter-claims: it wants the company to serve the common good, its 'collective conscience' no longer accepts that the company should have no other goal than profit, without a care for the public or general good. The company's service is thus measured against a general objective common to all who, from within or without, contribute to the well-being of the company; this objective is the 'common good'.[134]

In whatever way such a 'common good' might be generally defined, its observation has been ensured by the introduction of government controls and many forms of public intervention. Apart from the classical instruments of socio-economic policy and present-day economic planning, various alternative measures have been tried in Belgium. These include nationalisation and the formation of exclusively public enterprises (of little actual importance); enterprises with mixed public and private capital; temporary (and mostly minority) shareholdings by the Nationale Investeringsmaatschappij (National Investment Company), which is itself a mixed enterprise; government control (the Coal Industry Directorate); and control on a basis of equal representation of the parties concerned (the Gas and Electricity Agreement). Some of these arrangements have already been discussed in Part I, Chapter 2 of this book. (See pp. 58–61.) There are also special measures to protect the public in particular sectors such as banking and mutual funds, where the *Commission Bancaire* plays an important supervisory role. (See p. 177.)

There is now a trend to bring in certain new measures (some already discussed in earlier sections of this Chapter), such as legislation for the harmonisation of accounting procedures and for the publication of annual accounts; reform of the law concerning *reviseurs d'entreprises* (auditors); government participation in the supervisory and executive organs of the company, jointly with the workers and the owners of capital; and the formation of an economic magistracy.

BRITAIN

The function of the law in relation to a company's 'responsibilities' to the country as a whole has been in general to encourage rather than compel it to act in certain ways in order to achieve specific economic ends. Thus, exports are encouraged by the Export Guarantees Acts 1945 to 1967 which authorise

---

[134] See Baron Boel, 'L'entreprise privée, catalyseur de progrès', *Industrie*, No. 9, 1964, p. 593; and also p. 142 above.

the Board of Trade to guarantee payment for exports up to £2,000 million in aggregate at any one time. To achieve a similar end the government recently requested bankers to give priority in making loans to firms engaged in exporting. The Capital Allowances Act 1968 is designed to encourage firms to modernise, and enables them to set off against income or corporation tax capital expenditure on scientific research, industrial buildings and machinery and plant. To deal with the problem of regional unemployment incentives are offered for businesses to be set up or expand in 'development areas' by the Local Employment Acts 1960 and 1965, as amended by the Industrial Development Act 1966.

However, the Prices and Incomes Act 1966 has been a step towards compulsion in the area of public responsibilities of manufacturers. The power of the government to refer proposed price increases to the National Board for Prices and Incomes, and to create a standing review of some prices, for investigation as to whether the increases are in the national interest, as well as the power to stop a proposed increase, means that private enterprise is now under a general duty to adjust prices in the national interest as well as profit for the company.

On the other hand it has been recognised for some time that nationalised industries are not governed solely by the same responsibilities as private companies. In addition to their ordinary economic and commercial obligations, they have responsibilities of a national and non-commercial kind. Their plans for development and capital expenditure are discussed with the government, and in fixing their prices they must give weight to the considerations of the national interest brought to their attention.[135]

The power of companies to make direct contributions to charities and political parties depends upon their objects clause and the *ultra vires* rule which requires expenditure to be for the benefit of the company. Under the 1967 Act[136] contributions exceeding in aggregate £50 must be disclosed in the directors' report.

There have been few attempts in England to analyse the responsibilities of a company to the country as a whole, but several people have attempted to show that the relationship of a company to the nation is an important consideration for directors.[137] Several industrialists have attempted to show how a company fulfils any responsibilities which it may have. One common view is that a company fulfils such responsibilities by acting in its own self-interest, for, as the late Charles Wilson, one-time President of General Motors, succinctly put it: 'What is good for General Motors is good for America.' Sir Reay Geddes, the Managing Director of the Dunlop Company, has given a more detailed statement of how a company fulfils its responsibilities in his address 'An Approach to the Philosophy of Company Law'.[138] He pointed out that a company does so by supplying a product people want, by creating

---

[135] *The Financial and Economic Obligations of the Nationalised Industries* (1961), Cmnd 1337.
[136] Sec. 19.
[137] See for example Percy, *The Unknown State* (1944) and Goyder, *The Future of Private Enterprise* and *The Responsible Company*.
[138] Given to the Institute of Bankers on 20 March 1967.

jobs, by paying about half its profits to the state, by collecting taxes from individuals and generally adding to the economic life of the community; secondly, by subscribing money to causes to which it attaches importance; and thirdly, by allowing employees to take part in community activities.

Some object to the method of fulfilling responsibilities outlined by Sir Reay Geddes, because it allows too much power to the directors to do what *they* consider to be in the national interest. It has been argued that it is not a sufficient justification to say that the company supplies a product people want, since such a product may involve a wasteful use of scarce resources. It may be produced solely for the domestic market although the raw materials have to be imported on a large scale. Moreover, it is said, the directors should not be free to donate money to causes which they regard as important since these may be detrimental to the national interest. On the other hand, it seems that to impose obligations such as these on a company would inevitably involve a great deal of government intervention and be a serious threat to private enterprise and initiative.

Any codification of the 'responsibilities' of companies to the country as a whole would surely be impossible, since these 'responsibilities' are too un-certain and too varied. Moreover, it may reasonably be argued that, in general, companies do act in a responsible way, so that codification is un-necessary, unless drastic departures from modern business practice are thought desirable. A blanket clause, such as 'The company shall have regard to the public interest', would avoid the need to specify these 'responsibilities' but would be unsatisfactory for other reasons. The 'public interest' is a highly un-certain and by no means immutable concept, particularly when applied to economic conditions, and the ordinary courts would not be qualified to apply it. It may be asked whether there is one single national interest or a variety of competing interests for various sections of the community. Sceptics may wonder whether the 'national interest' might not be equated with the interests of the group predominant in power at a given moment—the political counter-part of the 'General Motors' argument. Again, since companies are managed by their directors and many directors genuinely believe (with Charles Wilson) that what is good for their company is good for the country, a blanket 'public interest' clause would probably not affect the usual outlook and behaviour of firms. Finally, the scope of directors' duties is already uncertain; a blanket clause of this tenor would add to the uncertainty and make it more difficult for members to control their directors.

FRANCE

Generally speaking, the public interest is not directly represented in the French firm. In actual fact, it is very heavily protected by the expedient of the traditional 'controlling' methods of French administration. (See above, p. 169, and also p. 83 for 'planning contracts'.) Employers continually com-plain that the administration starts by prohibiting everything and then makes individual exceptions. The most recent topical example has been the price freeze. (See p. 104 above.) Such control is particularly effective when implemented by such expedients as subsidies, the controlled movement of foreign capital and the granting of credits from FDES (Economic and Social Development Fund) and other public or semi-public credit organisations. All government decisions and controls must be guided by the Plan, which is prepared in collaboration with the various economic interests concerned and approved by parliament.

The supervision already exerted in the public interest by the state is such that it probably has not been thought necessary to introduce it into the firm itself. Some proposals have, however, been made to this end. Bloch-Laîné's suggestion of giving a government commissioner or magistrate acting powers has already been mentioned on p. 188 above. (There is already a government commissioner for the banking sector.) The CJP suggested in 1962 the appointment of a 'professional' administrative director. 'We believe that this supervision should be entrusted not to ill-prepared civil servants, nor to bank representatives, but to delegates of "professional" organisations such as have recently been set up. In our opinion, every quoted company employing more than 500 people (including the payroll of subsidiaries) or having a pre-tax turnover of more than 30 million new francs or a capital (including reserves) of more than 10 million francs, should include in its administrative board a director from the appropriate industrial sector who would have power first to "observe", then to "object" and finally to "veto".'[139]

ITALY

The Italian debate on the representation and protection of the public interest is lively—somewhat more so, in fact, than that on the relationship of the firm to employees and (a fortiori) consumers. The ways in which the state operates in the economic field and particularly how it participates as a shareholder in private concerns has already been described in Part I, Chapter 2 (see pp. 64–65 above). In another sense, the protection of the public interest is the aim of special legislation applying to certain economic sectors or classes of firm such as banking and insurance. These questions are not discussed in the company law reform draft, though opinion is by and large in favour of the introduction of special rules for companies controlled by the state or by a public authority.

THE NETHERLANDS

Dutch law makes no provision for the appointment to company organs of persons representing the public authorities. A minority of the Verdam Committee did favour new legislation making it possible to appoint supervisory directors in the public interest. Some people would like to see it laid down by law that supervisory directors, in the exercise of their duties, should take the public interest into account. The Verdam Committee thought that these matters should be included in the general definition of the duties of a supervisory director. It proposed the following text (in Art. 50, paras. 2 and 3 of the draft Bill): 'It shall be the task of the supervisory directors to supervise the management's conduct of the company's operations and the general

[139] CJP study paper, CREE Document No. 58.

course of business. They shall assist the management with advice. The articles of association may define the duties of supervisory directors in more detail. The management shall be bound to provide the supervisory directors in due time with the information they need in the exercise of their duties. Within the limits of the public interest, the supervisory directors shall carry out their duties on behalf of the company's interests as a whole and of the enterprises associated with it.' Various objections have been raised to the inclusion of this subject in the general definition of supervisory directors' duties, particularly because the term 'the public interest' is felt to be too vague and capable of widely differing interpretations.

SWEDEN

Apart from the comparatively few companies owned by the state or a municipality, the Swedish public has so far made no demands for any direct influence on manufacturing firms and has been content to rely on the effects of legal and economic measures concerning the conditions of competition. The social democrats have always considered that it would disturb the existing equilibrium if the community—apart from its own enterprises and its strong arsenal of instruments for economic policy—were to have a direct influence over privately owned companies. The question, however, has recently become more immediate because public loan capital has been placed at the disposal of industry for relocation and to ease and accelerate structural change in certain vulnerable sectors. There are also, of course, Swedish proponents of socialisation in the sense that the community should take over the ownership of certain industries and thereby supersede the former owners' exclusive right to make decisions. The only example of the actual representation of the public interest is the appointment of government representatives to the boards of insurance companies (see above, page 232).

Section F: The Location of Interest Representation

How far is a board of directors (in any existing or proposed form) an appropriate site for the representation of the interests considered in this chapter? If it is thought inadequate, in what other way could these interests influence firms?

In *Belgium*, apart from family owned companies where the board constitutes a body truly representative of the shareholders, the board of directors is usually representative only of the controlling shareholder(s). As pointed out under Section B, pp. 178–179, this situation can to some extent be improved by providing for proportional representation of shareholders on the board, thus giving a voice to the interests of minority shareholders. Employees are not represented on the board of directors and the company law reform committee has not proposed any changes in this direction. (A government Bill, which never became law, was tabled in 1947 providing for the election of at least two members of the board of directors from among the company personnel. See above, p. 20.) Many lawyers feel that employees should not be represented on the board of directors but in special organs in which they could better negotiate and bargain with the employer than on the board. At company level this has been, to some extent, achieved through works councils. (See above, p. 202.)

The position in *Britain* is as follows. The representation of inside interests. that is to say the interests of shareholders, are found in the meetings required to be held by the Companies Acts,[140] and in the power of one tenth of the shareholders to requisition an extraordinary general meeting.[141] At present, however, there is no formal arrangement for the location within a private enterprise company of outside interests. Neither the employees, consumers nor the public authority are accepted as yet as having any right of internal representation. But the feeling is growing in certain quarters that there should be some machinery to represent such interests. For examples, a few of the proposals for worker-representation suggest that it should take the form of a supervisory committee of some sort related to the German *Aufsichsrat*. Other proposals appear to prefer such representation to take place on the board of directors. The Industrial Expansion Act 1968 provides money to be used to finance the development of industries and to improve their efficiency. It does not, however, establish any requirement that the government are in any way represented on the board. Presumably the public interest in such an investment will be protected by the negotiations between the Industry Board and the company.

Creditors of a company are outsiders and are not formally represented in the company's government. Financial factors to some extent serve to protect their interests and in the last resort they have power to wind up the com-

[140] 1948 Act Sections 130 (the statutory meeting to report on the details of the flotation of the company) and 131 (the annual general meeting).
[141] 1948 Act Sec. 132.

pany.[142] A creditor who has taken a debenture may have the power to appoint a receiver and manager to replace the board of directors. But such representation of creditors' interests does not exist whilst the company is a going concern.

The nationalised corporations make limited provision for consumer representation through the consumer consultative committees. These bodies have been attacked as being too closely linked with the corporation[143] and for other reasons mentioned on pp. 229–230. It seems that, in practice, they operate as little more than a channel of communication between consumers and the nationalised industries.

Public corporations are required by their constitutions to pay attention to the safety and welfare of their employees and have also established negotiating machinery with the trade unions, as outlined by Professor Hugh Clegg in his *Nationalisation and Industrial Democracy* (1951). Professor Clegg also comments on the fact that these public corporations are obliged to have works committees, which in private industry would be left to the goodwill of the proprietors.

As far as the location of representation of the two kinds mentioned here is concerned, in the nationalised industries they may be described as being advisory to the 'line management' and no more. The public interest is represented through parliamentary control and the power exercised by the appropriate Ministers over the various boards.

Various proposals have been made in *France* for putting shareholders and workers on an equal footing for the purpose of supervising the management. The part of the Capitant Amendment which did not go through (allowing for joint meetings between the supervisory board and the works council), and also the fact that two members of the works council may attend administrative board meetings in a consultative capacity, have already been mentioned. (See pp. 190 and 208 ff above.)

The employers are hostile to employees being brought in at decision-making level. In Maurice Hannart's opinion,[144] 'The board should consist only of members appointed by the general meeting, to the exclusion, therefore, of all employees of the company as such. Any other arrangement would be bound to lead to a confusion of responsibilities.' Even the CJP, who have proposed a half-way solution, are at bottom equally firm. 'We accept the representation of labour in administrative boards, up to half the number of members, with the Chairman having for all purposes a weighted vote equal to the labour votes. . . . But we reject the proposal that a firm's own employees should join the board. In this way the mistake of allowing the participation of the works council in the administrative board would be remedied. Such participation is neither its proper job nor its proper responsibility.'[145]

ACADI has indirectly associated itself with M. Capitant's proposal by

---

[142] 1948 Act Sections 222–224.
[143] Professor J. A. G. Griffith (1950), *Political Quarterly*.
[144] Hannart, op. cit. (see footnote 49, p. 151).
[145] CJP study paper, CREE Document No. 58.

suggesting an 'examination committee' composed partly of employee representatives or of experts chosen by employees, the labour representation varying according to the sector of industry and its 'technical and financial structure'.[146] This committee would express opinions that would be laid before the shareholders' general meeting. The management committee proposed by François Sommer[147] appears to be very much under the control of the management of the firm. It would have between ten and thirty members, two thirds of whom would be appointed by the management and the other third elected by the employees, divided into two electoral colleges. The employees would vote two candidates for each post and the management would decide which should serve on the committee.

On the union side, the CFTC has suggested[148] 'a joint committee of eight to twelve members which would consist of equal numbers of representatives appointed by the administrative board and the works council'. An original proposition of J. Dubois[149] should also be mentioned. He suggests that there should be set up in every 'commercial' company employing more than 500 people a 'general supervisory office' dependent only on the general management. This 'office' would have powers to investigate any question at all times and at all levels of the firm. All its functions would be carried out by a 'commissioner' appointed by the works council, to which reports would be made.

The whole question is now in the melting-pot, as part of the wide-ranging debate on 'participation' sparked off by the Spring crisis of 1968. New proposals by M. Capitant, in his capacity as Minister of Justice, have caused a great stir among the employers. (See Section C above, *passim*.)

In theory, under the new *German* law, power resides with the annual general meeting to determine the disposal of profits, to dismiss members of the administrative or supervisory boards, to change the articles of association, to increase or decrease the capital, or even to dissolve the company. The increased influence of the meeting as regards both profits disposal and the creation of reserves dates only from 1967, when the law came into force. There are, in addition, increased safeguards against the use of proxy and multiple voting rights.

The supervisory board has important controlling powers over the conduct of the company and its management, with a clear division of responsibility between it and the administrative board, although in practice this distinction is sometimes a little blurred. For instance, in a subsidiary 'in many cases the administrative board of the dominant company is represented by one of its members on the supervisory board of the dependent company'. (Würdinger.)

The supervisory board now has power to determine the kind of business that the company may undertake, although the administrative board may get unwelcome decisions overruled by a vote at the general meeting—an

---

[146] 'De quelques problèmes relatifs à l'entreprise', *Bulletin de l'ACADI*, No. 191, June 1964.

[147] F. Sommer, *Au-delà du salaire*, Robert Laffont.

[148] J. Tessier in *Travail et Methodes*, February 1966.

[149] Dubois, op. cit. (see footnote 50, p. 151).

unlikely eventuality. The supervisory board can also, if necessary, summon the general meeting, scrutinise the annual report and accounts before publication, represent the company at law and approve the granting of credit to administrative directors, senior managers and its own members. It has a minimum membership of three, elected by the general meeting; its size depends upon the capital of the company. The number of members should be divisible by three, though this rule does not apply to the mining and iron and steel industries where the laws of co-partnership apply. No individual may hold more than ten seats on different supervisory boards, of which five do not count towards the maximum if they are on the boards of subsidiaries. No member may now be a legal representative of a subsidiary or of another company to which one of his directors belongs.

The administrative board is now obliged to report policy and management decisions to the supervisory board, to disclose the return on capital, as well as turnover and other key facts, and any dealings which affect the stability of the business. No single member of the supervisory board may be left in ignorance of any matter that could influence the company's situation.

The traditional *Italian* attitude to the question of the location of interest representation, which seeks a balance of power between shareholders' meeting, board of directors and *collegio sindacale* (the supervisory organ), is retained in the reform draft. However, the draft proposes a strengthening of the position of the *collegio sindacale* to make up for the diminished influence of the shareholders' meeting. Art. 23 provides that the chairman of the *collegio* should be chosen by the Court (or by the public authority proposed for the supervision of quoted companies in Art. 33 of the draft) and lays down qualifications and limitations aimed at guaranteeing the independence of the *sindaci vis-à-vis* the management. The introduction of external supervision by a public authority (see Chapter 4, p. 278 below) would also give renewed authority to the shareholders' meeting.

Those in *the Netherlands* who consider it necessary for the interests of certain groups to be represented in company decision-making think the supervisory board is the most suitable place. The bare majority of the Verdam Committee suggested, for example, that the interests of employees might be represented by appointing one or more employees to the supervisory board. A few members of the Committee also suggested that the public interest might be represented through the supervisory board. (See pp. 225 and 236 above). It is widely held, however, that members of the supervisory board should not represent distinct interests, since this might easily lead to division and dissension on the board and thus to the undermining of its authority.

Swedish discussion on both the 'supervisory function' and the location of interest representation has been to some extent influenced by the German two-board system but any use of the latter as a model for Swedish practice would now appear to be out of the question, since the basic idea was discarded during the committee work on the current Companies Act. There is now a tendency to regard professional management as having the role of a 'contractor', running the enterprise at the behest of the most interested participants. These interests might therefore be enabled to exercise their influence through an indirectly recruited assembly of representatives, mainly with advisory functions, but with the authority to appoint, for a long term of office, the executive management. The whole question has, however, recently become the subject of vigorous debate, as mentioned on p. 226 above.

Chapter 3

PARTLY OR QUASI-INDEPENDENT UNITS
OF THE FIRM

*What kind of control, formal or informal, is
exercised by companies over their own divisions
and subsidiaries and over other firms? How far
do such 'subordinates' pursue objectives distinct
from those of the organisation which controls
them? How are their chief executives and their
structure of interest representation affected by
their subordination? What has the law to say
about these matters—and should it say more?
What of the 'multinational' corporation?*

BELGIUM

A number of financial groups exercise control over key industries of the
Belgian economy by various forms of shareholding and financial participation. It is the aim of these groups to wield financial control over a number of
firms in a single or in a narrow range of industrial activities. The enterprises
concerned retain considerable independence in matters of investment, production, marketing and personnel policy. The holding companies do not
usually interfere with the research activities of the firms under their control.

The overall policies of the financial groups have been severely criticised in
recent years, particularly for the conservatism demonstrated by investment
in traditional industries producing semi-manufactured goods and a lack of
interest in sectors of high technology. The holdings are also accused of showing little enthusiasm for the promotion of national economic objectives and
of being unwilling or unable to collaborate with the government for these
ends. It is not always properly understood that the main concern of the holding companies is maintain and strengthen their financial control rather than
to direct the actual operations of the companies under their sway. There is,
moreover, a good deal of secrecy about their structure and the extent of their
power and influence. This is a particularly sensitive point at a time when there
is widespread demand for greater publicity about the activities of firms.

Some changes are, however, now becoming evident. The holding companies are beginning to take more interest in scientific research and in its co-ordination and also in more advanced industrial activities such as nuclear energy, electronics, precision engineering and chemicals. They are providing rather more information about their activities. They are simplifying their structure by eliminating the maze of indirect holdings and are collaborating more closely than in the past with government agencies.

In the 1950s the FGTB (the socialist trade union organisation) put forward proposals for transferring the powers held by the financial groups to the state, either by direct nationalisation of key sectors of the economy or by arrangements that would ensure that the groups co-ordinated their activities with national planning.[1] These proposals came to nothing, partly because of insufficient parliamentary support and partly because the FGTB shifted its own position. (See Appendix A.) The Christian trade union body (the CSC) believes that a number of steps could be taken to compel the groups to have proper regard for national objectives. It has advocated[2] that specialised and industrial holding companies should be encouraged to set up stronger vertical and/or horizontal autonomous industrial concentrations and that the power and influence of the government on the policies of the groups should be strengthened by, for instance, the establishment of a supervisory institution, not unlike the Banking Commission; the involvement of the groups in government economic planning; and by government capital participation in private enterprises. (The CSC also calls for changes in the management structure of companies (e.g. a tripartite board, as mentioned on p. 203); restrictions on the number of directorships held by one person; and more obligatory publicity.)

An official committee on the financing of economic expansion has been charged by the government to work out proposals regarding the participation of holding companies in national economic, financial and scientific planning; the appointment of *reviseurs d'entreprises* (recognised auditors) in every holding company; and better disclosure concerning their activities for the benefit of investors.

BRITAIN

Under English law Company A is the subsidiary of Company B if Company B is a member of Company A and either controls the composition of its board of directors, or if Company B holds more than half in nominal value of Company A's equity share capital, or if Company A is the subsidiary of a company which is itself the subsidiary of Company B.[3] If a company is not a subsidiary within this definition, then the sole obligation[4] of a company holding shares in another is to disclose in its accounts if it holds more than one tenth or more of either the nominal value of all the shares or any class of shares of that company, the name of the company and its country of incorporation, and details of the shares held.

[1] *Holdings et démocratie économique*, Liège, FGTB, 1956, pp. 203–206.
[2] *Onderneming en syndicalisme*, Brussels, CSC, pp. 51–52.
[3] Companies Act 1948 Sec. 154.
[4] Companies Act 1967 Sec. 4.

A subsidiary does not merge legally with its holding company but maintains an independent existence. The effect of this is that, in the absence of ordinary agency relationships, a holding company is not liable for the acts of its subsidiary, and the fact that it is a wholly owned subsidiary does not give rise to a presumption of agency. The subsidiary company has its own objects which may be quite different from those of its holding company. The powers and duties of the directors of a subsidiary are the same as those of an ordinary company, and in the case of a subsidiary with independent shareholders it appears to be a breach of duty for the board to act solely in the interests of the holding company.

Various abuses have appeared in connexion with subsidiaries. For example, it is possible for an established company with a high credit rating when engaging in a speculative enterprise to form a subsidiary for the purpose with fairly small capital to keep its possible losses to a minimum, although this may cause injury to creditors who dealt with the subsidiary largely on the basis of its 'family connexions'. Nevertheless, in theory, the creditors have no claim against the parent company. It has been suggested that such activities should be prohibited, but it is difficult to see why a limited company should be the only form of business organisation that is not allowed to limit its losses in this way. The subsidiary can be used to overcome difficulties of the *ultra vires* rule and shareholders may find that they are investing in businesses far removed from the original objects clause.

The 1948 Act contains only a few provisions on the legal relationship between a holding company and its subsidiary. A subsidiary cannot, subject to certain limited exceptions, be a member of its holding company.[5] The restrictions on the provision of financial assistance by a company for the purchase of its own shares extends to the purchase of shares in its holding company.[6] Similarly, the prohibition of loans by a company to its directors extends to loans to directors of a holding company.[7]

'Group accounts' are required.[8] The holding company's balance sheet and profit and loss account must give a true and fair view of the financial position of the whole group. Basically one set of accounts for the whole group should be prepared, unless some other form would be more informative. Under the 1967 Act[9] these provisions have been extended: the parent company's accounts must state the name of the subsidiary, its country of incorporation and details of shares held, including the proportion of issued shares of each class held. The accounts of the subsidiary must disclose the name of the ultimate holding company and its country of incorporation. However, in both of these cases disclosure may be withheld with the consent of the Board of Trade where the company in question is a foreign corporation and disclosure would be harmful to the business of the holding company. These provisions, to some extent, enable the outside creditor to discover the financial position of a subsidiary and its indebtedness to various members of the group, but they provide him with little more protection; the shareholder is rather better off.

[5] Companies Act 1948 Sec. 27.   [6] ibid. Sec. 54.   [7] ibid. Sec. 190.
[8] ibid. Sections 150–153 and Eighth Schedule Part II.   [9] Sections 3 and 5.

The Jenkins Committee recommended[10] that the definition of a subsidiary should be based solely on membership and control. Because of the growth of non-voting and restricted voting equity shares, a company may hold more than one half of the equity shares without having control. It also recommended that where shares are held on trust for a company no votes should be exercised in respect of those shares, and that a subsidiary which was a member of its holding company before it became a subsidiary should be permitted to continue to be a member but should have no right to vote in respect of any share it might hold in its parent company.

At present there are no regulations concerning branches or divisions in companies. A company is free to set up whatever administrative structure it regards as appropriate, and this is usually determined by consideration of matters other than company law. There have been no serious objections to the present structure of parent and subsidiary companies and no reform has been proposed.

FRANCE

Little attention has been given in France to the questions raised in this chapter. Most people tend to think that the total dependence of the subsidiary on the parent company is inevitable. A report, for instance, of the CJP branch at Niort (February 1964) states: 'The dependence of the subsidiary on the parent will be complete both on the financial level (especially for the financing of investment) and on the current business level. It is the parent that provides the capital and has set up the board of directors; it may also be the principal supplier of the client.' It is certainly true that a number of 'subsidiaries' have been formed solely to get round a fiscal or company regulation or to find a new chairman's post for a senior executive of the parent firm.

The necessity for such total dependence is by no means self-evident to François Bloch-Laîné. 'When a subsidiary belongs entirely to its parent company, or has no other shareholders whose power balances that of that company, ought its principal shareholder to be the master of all its decisions? What standing can it have in the eyes of its employees and third parties if its directors are no more than a façade behind which the true powers operate? This is a very difficult problem. Let us now merely note that the "government" of a firm, if it is to be more firmly based than it is today, will unquestionably have more difficulty in adapting itself to situations brought about by external connexions than from internal links between ownership and management, or because of its intrinsic or national standing.'[11]

In present circumstances, the directors of subsidiaries have practically no independence. If there is only one parent company the directors are in office merely by the good will of the parent; if several companies share the ownership of the subsidiary, the directors must constantly 'cover' themselves on several sides, thereby harming the efficiency of their business.

The activities of big foreign groups have recently heightened awareness of these problems in France. If the government does not want to witness the disappearance of an independent French economy it will try, for instance, to

[10] *Report* paragraph 156.
[11] F. Bloch-Laîné, *Pour une réforme de l'entreprise*, Paris, Editions du Seuil, 1963.

prevent the decision centre of the French car industry from passing by stages to Detroit, or elsewhere—a problem which arose over the Fiat–Citroën negotiations. Some mechanism will doubtless be set up in the future to allow subsidiaries to act in harmony with the national interest and not just that of the foreign parent company.

There has recently been some progress in the protection of the various interests involved in subsidiaries. According to the proposals of Maître Aussedat at the National Assembly of Notaries in July 1966, French legislation is moving towards 'a new regulation for company groups considered as such, that is to say, considered as juridical entities in fact and in law'.

The new law on commercial companies has introduced some specific solutions. As regards cross-shareholdings, the law limits to 10 per cent the level of holding that two companies may have in one another. As soon as this level is exceeded, they lose their voting rights on the excess and only one of the companies may keep its holding, the other having to dispose of its stocks unless both agree to reduce their share below the 10 per cent level. This measure is designed to prevent company capital becoming unreal and fictitious; it ensures the protection of the interests of creditors and even, incidentally, those of the two partners. Parliament, however, has not dealt with links between companies other than through shareholdings. Secondly, a subsidiary has been defined as a company in which another company owns more than half the shares. This definition will probably have to be extended, because even with a holding of less than 50 per cent one company can completely dominate another. However, one company is deemed to hold a share in another when it owns between one tenth and one half its capital. Thirdly, shareholdings must be disclosed. The administrative board and the auditors must list holdings in their annual report and give an account of the activity of subsidiaries by sector and make clear their financial results. In the same way, certain companies are obliged to declare the composition of their portfolios.

Many points, however, still need to be clarified. According to Maître Aussedat, 'It does not seem possible to fit the organisation of groups of companies into too strict systematic regulations, which would run the risk of becoming out-of-date overnight. . . . It thus appears necessary to provide companies with a kind of legal framework which could be variously filled in according to their economic needs and profitable operation. I believe that such a law should contain, apart from a new definition of a "subsidiary", provisions relating to the control and supervision (an essential notion in this matter) of group interests, the withdrawal or appropriate compensation of disagreeing shareholders, the buying-back of shares, majority abuses, limitations of the right to vote, one-man companies as a means of forming subsidiaries, guarantees designed to safeguard the interests of third parties, balance sheets and consolidated accounts, the special civil and criminal responsibility of directors, the strengthening of the powers of auditors, etc.'

GERMANY

The ever-increasing importance of business concentration in the West German economy has been reflected in Part III of the 1965 Act (Sections 291–338) in which, for the first time, a coherent system of combine law has been laid down. The purpose of the new regulations is, according to the original draft Bill, 'to approach business link-ups in a juridical manner and to ensure that their existence is known, for the protection of shareholders and the harmonisation of managerial power and responsibility'. Another specific aim of the Act is to guarantee the rights of independent companies and their shareholders within a kind of 'combine constitution' and to protect them from harmful effects without hamstringing the concentrations themselves.

It remains to be seen, however, whether these measures will have much influence on existing link-ups or those that come into being. In any event, the Bill assumed that it is not the object of company law to oppose combines as such. 'A combine may be economically and socially desirable, since it may be only through the grouping together of several firms under combined control that production and sales can be rationalised. On the other hand, a combine may also be dangerous (for competition, for example) and may put the dominant company in a position of economic power which may be quite out of proportion to its capital holding and undesirable for sociopolitical reasons. Company law cannot distinguish between those combines that are desirable and those that are undesirable from the economic or socio-political points of view since the relevant criteria lie for the most part outside its scope.' However, the fact that some 70 per cent of West German AG are in some way connected with combines proves the economic importance of these links and justifies the efforts of parliament to bring this important area under comprehensive legal control. The powers of control as provided for in the Act are generally limited to combines in which an AG or a KGaA is involved. It may, however, be taken that these regulations, in an appropriate form, will serve as a model when the projected reform of the GmbH and the debate on a comprehensive 'enterprise law' are undertaken. It is especially interesting that parliament did not limit itself, when drawing up the revision of the law on company link-ups, to combine law in a narrow sense but took as its guiding concept that of the associated company, the various forms of which are exhaustively listed in Sec. 15 of the Act, without any general definition being attempted. In any case, we are here concerned with legally independent firms, whose relationship to one another is characterised by various and sometimes overlapping factors, briefly outlined in the following paragraph.

Firms under majority control and those having a majority interest are mentioned in Sec. 16. The law applies to such firms when the majority of the shares of a legally independent company belong to another company or when another company is entitled to a majority of the voting rights. It is deemed that the majority-owned company is dependent on the company holding the majority. Sec. 17 deals with dependent and dominant firms. The dominating influence which one company can exercise over another may be of various kinds and may, for example, be based on a majority interest or on a contractual agreement. A situation, however, may also arise in which one firm is permanently subject to the will of another for purely factual reasons. A 'combine' (Sec. 18) exists when legally independent firms are grouped together for economic purposes under a unified administration. A combine based on equality entails no relationship of dependence among the firms in the combine, but the 'subordination combine', which is commoner in practice, is characterised by the fact that the leading firm is at the same time the dominant company in the combine. In the case of firms with cross-shareholdings (Sec. 19), a dominant/dependent company relationship is deemed to exist when either firm owns more than a quarter of the shares of the other. In addition to the group of contracts listed in Sec. 292 of the Act, which include contracts for the pooling of profits and for the deduction of part of the profit, as well as industrial lease and cession agreements, the Section also specifies two other forms of contract which are of particular importance. These are the type of 'dominant' agreement under which an AG or KGaA puts itself under the control of another firm, and the type of profit deduction agreement which obliges an AG or a KGaA to make over its total profit to another company.

The provisions of Part III of the Act apply to all the matters which parliament considered under the general heading of 'associated companies'. A few of the legal requirements which parliament has laid down for various types of business connexion will now be briefly summarised. 'Dominant' and profit deduction agreements are valid only if they are confirmed by a majority representing three quarters of the issued capital at the general meeting, after other obligatory conditions, such as the prior publication of the contents of the agreement, have been satisfied. The contract is valid only after it has been entered in the business register. External shareholders are protected by being given the choice of remaining in the dependent company with a guarantee of suitable compensation or of placing their shares at the disposal of the 'dominant' firm in exchange for an appropriate settlement (Sections 304 ff). If there is no 'business agreement' as such, the provisions of Sections 311 ff on *de facto* combines take effect. These oblige the directors of a dependent company to submit a special detailed report every year on the company's connexions with associated firms. This is intended to protect a dependent AG or KGaA from being compelled to take measures or make deals which would be disadvantageous to it. In addition, far-reaching liability provisions mean that, overall, the *de facto* combine will increasingly lose ground to contractual combines. This is not, of course, a direct aim of the provisions of the Act, which is 'neutral towards combines'; nevertheless, from a legal point of view, this is a not undesirable development.

Other new measures introduced by the Act require that combines should produce annual balance sheets and business reports and the (not uncontested) obligation to disclose interests when these are greater than 25 per cent (Sections 20 ff). This requirement accords with the wider disclosure provisions of the new Act and means that any business link-up must be declared as soon as a firm—irrespective of legal form—owns more than 25 per cent of an AG. The latter, for its part, must immediately publish the fact of the interest in the company papers and give the name of the owner. These regulations will certainly make for more effective information on interests and link-ups for shareholders and creditors. On the other hand, it should not be overlooked that serious and almost unavoidable difficulties will thereby be put in the way of mergers which, under certain circumstances, are economically necessary and desirable. This proves how far parliament, when weighing the arguments, has come down in favour of more disclosure and thereby greater protection for shareholders and creditors.

ITALY

There is a widespread feeling in Italy that stricter regulations concerning subsidiaries are needed. The most important question is thought to be that of the protection of shares from 'watering' by cross-holdings. The reform draft therefore provides, in Art. 5, for a stiffer discipline in these matters than is to be found in Art. 2360 of the Civil Code. It also offers a more accurate definition of what is meant by 'control', the operative concept being that of 'predominant influence', including informal control gained through contractual obligations. Another interesting provision is that of Art. 10 of the draft: 'A company cannot vote in the meetings of companies which own its shares, up to the limit of nominal value for which a cross-shareholding exists. A company controlled by another company cannot vote in the meetings of the latter.'

No explicit consideration is given in the draft to differences of objective pursued by a company and its subsidiaries. However, Art. 4 limits the maximum amount of its own capital that a company may invest in shares of other companies to 50 per cent. If investments exceed this amount, the company must sell the shares within three months. Only financial holding companies are exempt from this requirement but special disciplines and supervision arrangements apply to them in other respects. The draft makes no provisions concerning other problems of the relations between parents and subsidiaries and in this respect differs considerably from the new German law. However, Art. 28 does contain another provision which deals with control over other companies. This requires that the balance sheet must specify the level of holdings in controlled or 'linked' companies. (According to Art. 4, a 'linked company' (società collegata) is a company in which another has a shareholding of more than 10 per cent.) A summary of the essential facts concerning the balance sheets of controlled or linked companies must be attached to the balance sheet.

THE NETHERLANDS

Dutch law has nothing to say on the issues considered in this Chapter nor did the Verdam Committee make any overt proposals. In the statutory provisions proposed by the Committee, however, inter-company relationships within a group are occasionally taken into account, in connexion, for example, with consolidated annual accounts and a central works council. (The government bill on accounts, mentioned on p. 174 above, takes this line.) The members of a group of companies (i.e. of a 'concern') are thus in general subject to the normal provisions of company law.

SWEDEN

The Swedish Companies Act has only to a limited extent considered the special problems arising when two companies enter into a joint venture. Combinations of joint-stock companies and firms with other legal forms have not been dealt with at all.

Parliament's chief aim has been to prevent a parent company paying dividends which arise from internal transactions between the parent company and its subsidiaries and which do not correspond to group profit-making. It has, on the other hand, paid very little attention to the organisational problems which occur when a subsidiary is united, more or less completely, with the parent company but legally remains a separate unit; nor has it thought it necessary to deal with questions concerning the protection of the rights of minorities and creditors of the subsidiary in situations when the controlling company exercises its power over the terms of the agreements arrived at by the subsidiary. In these cases general rules have to be applied which have no special relevance to groups of companies.

Strictly according to the law, a parent company should give its instructions to the management of a subsidiary by bringing its influence to bear as a shareholder at shareholders' meetings. The management of a parent company is not entitled to give direct orders to the management of a subsidiary. Matters are, however, quite different in practice. Most managements of parent companies see nothing wrong in giving their orders directly to the administrative unit of the subsidiary ignoring, in fact, the shareholders and the board of directors.

There is a great deal of variation in the independence of subsidiaries. In some cases the subsidiary is completely integrated in the organisation of the parent company; in others it is used deliberately to set up a unit with a fair degree of administrative independence. In neither case are the legal aspects in practice considered, in spite of the fact that, according to law, the shareholders' meeting of the subsidiary has to approve the annual report and dividends and appoint a board of directors and auditors.

There is no provision in Sweden, as there is in Germany, for agreements laying down the relationship between parent company and subsidiary. Furthermore, Swedish law, unlike German, actually contains obstacles to the conclusion of such agreements. If the subsidiary is not fully owned by the parent company, the latter is not permitted to discuss whether such an agreement should be entered into at the shareholders' meeting of the subsidiary. The minority holding within the subsidiary has the sole right to decide upon agreement between the companies. In such circumstances it is understandable that Swedish parent companies have not burdened subsidiary shareholders' meetings with these problems.

As regards the objectives of parent and subsidiary companies, whenever the making of administrative decisions is highly decentralised within the parent firm, there is generally a harmony of main specific objectives among the companies. This will be obvious in groups of companies active in similar industrial sectors, with central managements familiar with the sectors. It will be less self-evident among companies which have different production structures, grouped under a holding company. In this case the central management chiefly represents financial interests and cannot be expected to take part in the formulation of the specific objectives of the companies in the group.

On the whole, the Swedish parliament has not 'taken note' of the relationship between parent companies and subsidiaries. It seems to be widely thought that detailed regulations in this area would only complicate practical solutions of high-level administrative problems. As for the freedom and accountability of chief executives, the managing director, under the Swedish Companies Act, is responsible to the board and the latter to the owners. Consequently, the manager of the subsidiary is usually responsible directly to his board, which is composed of representatives of the parent company. The degree of independence varies according to the personalities of the people involved, the financial position of the subsidiary, the traditions of the industry, etc. Other, particular, problems arise when the parent company and the subsidiary are located in different countries, but even in this case Swedish industry has not sought more detailed legislation.

AN AMERICAN VIEW OF THE MULTINATIONAL CORPORATION

There is a growing body of American literature on multinational corporations that is significant in two respects. It indicates a major institutional trend; it also indicates an intellectual awareness of this trend. Trend and awareness of trend are occurring almost simultaneously, an unusual concomitance. The trend towards the institutionalisation of international business in the form of multinational companies brings into play new functions and uses for the corporation as it has developed in American law and managerial practice. The aware observers of this institutional trend are already at work on the problem of interpretation, of trying to get the trend in perspective and to see what it means not only for the world of business but also for the makers of public policy.

'Transnational' and 'international' business

As an increasingly important institution of international business, the multinational corporation has a significance that transcends the scope of *international* affairs, reading that term to mean the relations among the sovereign states of international law. Multinational corporations move in the world arena not at all as entities with legal status on the same level as sovereign states, which are the only 'actors' on the world scene that constitute the 'subjects' or makers of international law in the classic sense. In contrast, these private companies are the mere 'objects' of international law, a body of law which defines their rights and duties according to sovereign pleasure. Business corporations, like natural persons, cannot even claim, in the traditional schools of international law, the status of non-state actors, a status that is usually reserved to public international bodies. It is true that some eminent publicists have urged that international law is undergoing fundamental change. The classicists who regarded only states as governing units of the international system have been challenged by these publicists to take a more realistic position in the face of trends that point strongly towards the common law of a world community. The making of this common law, now assertedly in progress, involves both natural persons and corporate entities. The rights and duties of non-state *private* actors in world affairs, in this more recent

252

view, inhere in the individual and his voluntary associations, and are not derived solely from state action.

The rise of this new school of jurisprudence can be traced in such works as Phillip Jessup's *A Modern Law of Nations* (1948) and his *Transnational Law* (1956); and in *The Common Law of Mankind* (1958) by Wilfred C. Jenks. These and other writers point to several trends, all of which are of importance to students of the future status of multinational corporations. In the first place, there were the joint Allied tribunals after the second world war which found enemy officials personally responsible for crimes against humanity. Secondly, there have been multilateral declarations and conventions designed to secure the international protection of human rights, even as between governments and their nationals. Thirdly, international agencies to promote individual welfare throughout the world have multiplied. Finally, as Percy E. Corbett has indicated, there has been 'a concurrent growth of common national patterns in the regulation of worldwide business and a broad movement toward the unification of private law to facilitate the interchange of personnel, goods, and services'.[12] On this latter point, one might go even further and note the repeated assertions by the leaders and proponents of unfettered trans-national business that inter-*national* controls—notably in the rise of nationalistic and common-market barriers to trade—are retrogressive; they deter the natural growth of a common law of world enterprise and pose the outmoded power of sovereign entities against the emergent energies of corporate creative forces in world affairs.

For these reasons, it is wise to use the term 'international business' with caution and appropriate reservations. The multinational corporation of the future will hopefully be the instrument of *transnational* enterprise that serves mankind individually and collectively, and not primarily the instrument of an international system of sovereign states nor of any state exclusively. That this ideal can be realised only in the somewhat distant future may be taken for granted. One dare not 'underestimate the resistance that still guards the sanctuary of state sovereignty in East and West alike' and, 'given the existing conflict of ideologies and political objectives, any rapid advance to a common law of mankind interpreted by supranational courts and commissions and enforced by supranational agencies is a remote prospect'.[13] Yet short of any such radical transition to some kind of world order under law, it seems undeniable that transnational business in the form of the multinational corporation could have far-reaching effects to modify the extremes of theory and practice in the international system. These effects could go beyond the carving out for transnational business a place of honour in the world arena, a position, that is to say, which is solidly grounded on the service to mankind that multinational corporations can and must perform, and on universal recognition of that service. It is undoubtedly true, as Corbett has reminded us, that it will take time for the 'hard crust of the state' to be broken through in legal theory and in international practice so that due recognition will at length be given to all groupings—including, of course, states but not less the essential

[12] P. E. Corbett, 'International Law', *International Encyclopedia of the Social Sciences*, Vol. VII, pp. 550–1.
[13] ibid.

non-state entities—that work towards a better life for individual human beings. But that time may come sooner than most expect it.

The term 'transnational business', though not in general use, thus signifies the forward look in multinational corporate operations. 'Transnational' means, according to *Webster's Third International Unabridged Dictionary* (the word appeared only in a footnote in the Second Edition), 'extending or going beyond national boundaries'; and certain usages were cited: '. . . an abatement of nationalism and the creation of transnational institutions which will render boundaries of minor importance' (from *The New Republic*), and Edward Sapir's comment that 'by the diffusion of culturally important words . . . transnational vocabularies have grown up'. In the *Random House Dictionary of the English Language* (1966) similar note is taken of a recent usage: '. . . a transnational program for improving the economy of Europe . . .', and this definition is found: 'going beyond national boundaries or solely national interests'. That is the significance of the transnational business of the multinational corporation.

The key word in that last definition is 'solely'. In our present stage of political development for the world arena as a whole, men's purposes will generally polarise about national—even extremely nationalistic—institutions. But men's mandates directed through nation states are not necessarily nationalistic and tribal in character. The corporation, as a modern social institution, will for a long time to come have societal obligations that are spelled out primarily in terms of the constitutions and laws of sovereign states; the reason is that mankind today generally expresses its demands on all social institutions in this way, and in the United States—as Berle, Miller and others have shown—the American demands upon the corporation are considerable. Not only does American constitutional law veer towards the doctrine that corporations, like public governments, must respect the constitutional rights of individual persons; in the more positive role, 'the corporation has proved a vital (albeit neutral) instrument and vehicle' of what Berle calls 'the central mass of the twentieth-century American economic revolution' with its driving forces of immense increase in productivity, the massive collectivisation of property devoted to production and the concomitant decline of individual decision-making and control, the massive dissociation of wealth from active management, the growing pressure for greater distribution of passive wealth (shareholding), and the assertion of the individual's right to live and consume as he chooses.[14]

These driving forces in the American economic revolution of our century represent, to be sure, only the mandates of one among many sovereign states. In others the demands made upon corporate institutions sometimes reflect little concern about individual rights. The point is that despite the contemporary resurgence of nationalism, men everywhere do reach for all possible institutional instruments—including the modern corporation—for auxiliary means to whatever ends, modernisation, development, learning to live in the global environment of our time, and so on. The multinational corporation will be expected to serve purposes that are not necessarily definable in nation-

[14] A. A. Berle and G. C. Means, *The Modern Corporation and Private Property* (revised edn.), New York, The Macmillan Co., 1968, p. xxv.

alistic terms. And indeed the very presence of such corporations on the world scene may do much to mitigate the extremes of nationalism.

These observations on the use of variations on the stem word 'national' in discussing the future of the multinational corporation are intended as warnings against any assumption on the part of the reader that when 'international business' is spoken of in later pages any inference can fairly be drawn that inter-*national* or state trading is referred to. Often, the proper term would have been transnational business, but current usage has been allowed to supersede precision of expression.

The US multinational company defined

The multinational company, as a focus of business and public policy interest, is a relatively new phenomenon in the United States, as compared with Europe. In general, foreign trade and commerce has always been a relatively minor part of American business, as compared with business in most European economies; and that part of US trade and commerce assignable statistically to multinational corporations is even a smaller fraction of the whole. The import and export of products and services across national frontiers is carried on by many kinds of business unit, most of which cannot be designated multinational companies.

Capital movement abroad now proceeds at an unprecedented scale under the aegis of these companies, and problems of repatriation of profits arise, together with a whole range of managerial issues, the movement of capital,[15] technology[16] and manpower.[17] It therefore becomes necessary to define the term 'multinational company' for purposes of analysis. For a preliminary definition we may reserve that designation for a company with its home and headquarters in one country and bases in other (or host) countries, where

[15] See Emil L. Nelson and Frederick Cutler, 'The International Investment Position of the United States in 1967', *Survey of Current Business*, October 1968. For earlier years, see Charles E. Silberman and Lawrence A. Mayer, 'The Migration of US Capital', *Fortune*, January 1958; Samuel Pizer, 'Expansion in US Investments Abroad', *Survey of Current Business*, August 1962; 'The Global Stake of US Business Abroad', *Fortune*, December 1963, with charts; and issues of the *Survey of Current Business* published by the Office of Business Economics of the US Department of Commerce, Washington, DC, as well as surveys by the economics department of McGraw-Hill Publications, New York, NY. Direct government control of capital exports has been vigorously opposed by the Balance of Payments Advisory Committee of the US Department of Commerce, but several hundred companies participating in a voluntary balance of payments programme have effected a reduction of the dollar outflow. Cf. William F. Butler and John V. Deaver, 'Gold and the Dollar', *Foreign Affairs*, October 1967; Richard N. Cooper, 'The Dollar and the World Economy', in Kermit Gordon (ed.), *Agenda for the Nation*, Washington, DC, The Brookings Institution, 1968, pp. 475–508.

[16] See Jack Baranson, 'Transfer of Technical Knowledge by International Corporations to Developing Economies', *American Economic Review*, Vol. 66, No. 2, May 1966, pp. 259–267, and sources there cited. The paper treats of technological transplants as to product design, production techniques, and industrial systems for planning, organising and carrying out a production plan, and of the obstacles to transference when developing economies have difficulty in absorbing foreign techniques.

[17] See Herbert B. Grubel and Anthony D. Scott, 'The International Flow of Human Capital', *American Economic Review*, cited in the preceding note, pp. 268–274, and the discussion of this paper and Baranson's by Stephen Hymer, Burton Weisbrod and Harry G. Johnson at pp. 275–283.

the company carries on manufacturing or other business activities through direct local investment. Such 'roots' overseas are a key characteristic of the multinational company. It lives and operates in other countries, under their laws and customs, as well as those of its home country. This fact alone brings in its train a sequence of managerial questions that do not arise in purely domestic operations.[18]

The multinational company carries on industrial, commercial and financial activities abroad that directly involve corporate managerial responsibility on an international basis. Some components of the company must straddle political boundaries. Other components may be limited to domestic operations and staff functions. In the multinational company operating or staff functions, or both, will be assigned to one or more of the components at company headquarters in the home country. Organisational types differ widely. In some companies there is an 'international' division, department or allied company. The trend towards integration of all functional components of a corporation under combined domestic and foreign operations has been noted by some writers. If this is so, it is significant as a development parallel with the trend in national politics everywhere in the world today, when the line in every country between domestic and 'foreign' affairs becomes more and more hazy.

The minimal number of host countries required for accurate designation of corporate multinationality must be an arbitrarily set figure; but let us assume that 'multi-' refers to at least three nations: the home country and two host countries. Strictly speaking, a corporation with a single foreign base is not multinational, though its business activities could certainly be described as international. Such a two-nation spread could apply to a very large business operation. But if one elects to focus attention, not upon the international business activity as such, but rather upon the organisational, procedural and policy issues that arise from business activity carried on under a number of foreign jurisdictions, then it would seem better to aim for some statistical universe of companies that are truly multinational.

[18] In the US federal system, where most companies are incorporated under state and not under federal law, a 'foreign corporation' is one which, from the point of view of a State of the Union, is not chartered by that State but does business there under conditions prescribed by the host State. At first glance there would thus seem to be a close parallel with the conditions under which an American multinational company does business abroad. But there is a basic difference between the two situations. The doctrine of 'unconstitutional conditions', enforced in US federal courts against State governments which attempt to exclude or restrict the operations of 'foreign' corporations chartered by another State, has no close parallel in the law of nations governing the operations of multinational corporations in sovereign host countries. The doctrine of unconstitutional conditions, for example, is available as against hostile State action such as prescribing as a condition for entry to do business there that a foreign corporation shall not resort to federal courts for the enforcement against state officials of corporate rights protected by the federal constitution and statutes. Corporations are 'persons' protected notably by the due process and equal protection clauses of the 14th Amendment of the US Constitution. This supremacy of federal law having no parallel in the world arena where transnational business is carried on, one must distinguish sharply—even in the US federal system where the States are sometimes loosely described as 'sovereign'—between the US domestic market and the international marketplace. The American domestic market is continental and vast, but it is governed by a firm rule of federal law that is non-existent in the world arena.

The question of company size then arises. A list of the world's largest companies is not identical with a list of the largest international corporations; size and multinational distribution of corporate activities are not necessary correlatives.[19] Some of the largest companies are limited to domestic operations and, regardless of the size of their import and export business, these would not qualify as multinational companies under the suggested definition. On the other hand, some relatively small companies may have roots in numerous foreign places. The usual lists of the world's largest corporations

[19] The 'size' of a firm—however measured—is rarely an index of its effect in the international economy and the world arena unless the effect is narrowed to precise qualitative specifications. 'Size' requires careful specification of the thing measured and the relevance of that characteristic of a firm to discussion in hand. *Fortune*'s annual lists of the largest US and foreign industrials rank the companies primarily by sales; data are also provided for these companies' ranks according to assets, net profits, invested capital, profit as a percentage of both sales and invested capital, and earnings per share. There are also tables on who did best and worst among the 500 in the United States by several different standards. To show industry medians industrial groupings are based on classifications established by the US Bureau of the Budget as follows: motor vehicles and parts; farm and industrial machinery; pharmaceuticals; apparel; aircraft and parts; metal products; appliances and electronics; measuring, scientific, and photographic equipment; metal manufacturing; office machinery (including computers); chemicals; rubber; textiles; mining; publishing and printing; soaps and cosmetics; glass, cement, gypsum, concrete; petroleum refining; shipbuilding and railroad equipment; paper and wood products; food and beverage; and tobacco. Moving over from the industrials to the commercial banks, *Fortune* in 1966 showed rankings of the fifty largest according to assets, deposits, loans, number of employees, earnings, capital funds, earnings as percentage of capital funds, and earnings per share. The fifty largest life insurance companies were ranked according to assets, life insurance in force, increase in life insurance in force, premium and annuity income, net investment income, net gain from operations, and number of employees. For the fifty largest merchandising firms the ranking was according to sales, assets, net profits, invested capital, number of employees, net profit as percentage of both sales and invested capital, and earnings per share. The fifty largest transportation companies were ranked primarily according to operating revenues, but with other ranking according to assets, net income, invested capital, number of employees, net income as percentage of both operating revenues and invested capital, and earnings per share. The fifty largest utilities were ranked primarily according to assets, but with other rankings according to operating revenues, net income, invested capital, net income as percentage of invested capital, number of employees, and earnings per share. *Fortune*'s lists do not provide rankings of immediate relevance to categories of multinational companies, even though many companies on the US and foreign lists are multinational on the definition suggested here. Nor are the highly aggregative data in *Fortune*'s directories adequate for drawing conclusions about the size distribution of firms for purposes of growth analysis, antitrust policy, etc. See R. E. Quandt, 'On the Size Distribution of Firms', *American Economic Review*, Vol. 56, No. 3, June 1966, pp. 416–432; also R. J. Monson, Jr and A. Downs, 'A Theory of Large Managerial Firms', *Journal of Political Economy*, Vol. 736, June 1965, pp. 221–236.

The actual count of the world's most *important* multinational companies is an elusive question, reminding one of Oskar Morgenstern's attack on the tendency toward 'specious accuracy', and a pretence that things have been counted more precisely than they can in fact be counted, in his work *On the Accuracy of Economic Observations*, Princeton University, 1950. In the revised edition of this work (1963) Morgenstern cited the classic case of such specious accuracy: the man who claimed a river was 3,000,021 years old on the ground that twenty years earlier the river's age was given as three million years. As an example of 'functional speciousness' he cited the example of the exchange rate of a country with exchange control: the official rate might be stated quite accurately to any number of desired decimals while the vast majority of transactions take place at different rates that are neither disclosed nor determinable.

are not, therefore, reliable guides to the question in hand. There is something to be said, however, for concentrating attention on some of the largest companies that do in fact operate in a number of host countries. Studies based upon the observation of such companies can be quite useful for the purpose of assessing the role of the multinational corporation as a contemporary business institution in the larger international economy and in the arena of world politics.

General conclusions about the business performance and the public policy implications of multinational corporations as a whole cannot, of course, be derived from such a sample. One needs a larger canvas, as indicated in a special report by *Business Week* (20 April 1963) on US multinational companies. There it was estimated that at least 3,300 companies could be so designated, on the grounds that they were rooted abroad as well as at home in at least one host country in the form of a manufacturing base or otherwise through direct investment. If one specified at least two host countries as the criterion, the figure would be much reduced.[20] *Business Week* specified a second criterion

[20] There is no single official source for determining the number of multinational companies based in the United States. The most recent relevant census was conducted in 1957 and published by the US Department of Commerce in 1960 under the title *United States Business Investment in Foreign Countries* by Samuel Pizer and Frederick Cutler. This is a survey of 2,800 companies having at least one foreign affiliate in which at least 10 per cent of equity interest was held by the US company surveyed. The top ninety-six companies, each with such an investment abroad of $50 million or more, accounted for $18 billion of the total investment of $25 billion for all 2,800. The next sixty-seven companies accounted for $2 billion. An updating of this study is under way at the US Department of Commerce. For more recent data, see the Department's *Survey of Current Business* and its 1963 publication, *Balance of Payments Statistical Supplement*. See also 'The Balance of Payments Payoff of Direct Foreign Investment', *Michigan Business Review*, July 1962. Clues to the numbers of US multinational companies and to the trends in international business are to be found in certain reports of consultant firms. A report in 1965 by Booz, Allen & Hamilton, Inc., management consultants, on the foreign activity of American firms showed that in 1964 there were 761 new business units started or acquired by US companies overseas, as compared with 718 for 1963, 584 for 1962, and 560 for 1961. *US News and World Report* (7 June 1965) stated that this report was a continuing study—covering 2,042 US firms undertaking 5,244 new foreign activities. The report showed that new business units started or acquired by US companies overseas in 1964 topped those of other recent years, but licensing moves and expansions dipped below 1963 levels. Declines in the extensions of previously existing US business units abroad and in the signing of new licence contracts held the 1964 total number of new foreign activities to 1,211, off a shade from the 1,224 of 1963. Total new activities were 1,107 in 1962 and 1,155 in 1961. Western Europe's share of new activities eased to 48 per cent of the total for the second half of 1964, from 52 per cent in 1961; joint ventures accounted for 41 per cent of new units in the second half of 1964, up from 36 per cent in 1961, with wholly owned subsidiaries and branches losing ground as ownership forms. Booz, Allen & Hamilton described its data as 'conservative', since some new activities not publicly acknowledged were omitted. A consistent compilation procedure makes its data useful, however, in drawing comparisons and analysing the direction of activity. In December 1966, the firm reported that new business ventures abroad by US firms were at the lowest level in six years. During the first half of 1966 there were 469 new business establishments, expansions and licence agreements registered by US firms abroad. The previous lowest level for a similar period was said to be 495 new activities in the first half of 1962.

Cf. Howe Martyn, *International Business: Principles and Problems*, New York, The Free Press of Glencoe, 1964, Ch. 4, The Extent of International Enterprise and sources there cited, and also Sidney E. Rolfe, *The International Corporation*, a Background Report prepared

that reduced its estimate: only a company with 'a genuinely global perspective' would meet its test for the truly multinational corporation. The managements of such firms, 'make fundamental decisions of marketing, production, and research in terms of the alternatives that are available to it anywhere in the world'. The demarcation line between 'domestically oriented enterprises with international operations', on the one hand, and the 'truly world-oriented companies', on the other, was drawn in this way on what is essentially a normative basis.

Normative criteria for a definition

Such a normative approach to the definition of corporate multinationality has its uses, and is indeed an indispensable approach to qualitative analysis. For purposes of defining the statistical universe of multinational corporations, however, it presents insurmountable difficulties. Perhaps all companies engaged in transnational business *ought* to have global perspectives, and it might be hoped that their managers would see the enterprise as a 'global entity', as *Business Week* suggested, regarding the foreign and domestic interests of a company as 'interwoven into a web of carefully integrated parts', allocating its capital, manpower and other resources on a global basis.

Yet such subjective qualities in corporate management are often inaccessible, not only to the outsider but even to one close to policy centres. Non-qualifying executives, without a truly global (or regional) outlook, may still be managers in companies with quite substantial international operations. Success in such operations may or may not demand global perspectives. Judgment on 'success' itself can hardly be limited to the reading of balance sheets, ranking by sales, the estimates of market position, the indices of economic growth, etc. Judgment may embrace more than a company's place in the world process of production; it may include assessments of the multinational corporation as a participant in the world power process.

This assessment will depend upon a view of the place of multinational companies in the world arena as stabilisers or disturbers, as the case may be, of a system of world order and of a dynamic, epochal, trend towards preferred goals for the human race. Nation states and other public organisations are not the only actors in this great drama, the outcome of which may well decide the fate of the free enterprise promised in the long-range policy of a multinational company.

The normative criterion, then, while irrelevant to the task of setting the boundaries of a statistical universe of multinational companies, is highly relevant in getting at their function. This function is still undefined, and is perhaps indefinable, except on certain value premises and in the context of fairly well-developed conceptions of world processes, political as well as economic. When one moves into these wider assessments of the global role of multinational companies, it is not enough to speak only of global *business* perspectives in any narrow sense of that term. With the multinational corporation, as with the modern corporation in general, the meaning of 'business' is undergoing profound change.

for the XXII Congress of the International Chamber of Commerce, Istanbul, 31 May–7 June 1969 (Paris, ICC, 1969), Ch. 2, Some Statistics.

The ultimate goals, a firm's objectives, are also various. A single-minded pursuit of profit, to the exclusion of benefits, say, to underdeveloped economies or to society generally, may be the drive behind some of the most influential multinational corporations. The preferred outcomes in managerial decision-making in these companies must be a part of any comprehensive study, and not the ground for including or excluding them from a survey of the institutional development one seeks to understand.

As to the kinds of business multinational firms engage in, it is again necessary to take a comprehensive view. There is a tendency in some commentary on the subject to limit enquiry to industrial corporations. In addition to manufacturing and mining, the business of banking, merchandising, insurance, transportation, communications, construction, public utilities, and services such as advertising, public relations and management consultancy, are also important in a comprehensive survey.

The question of organisation of a company's international operations must be kept open if one is to be comprehensive. Some writers would reserve to the multinational category only those companies in which the top management takes direct responsibility for overseas operations. If this were to eliminate corporations which delegate that responsibility to an 'international division' or a domestic subsidiary or affiliate, the exclusion may be unrealistic, especially in cases where a firm is under pressure to integrate.

The identification of all truly multinational companies runs into still other hazards. Do we look only into the 'private sector'? How should we draw the line between the public and private sectors, especially in the case of joint ventures? Because of the predominance in the world today of 'mixed' economies it is often necessary to soften with a 'quasi-' any precise description of private corporations, especially the largest ones. For operations within countries at early stages of economic and political development, multinational corporations may face the necessity of engaging in joint ventures that involve clearly public national[21] and international organisations. In the long run, the

[21] See 'More US Companies Choose Joint Ventures for Expansion Abroad; Growing Nationalism Forces Ownership Sharing . . .', *The Wall Street Journal*, 30 March 1965: 'In Mexico, Japan or India you have no alternative' to pooling investment capital with national governments, according to one US executive with a score of joint foreign ventures. On the general subject see Wolfgang Friedmann and George Kalmanoff (eds.), *Joint International Business Ventures*, New York, Columbia University Press, 1961; and Johannes Meynen, Wolfgang Friedmann and Kenneth Weg, 'Joint Ventures Revisited: A World Business Symposium', *Columbia Journal of World Business*, Vol. I, No. 2, Spring 1966, pp. 19–29.

A 1966 survey by the National Industrial Conference Board shows that international joint business ventures are multiplying rapidly and are expected to continue doing so during the next decade. The survey, conducted among 146 business officials in fifty-four countries, disclosed that joint ventures were considered beneficial because they 'unlocked' new markets, provided technology, skills and capital, opened world trade and narrowed the economic and political gap between poor and rich nations. Though underdeveloped countries would be the first to gain by joint ventures, all countries would ultimately share in the benefits. Those questioned believed that one of the strongest appeals of joint ventures was the substantial reduction in economic and political risks of foreign investment. The presence of a local partner not only guarded against outright expropriations in unstable countries but also offered protection against nationalistic sentiment, many executives emphasised. The study, which lasted three years, disclosed especially strong support for joint ventures in developing nations, where money and technology are short. 'Besides providing capital and technology,

autonomy of management in a given economic and political context may prove to be far more decisive for the future role of multinational corporations than the question of their ownership. 'Property' is a fluid concept, and the fluidity is influenced above all by developments in the whole corporate business system itself.

It is obvious from these observations on the problem of identifying a statistical universe of 'multinational companies' that too clear-cut a definition is likely to be misleading. The consequences can be unfortunate for any assessment of the larger institutional roles of these companies. To focus upon but one type of company, or upon a few aspects of multinational corporations in general, can lead to unreliable conclusions for policy purposes. In order to avoid errors of judgment of this kind it is highly desirable that there be exhaustive statistical analyses of the whole subject. At the present time there are no studies of this kind available. One must, accordingly, reserve judgment upon many normative issues connected with the subject, especially issues of public policy.

Before turning to these policy matters a few comments are in order concerning the statistical method of comprehending the multinational corporation. One would like to see certain kinds of distributions, for example. Multinational companies can be distributed, for purposes of analysis, along several different continua. There is, first, a continuum in terms of size, as already indicated. There are, in addition, possible continua based on degrees of public and private ownership, on degrees of integration of overseas operations into the organisational structure of the home-based company, on the kinds and amounts of investments[22] in overseas operations (direct or

joint ventures bring together high-calibre individuals of different nationalities and promote an endless two-way flow of all kinds of human, political and economic experiences', a Brazilian executive commented. Among the major hazards involved, the survey listed divergent objectives and management practices, lack of mutual confidence and respect and failure to anticipate and resolve conflicts of interest before agreements were signed. Since shared ownership went hand in hand with shared management and profits as well as a loss of the essential freedom and control, not all companies were sold on joint ventures and accepted them only when policies of a host country made them mandatory, the NICB found. Other companies questioned granted that there were advantages in sharing risk and technology, but they insisted on a majority equity or extensive contractual safeguards to protect their financial and management interest. The acceptability of a joint venture depended largely on the kind of enterprise contemplated. Many executives surveyed stressed they would consider forming joint ventures in manufacturing but not in mining or other extractive operations. These executives preferred to avoid conflicts of interest caused by the general instability of raw material prices and governmental pressures to bring national resources under national control.

[22] Annual data on the US foreign investment position, indicating total amounts, but not the numbers of companies, are reported in the US Department of Commerce's *Survey of Current Business*. See also Samuel Pizer and Frederick Cutler, *US Business Investments in Foreign Countries, A Supplement to the Survey of Current Business*, US Government Printing Office, Washington, 1960, for the historical background. Also, *The European Market: A Guide for American Businessmen*, New York, The Chase Manhattan Bank, January 1964, and 'US Investment Activity in Europe During 1965', in *Report on Western Europe*, No. 40, March–April 1966, and corresponding articles in succeeding issues. These are bi-monthly issues of the Economic Research Division of Chase Manhattan. The figures are not broken down by company but by branches of industry. Further refinement would be necessary for a continuum of companies based on direct investment in overseas operations. A more detailed

portfolio, for example), and on the kinds and degrees of autonomy of operation extended to overseas subsidiaries and affiliates. Other indices can be used in order to distinguish types of capital movements through corporate channels as compared with other means (e.g. the action of public national and international organisations).

These are but a few of the possibilities open to analysts. At a higher level of abstraction the role of multinational companies in the total flow of international transactions can be measured. S. J. Brams[23] has shown, for example, that it is possible to conceptualise the relations of nations in the form of transactions in the public and private sectors. Systematic, empirical analysis of transactions flowing among selected nations can be indicative of relationships in the international system generally. He has found that the flow in trade relations tends to be far more erratic than diplomatic and organisational relations, and thus possibly suggestive of changes or disturbances in the international system.

Policy issues: some fundamentals

Two kinds of policy issues are posed by the rise to prominence of the multinational corporation as a major business and social institution. Within the company itself there are corporate policy issues to be formulated and decided by its board of directors and executed by its managerial staff. At government level, on the other hand, there are issues of public policy concerning this kind of business organisation and its international activities.

The issues of both corporate and public policy pose certain basic problems that need attention at the threshold of enquiry. How is the multinational company to be classified for legislative and administrative purposes? What kind of an organisation is it? What are its identifying aims and other characteristics? Whose instrument is it? Very much the same basic problems confront the internal corporate policy-makers. They must decide, for example, whether to treat the multinational company as an extended domestic company that moves into the international market and the world arena, or as an organisation different in kind. Do its purposes and functions require radically different approaches to the managerial issues ordinarily confronted by the purely domestic corporation? Is there not a range of issues for the internal government and public regulation of the multinational corporation that differs in kind from that applying to other kinds of business units?

Policy-makers may elect to take the basic position that the multinational corporation is simply a special case of business companies in general; or they

study of American corporate investments abroad is Judd Polk, Irene W. Meister and Lawrence A. Viet, *US Production Abroad and the Balance of Payments: A Survey of Corporate Investment Experience*, New York, National Industrial Conference Board, 1966; this study was 'based on an intensive examination of the corporate balance of payments of a hundred of this nation's leading manufacturing enterprises', which remain anonymous. Cf. *US Manufacturing Investments Abroad and the Government Program for Balance of Payments Improvement*, Washington, DC, Machinery and Allied Products Institute and the Council for Technological Advancement, 1965. *The Exchange Magazine*, January 1963, published a sample survey of the foreign operations of US companies on the New York Stock Exchange.

[23] Stephen J. Brams, 'Transactional Flows in the International System', *American Political Science Review*, Vol. 60, No. 4, December 1966, pp. 880–898.

may take the very different position that the multinational company is a new genus and that the purely domestic enterprise is a species, albeit the more numerous class. The choice of such a major premise in arguments for public control and for internal corporate policy can have profound consequences. To proceed on the assumption that the multinational company is a kind of overgrown and extended domestic company, for example, is a naive approach to the problem of business objectives. The ends to be served by business enterprise may more naturally be sought in global than in nationalistic perspective.

The multinational company's activity is like that of a stream seeking its outlet into the sea. It seeks a natural course into the world of trade and commerce. Intercourse in this larger market is impeded by political boundaries and protectionist tendencies in public policy; a truly worldwide orientation of public and corporate policy may appear in both host and home countries to be distorted thus disturbing the natural flow of international business. (To use words like 'natural' and 'distort' in this way betrays a bias, of course, just as nationalistic preferences today typically bias the aims and activities of the international company.)

Whose instrument?

There are overriding considerations in both public (and corporate) policy-making that go straight back to the question: Whose instrument is the multinational company and what purposes is it to serve?

Realistic appraisal of the future direction of transnational business conducted by this kind of enterprise depends upon facing this question candidly. If it be assumed, along lines of traditional thought about corporations, that the immediate property interests of stockholders must be served above all, then very different conclusions are to be drawn for both corporate and public policy than if other assumptions are made. In assessing the future of multinational corporate operations in the underdeveloped parts of the world, to take another case, the assumption that the corporation is primarily an instrument of development leads to very different policy conclusions than if the assumption is that profitability is the primary goal. Or, to take a third case, if it were assumed that multinational companies are to be the instruments of their home nation governments in the world struggle for power, then both corporate and public policy governing corporate activities will again be different.

A further case may be posited. Although it is hypothetical and necessarily based on some construct of an international system that is emergent and not yet clearly describable, it is quite possible that this position will eventually be decisive for many companies. If we assume the necessity for an industrial international system—as described later—as the basis for international business in the future, it is reasonable to argue that the multinational corporation must be in part, at least, an instrument for the maintenance of that system.

Corporate goals

Descriptively and objectively what are the operational goals of most multinational companies? No one has the answer to this question, any more than one has to that of corporate goals in general. The tentative conclusion may be drawn, from incomplete evidence but extended observation of corporate managers in action, that these goals are mixed. They are the goals of directors and executive managers who are human beings subject to all the conditioning influences of their environment. They are goals, moreover, that vary from company to company and, within a given company, from year to year. They do not conform to any preconceived economic, ethical or political doctrine.

As the present writer has said elsewhere,[24] the modern corporation as an institution becomes more comprehensible when the diverse aims of corporate policy are examined realistically, as well as in terms of ideal models. Here we must distinguish what Walter Lippmann spoke of in *Public Opinion* as 'the world outside and the pictures in our heads', or what Louis J. Halle[25] speaks of as the 'chaotic existential world' as contrasted with that more comfortable 'orderly conceptual world' that all of us inhabit at the same time. The pictures in our heads are of course unavoidable and are in fact of no little utility as props in thought and in empirical enquiry. The real trouble, as Will Rogers used to say, 'isn't what people don't know, it's what they do know that isn't so'. The trouble with the dogmatic conception of the business corporation as an organisation devoted exclusively to making profits is that this isn't so.

It is now generally conceded that 'profit maximisation' is not, alone, a scientifically sound designation of corporate purpose as seen in directors' and executives' actions and corporate behaviour generally. Time is a qualifying factor. Immediate profitability is not the same as profitability over a long time-span. The survival and health of the enterprise are other kinds of institutional goals that do, in fact, govern policy, despite intellectualistic objections to the implied reification of the corporate entity as though the real persons connected with it were of secondary importance. In practice, they are, whatever theory may require of corporate policy-makers.

The point is made emphatically, at least in the case of US corporations, with respect to current trends in corporate giving and concepts of corporate social responsibility. Against the resistance of conventional wisdom about the primacy of stockholder interests, directors and executive managers have deliberately widened the range of corporate goals to include diverse forms of strengthening of the company's environment. Nor are the expressed aims in the execution of corporate social responsibilities limited to the sphere of 'enlightened self-interest'. Outright philanthropy is often cited as the purpose of corporate giving, and it is hard to find instances of stockholder dissent.

Multinational companies are doubtless organisations oriented to economic production, as distinguished from what Talcott Parsons[26] has called 'integrative' and 'pattern-maintenance' organisations and those which are oriented to political goals. 'Production', however, is understood in the full economic

[24] R. Eells, *The Meaning of Modern Business*, New York, Columbia University Press, 1960, Ch. VI, 'Corporate Goals'.
[25] Louis J. Halle, *The Society of Man*, New York, Harper & Row, 1965.
[26] Talcott Parsons, *Structure and Process in Modern Societies*, Illinois, The Free Press of Glencoe, 1960, pp. 44 ff.

sense as 'adding value' and not as limited to specific branches of business; it covers a wide and undefined range of companies. Unlike integrative organisations, such as those concerned, like law courts, primarily with the adjustment of conflicts, and, like political parties, primarily with placing their elites in positions of power, the multinational corporation makes its primary, but not exclusive, goal economic. Every organisation contributes in some way, as Parsons observes, to every primary function if it is well integrated in society.

Economic *primacy* in the multinational company thus leaves plenty of room for other organisational purposes. Pattern-maintenance organisations, such as churches and schools, are concerned primarily with cultural and educational functions. But it cannot be said that they alone are so concerned, and that business corporations, with primary economic interests, are without similar concerns.

Configurational analysis

The real functions of organisations[27] generally, and of multinational corporations in particular, must be sought in their social setting and the human motivations of those who determine policy. The supposed goals of the multinational company, as conceived by social theorists, public officials, and even by those close to its operations, may be at odds with the functional realities. It is ordinarily supposed that the 'business' function predominates and determines the shape of corporate policy. As indicated above, however, the makers of policy may have quite latitudinarian ideas about the meaning of modern business. And the configurational analysis of a multinational company may show up causal mechanisms that preconceptions have not allowed for.

Configurational analysis for the purpose of revealing both real and ideal functions of contemporary multinational companies is of three kinds. The *internal organisational system* of these companies shows up in the total configuration of relationships between those who may be called the constituent members of a company's whole financial and operative structure and the internal governmental system of the company. The *institutional system* is revealed in the configuration of relationships between the company and its social setting. Finally, the *technical system*[28] appears in the configuration of relationships between the company and its technology.

We shall be concerned here mainly with the institutional system, although brief comment will first be made also on the technical and internal organisational systems of multinational corporations. Significant ecological mechan-

[27] The term 'organisation', as used here, refers to what Stanley H. Udy, Jr, in 'The Comparative Analysis of Organizations' (James G. March (ed.), *Handbook of Organizations*, Rand, McNally & Co., Chicago, 1965, pp. 678–709), calls 'any group of persons plus the system of roles defining their interactions with one another' and to what in his article he designates in particular as 'organizations with objectives which are explicit, limited, and announced'. In this Section I have followed Udy's method of enquiry to some extent.

[28] The scheme used here, with adaptations, is Udy's, and, as he says, 'social setting' and 'technology', for purposes of this threefold configurational analysis, are not on the same level of abstraction since any technology employed by an organisation exists in the same social setting as does the organisation. In the case of business corporations the wisdom of considering separately its operation in the context of rapidly changing modern technology is obvious.

isms are involved in the institutional system. There are external pressures that elicit active strategic responses on the part of a company. There are also adaptatory changes in structure and corporate policy in passive response. The effect of external pressures on the multinational corporation can be seen in its authority structure, in its communications and in its policy patterns.

It seems probable, for example, as to the *internal* organisational system, that the authority structure of the multinational company will as a rule exhibit characteristic responses to the highly diffuse authority structure in the world arena, as contrasted with the more centralised and unitary authority structure of nation states that constitute the framework for purely domestic corporations. The decision-making apparatus of a multinational company is necessarily decentralised, regardless of the rapidity and ease of world communication, because of the multiplicity of sovereignties that break up the international marketplace. Local conditions vary so greatly that local managers need discretionary authority[29] beyond that required within a unitary (or highly centralised federal) system of national government under a common rule of law. On the other hand, this diffusion of world authority impels the headquarters management of a multinational company to create special devices and conditions, within the total company organisation, which will reduce diseconomies of scale. The internal communication systems[30] of such companies, and their methods of control to induce unity of effort and common corporate purposes, are characteristic ecological responses to the external pressures to which international business is exposed.

These ecological considerations demand closer attention than they have been given by public policy-makers concerned with the regulation of transnational business. It should be understood that the managers of multinational companies are confronted with the necessity of creating and maintaining, in comparatively chaotic surroundings, vital organisations for doing much of the world's work.

The internal structure of the multinational company also faces unique issues. Some of the problems involved have been indicated. Comparative studies of multinational corporate policies are rare and are badly needed[31]

[29] William R. Dill, 'Environment as an Influence on Managerial Autonomy', *Administrative Science Quarterly*, Vol. 2, 1958, pp. 409–443.

[30] Harold Guetzkow, 'Communications in Organizations', in March (ed.), *Handbook of Organizations*, pp. 534–573. Cf. W. P. Davison, *International Political Communication*, New York, Frederick A. Praeger, Inc., for the Council on Foreign Relations, 1965, especially Ch. IV, 'Communication and Organization'. The common problems of business and political communication in the world arena have been little studied with reference to the organisation of multinational companies.

[31] Udy's otherwise admirable paper on the comparative analysis of organisations has little to say on the internal organisational system, or what the present author calls corporate government. Udy's position is that 'independent variables of comparative studies of internal systems by and large coincide with the dependent organizational variables of the institutional and technical studies' (p. 702) which he had surveyed earlier in the paper. But it is not at all clear that the comparative analysis of multinational corporate governance is thereby ruled out as less promising than other methods of approaching the subject. He cites no efforts of this kind in the field of transnational business and, in fact, it is a little explored one. Udy's suggested 'three strategic analytic aspects' of what he calls 'the administrative system' (i.e. 'a designed pattern of roles') of an organisation would be useful tools of enquiry in the exploration of this field. The three aspects are authority, communication and

for the use of corporate and public policy-makers. In neither sphere does adequate attention seem to have been given to certain issues of increasing significance in the United States. On the other hand, we do have some useful studies of corporate government, especially in its administrative aspects, which could easily be extended in method to the comparative study of multi-national corporate polities. A good example is the work of R. Bendix on varieties of internal company 'bureaucracies' designed or adapted to meet expectations inherent in local external social systems.[32]

Only a brief comment is possible here concerning the *technical* system, i.e. the pattern of relationships between technology and the internal organisational system of the multinational company. The effect of technological development can be seen in both a company's communication patterns and in its authority structure. But there are also important psychological implications for members of the firm. Udy,[33] in surveying the literature on these points, raises doubts about the universal applicability of the argument made by some writers that there is 'a general "assembly-line syndrome" in which mechaniza-tion "breeds" bureaucracy, inhibits communication and social interaction on the mob, and subjects the worker to severe psychological stress' and urges the need for much more careful comparative analysis of the actual situations. For multinational companies, some of which must carry on manufacturing operations in sharply differing social environments and must be prepared, furthermore, to counter unfounded propaganda that inhibits operations, the need is particularly urgent. In the broader picture, the technological impact upon all kinds of transnational business operations has been so great, and will continue at so great a rate of change, that both public and corporate policy-makers face a lack of expertise in this field. The traditional dogmas will not do. Neither business firms nor nations dare let themselves be saddled with policies rooted in conventional wisdom about the technical system that hampers enterprise (economic or political) in the world arena.

We turn now to the *institutional* aspects of configuration analysis, that is to say, the relationships between the multinational corporation and its social setting. The relevant social setting in this case is the international system, of which business corporations are an important part. That system, of course,

differentiation. 'Differentiation' refers to 'the pattern and mode of segmentation of roles, both one from another as well as from personality characteristics' (p. 703), with more detailed reference to the number of administrative roles differentiated, the extent of role conflict in the system, variables relating to the degree of specificity of jobs, the formality of the system of rules, and the extent to which performance is emphasised in contrast with ascribed qualities. As to 'group structure and membership', another general heading for what Udy finds to be a probable taxonomy for the internal organisational system, he mentions degree of fragmentation in the overall structure, the degree of separation from one of the fragmented groups to another, the rates and modes of interaction and cohesive-ness, supervisory style, formal and informal organisational types of interpersonal relation-ships, and various characteristics and qualities of organisation membership.

[32] See Reinhard Bendix, *Work and Authority in Industry*, New York, John Wiley & Sons, Inc. and London, Chapman & Hall Ltd., 1956, especially Ch. 4, 'The Bureaucratisation of Economic Enterprises' and Ch. 5, 'The American Experience'. Also Bendix, 'Industralisa-tion, Ideologies, and Social Structure', *American Sociological Review*, Vol. 24, 1959 pp. 613–623.

[33] Udy, 'The Comparative Analysis of Organizations', cited, at pp. 699–702.

will profoundly affect the future of the corporation as a social institution.

The multinational corporation in the international system

The long-range test of the usefulness of the corporation as a social institution will be its viability in the future structure of world society. The corporation as a purely local and domestic form of business unit will, of course, persist in countries where corporate capitalism is encouraged, simply because business organisation in corporate form functions so well in such an economy and is protected by municipal law. In the world arena, however, different conditions prevail and more stringent requirements for survival apply. The decision process in multinational companies operates under especially exacting requirements of perspective-accuracy for executives. 'A decision is always a choice among alternative perceived images of the future'.[34] A dependable 'image' of the international milieu of the future, and above all of the political configuration of that milieu, is therefore a prime requisite for long-range strategic decision-making in multinational corporations.

The contours of international political systems[35]—past, present and future— are now the subject of intensive study; but unfortunately there is still no consensus among the specialists in this field that business executives can take as a major premise in estimating trends in the international system they are likely to be working in. While it is true that multinational corporations may well be among the formative influences on the international system of the twenty-first century, as of today the future of the multinational corporation as a viable economic institution depends heavily upon the nation-state international system now regnant. Political analysts for multinational corporations must accordingly watch with care the development of contemporary international systems theory for guidance in working out their own estimates of current and future configurations of power and authority in the world arena, as these configurations are likely to affect a company's operations. The literature is extensive. As an example of the thinking required for long-range estimates of the 'fit' of the multinational corporation, as a social institution, into the emergent world setting, we may turn to a study of the international implications of industrialism.[36]

In this study, George Modelski has characterised 'Agraria' and 'Industria' as two major types of international systems in world history, and asks what kind of international structure is consistent with each of these systems. Historically, 'Agraria' has predominated but now 'Industria' is emerging as

[34] K. Boulding, 'The Economics of Knowledge and the Knowledge of Economics', *America Economic Review*, Vol. 56, No. 2, May 1966, p. 7.

[35] George Modelski, in the article cited in footnote 36 below, has pointed to the necessity of keeping in mind the 'universe of international systems, past, present, future and hypothetical' for the proper study of international relations, including among those systems 'a large number of hitherto ignored species' that are exotic to the Westerner with eyes fixed on the nation-states system which emerged at the end of the Middle Ages. On the present status of studies of international systems, together with bibliographies, see Chadwick C. Alger, International Relations, *International Encyclopedia of the Social Sciences*, Vol. VIII, pp. 60–68, and Morton A. Kaplan, Systems Analysis: International Systems, ibid., Vol. XV, pp. 479–486.

[36] George Modelski, 'Agraria and Industria: Two Models of the International System', *World Politics*, Vol. XIV, No. 1, October 1961, pp. 118–143.

the dominant type throughout the world with certain implications for the future of the multinational corporation that Modelski does not spell out but at which one may hazard some guesses.

Agraria—the type of international system which operated in more or less pure form in most of Arnold Toynbee's twenty-one historic civilisations—has had characteristic functions, structures and principal actors. It was a system that predominated after the passing of primitive conditions and the rise of towns and 'civilisation' but before the appearance of tremendously increased sources of industrial energy (through the harnessing of steam, oil, water and atomic energy) gave rise to Industria. Both primitive and agrarian systems were relatively small and heterogeneous while the industrial international system is both large and homogeneous.[37] Even the Graeco-Roman international system of antiquity hardly exceeded a population of 113 million in A.D. 200. The Western international system, beginning in Europe about A.D. 700, remained for centuries at a level below 100 million but it began a steep upward climb in sixteenth century Europe and within the past century has risen to nearly 1,000 million in the West and now exceeds 3,000 million as it extends throughout the world.

Agraria was (and still is, where it persists) a system in which power was tightly held by traditional elites, while Industria mobilises whole populations for political and industrial purposes.[38] Industria, moreover, exerts a strong levelling-up influence on 'underdeveloped' states either to industrialise or be eliminated by absorption.

These two major types of international system exhibit characteristic functions through identifiable actors in the system and by means of certain mechanisms that allocate actors and facilities to international functions. This division of labour in international systems is of particular interest to the student of multinational companies. There is very little specialisation in Agraria, while Industria requires a complex and elaborate division of labour. The very homogeneity of Industria as a whole system gives rise to complex new international functions, i.e. to functions that must be (or can most effectively be) carried on at the international level. In Agraria, heterogeneity was and is observable in the carrying on of most functions at the national level.[39] In the industrial international system functions are numerous,

---

[37] Homogeneity, in Modelski's terms, refers to both the relative sameness in cultures and traditions in the different societies of the international industrial system as compared with Agraria, and to the absence of a class structure which, in Agraria, makes 'subjects of most of a country's populations' whereas in an industrial society 'the whole population is mobilized for interaction' with other industrial countries.

[38] Modelski, op. cit., p. 131, characterises a member (an industrial state) of the industrial international system this way: '(1) national power based on industrial organization, large in extent; (2) political community coextensive with the population; (3) rational authority of the committee type; (4) an international culture pervading the whole society.' By way of contrast, the Agrarian model tends to require a member state to have: '(1) power based on land or commerce and limited in extent; (2) a narrowly based political community founded on kinship and centred on the prince and the great families; (3) traditional authority, typically focused on the landowner-merchant prince; (4) acceptance of the great tradition as bearer of international culture.'

[39] In Agraria, Modelski observes that 'the functions necessary for the operations of the international system, international trade and its regulation, decision-making and the

specialised and cover a very wide range of activities. The actors are not a few princes, diplomats and family heads. Not only states, but also international organisations (both governmental and non-governmental) and private firms and individuals are widely engaged in these wide-ranging actions.

An outstanding, and in some respects crucial, characteristic of Industria is the 'market for security'—the system within which security against aggression and violence can now be inexpensively bought and sold, demanded and supplied—in the nuclear missile age. The cost of security for small states was heavy, and often prohibitive, in Agraria. Deliverable security in Industria is becoming relatively cheap.[40] But military power, in nuclear terms, is not the decisive determinant of status in the pecking order of Industria. Power in Agraria rested on land and commerce, in Industria it rests on the output of industrial goods and services. Proficiency in science, technology and management is valued highly. 'High status accrues to those who assume valuable functions (for instance, as mediators and trade intermediaries or in banking as does Sweden, Canada or Switzerland)', Modelski observes.[41] But while it is true that there are increased opportunities for small states to perform such functions in Industria, there are also increased opportunities for non-state actors in the world arena and the international marketplace.

This is a point that Modelski does not make, nor is it usual to have it made by contemporary commentators on the emerging international system. The reason for this is partly the inertia of conventional wisdom about the identification of actors on the world stage. So long as non-state actors are relegated by definition to the role of mere 'objects', and not primary 'subjects' of international law, the role of multinational companies is apt to be overlooked. Yet the transnational business operations of multinational companies contribute substantially, even indispensably, to the necessary specialisation of function in Industria's division of labour. For the home and host countries the multinational company contributes towards the industrial basis of power, and for the industrial international system as a whole it contributes towards essential system-maintaining processes.

To the extent that the multinational company of the future continues to make these contributions, and at the same time can operate profitably, it will be a mainstay of the international system. To the extent that it fails so to contribute, its future may well be in doubt even if some degree of profitability can be sustained. For the international industrial system has four outstanding characteristics[42] from which criteria may be drawn for assessing

allocation of rewards, international communication and determination of the rules of international order are fused in combined roles, especially in the rulers of powerful states'. Also there are few facilities for these functions and no specialised mechanisms for diverting resources to international functions. Modelski, op. cit., pp. 132–133.

[40] 'Any power armed with nuclear missiles can safeguard the independence of a small country wherever it is situated. No state can lose its freedom against the opposition of one great power; the more such powers there are, the smaller the chance of great power collusion. . . . By a great paradox, the overwhelmingly superior power of the nuclear-equipped states may give to the smaller power a new lease of life, and to the industrial international system a hope for stability.' Modelski, op. cit., p. 143.

[41] Modelski, op. cit., p. 135.

[42] ibid., p. 139. Modelski does not pursue the subject into the area of multinational companies and would not, therefore, necessarily agree with the criteria I have formulated.

the long-term viability of the multinational company as a social institution.

The first of these characteristics is the highly developed international division of labour which requires not only states and international governmental organisations as actors but non-governmental organisations as well. In this latter category profit-making firms are as essential as non-profit organisations. The profitable multinational company is a necessary actor because it offers one of the best instruments for diverting the flow of capital to areas where development is needed. That flow has to be aided by national and public international bodies (such as the World Bank and UNCTAD) but these alone cannot do the job. The same thing applies to scientific and technological advance into underdeveloped areas. One criterion, then, for the viability of the multinational company as an institution is its performance as a major actor in the international division of labour, and not merely its success as measured by profitability.

The second characteristic of the industrial system has to do with the nature of international authority. That authority is determined not by tradition and 'charisma' but by achievement. A second criterion, then, for the viability of the multinational company is its recognition of the need for such authority at the international level and its support of ways and means to achieve it. Support for both public and private sector international institutions is required.

The third and fourth characteristics are what Modelski calls 'system integration through ideological loyalty to an international order' and 'large-scale and specialised procedures for the diffusion of culture'. As to the first of these, international solidarity is difficult to achieve in any segmented society, and not least in a world of nearly 200 sovereign or so-called sovereign states. The problem has yet to be solved, in terms, perhaps, of a few groups of powers each centering on some super-state, or of some still to be discovered universalist principle to which all could rally. The indicated criterion for multinational corporations is co-operative effort to find the solution or at least to cleave to the more viable tentative one (such as 'free-world' solidarity). As to the maintenance of international communications and the 'culture' of the international industrial system, the multinational company must shoulder its share of the responsibility along with diplomatic and other information and negotiatory networks, the world press and transnational scientific, educational, cultural and other associations.

The survival value of the multinational corporation in the emergent international system can in this way be assessed, as can national and international public policies governing the function and operations of this significant institution. It is submitted that purely nationalistic grounds for assessing the value of the institution are inadequate, and that standards of performance and statutory regulation based solely on national considerations will not suffice.

Yet this multinational company does not and cannot have its 'home' in the international system as such. There is not now and there will not soon be a world government to define the *siège social* of a multinational corporation in non-national terms. The nearest one can expect to come towards internationalisation of the seat of its business operations, at least for the fore-

271

seeable future, is common market action or continental action such as that made possible by a far-flung federal system. The multinational company must thus look two ways: towards the strengthening of its own home country as well as the maintenance of the international system. Dilemmas for both corporate and national company policy arise under such circumstances and must somehow be faced.

Chapter 4

PUBLIC CONTROL

To what extent and by what means should private enterprise be subjected to some degree of control in the public interest? Are proposals for 'social audits' or 'efficiency audits' under consideration? Should there be a public authority to conduct enquiries into companies at the request of shareholders, employees or state agencies?

BELGIUM

With the exception of special sectors, such as banking, investment, transport, electricity, insurance and mining, where direct public control is already enforced under one form or another, and certain groups of companies, such as holding companies for which it is currently demanded by the unions (see Chapter 3, p. 244 above, and Appendix A, p. 340 below), such public control is generally regarded in Belgium as something that should be introduced as an *a posteriori* measure against instances of existing abuses. This is shown by the law of 27 May 1960 on the abuse of economic power. This law seeks to prevent economic power being used to inflict harm upon the public interest by means of practices that weaken or restrict the normal play of competition or that hamper either the economic freedom of producers, distributors or consumers, or the development of manufacture or trade.

It may be mentioned here that in the case of contributions in kind to a company at the time of incorporation, or in the event of a subsequent increase in capital, the intervention of a *reviseur d'entreprise* (auditor) is prescribed by the law of 30 June 1961 to make sure, in the interest of other shareholders and of the creditors of the company, that the assets contributed to the company are appraised and compensated for in a reasonable and proper way.

In certain very exceptional cases, such as when the general meeting decides to change the rights of certain categories of shares or to replace one category of shares by shares of another kind, the law provides for the intervention of the courts. Decisions of this kind are valid only if subject to the fulfilment of certain requirements as to notice, presence and voting (Art. 71(a) of the Code on Commercial Companies). Moreover, if any proposed change of this sort is not approved, in each category of shares, by at least one third of the outstanding shares, it can be put into effect only after ratification by the Court of Appeals (Art. 71(b)). Apart from these legal requirements, the courts have intervened, reluctantly, whenever the activities of a company have been paralysed by long drawn out conflicts of interest between two groups of shareholders. (See also p. 177.)

BRITAIN

Although the Stock Exchange exercises some private (and therefore voluntary) control, there is very little public control over private enterprise. The government offers inducements and incentives but wields few compulsory powers.

Theoretically, the public interest in Britain is safeguarded in the main by the Board of Trade, the principal ministry concerned with the supervision of companies. Its powers are contained in the Companies Acts 1948 and 1967. These powers, basically, are concerned with the investigation of a company's affairs where there has been fraud committed on the shareholders or outside creditors. There is no power to intervene where the activities of the company are prejudicial to the national interest. The Board also has power, in the circumstances specified in the Monopolies and Mergers Act 1965 (see p. 100 above), to refer to the Monopolies Commission every merger of two or more companies which is likely to result in monopoly powers—that is, that the resulting combination is likely to control at least one third of the market or the value of the assets taken over exceeds £5 million. Where the report of the Commission shows the existence or potential existence of a situation which will operate against the public interest, the Board of Trade may make orders to remedy the actual or potential situation. (The Labour Party Report *Industrial Democracy* mentions the Monopolies Commission as one body through which worker protection might be achieved. As already mentioned, the Party report issued in August 1969—*Labour's Economic Strategy*—suggested that a ministerial investigation might be held when a representative body of employees considered a company was defaulting on its obligations to them. See p. 204. On the general question of public control, see also p. 185.)

The Industrial Reorganisation Corporation was established by the Industrial Reorganisation Corporation Act 1966. The Corporation's functions[1] are to promote industrial efficiency and profitability and to assist the economy of the United Kingdom by promoting or assisting the reorganisation or redevelopment of any industry or, if required by the Secretary of State, the establishment of any industrial enterprise. With Treasury approval the corporation may invest or lend up to £50 million, and it may borrow up to a limit to be fixed by the Secretary of State. This money may be used to provide any finance necessary for mergers or development. Such wide powers have given rise to apprehension in some quarters but it would not appear to be justified.[2]

The Industrial Expansion Act 1968 has conferred upon the government

[1] Sec. 2 of the Act.
[2] See for example R. H. Grierson, 'General Licence to Roam', *The Times*, 29 June 1967.

power to invest, with the approval of Parliament, up to £100 million in schemes which are calculated to improve the efficiency and profitability of an industry, to promote technological improvement or to maintain capacity. The money may be advanced by way of loan, by guarantee, by purchase of part of a company's fixed assets and its business as a going concern or by the acquisition of shares in a company. This last power, to acquire shares, is the most controversial since it is felt to be the thin end of the wedge of 'nationalisation by the back door'. However, whether this fear is justified can be seen only after the scheme has been in operation for some time. The basic idea of advancing money and supplementing the private capital market at times of high interest rates and shortage of money appears to be quite reasonable.

The National Board for Prices and Incomes, established by the Prices and Incomes Act 1966, represents a direct attempt to control prices in the national interest. The leader of the Conservative Party, Mr Edward Heath, stated in a speech at Newcastle on 14 September 1967 that this Board would be reconstituted as a Productivity Board if the Conservatives were returned to power. How far the present compulsory control of 'unjustifiable' price increases will be retained by any government is not clear.

There have been few proposals for the reform of company law arising from a study of public control and these have, on the whole, taken the form of proposals for greater consultation between the government and private enterprise, or government participation in decision-making rather than proposals for complete centralised state control over sectors of the economy. For example, George Goyder, in *The Responsible Company*,[3] proposed that the public interest should be represented on the boards of companies and that companies should be subject to a 'social audit'. However, neither of these proposals has received wide support.

At present there is no overall body exercising general control over companies in the public interest. In addition to the government agencies mentioned above which influence or control developments in various ways, there are numerous private organisations which are designed to promote the interests of various sections of the public such as trade unions and consumer associations. But it is generally accepted that public control and intervention is being extended in the United Kingdom by a variety of methods and bodies. It has been suggested, with some justification, that this method has led to overlapping of jurisdictions and to inconsistencies. The most obvious of these difficulties is provided by the uncertain relationship between the Monopolies Commission, designed to keep businesses from becoming too large, and the Industrial Reorganisation Corporation which is empowered to promote mergers. The recent proposal of the Royal Commission on Trade Unions and Employers' Organisations for a Commission for Industrial Relations, which has been acted upon by the government, adds yet another body to the many already acting to protect the public interest in this field. It is perhaps time to stand back and see whether the whole structure of these organisations might not be rationalised. Be that as it may, the trend towards wider public control has so far not produced any proposals for the reform of company law.

[3] See also Professor M. Fogarty, *Company and Corporation—One Law?*, at p. 15.

FRANCE

The *a priori* type of control traditional in France, such as the obligation on firms to obtain government authorisation before setting up in business has already been described. (See p. 169 above.) This control is reinforced by the important part played by the state in the banking, finance and monetary sector and in the financing of investments. More and more people, however, especially heads of firms and those who are concerned with management efficiency (Octave Gélinier, for example), want these arrangements to be gradually replaced by *a posteriori* controls.

The criteria by which these public controls are exercised are decided in the Plan; but because French planning is essentially flexible and indicative it is also responsible for seeing that the various interests involved in the life of the country share in the definition of the objectives. François Bloch-Lainé recalls that some people would like business and the professions to be invited to participate in the Plan as 'homogeneous units'. He points out, however, that 'if the state waited for industrialists and their employees to agree among themselves on important questions before discussing them with the state, the discussions would become long drawn out or be, most often, sterile'. The unions are particularly in favour of anything which could improve their participation in the preparation of national objectives. Lacking the means and specialised knowledge, they would prefer to use their influence in this direction rather than seeking closer involvement with firms. As for state intervention in the firm, there are the suggestions for a government commissioner (see p. 188 above). Anything which threatens to bring the state into the company is vigorously criticised by 'neo-liberals' and the employers. The 'Giscardiens', for example, are strongly of the opinion that the government should intervene in the execution of the Plan only by general measures and not by particular decisions. Pierre de Calan thinks that any power of intervention given to state representatives would be harmful because it would not correspond to direct responsibilities. 'Furthermore, the authority of the representatives, once involved directly with the firm and its everyday business, would be compromised rather than enhanced'.[4] Even the CJP believe that the public powers of the Plan have enough means of control, constraint and encouragement to render unnecessary the delegation of state representatives within the firm.[5]

With regard to socal and efficiency audits, it may be recalled that as long ago as 1944 a group of heads of firms[6] suggested in the 'Plan Commun 44' that 'every head of a firm should be subject to a "tripartite professional jurisdiction", composed of employers, salaried staff and workers, before which he could be called, within certain limits, to answer for serious administrative errors, for actions against the general interest or for infractions of professional regulations. He would be exposed to sanctions which could go so far as his

---

[4] P. de Calan, *Renaissance des libertés économiques et sociales*, Paris, Plon, 1964.

[5] M. Brissier, *Réflexions et propositions sur le livre de M. Bloch-Lainé Pour une réforme de l'entreprise*, Bureau d'Etudes du CJP, October 1963.

[6] 'Plan Commun 44—Contribution à une réforme de l'entreprise', *Le Quotidien Juridique*, No. 111, 17 October 1964, CREE Document No. 1042.

dismissal'. This structure (an example of a kind of corporatism) would be headed by a government representative with a right of initiative and veto. J. Dubois[7] has proposed the establishment of a 'Magistracy of Economic Conscience'. This would have the right to compel commercial companies with more than fifty employees, and groups such as trade associations or unions, to 'cause to resign' or dismiss 'any chairman, director, general manager, manager or partner who was individually or collectively responsible for an economic action which, although not criminal, did not appear to have been dictated by his conscience alone'.

The proposals of François Bloch-Lainé for an economic and social magistracy, as a means of appeal against the decisions of firms, have aroused particularly lively reactions, both for and against. The unions are very much in favour. 'The economic magistracy', Georges Levard has said,[8] 'will play a more and more important part as the reform of business progresses'. The Club Jean Moulin affirms the necessity of 'establishing new magistracies charged with defining the limits, the rights and the obligations of the market, arbitrating in certain business disputes, advising on the application of an incomes policy and ensuring the objectivity of information'.[9]

The employers are hostile to anything which threatens to limit freedom in business. 'Generally speaking', writes Maurice Hannart, 'we feel a definite distrust towards compulsory arbitration procedures, because the prospect of recourse to it causes the opposing parties to exaggerate and harden their positions and, on the other hand, to abdicate some at least of their responsibilities.' He favours, however, the formation of a new magistracy charged with watching over 'the compatibility with the national Plan of agreements between employers' and employees' organisations'. Obviously, this would be a means of putting a brake on pay rises. The CJP do not believe that such conflicts should be settled by an economic magistracy. Where it is a matter of legal interpretation, they consider the usual machinery of the courts to be capable of handling any problems.[10]

François Bloch-Lainé thinks that 'a court could be formed, at the highest level, composed of members of the Council of State, members of the Court of Accounts and experts designated by the Economic and Social Council. The latter would represent employers, employees and consumers. This court would be assisted by special representatives drawn directly from important state institutions or from among the Plan commissioners'. Such a court would be merely advisory. J. Dubois goes much further.[11] His 'Magistracy of Economic Conscience' would have a 'Supreme Council elected for life by all the members of this magistracy, by secret ballot. It would itself fix the membership requirements and make all nominations and promotions. It would thus be completely independent of the political power structure and every social group.'

---

[7] J. Dubois, *Recherche d'une plate-forme de politique économique de synthèse pour la France pendant les 15 années à venir*, July 1963, CREE Document No. 125.

[8] 'Débat sur la réforme de l'entreprise', *Revue de l'Action Populaire*, No. 175, February 1964.

[9] C. Bruclain, *Le socialisme et l'Europe*, Paris, Editions du Seuil, 1965.

[10] Brissier, op. cit.

[11] Dubois, op. cit.

ITALY

One of the new and most widely debated features of the Italian reform draft is the establishment of a public authority to control quoted companies. It has long been recognised that the internal control of the *sindaci* was insufficient to protect investors and that the control that a court can exercise on the drafting of a memorandum of association or over the management—when a tenth of the shareholders requires it (Art. 2409 of the Civil Code)—is limited to the formal legality of company decisions.

Under the proposed public authority, the kind of control already exercised over banks and insurance companies would be extended to all quoted companies. It would, however, be a less pervasive control, very similar to that of the American SEC. According to Art. 47 of the draft, the public authority would have the power to ask a company for information and documents; to inspect the company's books; to fix the criteria to be followed in a balance sheet; to ask for more detailed information to be given by directors to the shareholders' meeting which has to approve the balance sheet; to make observations and comments on the balance sheet and directors' report, which would be read during the shareholders' meeting; to ask for a shareholders' meeting to discuss directors' liability to the company (a power granted under present legislation to a minority of one fifth of the shareholders); to ask for remedy in the courts against irregular management (as shareholders may according to Art. 2409 of the Civil Code); to appeal against a company's decisions (a power now held by every individual shareholder under Art. 2377 of the Civil Code but which, in Art. 13 of the reform draft, would be limited to a minority of one fifth of the shareholders); and to publish in the quoted companies' Bulletin its reports and observations on the management of companies. Art. 48 of the reform draft would give the proposed public authority power to intervene with regard to directors' proposals concerning dividends to be distributed to *azioni di risparimio* (see p. 194 above), or the share exchange ratio in a merger, or the exclusion of pre-emptive rights. The authority could invite directors to amend their proposals and, if they did not do so, its remarks would have to be read to the shareholders' meeting.

The powers of the proposed public authority clearly demonstrate that its control would be exercised on behalf of shareholders and, perhaps also, of the financial market in general, but not of other wider interests. This intention is demonstrated also by the fact that the agency is to be organised by and be dependent upon the Banca d'Italia. The view that such a control over companies should be entrusted to a 'technical' rather than to a 'political' body has therefore prevailed. In the preceding debate the opposing view was that expressed by those (mainly the Socialists) who would have preferred such a public authority to be linked with the national planning institutions and be dependent upon the Ministry of the Budget.

THE NETHERLANDS

Opinion in the Netherlands is generally not in favour of public control *within* a company, as opposed to external control by the state, although a minority of the Verdam Committee did support the appointment of supervisory directors in the public interest (see above, p. 236). There have been no proposals for nationalisation. The government Bill on the presentation of annual accounts (see p. 174 above) has taken up the Verdam Committee's suggestion that an independent auditor should be appointed by companies with an issued capital of at least Fl. 500,000 or by those which are required by law to deposit their annual accounts with the *Handelsregister* (see above, p. 173). Proposals for giving the Social and Economic Council certain powers in respect of the appointment of supervisory directors have been mentioned on p. 226 above.

At the moment the law (Arts. 53 ff of the Commercial Code) grants a right of appeal to a public authority for an enquiry into the management's conduct of a company's business only to shareholders who represent at least one fifth of the issued capital, or such less amount as may be laid down in the articles of association. The court will reject the petition if it is not shown that strong reasons exist to doubt the correctness of the management or the conduct of the company's affairs.

The Verdam Committee proposed that the law should widen the opportunities for instituting an enquiry. It suggested: (*a*) that enquiries into companies not permitted to issue bearer shares should be allowed; (*b*) that the percentage of capital representation required by Art. 53 of the Commercial Code should be reduced from one fifth to one tenth and, in addition, that an absolute minimum of Fl. 500,000 should be fixed; (*c*) that holders of depositary receipts should have the same rights as shareholders to call for an enquiry; (*d*) that recognised central organisations of trade unions should also have the right to demand an enquiry; and (*e*) that the public prosecutor should be empowered to institute an enquiry.

The Committee also proposed that requests for enquiries should be dealt with by a special division of the Court of Appeal in Amsterdam (the *Ondernemingskamer*), which they suggest should also be made responsible for settling disputes in connexion with annual accounts (see p. 173 above). If the *Ondernemingskamer*, in dealing with the request, decided that strong reasons existed to doubt the correct management and proper conduct of the company's business, it would appoint a number of persons to hold an enquiry. These persons would be given wide powers for this purpose, such as the authority to inspect the company's books and records. The *Ondernemingskamer* would decide whether the report resulting from the enquiry should be made available for public inspection or merely brought to the notice of specified interested parties. If the report showed mismanagement of the company or irregularities in the conduct of its business, the *Ondernemingskamer*, upon application by the original petitioners, by other parties concerned or by the Attorney-General at the Court of Appeal in Amsterdam, would have the power to order that: (*a*) resolutions of the management, of the supervisory board, of the shareholders' meeting, or of any other organ of the company, be stayed or rescinded; (*b*) members of the management or supervisory board be suspended or dismissed; (*c*) other managers or supervisory directors be temporarily appointed; (*d*) temporary arrangements be made to depart from the articles of association; or (*e*) the company be wound up. If the *Ondernemingskamer* rejected the petition for an enquiry it would be able, if the petition were shown to have been unreasonable, to order the petitioners to pay damages to the company concerned. A Bill to widen the opportunities to institute an enquiry, following the Verdam Committee's proposals, was being considered in Parliament at the time of going to press.

SWEDEN

There is general agreement in Sweden that the need for interested parties to have information about and control over the activities of large companies has increased over the years. Opinions differ widely, however, about how this need should be met. Industrial circles usually judge the present means of control to be sufficient. At a political level, however, more direct means of regulation and joint action have been advocated. The instruments of control available to the community have so far been of an indirect kind, such as the guidance provided by general economic and fiscal policy and competition legislation. Parliament has seen to it that company auditing is efficient and carried out by authorised chartered accountants. Companies, moreover, are subjected to ever more intensive scrutiny by the press, radio and television. In the first few years after the war (and again in the late 1960s) some sectors of industry were investigated by state commissions but the social aspects of the performance of industry can be said to be fairly well cared for by the political parties, the trade unions, the press and radical authors. There is a special Swedish 'Ombudsman' for matters relating to competition, who hears complaints on restrictive practices. A state commission has also proposed the appointment of an 'Ombudsman' to look after the interests of the consumers. There is a special Labour Court where conflicts related to collective agreements are dealt with. No special authority for the problems of shareholders has been proposed. The current trend is for 'small' shareholders to organise themselves in order to protect their interests more effectively.

Part IV

THREE SPECIAL CASES

1. JAPAN

The social responsibilities of business administrators have recently been studied from various points of view. There are two main reasons for this activity. The ownership of shares has been widely spread among large numbers of people, making it almost impossible for the administration of any business to depend solely on individual owners. On the other hand, the increasing complexity of large-scale business administration has created a need for 'professional' management. This has resulted in the separation of ownership and management and the development of a conspicuous tendency for business to be controlled by management. Moreover, the economic power now exercised by the big enterprise, both absolutely and relatively, has grown so vastly that its resulting social effect can never be taken lightly. In the economic world of today a small number of large firms has an overwhelmingly powerful position and wields a monopolistic influence which tends to nullify the salutary effects of free competition so highly commended by classical economists. The result is that some big enterprises and groups pursue their policies and objectives unchecked by the processes of a competitive market. Their unilateral decisions on price, production, investment and employment affect the interests and welfare of the people and the area concerned, as well as the life of the nation as a whole. The social significance of vast economic power exercised by large companies and the responsibility borne—or mission undertaken—by their administrators are indeed worthy of serious study. In brief, the problem is to determine what attitude or method the administrators of large private firms (now free from both the one-sided subjugation to owners or shareholders and the impersonal control of a free market) should adopt in the fulfilment of their social mission as responsible, independent managers.

THE SEPARATION OF OWNERSHIP AND MANAGEMENT

The conditions just outlined have reached an advanced stage in Japan. A survey of the dispersal of the shares of big companies was made in 1958.

There were 4,050,000 shareholders of 120 large corporations, an average of 33,000 shareholders per corporation. Of the 120 corporations, 101 had more than 10,000 shareholders, twenty-five had more than 50,000 and four had more than 100,000. When the shareholders of the same 120 corporations were classified according to ten major types, it was found that individuals possessed 1·5 per cent of the total share value, banks and insurance, trust and investment companies 18·6 per cent and other agents 1·1 per cent. The total of these figures amounts to only 21·2 per cent. The percentage of individual shareholders is strikingly small.[1]

According to another survey, the percentages of share ownership of 346 big corporations listed on the Tokyo Securities Market in 1961 were as follows: 33·0 per cent by financial agents, 2·8 per cent by investment companies, 17·4 per cent by business companies, 45·2 per cent by individuals and 1·6 per cent by foreigners and others. The proportion held by individuals was less than half the total. By contrast, a high proportion was held by legal persons, including financial agents. Moreover, the share of individuals seems to have fallen since the war: the pre-war percentage of financial agents was 11·2 per cent and that of individuals 53·0 per cent. The weight of shareholding by legal persons, including financial agents, was also small after the war.[2] These results show that the conditions for the separation of ownership and management, as a consequence of the dispersal of ownership, are now firmly established in Japan.

In seeking the decisive factor which set the scene for these changes in the Japanese economy, there is no need to look further than the policy of democratisation enforced during the American occupation after the war. The breaking up of the financial combines, and the dismissal of all the business leaders who had been closely connected with the wealthy governing class and its dependants, put an end to a world of self-righteous paternalism and allowed a number of well trained or experienced business administrators to come to the fore. Hand in hand with these changes, a programme for the unionisation of industrial workers was launched. In order to cope with a labour movement which resorted to collective bargaining, business administrators were compelled to cultivate a new social attitude which required them totally to abandon the concept of employer/employee relationships that had been prevalent in pre-war Japan. In this way, the importance which the business administrator had acquired as an owner rapidly diminished in the post-war years. Study of the control of industry after 1950 shows the percentage of corporation shares held by executives and other senior members of corporations to be as low as 2 or 3 per cent of all shares. Thus, the possibility of controlling an enterprise on the basis of ownership has, for all practical purposes, been reduced to nil.[3] In a word, the administrators of large companies have held their own since the war by dint of proven administrative talent and of the social esteem they have thereby earned and not by any right or prestige of ownership.

[1] Kuniyoshi Urabe, *Kigyo-keitairon* (*The Structure of the Enterprise*), Moriyama-shoten, 1958.

[2] Statistics from Research Department, Nikyo Securities Co., and Ministry of Finance.

[3] ibid.

THE CONCENTRATION OF ECONOMIC POWER

If the Americans went somewhat too far in the enforcement of economic democratisation, the policy of the dispersal of economic power was nevertheless quite successful. In the process, however, of economic recovery through the rapid absorption of new technology, a new concentration of economic power in a few big enterprises has occurred. A number of studies has pointed to the danger that this recovery may entail something akin to the restoration of the pre-war financial combines.

In 1966, companies with more than 1,000 employees represented only 3 per cent of all companies in Japan (excluding those with fewer than three employees), but accounted for 19·2 per cent of the total number of employees of all firms employing more than three people, and for 34·2 per cent of total added value. If the concentration of general economic power is examined on the basis of the corporation unit, it is found that, in 1962, of a total of some 150,000 companies, 422 large firms (0·3 per cent) had a capital of more than 1,000 million yen (some £1·15 m.). These accounted for 26·0 per cent of all employees, 61·5 per cent of all tangible fixed capital and 51·8 per cent of total net corporation profit, whereas the small and medium-size firms with a capital of less than 100 m. yen (about £115,000) (98·8 per cent of all companies) accounted for 61·3 per cent of employees, 24·2 per cent of tangible fixed capital and 34·6 per cent of net corporation profit. Of 154 principal industries examined for their degree of concentration in production, in thirteen of them the five largest corporations together accounted for the whole of the industry's production; in ten for 90–100 per cent; and in two for 70–90 per cent. In other words, in twenty-five industries the five biggest corporations account for 70 per cent or more of production. If we take the ten biggest corporations, we find that they account for 100 per cent of production in twenty-two industries and for 75 per cent in eighty—that is, in the majority of the various industries.[4]

These facts not only show that a small number of big corporations in various industries is dominant in production, but also point to the powerful sway they hold over the industrial world through financial influence, the mutual holding of shares and the interchange of executives and staff members. All these factors give the big firms (*zaibatsu*) an important role in the moulding of the economy and the lives of large numbers of people. Opinion both at home and abroad regards this situation as something which can no longer be taken for granted. Indeed, the power and influence of an oligopolistic industrial structure is now severely criticised.

When the Japanese economy, having stabilised itself, began to expand about fifteen years ago, leading industrialists started to think more profoundly about their mission and often themselves declared the importance of their social responsibilities. The Keizai-Doyukai (Japan Committee for Economic Development),[5] one of the most progressive organisations of businessmen,

---

[4] Kosei Torihiki Iinkai (Fair Trade Commission), *Nihon no Sangyo Shuchu* (*Industrial Concentration in Japan*), Tokyo Keizai Shimpo-sha, 1964.

[5] The Keizai-Doyukai was founded in 1946. Businessmen join it as individuals and a large part of the membership is youthful and at middle management level. It serves as a meeting-

took up this question at its national convention in 1955. At its convention in 1956, a declaration was made on 'The Social Responsibility of Business Administrators: Awareness and Practice'. This called the attention of managers in general to such matters as the significance of business as a public organ, the importance of their awareness to their responsibilities to shareholders, employees, consumers and the general public, as well as to practical means for fulfilling them.

It is now evident that Japanese businessmen have a new attitude towards the objective conditions of their position. They are not satisfied with the concept of business as a purely private affair, proclaim its public importance and look forward to its establishment as an integral part of society as a whole. These progressive ideas are, of course, a direct result of the enlightened philosophy of management which was brought over from the United States after the war; how far they have permeated is examined in what follows.

PRE-WAR JAPANESE BUSINESS

The ideological background of industry in pre-war Japan could be said to be devoid of such concepts as an independent sense of responsibility or of social mission among businessmen. That this was so may be ascribed to the fact that the capitalism of Japan had always been firmly based on government intervention and the control of financial cliques. Coming into the industrial world far later than other advanced countries, Japan had largely to depend on government protection or support to overcome her backwardness. Typical examples of government intervention were the various factories set up in the early days of the Meija Era (1868–1912) and later sold to private interests, the munition and arms factories built and operated by the government till the closing years of the Taisho Era (1912–26), the counter-measures taken by the government against the panic which took place at the beginning of the ensuing Showa Era and the enforcement of a controlled economy during the last war. For some years after the end of war, the government had to adjust the demand for and supply of food in a market disturbed by its shortage.

These historical facts not only distorted the development of free enterprise but also greatly affected the outlook of businessmen. Independence and self-criticism were weakened, and it became natural to compromise or to depend on government control or intervention. To be fair, however, businessmen had little choice but to come to terms with a pattern of government control which sprang from the nationalism and militarism prevalent in Japan at the time.

For many years before the war, the financial combines—monopolistic bodies based on family and social relationships—set up holding companies in order to establish affiliated firms through which they could exercise their influence or control. Just before their break-up after the war, the four biggest combines (Mitsui, Mitsubishi, Sumitomo and Yasuda) possessed 24·5 per cent, and the big ten combines, including these four, 32·2 per cent of

place and study centre. The other main business organisations in Japan are more formal in character. The most important are the Keidanren (Federation of Industry), the Nikkei-ren (Federation of Employers' Organisations) and the Nihon-shoko-kaigisho (Japan Chamber of Commerce and Industry).

total paid-up corporation capital. Moreover, they had absolute control of the majority of such important industries as heavy chemicals, shipping and mining, of finance and of foreign trade. The entire Japanese financial world was, to all intents and purposes, under their dictatorship. According to the report of the Holding Company Liquidation Commission, the four giants alone had 49·7 per cent of the paid-up capital in finance; 32·4 per cent in the heavy chemical industry; 60·8 per cent in shipping; and 12·9 per cent in commerce.[6] In such a situation, the medium-size and small firms under the control of the combines also developed as 'family' organisations. Thus, the basis of many pre-war enterprises was similar to a family constitution—an enterprise was identified with a family. The businessman sought to run his company in rather the same way as he saw to the continuity and prosperity of his family—and he and his employees were considered members of one and the same family. Such an attitude certainly fostered habits of loyalty but something of family selfishness and paternalism lurked behind it. At any rate, it had nothing in common with modern ideas of service to the community.

It does not follow, however, that there existed no 'business ideal' to stand in contrast against the principle of profit for profits' sake in pre-war Japan. Particularly in the Meiji Era, profit-making was regarded as despicable. The tone was set by the same Confucian principles which had formed the basis of the four classes in feudal Japan—knights, farmers, artisans and merchants—and by the industrial development policy pursued by the government in a spirit of patriotism. It is true that patriotic sentiments soon afterwards become powerful in the nation as a whole; but such high-mindedness was more something of a defence mechanism against excessive government control or intervention and, as far as businessmen were concerned, was an outward gesture rather than a spontaneous expression of their sense of responsibility.

The expression *uchi no kaisha* ('my home company') is still quite often heard in modern Japan—not just from executives but also from ordinary employees. A symbolic phrase of this sort is a relic of the idea of the business as a family affair and, indeed, of 'family' structures applied to all aspects of social life in pre-war Japan. In other words, the head of a business was considered the patriarch of a family and its employees as blood relations. The capital/labour relationship was summarily dealt with by the paternalism of the employer and the slavish fidelity of his employees. The benovolent paternalism of the employer became formalised in welfare and recreation facilities for employees and the system of grading wages by seniority. The employee's loyalty became devotion to one job for life and a fatalistic attitude of compliance. Thus, the relationship between the entrepreneur and his employees was vertical or, in other words, feudalistic.

The dissolution of the financial combines and the rapid unionisation of industrial workers which accompanied the wholesale democratisation of the economy and industry of Japan marked the end of the traditional business system based on the family. The relationship between capital and labour emerged as a negotiation between equals and businessmen acquired an entirely new conception of their role. Naturally enough, many Japanese businessmen now devote much energy to the promotion of the welfare and recreation of

[6] Hitoshi Misono, *Nihon no Dokusen* (*Monopoly in Japan*), Shisei-do, 1960.

their employees; but these efforts are now motivated rather by economic considerations, to supplement, at the company's expense, the inadequate benefits of a national social security system that is still in its infancy.

What do the Japanese businessmen of today think about their management responsibilities? Some insight into this has been given by a survey commissioned by the Keizai-Doyukai, based on questionnaires sent to 1,447 large firms. The rather poor response rate of about 27 per cent may perhaps reflect a certain reluctance to think deeply about the principles of business. The results of the survey are summarised in the paragraphs that follow.

In the traditional view, the pursuit of *profit* is considered to be the main purpose of any business. According to the survey, only 35·7 per cent of the respondents still thought this to be so. The others allowed profit a functional value as a measure of the contribution a company may make to the national economy or to some loftier purpose. In other words, they valued profit only for the secondary service it performs, not as an end in itself. This is a clear result of the separation of ownership and management. The point is further clarified by the attitude towards *shareholders*.

27·2 per cent of the respondents considered that the shareholders were the owners of a company, and that it was the duty of management to act in such a way as to secure the maximum profit for them. 33·0 per cent thought that managers sometimes behave as though they disregarded the shareholders, in the apparent belief that they were promoting the latter's long-term interests. 33·8 per cent replied that, though it was true that shareholders were the owners of a company, their importance was becoming relatively less and their interests could be considered only in a wider context. Thus, the percentage of respondents who considered their duty to shareholders as an absolute imperative was lower than that of those who still claim to regard the pursuit of profit as the ultimate business objective. From this it may be inferred that the shareholder is no longer an entrepreneur, but merely a lender of funds like a banker. Thus, the immediate purpose of a dividend policy is to maintain the market price of shares at a level high enough to prevent shareholders from parting with their stocks. It is also evident that, for managers, the profit motive, as an incentive to enterprise, is declining in importance.

On the question of '*social welfare*', only about 3 per cent of the businessmen in this sample thought it would be automatically realised if every company devoted itself wholeheartedly to the pursuit of profit. As many as 93 per cent considered it could be realised only when it was a conscious aim and that this aim would be pursued only when businessmen become aware, by their own efforts or under external pressure, of their social responsibility. The remaining 4 per cent held the view that social welfare would be promoted only when private enterprise was directly guided or encouraged by the government or other public authorities. (The question of course arises of what is meant by 'social responsibility' and by the social duties of businessmen. 'Society' seems to be interpreted in two ways in discussions on this subject. It is taken to mean either a comparatively small group of people directly interested in the

company—shareholders, employees and customers, or a local community—
or a much larger community such as the nation, in which business plays an
important economic role. The questionnaire concentrated on the first
definition.)

As regards attitudes toward *employees,* as many as 95·7 per cent of the
sample said they felt responsible not only for the payment of wages but also
for the provision of facilities to raise their employees' living standards and
improve their welfare in general. Indeed, concern on this point could be rated
very high but it is doubtful whether this should be taken as evidence of a full
appreciation of 'social responsibility' in a modern sense. As already explained,
Japanese business still remains powerfully influenced by paternalistic sentiments derived from the idea of the company as a family, an attitude quite
different from that in modern Europe and America. Traditional motives of
this sort encourage Japanese firms to provide housing, dormitories and
medical services for their employees. Moreover, since the social security
system is underdeveloped by comparison with that in European countries,
businessmen consider it a managerial necessity to grant their employees
various fringe benefits at their own expense, in order to secure and retain
sufficient labour.

The survey, when considering the interest of *consumers,* did not take up the
question of price but limited itself to such topics as 'model change' and the
'merits or demerits of certain types of advertising'. Nearly all businessmen
assert the social importance of non-price factors and dwell enthusiastically on
such matters as the enlightening effect of commercial advertising and 'model
change' as vital factors in economic development. Few, on the other hand,
will willingly reduce their prices. They may constantly complain of the
anarchic state of *competition* but will still treat price as something for themselves to settle on their own. These attitudes testify to the oligopolistic state of
Japanese industry and to the shift from price competition to non-price
competition.

It has already been pointed out that in pre-war days government intervention in private enterprise was so deep-rooted, and the monopolistic
influence of the financial combines so extensive, that the attitude of businessmen to free enterprise and consequently their conceptions of competition, the
essence of the free market, were quite ambiguous. After the war, the old
financial combines were disbanded and the excessive concentration of
economic power was abolished by the anti-monopoly law. But a lingering fear of
excessive competition remained. (There has been, of course, a tendency in the
last few years to adjust or combine business interests with the object of re-
organising industry in order to make a good showing against *international*
competition.) The survey we are considering showed that 64·2 per cent of the
respondents were in favour of competition because it is the 'mother of
progress'; 30 per cent were somewhat defensive as they considered competition likely to bring disorder and confusion; and 4·5 per cent believed that
competition aggravated unfairness, as different companies start their business
in different conditions. Thus, as many as a third of those who replied had a
negative attitude to competition. Even those who were more positive did not
necessarily support free competition in the sense of the classical economists.

Their support, in other words, was conditional and different in degree according to the level of concentration in their particular industry.

The survey also revealed that more than 80 per cent of the respondents considered 'restriction of competition' was unavoidable if the development of industry was to be stable. 84·4 per cent thought that competition should be restricted by cartels and two out of three that government intervention was necessary for the effective operation of a cartel. More than half favoured restrictions on price formation, more than a quarter on plant investment, 23 per cent on the volume of production and 17 per cent on exports. Price restriction, direct or indirect, is obviously generally supported by the Japanese businessmen in this sample. Most of them would like to see such cartels run by employers' organisations, probably because the latter worked well before the war under government protection. It seems, however, that views on this point differ according to considerations of scale: generally speaking, the large companies put a high value on employers' organisations whereas the medium and small firms have complaints and criticisms about them. Under the present anti-monopoly law, cartels are illegal with the exception of those that are particularly provided for in legislation. Consequently, businessmen in the main consider the law to be an undesirable restriction. Hardly any respondent to the survey thought it should be made stricter or be applied more strictly. Only about 15 per cent were in favour of maintaining the status quo and more than 82 per cent thought the law should be moderated or its application made more lenient.

These complacent attitudes to cartels appear inconsistent with the ideas of social responsibility to which businessmen have recently given so much support. Moreover, Japan has now emerged into a world of free international trade and free capital movements. The arguments for and against the anti-monopoly law are therefore in the melting-pot. Our own view is that the law will lose the respect of informed public opinion if it is amended in a manner that narrowly favours the interests of individual firms. The business world must put forward far more comprehensive and persuasive arguments for the adjustment of the law, if it wants the public to believe its talk of social responsibility to be sincere. Under the prevalent oligopolistic economy the open establishment of cartels would be a drastic measure. Prices would no longer be 'given' but arbitrarily administered by a corporation and its allied interests. Such a situation would naturally call in question the social responsibility of the company concerned. The firm would therefore have to clarify its price-setting policy so that the public would be convinced of the reasonableness of its decisions.

Before concluding, it may be useful to consider some other points of view on these questions. The Sohyo, for instance, the largest of the Japanese trade union federations, is traditionally marxist. It wishes to continue to fight the class war and is therefore hostile to attempts at a redefinition of the businessman's role in society. (It declined to take part in the survey just summarised.) It goes along with marxist social scientists who utterly refuse to admit the facts of the separation of ownership and management and of management control and regard such expressions as 'the awareness and practice of social responsibility by businessmen' as meaningless. Such people have no doubt at all that a handful of capitalist financiers controls the business world with the banks as citadels for economic exploitation. They even think that the dispersal of shares, far from effecting a separation between ownership and management, makes it easier for capitalist financiers to exert their influence. If marxists admit that the operation of business has been transferred to professional administrators, they still consider the latter's power as being limited to the mass of small shareholders while the administrators themselves remain completely subordinated to the giant financiers.

Scholars who support private enterprise have given a warm welcome to the new willingness of businessmen to shoulder social responsibility. By studying the latest trends in management thinking as developed, for instance, by Berle and Drucker, they are trying to lay down some theoretical foundation for the businessman's social role. Their work would be stronger, however, if it paid more attention to modern large-scale private enterprise as represented, say, by firms of national dimension; it is too often limited to small Japanese communities consisting of a variety of interested groups, and their concern, as far as managerial policy goes, seems mainly to be with the distribution of surpluses within these groups. On the union side, the Sohyo's main rival, the Domei, long ago discarded Marxism and exemplifies the new labour movement matching the endeavours of employers to keep up with modern economic developments at company, industry and national level. Recently, however, it has not been eager to participate in affairs at the level of the firm, preferring to be involved in planning at industry level as seen in the broad context of the national economy. Such an attitude, it may be observed, seems entirely unacceptable.

There are two main currents of thoughts among orthodox economists, or modern economists who are not influenced by marxism. Some of them oppose the view that businessmen should be aware of a social role and should accordingly pay attention to objectives other than profit-making. They believe such an attitude to be contrary to the principle of the social distribution of work and harmful to the efficient running of business. (In this they are, curiously enough, in line with the marxists.) They put their trust in the power of competition and the free price mechanism. They are, as it were, the Japanese counterparts of the Chicago School of Hayek and Freudman. The economists of social-democratic persuasion, on the other hand, recognise the significance of the separation of ownership and management and put a high value on the incipient awakening of a sense of social responsibility among businessmen—indeed, they look forward to fostering it still further. Their interest, they believe, should not be confined to the problems of economic distribution in a small community but should extend to industrial structure, economic growth and national stability. They place great emphasis on the importance of the role to be played by large companies and the relevance of the latter's sense of social responsibility as related to such questions as national industrial planning, investment and employment. Moreover, they believe that business responsibility will be guaranteed if consumers' organisations as well as trade unions are represented within the enterprise and are permitted to take part in planning and policy decisions.

CONCLUSIONS

There is no denying that a new type of businessman has emerged in Japan, aware of the important role he is expected to play and conscious of his social responsibility. His attitudes are, however, still tinged with old, paternalistic ideas, particularly with regard to labour relations and competition. His confusion of thought may be traced to the confrontation between a distorted economic system, which had laboured under government intervention and the monopolistic control of financial combines, and the new freedoms encouraged after the war. Consequently, many Japanese businessmen have still not yet succeeded in acquiring a vigorous feeling of independence and in cultivating an ethical sense of responsibility. There is still too much easy-going reliance on government direction and mere lip-service to a social role. There is an urgent need to enquire into business philosophy or ethics to provide a base for the practical fulfilment of social responsibility. (In Europe and America, Christianity seems to go a long way in answering such a need.)

Judged by the results of the survey summarised above, Japanese businessmen appear inconsistent in their understanding of social responsibility. This inconsistency seems to spring as much from inadequate training and practical experience in new managerial techniques as from ideological or cultural confusion. It is only during the last decade that the science of management has been introduced into Japan from the United States and that firms have begun, consciously and publicly, to base their policies on these new techniques. We look to the future for better things. Japanese businessmen must now clearly explain to a critical public, both at home and abroad, how they propose to put their 'social responsibilities' into practice.

2. INDIA

INTRODUCTION

The historical roots of present-day Indian thinking about the corporate sector of the economy lie in the socio-economic ideology of the Congress Party, evolved during the most acute phase of the struggle for independence some thirty-five years ago. The basis of this ideology was the essentially egalitarian concept of economic order, then held by the dominant leaders of the liberation movement, which was later to be formalised as the 'socialist pattern of society'.[1] The beliefs of the Congress leaders were subsequently backed up by considerable practical evidence that, in the circumstances then prevailing, the resources of organised trade and industry could best serve the fuller and more balanced development of the national economy by large-scale state initiative and the active participation of the state in economic enterprises.

The early company law reformers grew up with these ideas. They were not, however, concerned with making any basic changes in the 'classical' concept of the joint-stock company or the tradition of company law which they had inherited from the Anglo-Saxon world. Although many of them might have shared, in an abstract philosophical sense, the views of the dominant section of the Congress Party on the future economic order, and on the role of trade and industry in the development and modernisation of the national economy, their primary anxiety at that time was how to deal with the growing mal-practices of company management which had become serious during the

[1] The famous resolution adopted at the annual session of the Indian National Congress at Avadi in January 1955 declared that 'planning should take place with a view to the establishment of a socialistic pattern of society, where the principal means of production are under social ownership and control'. (Indian National Congress, *Resolutions*, 1955–56, p. 1.) This resolution followed a series of policy declarations by the All-India Congress Committee, the National Development Council and the government in Parliament during the second half of 1954. It must not be forgotten, however, that these declarations saw an important role for the private sector in the national economy. The Avadi resolution laid it down that 'the private sector or the non-state and voluntary enterprises . . . will continue to have importance', and, in the course of his report as the outgoing President of the Indian National Congress, Prime Minister Nehru himself stated that '. . . the main purpose of a socialised pattern of society is to remove the fetters to production and distribution. . . . It becomes therefore necessary to have a private sector and to give it full play within its field.' Throughout these statements runs a curious blend of ideology and pragmatism—the hallmark of India's mixed economy.

293

inter-war years.[2] They sought to do this by providing structural and procedural checks and balances in the organisation and working of joint-stock companies, without impairing the classical framework of Anglo-Saxon company law. Most of the reformers were keen adherents of the traditional liberal faith in disclosure as an effective restraint on reprehensible and anti-social conduct; but, apart from aiming at increased publicity for major company decisions, they also devised measures to ensure greater powers for the general body of shareholders and closer supervision by the latter over decision-making by the management.

The leaders of the reform campaign at this stage were confined to a few shareholders' associations (notably the Bombay Shareholders' Association which was a pioneer in the struggle for the recognition of shareholders' rights and privileges), a few leading company lawyers and commercial journalists in Bombay and Calcutta and some leading members of the Congress Party.

The first glimmerings of the 'new thinking' on joint-stock companies and company law were discernible in the report of the Company Law Committee which the Government of India set up in 1950 with Mr C. H. Bhabha—a distinguished commercial banker—as Chairman and the present author as Member-Secretary. Chapter II of this document, halting and hesitant as it was in outlining the main points of the report, appears nevertheless to have been of germinal importance and to be worth recalling even now. The following passages illustrate the Committee's approach:[3]

'Some witnesses . . . seem to assume that our task necessarily presupposed that we should take a view of the role of private enterprise in the economic development of the country . . . and then formulate our recommendations. . . . Other witnesses suggested more explicitly that our recommendations should conform to particular economic policies which, in their opinion, represented the avowed aims of the present Government and the welfare state, while still others pleaded for recognition of the importance of particular interests, e.g. labour, in the administration of the Companies Act.

'For the reasons which we explained . . . we have not adopted any such an a priori approach . . . The truth is that the Company Law is primarily

[2] Many authoritative enquiries and committees which reported between 1947 and 1952 deplored the weakening of business morality since the end of the war. See, for example, the reports of the Fiscal Commission (1949–50); the Industrial Finance Corporation (Second Report); the Income-tax Investigation Committee; the Planning Commission (First Five Year Plan), etc., and also N. K. Mazumdar (Special Officer, Ministry of Commerce, Government of India), Memorandum on the Indian Companies Act (1949).

[3] Government of India, *Report of the Company Law Committee*, 1952, pp. 10–11. This passage refers to the evidence of some well-known trade unions and professional associations, of which the following are typical. (i) 'Company law partakes of the character of both public law and private law, of substantive law and adjective law. It regulates the commerce and industry of this country and therefore vitally affects the public interest. It imparts rights and imposes responsibilities on private individuals and their associations and controls the economic system. Its contents will, however, differ with the character of society, past and present, or the one to be shaped in the future.' (Hind Mazdur Sabha, a leading trade union in Western India.) (ii) 'We are of opinion that labour is a partner in any business or industry in which it is employed. Though it does not contribute capital, it performs its functions by contributing labour which is as essential an ingredient as capital in the production of goods or rendering of service.' (Indian National Trade Union Congress.)

concerned with means and not ends. . . One should recognize the limitations of an enquiry such as ours which is concerned primarily with the mechanics of company management and not with the basic economic logic underlying it.

'The operation of private enterprise under current conditions must, however, be subject to the acceptance of certain broad social objectives and of some recognized standards of behaviour. . . The working of Company Law in any country must take note of this factor, which will become increasingly important in future.'

It is clear from this chapter (and, indeed, from other parts of the Report) that the Committee, although it was pressed to take a wider view of company objectives and management behaviour than was traditionally accepted, felt that this was too unorthodox a departure from the classical view to deserve serious notice. Hence its recommendations, though far-reaching and in many ways much in advance of the classical attitude, scarcely deviated from the basic framework of traditional thinking on companies and company law.[4]

The Companies Bill 1953 faithfully followed the recommendations of the Company Law Committee. During the parliamentary stages of this Bill in 1954–55, however, its provisions underwent some major changes and it is in many of these that the slowly emerging outlines of the 'new thinking' may be discerned. This was reflected not only in the large-scale structural changes which were incorporated in the Bill at its Select Committee stage but also in the reshaping of the traditional aim of many of the procedural provisions of the law.

The distinguishing features of this 'new thinking' were the statutory recognition given in the new Companies Act to the concept of the 'public interest' in company management and the concern felt for the twin goals of a reduction of inequality in incomes and of the concentration of economic power, in so far as these were affected by company management and practice. The present author has attempted elsewhere[5] to expound these aspects at some length. There is no need to dwell on them here but it should be mentioned that, although this 'new thinking' influenced many operative provisions of the Companies Act 1956, and was officially accepted in the formulation of basic government policies for the Act's administration and enforcement, neither its underlying aims and objects nor its administrative implications can be said to have won the willing allegiance of the business community. The important issues raised are still matters of continuing argument and debate.

It may be gathered from this brief account that only a few narrow sectors of Indian society were actively involved in the origin and growth of the new ideas. The major impulse came from some leading members of the ruling political party, a few members of the government and a group of senior civil servants associated with them in policy-making, legislation and the setting up of appropriate administrative institutions. The radical wing of the Congress

---

[4] ibid., p. 13. 'It is not, however, the province of company law to anticipate what economic policy should be, and we fully endorse the observations of the Cohen Committee.' (On the Cohen Committee, see Introduction, p. 26 above.)

[5] D. L. Mazumdar, *Towards a Philosophy of the Modern Corporation*, Bombay, Asia Publishing House, 1967, pp. 54–66.

Party created the political conditions necessary for putting the 'new thinking' into practice when, under the leadership of the late Pandit Jawaharlal Nehru, it resolved at its annual meeting in January 1955 to accept the 'socialist pattern of society' as the ultimate goal of the country's economic and social policies. This policy was formally ratified by the Indian Parliament shortly afterwards.

In spite of doubts and hesitations expressed in some quarters, a broad (albeit formal) consensus on the new policy emerged in the other dominant sectors of Indian society. The Federation of Indian Chambers of Commerce and Industry (the leading representative body of trade and industry) adopted a resolution at its annual conference in 1955 endorsing the declaration. Many other professional institutions recorded their formal approval. Although subsequent events after 1959–60 were to reveal that this consensus was largely superficial, it provided the necessary climate for the basic legislative and administrative measures adopted during the years between 1955 and 1960 which gave shape and direction to the new ideas. It may be worth while to add that although wide differences of views later became apparent even between senior members of the government—particularly after 1959–60—the Cabinet as a whole had endorsed all these major decisions which were implemented in the earlier years of the acceptance of the 'socialist pattern of society'. The few senior members of the Civil Service who were concerned with the problems of joint-stock companies not only played a leading part in the formulation of the policies underlying these measures but had also to carry the burden of enforcing the policy decisions. As was to be expected, the atmosphere in which they had to work from 1959–60 onwards became severely strained, and the enforcement of policies and administration of the law could not but be affected by the gradual erosion of the consensus on basic policies.[6] Whatever impact the 'new thinking' may have had on management practice during the life of the 1956 Act has arisen mainly from the commitment of a few civil servants who had been entrusted with the administration of company law to the policies underlying it and to the values which these policies represented. An appreciation of their role is necessary for a proper understanding of the forces at work at that time. They not only pioneered but also promoted the new ideas. It was the privilege of the writer to head this small group, drawn from different service cadres and belonging to different professions, from 1953 to 1963.

The new outlook on company affairs continues to be an active concern of the radical sections in Congress (now perhaps in a minority), of several left-wing opposition parties and of the Department of Company Affairs in the Government of India. However, the old sense of urgency which inspired the radical elements of Congress has largely abated. The interest of the opposition parties on the left has become increasingly political and combative, in contrast with the zeal for reform and reconstruction which they displayed in the years between 1953 and 1960. The voice of the Department of Company Affairs has been progressively muted and the sense of commitment of its senior members to the basic values underlying the 'new thinking' has been

[6] See *Annual Reports on the Working and Administration of the Companies Act, 1956,* particularly for the years ending 31 March 1957 (pp. 1–2), 1958 (p. 1) and 1960 (pp. 1–2).

continually diluted. Nevertheless, these circles maintain a degree of their former active interest in the implications of the new ideas for company affairs in general.

The legal profession, on the other hand, has remained largely unaffected, with a few notable exceptions, particularly in the Calcutta and Madras areas. Most company lawyers have continued to adhere to 'classical' tradition and attitudes, typified by their predominantly legalistic view of managerial behaviour and company practice, and their purely formalistic opinions on many basic provisions of the new company law.

No substantial enquiry into the structure of working of company law has been held since the Company Law Committee reported in 1952,[7] although a number of *ad hoc* committees of enquiry have expressed views on many aspects of management and practice. The most important of these was the Commission of Enquiry on the Administration of Dalmia Jain Group of Companies,[8] presided over by a distinguished former Judge of the Supreme Court of India, which in the course of its detailed investigation into the affairs of these companies recommended further amendment of the Companies Act 1956. These recommendations were intended primarily to close loopholes in the Act, which in the view of the Commission permitted the abuse of some of its provisions, and the indulgence by some groups of companies in dubious practices which the Act had attempted to control. More recently two other Committees were set up to examine the incidence of monopolistic and restrictive practices in the corporate sector[9] and to consider the future of the managing agency system,[10] the traditional form of company management in India. Important as were the recommendations of these two committees, they did not impinge directly on the structure or working of the Companies Act, being concerned with two major aspects of company practice and management which had been the subject of continuous and widespread debate since 1952–53.

Other professional people—accountants, executives and company secretaries—though relative newcomers and (with the exception of the accountants) not yet fully institutionalised, have taken a much more lively interest in the 'new thinking' than their colleagues in the very much older legal profession. Their views have, however, been largely confined to professional issues of accountancy, management and the mechanics of company administration. From time to time, however, they have shown a perceptive understanding of and interest in the impact of these issues on the relationship between company practice and society in general.

Trade unions and other workers' movements played a significant role in the evolution of the new ideas in the formative stages of the new Companies Act between 1950 and 1955. Indeed, several provisions of the Act, particularly those relating to company management, owe a great deal to the constructive

---

[7] But see 'Conclusions', p. 319 below.

[8] Government of India, *Report of the Commission of Enquiry on the Administration of Dalmia Jain Companies*, 1962, pp. 797–815.

[9] Government of India, *Report of the Monopolies Enquiry Commission*, 1965.

[10] Government of India, *Report of the Managing Agency Enquiry Committee*, 1966. (On the managing agency system—abolished as from April 1970—see p. 308 below.)

suggestions and recommendations of trade unions.[11] In recent years, however, union interest seems to have shifted more to industrial relations, to wages and participation in profits, not to mention their unending competitive struggle to secure the allegiance of workers. The earlier demands for participation in management voiced by some sectors of the union movement now seem less insistent. Employers' organisations, banking and other investment institutions have clung tenaciously to the classical tradition and have shown little interest in innovation.

The contribution of social scientists has been conspicuous by its absence. Apart from economics, the social sciences in India have yet to reach the necessary degree of sophistication. Senior Indian economists, following the example of their British colleagues, have till recently taken little interest in the study of analytical institutional economics. Furthermore, neither the economists nor the other social scientists have so far learned to regard the joint-stock company as the most dominant socio-economic institution in the organised sector of the Indian economy, much less as a significant system of power. It is only during the last ten years or so, as a by-product of the interest taken in company affairs by legislators and administrators, that some statistical and descriptive studies have been undertaken.[12] It is to be hoped that, with growing interest in the study of corporate economics, these pioneering efforts may stimulate further studies in depth and provide the essential raw material for a more meaningful investigation into corporate management and practice in the future.

The only significant public opinion groups which can claim to have made any contribution to the new developments are shareholders' associations in the leading centres of commerce and industry. The most important of these and one which has to its credit a remarkable record of constructive effort over many years is the Bombay Shareholders' Association. In recent years its influence has somewhat declined, mainly because of the many stockbrokers who have joined this association, and whose interests and points of view do not always coincide with those of shareholders. As a result, its approach and attitude towards company matters and company law has become somewhat blurred and less cohesive.

---

[11] The far-reaching amendments to Chapter III of the Companies Bill, 1953, on managing agents, introduced at the session of the Joint Select Committee of Parliament held in August and September 1954, were inspired by a resolution passed at the 1954 annual session of the Indian National Trade Union Congress.

[12] See P. S. Lokanathan, *Industrial Organization in India*, London, Allen & Unwin, 1935, and D. H. Buchanan, *The Development of Capitalistic Enterprise in India*, New York, The Macmillan Co., 1934. The more important of relatively recent publications are: M. M. Mehta, *Combination Movement in Indian Industry: A Study in the Concentration of Ownership, Control and Management in Indian Industry*, Allahabad, Friend's Book Depot, 1952, and *Structure of Indian Industries*, Bombay, Popular Book Depot, 1953; N. Das, *Industrial Enterprise in India*, Bombay, Calcutta and Madras, Orient Longman, 1956; *Concentration of Economic Power in India*, Allahabad, Chaitanya Publishing House, 1962; R. K. Hazari, *The Structure of the Corporate Private Sector*, Bombay, Asia Publishing House, 1966. See also the publications of the Research and Statistics Division of the former Department of Company Law Administration, of which the author of this Chapter was Secretary between 1955 and 1963. The more important of these are *Managing Agencies in India (First Round: Basic Facts)*, 1958 and *The Corporate Sector in India*, 1960.

The press and other mass media might have been expected to influence thinking on company matters but the conditions in which the Indian press functions, and its close links with trade and industry, make it difficult for it to express any views which might appear to be critical of the practices of leading businessmen or business houses, on whose support it still leans heavily. Besides, economic journalism, even of the generalised type, is still in its infancy in India. Professional journalists by and large lack the specialised and sophisticated training needed for competent study and analysis of company practice and finance and their relationship to society, and a specialised cadre of journalists who can be expected to handle with knowledge and confidence company data and the statistics of finance and investment has yet to emerge.

CORPORATE DISTINCTIONS

Different forms of private enterprise

The two major classes of companies recognised in the Indian, as in the English,[13] Companies Act are (i) private companies and (ii) public companies. Like the English Act, it also provides for a class of non-profit-making companies, i.e. companies whose objects are limited to the promotion of commerce, art, science, religion, charity or any other useful object and which intend to apply their profits, if any, or other income, in promoting their object and which prohibit the payment of any dividend to their members. There is no distinction, as in English law, between exempt and non-exempt private companies. On the other hand, the Indian Act (Sec. 43A) recognises a new type of private company, popularly known as a 'deemed public company'. In private companies of this category not less than 25 per cent of the paid-up share capital is held by one or more bodies corporate. For all practical purposes the duties and responsibilities of such companies are the same as those of public companies and the provisions of the law relating to public companies broadly apply to them.

Indian law also recognises a class of 'Government Companies' (similar to the so-called 'Crown Companies' in some other parts of the world), in which not less than 51 per cent of the paid-up share capital is held by the Central Government or by one or more state governments, or partly by the Central Government and partly by one or more state governments. Subsidiaries of a government company so defined are included in this category. The three principal distinguishing features of these companies are: (i) they are not under managing agents; (ii) the standard audit provisions of the Companies Act, which apply to all other companies, do not apply to them in as much as the audit of their accounts is carried out by auditors appointed by the Central Government under the general supervision and direction of the Comptroller and Auditor-General, whose instructions they must carry out; and (iii) that the Comptroller and Auditor-General is entitled to supplement the audit of the accounts of these companies and in fact does so in much detail.

[13] It should be noted that this chapter was written in the light of English law before the British Act of 1967 came into force. Reference may be made to the British sections in the earlier parts of this book for the changes introduced by the Act of 1967.

The line drawn between private limited companies and public limited companies so far as their objects, constitution, management and external control are concerned follow broadly the distinction between such companies in the English Act, with certain modifications. For example, the Indian, unlike the English, Act requires the accounts of all private companies to be audited by qualified auditors. On the other hand, the control provided for by the Act over the management of public companies or the remuneration of different classes of executives does not apply to private companies, nor do these sections intended to regulate the contracts, inter-company loans and investments of public companies and their subsidiaries.

The 'deemed public companies' under Sec. 43A of the Companies Act were a conceptual innovation, meant to bring the two principal classes of limited companies somewhat closer together as regards their status, privileges and liabilities. The amendment arose from the growing dissatisfaction with the use of private limited companies as a device for getting round the restrictive provisions applying to public companies and as channels of undesirable investment by public companies, whose freedom to invest and engage in financial transactions not directly connected with their interests had been severely restricted by the Act of 1956.

The general theory underlying the differentiation in the Act between private and public limited companies (the two principal classes) is that the public interest in the organisation and working of the latter justifies the exercise of a much wider and tighter supervision and control than is needed in the case of private limited companies in whose operations, it is assumed, the public are not normally so interested or concerned. This theory, inherited from the classical Anglo-Saxon tradition of company law, has, in the light of the Indian experience (and presumably that of other countries), become increasingly difficult to support. During the discussion on the amendment of the Companies Act in 1960, several prominent members of the Joint Select Committee of Parliament argued that the distinction between the two classes of companies as laid down in the Act of 1956 was unrelated to actual contemporary developments in company method and practice, served no useful purpose and should be abolished. These would-be reformers maintained that if there was to be any distinction between different categories, it should be between relatively small and larger companies, as, for instance, between the German AG and GmbH. The Minister in charge (the late Shri Lal Bahadur Shastri) favoured a classification based on size but eventually no action was taken because it was felt that to amend the law in this way would involve too drastic a departure from long-established legislation and practice. Be that as it may, many contemporary students and experts believe that it may now be time, in the public interest, to take a further look at this question. Experience of Indian company legislation and the working of joint-stock companies leads the present author to share this view and to feel that a good case can be made out for the rationalisation and simplification of the law, involving the abolition of the distinction between private and public companies in favour of a classification based on more relevant criteria, such as size or other related objective facts.

As far as enterprises in the private sector are concerned, the choice as to the form in which they should be organised is, of course, left to promoters and investors and the provisions of the relevant laws have nothing to say about how this choice should be exercised. In practice, however, apart from the sprawling unorganised sector of the Indian economy, with its many 'self-employed' businesses, the choice in the organised sector is between partnerships and limited companies. Because of the increase in the scale of business, in both manufacturing and trading, the number of companies has grown enormously. After the end of the second world war, many large partnerships were converted into private limited companies, particularly in the years between 1946 and 1950. The principle of limited liability was a very important factor, next only to the taxation laws, in this change-over.

The choice between private and public limited companies is largely determined by a complex of considerations in which fiscal laws, the size of the company, the nature of its business, the manner of its financing, the extent to which it is likely to depend on internal or external sources of finance and to which it has to apply to semi-governmental or private financial institutions and, above all, the stock exchange requirements, play a decisive role.

Public and private enterprise

The debate on the form of ownership of public sector enterprises goes back to 1950.[14] Shortly after Independence the issue assumed considerable practical importance as a result of the new government economic policy of establishing key and basic industries, often very large, in the public sector. Several committees and commissions debated the pros and cons of the different forms of organisation suitable for public enterprises, and a number of official and unofficial *ad hoc* studies were made of the practice in other industrially advanced countries. Opinion on this subject has varied from time to time and it is unnecessary in this context to go into the history of this debate. The present thinking seems to be broadly as follows. (*a*) If an enterprise is closely integrated with and forms part of the operational activities of a government department (e.g. a factory building coaches or locomotives for the Department of Railways), it may be carried on either as an independent wing of the department concerned or as a government company, depending on the comparative advantages of the two forms of organisation as seen by the departmental authorities. (*b*) For businesses or industrial undertakings which provide goods or services in the nature of public utilities (e.g. civil aviation) or relating to the infrastructure of trade and industry (e.g. electricity or road transport), the form of a public corporation might be desirable. (*c*) For other businesses or industrial undertakings which are engaged in the production and sale of goods and services—particularly where collaboration with private capital or private management is desired—the company form of organisation would ordinarily be considered to be the most suitable.

The differences between public and private enterprises organised in the form of companies do not arise from the provisions of the Companies Act—except in regard to audits (see above)—but from policies and attitudes towards

[14] See Government of India, *Report of the Indian Fiscal Commission*, Vol. 1, 1950, pp. 219–221. The debate continued intermittently until the Congress Parliamentary Committee under the chairmanship of Shri V. K. Krishna Menon reported in 1960.

their responsibilities. These differences are reflected in the articles of 'government companies'. As a rule, these provide, *inter alia*, for the appointment of the chief executives by or with the approval of the government and for government approval of contracts above certain ceilings (the latter fixed by the government), of the appointment of executives above prescribed salary levels, of capital increases, of the raising of loans, of capital expenditure beyond a prescribed ceiling and of the allocation of profits. Government companies are also subject to parliamentary control and to scrutiny of their accounts and other activities by the Public Accounts Committee of Parliament and the special Parliamentary Committee on Public Undertakings set up a few years ago.

Most people believe that the main differences between public and private enterprises arise from their objectives, how they operate and the different degrees of public control exercised over them. It is implicitly held that public companies must have wider business objectives than the maximisation of profits, that they should aim to earn no more than an optimum return from their investments, consistent with their responsibilities to their employees, the local community and the public interest, which may involve quite legitimate expenditure out of their income. Their constitutions and ways of organisation also provide, if not expressly at least by implication, that they must accept the obligation to follow national policies on the appointment and recruitment of personnel and appropriate levels of remuneration for top management, with due regard to the latter's competence and technical qualifications. It is also the prevailing view that public enterprises are under a special obligation to subject themselves to the public gaze and assume the liabilities imposed on them by the need for scrutiny of their accounts and of policies, both managerial and financial, by Parliament or any central public agency set up by Parliament. It is clear that people expect from public enterprise what the best undertakings in private enterprise would do of their own accord. In other words, the view taken in India of the attitudes, motivation and behaviour of public enterprises seems to approximate to the 'ideal' organisation and working of firms in the private sector—a point of view not very different from that observable in other advanced countries.

THE OBJECTIVES OF THE COMPANY

It has been increasingly recognised in recent years that, irrespective of legal provisions, the responsibilities of a company are not merely to its shareholders and creditors but extend to employees, customers and suppliers, and embrace within their scope also the interests of the local community and the national economy. The Companies Act 1956 was the most important single factor in developing this attitude. Other important influences have been the gradual development of professionalism in management; the example of the industrially advanced countries of the world, reinforced by that of foreign collaborators in Indian joint ventures; an increasing anxiety among large firms to project an acceptable 'image'; the gradually increasing impact of the new schools of management set up in different regions during the last decade; and the competitive effect of the broader social objectives officially accepted by companies in the public sector. It would be unrealistic to claim that such enlightened views are held by more than a few progressive businessmen. Most companies have yet to translate them into appropriate action.

The economic environment since the second world war has not been helpful. War-time controls and their aftermath, followed by continuing shortages and consequent restraints on trade and industry, both internally and externally, have ensured a highly sheltered domestic market. Foreign competition has been virtually non-existent and internal competition relatively weak except in a few consumer industries such as cotton textiles. The size and the productive capacity of the internal market has steadily increased but effective demand has at the same time continued to run ahead of production and supply. Indian management has never been forced to accept the usual social obligations to customers or partners in production, nor to strive for the high standards of performance which would help to transform the strictly economic process of marketing and distribution into socially responsible business.

The consumer

The desirability of reducing the cost of goods and services, while improving their quality and providing marketing facilities normally available to consumers in industrially advanced countries, is widely recognised and accepted by far-sighted business leaders. The urgent need to secure for Indian trade and industry a better reputation abroad has been emphasised, not only for the sake of the growth of Indian business but as an essential aspect of public relations in contemporary society. Little, however, has been done. Businessmen complain that they are hampered on all sides—by shortages of materials and equipment, the poor quality of labour in some industries and above all by taxation. Frustrated consumers argue that the government must intervene. But there are hardly any consumers' associations worthy of the name, even in the industrial and commercial centres, and the few that do exist in name lack the leadership and expertise necessary for dealing effectively with the problems.

The shareholder

There is at present hardly any statutory control over dividends or other monetary benefits to shareholders except in the case of one or two utilities such as electricity generation. Studies on income and price policy are still in their infancy.[15] There are, however, other factors which exercise some indirect control on dividends. A major provision of the Companies Act 1956 (Sec. 205) prohibits the declaration of a dividend by a company which has not made any provision for depreciation in its accounts. This gives statutory backing to the orthodox view, hallowed by many court decisions, that dividends may be paid only out of profits and not out of capital. The other indirect control is the demand of employees for a share in company profits,

[15] See Reserve Bank of India, *Report on a Framework on Incomes and Prices Policy*, 1967. This report was prepared by a steering committee of economists and others employed in Central Government departments and in the Reserve Bank of India, under the Chairmanship of Dr B. K. Madan, until recently Deputy Governor of the Bank.

which in Indian industrial parlance goes by the name of 'bonus'. Both the industrial courts and the Bonus Commission,[16] appointed by the government to go into the matter and lay down norms for the determination of profit-sharing, have accepted the legitimacy of this claim under certain conditions and up to certain limits. The recommendations of the Commission have been embodied in a statute. No other definitive proposal has so far been made for the regulation of dividends and other benefits to shareholders.

The employee

The wages of industrial labour and the conditions governing their fixing and regulation are dealt with in the labour laws and labour codes. The remuneration of other employees (middle management, for example) is also for all practical purposes outside the provisions of the Companies Act and is indeed free from all legal restraint.

The 1956 Act, however, deals at length with the remuneration of managing agents, directors and the most senior executives.[17] Very briefly, the position is broadly as follows. The aggregate marginal remuneration payable by a public company (or a private company which is a subsidiary of a public company) to its directors, managing agents, secretaries and treasurers and to its general manager may not exceed 11 per cent of annual net profits, exclusive of fees paid to directors for attending board meetings. If profits are nil or inadequate, minimum remuneration of not more than Rs.50,000 a year, in aggregate, may be paid to top managerial personnel, whether they are directors, managing agents or the general manager. Compensation in excess of these two overall limits must meet with the approval of the company, conveyed through a special resolution, and/or with the approval of the Central Government. Within the limit of 11 per cent of annual net profits, further ceilings on the remuneration of managing agents and whole-time directors have been imposed administratively; the law also specifically provides that the remuneration of an individual director may not exceed 5 per cent of annual net profits.[18] These provisions are more than twelve years old

[16] Government of India, Ministry of Labour and Employment, *Report of the Bonus Commission*, 1964, pp. 107–120.

[17] See Government of India, *Annual Report of the Company Law Advisory Commission for the year ended 31 March 1957* for a detailed summary of these provisions and of the principles evolved by the Commission, constituted under Sec. 410 of the Companies Act, on whose advice alone the government were competent to take decisions on these matters.

[18] In an earlier publication (*Towards a Philosophy of the Modern Corporation*, Bombay, Asia Publishing House, 1967, pp. 18–19 and 155–156), the author of this chapter has gone into the reasons for these unusual provisions in the Act of 1956. It is not necessary to discuss them again. However, as the Indian law represents a major departure from the classical tradition of the Anglo-Saxon countries, it may be worth while to reproduce the following brief extract in order to explain the nature of Indian thinking.

'All these provisions of our new Companies Act have been the subject of much comment not only in this country but also abroad. They have been attacked on the grounds that it is for shareholders to fix the remuneration of the management of companies and that administrative interference with managerial remuneration may be arbitrary, and may adversely affect the incentives to effort and risk-taking. And yet perceptive observers of the corporate scene in this as well as the Western countries have always recognised the fact that this problem of managerial remuneration or compensation, as it is called in some of the latter countries, provides a classic example of the unregulated use of corporate power, in the

and have been administered in consultation with and on the advice of a small body of eminent persons drawn from some of the major interests concerned in the working of joint-stock companies. Nevertheless, business is still not reconciled to their underlying objectives and fitfully continues to voice its opposition.

Recent studies in several western countries, and particularly in the USA, have shown that the problems of top managerial remuneration do not arise merely from the issue of legitimacy, but even more importantly from the fact that there is no competitive market in the higher echelons of the management profession, partly because of its characteristics and partly because of the methods of appointment and the conditions of employment. These non-competitive aspects are aggravated in India by a number of factors—the tardy growth of professional management, the prevalence of caste and family considerations in many private firms, the persisting hereditary character of top management in a disproportionately large segment of trade and industry, and the dominance of the ideological concept of equality on the part of elites generally, irrespective of their socio-economic or party affiliations. The provisions in the 1956 Act represent a rough and ready approach to this difficult problem and should be considered in the light of what has been said.

Development expenditure within the firm

The Indian Companies Act, like its English prototype, is neutral towards all internal development expenditure, whether destined for capital investment, research and development, employee training or the improvement of organisation and methods. Expenditure under the last three is given some indirect encouragement by liberal tax reliefs. Fiscal policy has varied from time to time but has never been deliberately designed to encourage the ploughing-back of profits rather than their distribution. Nor has the state ever made any claim to a share in ploughed-back profits, although, as already mentioned, the claim of employees to a share in earned profits, whether they are distributed or not, has been recognised following the recommendations of the Bonus Commission. (Towards the end of 1956, the then Minister of Finance, Shri T. T. Krishnamachari, proposed a Compulsory Reserves Scheme, under which companies would have been required to obtain Central Government approval for the use to which they put their reserves. The scheme was poorly

sphere of decision-making which calls for some effective measure of internal and external control. In a fairly well-publicised book on the Western methods and practices of corporate management in the USA, called *The American Stock-holder*, the financial commentator of a well-known Philadelphia journal attempted an analysis of the social consequences of the inevitable erosion of shareholder power on corporate management. "Executives", he commented, "had become an over-privileged class in a democratic society." The gravamen of his charge was that "with the restraining hand of shareholders atrophied, a tax-sheltered elite was inexcusably setting its own extravagant compensation [and that] the most serious consequence of this policy was not the diversion of corporate funds to personal use, but the impact which unduly high executive reward had upon the rest of society". In the light of this comment from a well-informed and sober critic of corporate methods and practices in this field, the provisions of our Companies Act, 1956, relating to managerial remuneration may well be said to blaze a new trail in thinking on the problems of corporate management in modern society.'

conceived and was soon found to be unworkable. It was abandoned by Shri Krishnamachari's successor.)

The need to increase company expenditure on research and development, and also on employee training, has been much emphasised in recent years and it is possible that such outlays will receive greater fiscal encouragement. However, the pace of technological advance and the scale on which industrial research has to be undertaken make it unlikely that the great majority of Indian companies will be able to take advantage of probably limited tax incentives. For many years to come, small and medium-sized firms will have to be assisted by industrial research in government or semi-official research institutes.

External expenditure

Expenditure incurred by companies in their relations with trade and research associations qualifies for tax relief but is relatively small as few associations offer costly services. By and large, trade associations function as if they were employers' trade unions and are mainly concerned with negotiating tax concessions and similar advantages. Apart from the research institutions organised and financed by the associations of leading export industries, several new research institutes have been set up by other associations of predominantly domestic industries during the last fifteen years. Progress in this area has been slow but steady. With regard to expenses incurred in relations with distributors and suppliers, it should be borne in mind that one of the earliest concerns of the Indian company law reformers was to try to prevent the marketing and distribution functions from imposing needlessly onerous burdens on consumers and the community. The 1956 Act lays down certain procedures for regulating the appointment of sole selling agents and their remuneration and also of buying and selling by managing agents of companies or their associates.[19] The Indian marketing and distribution system will have to be modernised before a more liberal view of expenditure on this account can be taken by either the government or others concerned.

Services to the community

Most large-scale industrial investment since 1951 has been covered by the Five Year Plans and has had to conform to Plan requirements both as to location and size. In some cases certain obligations on pricing policy have been imposed but only on the advice of a competent statutory body like the Tariff Commission and always with recourse to administrative arbitration. Any non-commercial services which companies may be asked to render to the community, either under the national plan or otherwise, are regulated through administrative machinery. Firms are not, for instance, generally required to accept unremunerative or not fully remunerative public service

---

[19] Sec. 294(1) and (5) of the Companies Act, 1956, require that the appointment of sole selling agents must have the prior approval of the company in general meeting and authorise the government, if necessary, to call for information about such agents. Sections 356–360 attempt to regulate the appointment of managing agents or their associates as selling or buying agents and also the terms and conditions on which managing agents or their associates can enter into selling or buying agency contracts with the managed companies.

responsibilities except in emergencies. In normal times leading businessmen frequently serve as voluntary part-time members of government commissions and committees and as paid members of the boards of public sector enterprises. These duties are more often regarded as a recognition of merit than as a burden and it is rare for either the companies or the individuals involved to be called upon to make much sacrifice. Business donations for education, research and charity are usually granted to institutions directly or indirectly controlled by the donor but other unconditional gifts are made from time to time. The record of a small number of Indian firms is not unworthy in this respect. Few business houses have so far set up non-family trusts or foundations, whose policy and management is not directly or indirectly influenced by their leading members, and it is only in rare cases that such organisations are run by competent independent trustees.

The legal definition of objectives

Following its English prototype, the Indian Companies Act of 1956 merely required the inclusion in the memorandum of association of a brief statement of the company's commercial objectives and the ancillary or incidental powers necessary to give them effect. An amendment[20] has provided that the objects clause should specifically distinguish between main objects, objects incidental or ancillary to the attainment of the main objects and other objects. It seems doubtful whether the purpose underlying this amendment, which clearly was to check indiscriminate diversification, will be achieved. The suggestion originally made by George Goyder in his book *The Responsible Company* that every company 'should be required by statute to add to its Memorandum of Association a general purpose clause expressing its purpose in terms of its obligation towards the shareholders, customers, workers and the community affected by the enterprise' has been considered at various seminars and conferences in India. The most important of these, held at the India International Centre in March 1965, was concerned with the social responsibilities of business. Mr Goyder and several other foreign scholars participated. The seminar broadly endorsed his views but expressed some scepticism as to the effectiveness of a general purposes clause of this type. It was thought that any such clause, phrased only in general terms, was likely to remain merely a statutory declaration of good intent. To achieve anything more, the proposed new obligations would have to be translated into operational terms and appropriate changes in company law (based on the operational concept of these aims and objects) made both in the substantive and the procedural provisions of the Companies Act. To a limited extent, the present Indian Act has done something of this kind with regard to remuneration of directors and senior management.

The doctrine of *ultra vires* has been invoked only in a few cases but nevertheless dominates the thinking of lawyers and judges, probably because of the influence it has enjoyed in the United Kingdom. If the objects clause of the Companies Act is extended in the manner proposed by Goyder, and suitable substantive and procedural amendments are made in the law, the purpose underlying the doctrine would appear largely to have been served.

[20] See Sec. 13 of the Companies Act, 1956, as amended in 1965.

This would be particularly true if the policy-making organs of a company included representatives not merely of shareholders but also of employees, customers and the general community, and if the law provided for consultation with these outside interests before a company took decisions which might directly concern them. Such developments, however, would have more to do with the 'new thinking' on the wider objectives of a company than any revision of the doctrine of *ultra vires*.

COMPANY ORGANISATION AND CONTROL

The powers and accountability of chief executives

When the 1956 Act was under discussion there was some debate about the powers of boards of joint-stock companies and the merits and demerits of both the Anglo-American and Federal German systems. The government undertook a tentative study of the latter, chiefly in the context of the relationship of labour to internal company management. In recent years, even in trade union circles, interest in the German model has noticeably declined. This does not mean that the unions considered the Anglo-American to be altogether satisfactory but by and large they now incline to the view that corporate accountability is best secured by their own activities, backed up by effective and vigilant shareholder participation and government control over decision-making in the more important areas of company management, such as trading and financial policies, managerial remuneration, investment and disclosure.

One particular aspect of the management structure of Indian companies, peculiar to the country, has received much attention in recent years. This is the 'managing agency' system, up to now the dominant form of company management. It involved a two-tier constitution, with the board of directors at the head of the hierarchy and 'managing agents' forming an inner core of management, theoretically under the control and supervision of the board but in practice leading them in decision-making. The system has been under attack for nearly twenty years and has been the subject of many investigations.[21] The latest official report[22] recommended its abolition in several well-established industries, but supported its retention in some others for the time being. The government, however, decided to do away with managing agencies altogether and, under the Companies (Amendment) Act, 1969, the system is completely abolished as from April 1970.

The Indian Companies Act deals elaborately with the appointment and dismissal of chief executives, whether they be managing directors, managing agents or general managers. By and large the terms of such appointments are

[21] The managing agency system is easily the most distinctive Indian contribution to the formation of institutions in the corporate sector and the greater part of the meagre Indian literature on the subject relates to it. The most comprehensive factual study of the system before the passing of the 1956 Act was undertaken by the Research and Statistics Division of the former Department of Company Law Administration (within the Ministry of Commerce and Industry). The study was supervised by Dr R. K. Nigam, under the instruction and guidance of the author, then Secretary to the Department.

[22] Government of India, Ministry of Law, Department of Company Affairs, *Report of the Managing Agency Enquiry Committee*, 1966.

set by company boards, subject to the provisions of the Act with regard to directorial and managerial remuneration which have already been described. Contemporary thinking on managerial remuneration has become much less rigid than it was at the time the Act came into force—largely, perhaps, because of dissatisfaction with the somewhat haphazard administration of the law and also because of the growing professionalisation of company management.

The traditional hierarchical system of management and the fact that major decisions still remain in the hands of managing agents, managing directors or general managers (many of whom, over a large area of Indian business, still constitute fairly well-knit family or caste groups) mean that the powers of chief executives in relation to third parties and their accountability for the actions of their subordinates are not live issues. The legal responsibility of directors (including managing agents and general managers holding directorial positions) for the major decisions of a company are, however, recognised in Indian company law in much the same way as in English law.

THE REPRESENTATION AND PROTECTION OF INTERESTS WITHIN THE COMPANY

Disclosure

Even before 1956 the attitude of Indian company law towards disclosure went far beyond the traditional limits of its English prototype. Indeed, several provisions of the Indian law, particularly those relating to company accounts, were much in advance of similar English and other foreign legislation. This was recognised by the Company Law Committee.[23] Until the period of 'new thinking', the law on disclosure was intended primarily to benefit shareholders and creditors. At first, shareholders' associations, the legal and accountancy professions and other bodies combined in their demands for greater disclosure, on the ground that it was in the interest of their clients. The concept of disclosure in the interest of employees and the national economy emerged later as a by-product of economic planning in the 1950s. The Act of 1956 greatly enlarged the scope and limits of disclosure, particularly with regard to company accounts and increased supervision of decision-making by the shareholders—the 'democratisation of management'. Many important areas of management and company practice, previously left entirely to the judgment of the board, were brought by the Act under the surveillance of the general body of shareholders, either through ordinary resolutions or 'special' resolutions needing a three-quarters majority of shareholders present at a meeting. It was also laid down that copies of all special resolutions and of certain categories of ordinary resolutions must be forwarded to any member of the company who might ask for them (on payment of a nominal fee) and also to the Registrar of Joint-Stock Companies. In this way much detailed information about the working of joint-stock companies was now readily available not only to the shareholders but also in offices of public record.

In recent years the business community has voiced even louder demands

[23] See p. 113 and pp. 467–472 of the Committee's report.

that these requirements be relaxed, on the grounds that they are costly and time-consuming; that most shareholders make little use of the resolutions they ask for; that neither the employees nor government departments make much use of the information contained in these records; and that the added publicity may sometimes needlessly expose companies to malicious attacks by hostile individuals or groups. No proposals, however, have been made for amending the legislation and it is doubtful whether the burden on companies is really still felt to be onerous. The question, nevertheless, remains whether much use is being made of the newly available information (even on company accounts) by any one, including the government. If it is not, is it worth while indefinitely to retain the present requirements of the law? In a sense, the answer would depend on the government's future attitude to company management and administration and on the public's attitude to private enterprise.

The shareholder

Before considering the position of the shareholder under Indian company law, it will be useful to recall a few points made earlier in these pages and developed more fully elsewhere[24] by the present author. (*a*) In several important areas management decisions are subject to the consent of the shareholders, by ordinary or special resolutions, depending on the nature and importance of the decisions. This control is, in particular, exercised with regard to the appointment, reappointment and remuneration of managing agents, managing directors and top managerial personnel, and in respect of contracts and other financial transactions of the management, especially inter-company contracts entered into between companies belonging to a group controlled by the same management. (*b*) Competition and other market forces do not operate effectively in the managerial field in an economy such as that of India. (*c*) The organs of public opinion and other forms of communication, many of which have close links with the higher ranks of business, cannot adequately protect the interests of shareholders and others. (*d*) Business must increasingly conform (within the pragmatic limits of administrative enforcement) with the basic values implicit in the accepted goals of national economic and social policy.

The Companies Act 1956 greatly extended the scope and range of *shareholders' meetings* and created conditions in which active shareholders could play a useful part and also exercise an indirect influence on company practice by taking advantage of the disclosure rules. Experience has shown, however, that the company reformers' naive faith in 'shareholder democracy' has largely vanished. Like any other form of democracy, it needs to be backed up by the continuous vigilance of a few men with enough time, money, trained assistance, knowledge and experience to build up the organisations necessary for shareholders' meetings to have any effective impact. (The present writer had personal experience of these problems when, shortly after the passing of the Act of 1956, he and some of his colleagues tried to revitalise a number of the existing shareholders' associations and to encourage the establishment of new ones.) Efforts have been made to devise other political

[24] Mazumdar, op. cit., pp. 31–32 and 51–53.

or economic substitutes to offset the powers of company management, such as joint advisory boards consisting of representatives of management, shareholders, employees and public authorities, or 'local meetings' open to representatives of consumers, workers and the community, including the local authorities.

Indian company law does not contain any special provision for the representation on company boards of any class of *capital suppliers*. Such an arrangement has not so far been thought necessary despite the increasing reliance of firms on external finance for their short-term as well as long-term capital requirements during the last decade or so. These requirements have in the main been met by the commercial banks and several public and specialised financial institutions, the most important of which are the Industrial Finance Corporation of India, finance corporations operating at state level, the Life Insurance Corporation of India, the Industrial Credit and Investment Corporation of India and the more recently established Industrial Development Bank of India. These institutional investors have not had to resort to statutory board representation in order to protect their legitimate interests and safeguard their investments in joint-stock companies. When one of these bodies grants financial assistance to a firm it usually enters into a specific agreement which, apart from the normal contractual safeguards (including the power to foreclose in an extremity), permits it to be represented on the board of the company to which a loan has been made. It is then left to the management and shareholders of the beneficiary firm to accommodate the representatives of the lending institution within the limits of their articles of association, which are amended, if necessary, for this purpose. These institutional investors have, like their British counterparts, on the whole refrained from taking any active interest in the management or control of any company, except when gross mismanagement may have threatened their investment. There has been little demand from any other source for the representation of capital suppliers on company boards. It has been generally assumed that the attitudes and values of institutional investors towards economic and social matters would inevitably lead them to take a limited view of their duties and responsibilities even if they were represented on boards.

The Act of 1956 hardly recognises a distinction between *committed and uncommitted investors*. Before 1956, special classes of investors could influence or control companies by holding shares with disproportionate voting rights, variously described as founder's shares, deferred shares, etc. The new Act provided that the share capital of companies limited by shares formed after it came into force could be of two kinds only—equity or preference. Ordinarily only equity shareholders have voting rights, in proportion to their holdings. Preference shareholders normally have no such rights, except when their dividends fall in arrears for two years. The Act also laid down (*a*) that no company formed after its coming into force could issue any equity shares carrying voting or any other rights as to dividend, capital or otherwise, disproportionate to the rights of holders of other equity shares; and (*b*) that existing disproportionate voting rights should be terminated within one year of the Act coming into force. Although the Central Government took powers to exempt companies from this provision in the public interest, or in that of

311

the company, or any group of its shareholders or creditors, it has exercised this power in one or two instances only.

The Act does not contain any special provision[25] for *minority rights* except in cases of oppression or gross mismanagement of company affairs by the majority, likely to jeopardise the interests of the minority. In the latter case the more important of certain elaborate provisions are contained in the following sections of the Act. Sec. 233A enables the government to order a special audit of a company's affairs, when the latter is not managed in accordance with sound business principles, or is run in a manner likely to cause serious injury or damage to the interests of the trade, or when its financial position is such as to endanger its solvency. Sec. 388B empowers the government to bring to the notice of a tribunal constituted under this section the conduct of the management of a company, and to ask for an enquiry into the fitness of the management to carry on the business, in the event of fraud, malfeasance, persistent neglect, or default in carrying out the obligations of company law; or where the company is not being managed in accordance with sound business principles or is being run in a manner which is likely to cause serious injury or damage to the interests of the trade. Sections 297 and 398 deal with the powers of the courts and the government to intervene in the event of oppression of its members, gross mismanagement or serious prejudice to its interests or prejudice to the public interest. Sec. 408 empowers the government to appoint not more than two suitable persons to the board in order to prevent the affairs of a company from being conducted in a manner which is oppressive to any section of its members, or is prejudicial to its interests or that of the public.

It should be said that, in the Indian context, these apparently drastic powers have not so far been regarded either as oppressive or constraining. They have been used effectively in a few cases only, and the leaders of the business community (and others close to the business world) have reluctantly recognised them as a necessary check upon certain elements which can still cause much damage to the reputation of business.

The employee

The old demands of left-wing trade unionists for employee representation on boards and other internal company organs, which received some support in recent years in official labour circles and from left-wing intellectuals and economists, appear to have been much less loudly voiced lately. Greater reliance is now put on institutions such as works councils and committees, joint consultative or advisory bodies within a firm, and on normal external union activities for the protection and advancement of workers' interests. Most of those directly or indirectly concerned with labour problems agree that, given the traditional organisation and structure of company management, this is the best way for labour to safeguard and advance its legitimate

---

[25] Nevertheless, Sec. 265 of the Act does give a company the option of adopting proportional representation for the appointment of directors. This compromise between English law and the compulsory provisions of company legislation in several states of the USA was embodied in the Act of 1956 after an amendment to provide for compulsory provisions of the American type was defeated at Select Committee Stage.

interests, with the support of suitable legislation. The government appointed a National Commission at the end of 1966 to undertake a comprehensive reappraisal of current labour legislation. This Commission has now reported but it is unlikely that early action will be taken on its wide-ranging recommendations, some of which concern very controversial issues.

The consumer

Although under Indian law there is no representation of consumers' interests within the firm, several provisions of the 1956 Act were intended to afford indirect protection to these interests within the limits of statutory provisions. These provisions concern such matters as the purchase and sale of goods and services by managing agents; the appointment of sole selling agents by directors; and contracts for the sale and purchase of goods by directors and managing agents.

The prevailing view is that consumers would be better protected by direct legislation on product price and quality and, to a lesser extent, by legislation directed against mergers, amalgamations, combinations and restrictive practices which are held to be contrary to the common good. (The difficulties of strengthening the bases of market competition have already been discussed.) Some legislation on quality and other services to which consumers are morally entitled was passed several years ago but it has by and large proved inadequate and ineffective. Because of this, more and more support has been given to consumers' associations and co-operative stores, particularly in metropolitan areas. These, however, have been severely hampered by continuing shortages of goods and services (and especially of basic consumer goods), in the face of accelerating demand. This is a major issue of economic policy and administration which can be hardly dealt with through company law or practice as such. Enlightened management could do a great deal to improve matters but unfortunately any sign of leadership on this score has been slow to emerge.

The public interest

A feature of the 'new thinking' on company management, practice and law has been the formal recognition given to the concept of the public interest, not only in several provisions of the Companies Act but also in the official formulation of policy relating to company affairs. In an essay written some time ago the present author pointed out that the more important sections of the 1956 Act which specifically mention the concept of public interest are generally in those areas of law where even conventional legal wisdom was disturbed at the likely consequences of the unhindered exercise of private rights by management or stock-holders. Indian law has now formally recognised the fact that there are circumstances when the joint will of management and stock-holders may have to give way to the requirements of public policy. This recognition may be traced in numerous sections of the 1956 Act—for example, those requiring compulsory provision for depreciation before dividends on shares or stocks can be paid; those dealing with the form and content of the balance sheet and the profit and loss accounts and those

313

concerning the presentation of these documents; and those dealing with the compulsory amalgamation or merger of companies in the public interest. The concept has been spelled out in such a way as not only to provide in certain circumstances for special procedures and action but also to authorise exemption from the general rules laid down in the Act.

An institutional step was taken in a recent amendment of the Companies Act, which set up the office of Public Trustee in order to enable the Trustee to take over the voting rights of shares and debentures held in trust from their trustees to be exercised in such manner as he may determine. The object of this amendment was to ensure that voting powers attaching to funds held in trust for the community or the public were exercised to promote the public interest and not to further those of private individuals who had formed tax-free trusts, ostensibly for 'public motives.' Whatever the theoretical justification for this amendment, however, it has so far had hardly any impact on company practice and is unlikely to have any in the near future.

The location of interest representation

Contemporary Indian thinking has not seen the boardroom as a suitable forum for the representation of the various interests involved in the conduct of a company's business. The increasing professionalisation of management is one important factor. It has already been mentioned that greater reliance is likely to be laid on new institutions to be set up within or outside the organisation of a company, integrated with the organisation on an advisory or consultative basis. Hence an important future task of management will be to assimilate the views expressed in these new institutions into the processes of policy formulation and execution. At the seminar mentioned above, much emphasis was given to this integrative role of management, as the following extracts from the Declaration adopted at the seminar will show:

'It should now be clear that it falls to management to see that the multiple social responsibilities of business are fulfilled. Each of the parties involved in business has no more than a partial interest in the enterprise; only management entrusted with its governance carries the overall responsibility for its success and growth. Management must be freed from one-sided dependence on any single interest, if it has to take a broad enough view of its obligations. Hence, our proposals for extending its formal accountability, but they will not in themselves suffice.

'With the growth of large-scale enterprise, management under any system of accountability and control necessarily acquires a high degree of autonomy in its decisions. While it must in practice reconcile the sometimes conflicting claims made on the enterprise by various interested groups, it is not merely their servant but has creative powers of initiation and innovation. How these powers are used depends essentially on the prevailing philosophy of management and the capacities and convictions of managers. . . . We want to promote a more enlightened philosophy of management which encourages responsible participation of all employees by respecting their dignity as human beings.'

PARTLY OR QUASI-INDEPENDENT UNITS OF THE FIRM

The special problems of dependent units would *prima facie* appear to arise from the fact that, in law, they are formally under the control of their parent firms. The managements of these companies are, therefore, formally subject to the overriding control and direction of the management of the parent companies, should the latter decide to exercise their rights. A similar problem used to arise with companies managed by the same managing agents. It was not unusual for as many as twenty or thirty companies to be managed by one or more associated managing agents, although the 1956 Act attempted in many provisions[36] to deal with these problems of agglomeration and the attendant and inevitable complications.

Indian thinking on subsidiaries and other quasi-independent units has, however, chiefly confined itself to the limited issues of the concentration of power. It is widely accepted that, whatever the legal or formal status of subsidiaries and other quasi-independent units, the objects which their management should pursue should be the same as, or similar or ancillary to, those of their parents; but their status should not have any effects, either in law or in practice, on the freedom of initiative or action, or the accountability, of their chief executives. Likewise, if the constitutions of the parent companies provide for the representation of all the participating interests, there is no good reason why the constitutions of the subsidiaries or other units under their control should not provide for similar representation.

PUBLIC CONTROL

The conviction that all companies set up under the terms of a public franchise, and dealing with the public in some form or another, and especially public limited companies as defined in law, are institutions in which the public are both directly and indirectly interested is central to the 'new thinking' on company affairs. Hence, the boardroom decisions of such firms should not merely conform to the technical requirements of the law but also take account of public requirements. It follows that all their major policy decisions should be based on the values implicit in the ultimate goals of national economic and social policy. Thus, in the Indian context, 'public interest' means not merely that of the national economy, as defined by state policy or legislation, but embraces all the other interests (quite apart from those of managers, shareholders and financiers) which are directly or indirectly affected by the operations of firms. It has never been suggested that this concept of 'public interest' implies that the 'external' interests are as relevant or as close to the day-to-day running of a company as are the more direct interests. It has merely been held that management should integrate all these diverse interests in a systematic and coherent manner, and take decisions founded on an integral and not a partial concept of the managerial function. How this is to be done is not a matter of law but of empirical judgment on the part of management.

In practice, of course, it is not always easy to define the area of 'public

[26] The more important of these are Sections 332, 370 and 372, which deal particularly with problems of management and investment.

interest' in individual decisions. Ordinarily, therefore, both law and practice leave it to the management of companies to act in the spirit of the law. But when a particular decision is clearly and seriously against the public interest, the administration has pointed out to the company management how they have failed to measure up to legal requirements. In situations like this the administration has taken its line from several sources, among them the following: constitutional provisions concerning the goals of Indian economic and social policy; authoritative statements on economic and social policy approved by Parliament; the advice of statutory advisory commissions and committees, in cases where these have been set up to assist the administration; competent expert advice on good company practice in relation to managerial, investment and financial problems; and the advice and opinions of trade and industrial organisations.

There has consequently been much more supervision of company management than is usual in the administration of similar measures in Britain or America, for instance. It has often been asked why India has chosen to follow this method of detailed regulation. The present author has endeavoured on many occasions in the past to explain the underlying theory of the Indian approach and will now limit himself to recalling some observations made by the late Shri Lal Bahadur Shastri (then Minister of Commerce and Industry and later Prime Minister), during the debate in the Indian Parliament at the time of the enactment of the Companies Amendment Act 1960.

Shri Shastri emphasised six main points. (i) Principles of social responsibility have won no more than limited acceptance—and that only in a comparatively small section of the Indian business community. (ii) The average company management has been rather slow in acquiring a sense of fiduciary responsibility. (iii) There is a lack of strong and well-organised financial institutions, with long traditions of public service and reputations to lose, for overseeing company flotation and management and, to some extent, thereby making the statutory regulation of company practice less urgent. (iv) The financial and economic press is weak and not wholly independent. (v) A vigorous and well-developed public opinion, such as would not tolerate unwarranted deviations from the accepted forms of company behaviour and practice, is also lacking. (vi) Comparatively slow progress has so far been made towards the professionalisation of management. Shri Shastri contrasted this situation with that in Britain, the USA and other Western countries, in which far-reaching changes in the character and quality of company management have evolved.

There is another aspect of this matter which should be mentioned.[27] Much debate took place in 1952 and 1955 on the institutions which were to be entrusted with public control over firms. Earlier, the Company Law Committee had expressed its preference for a statutory corporation on the lines of the American Securities and Exchange Commission, rather than ministerial or departmental control. The government, however, finally accepted the

[27] This debate began with the recommendations of the Company Law Committee (see *Report*, pp. 193–195) and continued until the conclusion of the parliamentary discussions on the Bill in the middle of 1955. (See Government of India, Department of Company Law Administration, *Selections from the Debates of the Report on Company Law*, 1955, pp. 51–55.)

recommendation of a Joint Select Committee of Parliament that, in order to exercise the wide range of control necessary in the Indian context, the authority should be a duly constituted department of government, under a minister. The minister in charge of the Companies Bill pointed out that the type of control over company affairs envisaged in the new Act would involve judgment on important public issues, many of which would go to the heart of the country's economic and social policy, and that it was therefore desirable for the government itself to assume direct responsibility. In the light of what has happened since, it is now possible to take a different view and, on balance, more people are inclined to do so. Their opinion is backed up by the fact that control over companies involves detached understanding and neutral and informed judgment with regard to company affairs, qualities not often found in civil servants (executive or judicial) and even less frequently in politicians.

The prevailing attitudes to the question of public control of companies in India may be briefly summed up as follows. The government and the Civil Service are in a sense committed to established policy, however much certain individuals may deplore the circumstances which made statutory controls necessary and however much they see the need for changing many of the provisions of the present law, particularly those which appear to serve little practical purpose. Business opposition to public control is sometimes based on ideological grounds—never very forcefully expressed—but is more often realistic and complains that the present legal and administrative requirements are complicated, time-consuming and irksome. There is, however, little inclination to challenge the basic philosophy underlying the present policies, much less to repudiate it altogether. Professional people are less vocal. Lawyers and accountants from time to time point out the system's defects and deficiencies and plead for simplification. Shareholders' associations seem no longer to take a strong line either way. Many of them now perhaps understand quite well that their members' interests cannot be protected merely by means of legal provisions and that they have to rely almost wholly on the administration to enforce the law, particularly when their interests are most closely affected. Public opinion is by and large indifferent to business affairs except when a scandal is in the news. Most of the organised political parties (except, perhaps, a section of the Swatantra Party whose economic and social views are not recognisably different from those of late nineteenth century liberalism) accept the need for the provisions of the Companies Act and their vigorous enforcement by the administration. In general, the whole question of company management and practice is no longer the live issue that it was in the 1950s. It is now the problems of growth and development, and the hardships and frustrations caused by failure to move ahead fast enough, that appear to hold the centre of the stage.

Social and efficiency audits

The idea of an 'efficiency audit' has been much discussed in recent years but little has emerged in the way of concrete and detailed proposals as far as the private sector is concerned. There has been some practical interest in public sector companies but progress has been hampered even here by the inability of the accountants and the management's financial advisers to work out the full implications and put a system to the test. Experiments have usually been no more than variations on the audit system operated in government departments under the control and guidance of the Comptroller and Auditor-General. An amendment of the Companies Act (Sec. 233B) provides that the government may order the audit of a company in suitable cases, but only if the company has been officially asked to record additional information in its books and accounts, with particular reference to the utilisation of material or labour and/or to other cost items as may be prescribed. Although this amendment was made about five years ago, no administrative orders have so far been issued. It would therefore seem to be primarily an expression of intent on the part of the then minister which does not appear to have been followed up.

The concept of a 'social audit' received a good deal of support at the India International Centre seminar already mentioned and the Declaration then adopted[28] recommended that a social audit should be introduced (on a voluntary basis at first) so that a factual assessment could be made by trained and professional observers of companies' 'social performance'. Such an assessment would, however, be meaningful only if undertaken by people trained not only in the social sciences but also in the mechanics of company management and finance, since they would be called upon to do for the 'social' performance of a company what the financial auditor already does for its financial. Since the recommendation cannot be implemented unless efforts are made to build up, from scratch, a force of auditors specially trained in the social sciences, it is hardly surprising that both business leaders and accountants have looked askance at this suggestion. It is nevertheless worth mentioning that several companies in the public sector have been already subjected to detailed study and assessment of their performance (in regard to matters such as prices, wages, research and development, public and human relations and employment stabilisation) by the Committee on Public Undertakings set up by the two Houses of the Indian Parliament some time ago.[29] The studies on several government enterprises undertaken by this Committee (and such staff as it has been able to command) cannot yet be said to constitute a real social audit, but they do contain much valuable raw material for such an audit and point to a possible institutional innovation which might help to strengthen the social outlook of management.

Rights of appeal

The Indian Companies Act provides for a right of appeal by shareholders to the Central Government and the courts and in this respect goes further than its English prototype. Under Indian law, this right is not confined to cases of fraud, malfeasance, mismanagement or oppression of minorities but extends, for instance, to the cases covered by Sec. 233A of the Companies Act. (See p. 312 above.) Furthermore, as has already been pointed out, the government has taken additional powers in Sec. 388B of the Act to refer to a tribunal the

[28] The text of this Declaration has been reproduced in the *Report of the Seminar on the Social Responsibilities of Business*, Manaktalas, Bombay, 1966, pp. 25–32.

[29] This Committee, comparable with the British Select Committee on Nationalised Industries, has already completed studies on a large number of government companies. Its reports are published by the Lok Sabha Secretariat, New Delhi.

cases of individual managerial personnel who are *prima facie* deemed to be guilty of malpractices or gross mismanagement, in order to seek their dismissal. Action under these two amendments can be taken only by the Central Government and cannot be initiated by shareholders or any other group. Nevertheless, the fact that the Act has provisions which go beyond the traditional limits of punitive action by governments or any central authorities, such as the American SEC, has damped down any demands for additional rights by either shareholders or employees. Many responsible people believe that the present powers are not only adequate but border on the excessive and that institutional changes should be made to ensure that they are used only in the public interest and not at the whim of an interventionist civil servant or minister.

CONCLUSIONS

This chapter has attempted to set out the views of those who take an active interest in company affairs in India. It should be stressed, however, that big business still remains a distant and, in many ways, a somewhat esoteric element in the modernised sector of the Indian economy. There remains, in many parts of the country, a gulf between businessmen and educated and thoughtful people, especially intellectuals. An important consequence of this psychological and moral alienation has been the lack of any close involvement on the part of intellectuals and others in business affairs and a corresponding failure to take a constructive interest in business problems and particularly in the organisation and working of firms. The ideas behind the 'new thinking'—largely worked out by sophisticated politicians, civil servants and professional people aided by the writings of Western scholars and the example of the best foreign corporate practice—have yet to impinge upon the average businessman whose conventional wisdom is still derived from the old-world practices of craft and marketplace. Only when this happens will there be a hope of building a bridge of understanding and assimilation between the two points of view.

Until recently, no scheme for the general reform of company law has so far been seriously considered in India and there have been no more than the suggestions for limited changes in particular aspects of the law, as outlined in this chapter. In 1967, however, a Working Group on Company Law Administration (under the chairmanship of the present author) was appointed by the Administrative Reforms Commission which was itself set up by the Central Government in 1965. This Group undertook a rapid survey of the whole field of the administration of company law in India and suggested some far reaching changes to improve its working and relate it more specifically to economic policy as pursued since the enactment of the basic legislation of 1956. No action has yet been taken on the Group's recommendations[30] but they cover such a wide field, of both law and administration, that it seems likely that, together with other suggestions for reform, they will form the basis of any future scheme (which cannot be delayed much longer) for the general reform of company law in India.

[30] *Report of the Working Group on Company Law Administration*, Administrative Reforms Commission, Government of India, 1968.

3. YUGOSLAVIA: A SOCIALIST ALTERNATIVE

INTRODUCTION

The institutional differences being what they are, it might be asked how a brief description of the organisation and administration of the Yugoslav enterprise, and of its practical everyday experiences, could contribute much of use to a book essentially concerned with company law and structure in capitalist countries. Nor can a chapter in a book produce ready-made and lasting solutions to the permanent human problems and conflicts of interest that at present bedevil modern industry. There is no 'golden key'. The answers must be sought in a process of continuous and systematic thought geared to practical action. If the relatively short experience of Yugoslavia can teach us anything, it is that the problems are far more complicated than they appear to be when seen from the viewpoint of modern social philosophies. To understand this is in itself useful; but this alone would not be a sufficient justification for this chapter. Its special contribution is, perhaps, that it will help to clarify some present trends and to define a range of possible solutions. Recent studies suggest that the relationships between the major organisational variables seem to be curvilinear, that is, the direction of the trend changes at a certain point. Is it possible to determine the trend if we never venture beyond the limits of our own particular culture? Does a certain institutional and cultural setting allow us to see the trend as a whole, including the point at which it changes? Or must we cross the borders of our own culture and compare contrasting environments? It would seem that we must. The theory of the enterprise can hardly be an exception when other social science studies are developing in a cross-cultural and cross-national direction. Such an approach will yield a deeper understanding of some basic aspects of social organisation and of the dynamics of the modern enterprise. It will also lead to a more adequate social philosophy of the enterprise as a basis for more viable practical solutions to its problems. If this chapter makes no more than a small contribution towards this aim it will have fulfilled its purpose.

THE FRAMEWORK

In dealing with its characteristics and problems, it must be borne in mind that the Yugoslav enterprise is one part of a wider whole. It is not possible here to give a full description of the Yugoslav economic system and social structure which would help to place the discussion in a complete perspective. However, readers are probably familiar enough with the basic facts and some cautionary remarks will suffice.

It is generally known that contemporary Yugoslavia is a socialist society founded on the social ownership of the means of production; that its economic structure is not based on central state planning but is decentralised, with a remarkable degree of market economy involving considerable, though limited, autonomy for business firms; and that Yugoslav socialism is not rooted in state control but in the principle of self-management. However, only a specialist can know to what extent the real economic structure of the country contains elements of decentralisation and centralisation, of market competition and government regulation, of state control and self-management. This question of 'how much' is often baffling for foreigners who make a close study of the Yugoslav economic and social system. Indeed, the question cannot always be answered satisfactorily, as the economic and social structure is intriguingly complex and cannot easily be reduced to ready-made formulae.

However, Yugoslav scholars *do* know that the relationship between various disparate elements of the economic and social scene is constantly changing. It is not the same today as it was fifteen years ago and is probably different now from what it was before the processes of the 'economic reform' began. Observation of these changes over a period would reveal a steady trend, despite all the shifts and hesitations—a trend towards more of a market economy, more autonomy for business firms, more self-management. In other words, the Yugoslav economic system, and the social system as well, is not a static and completed system, but is in a state of flux, developing towards the desirable type of economic and social structure we call 'the socialist society'. To understand this is to ward off the dangers of imprecise everyday language which, more often than not, makes no distinction between *the* socialist society and *a* socialist society. This essential point must be made clear if the heart of the subsequent discussion is to be properly understood. If the reader starts from the assumption that the Yugoslav economic system (and Yugoslav socialism in general) is a static system, he might interpret the rest of this chapter as an argument that the existing model does not work very successfully. Such an interpretation would be basically erroneous. We start from just the opposite assumption: that society and the economic system in Yugoslavia are undergoing vigorous development towards a new 'steady state' which is still far from being attained—and so is the model of the enterprise. It is hardly surprising that not all these developments run smoothly. The road is unmapped and much that has been undertaken has been empirical and hit and miss. Moreover, historical conditions have been unfavourable: a peasant society with heavy emphasis on the authority of and control by the state, a low general level of education, a relatively high rate of illiteracy, and so on. In view of the complexity of the problem it would be foolhardy to be dogmatic about the viability of the present model of the Yugoslav enterprise. This chapter has a far more modest intention: to illustrate certain phenomena and problems connected with the development of a new model of the enterprise, which are, or might be, relevant to a more general discussion on the modern business firm.

Finally, a word of caution about terminology. To make the discussion intelligible, terms have been employed that are customarily used in such discussions in the West. There is a danger that this could give the false impression that identical notions and phenomena also exist in Yugoslavia. This is not the case. For example, the term 'management' has no equivalent either in the language or in reality. When it is used in this chapter it should be taken merely as a rough approximation that can be applied to some aspects only of the phenomena to which it relates. The same holds good for other terms as well. The Western reader must beware of reading his natural preconceptions into the discussion that follows.

THE MAIN INTEREST SERVED BY THE ENTERPRISE

What is the main interest that the enterprise is supposed to serve? We shall begin with the institutional definition of the main interest, in spite of the fact that the real state of affairs always differs to a greater or less degree from the theoretical institutional framework. There is a sharp distinction between the Yugoslav and, say, the British enterprise from the institutional point of view, since a British enterprise serves the interests of an external group, the shareholders.[1] As recently as 1950 Yugoslav enterprises also served external interests—those of the state. Enterprises so far submitted to these external interests were reduced to technological and production units, executing centrally planned tasks that had their origin in the state budget, and paying their income into the same budget. Since the introduction and development of the self-management system, the institutional definition of the main interest has been radically changed: the enterprise is, in the first place, supposed to serve the interest of the members of the working collective and only indirectly the interests of society as a whole. This also means that the main interest lies within rather than outside the enterprise.

The interest of the working collective is expressed by the method of distributing the enterprise's income. The enterprise produces the goods and services demanded by the market; by selling them it earns its income. After covering business costs, taxes and other obligations, the balance of the gross income is distributed, as net income, into the funds of the enterprise and the personal incomes of the employees. In this way, as far as running the enterprise and distributing its income are concerned, all the rights (but not the influence) of any outside group are institutionally ruled out. Moreover, personal contribution remains the sole claim to participation in management and the distribution of income.

The situation, then, may be summed up in four points. (i) The main interest a Yugoslav enterprise is supposed to serve, as institutionally defined, is that of the members of the working collective, in order to maximise their personal incomes. (ii) The role of the public authorities is reduced in the main to enacting and enforcing the laws regulating the administration of enterprises and their taxation, taxes also being an instrument for directing their activities.

[1] George Goyder, *The Responsible Company*, Oxford, Basil Blackwell, 1961, Chapter 3.

(iii) There is no such thing as a capital market, although some kind of investment market does seem to exist. (iv) The financial resources invested in an enterprise do not act as 'capital'. Such finance carries no rights to participate in the management of the enterprise nor to benefit from the distribution of income in the form of dividends. These rights flow solely from employment with the firm and personal performance.[2]

CAPITAL SUPPLIERS

If the connexion between the enterprise and the state budget has been severed, and there is no capital market, who finances new investments? The whole answer cannot lie in self-financing as only very large enterprises can finance their own development. Nor will self-financing help us to answer the question 'who founds enterprises?' This is the problem we have now to consider.

Under the present regulations, enterprises may be founded by public authorities, economic enterprises, co-operatives, social and political organisations and groups of citizens. The regulations lay down that the task of the founder is to supply the initial assets necessary for the operation of the enterprise. These resources (regardless of who the founder is) are managed by the working collective of the newly founded enterprise and its organs. As already mentioned, such finance does not represent capital invested by the founder, and does not earn dividends, but is considered as a credit on which the enterprise pays interest and annual charges.

This is the legal framework. But who, in fact, does found enterprises? Are the founders predominantly the public authorities or other enterprises? No systematic data is available but it is nevertheless possible to state with a fair degree of certainty that the founders are, in the great majority of cases, public authority bodies. Why is this so and what does it mean?

At the moment, enterprises have little motive to invest their funds in the foundation (or enlargement) of other enterprises. Since investors have no claim to management rights or dividends, they can neither influence their investment nor win financial rewards (other than interest). On the other hand, high interest rates, especially in the conditions of inflationary pressure and legal insecurity as regards investments which prevailed until comparatively recently, scarcely make such investments attractive.[3] The pressing demands of employees to increase their relatively low incomes, which are fully understandable given increased living costs and much stronger aspirations towards a higher standard of life, work in the same direction.[4] For

---

[3] Some Yugoslav economists (including Dr D. Dubravčić, Dr F. Černe and Dr B. Horvat) use the term 'collective entrepreneurship' to describe such an institutional framework. In his book *Ogledi o jugoslavenskom društvu* (*Essays on Yugoslav Society*), Zagreb, Mladost, 1969, Dr Horvat has devoted a special section to 'collective entrepreneurship'.

[3] At present high interest rates on loans are attractive to the few big banks that inherited the so-called 'state capital' (assets of the Federal Government's former Central Investment Fund) and to privileged re-export companies. For example, these banks and companies, and not hotels or other tourist organisations, are the main investors in the Yugoslav tourist industry.

[4] The massive financial non-liquidity plaguing Yugoslav industry makes this pressure even stronger. Quite often many firms are unable to pay even these modest wages and salaries to their employees on the due date.

these reasons, investment by an economic enterprise in the foundation of a new enterprise (or in new plant in an existing enterprise) is often motivated by other considerations such as a desire to ensure the supply of raw materials.

The situation will be quite different when the founder is a public authority body. Non-economic motives will, of course, come much more frequently into play than will be the case when the investor is an enterprise. For example, the motives may be to provide employment for the population of a certain area (a chronic problem all over the country) or may have its roots in local politics, local patriotism, the personal standing of local personalities in the eyes of the electorate and so on. As an investor, a public authority body is in a better position than an enterprise. In a formal, and still more in an informal way, it may gain a considerable and even a dominating influence over the management of the enterprise. (The decisive influence upon the appointment of enterprise managers that has been and still is wielded by local communities will be examined later.) A public authority body, moreover, obtains, through taxation, a certain return on the financial resources which it has invested.

From the period of central planning until the economic reform, investment was undertaken by the state, which acquired the funds that were necessary from enterprises. Thus, more was taken from efficient enterprises. The functioning of state mechanisms of concentration and distribution of investment is of no interest here. It should be stressed, however, that this concentration of financial resources did not encourage enterprises to invest in other enterprises, as even the big ones were left with relatively small sums for investment after taxation.

It is scarcely necessary to say that such a policy inevitably hindered rational and efficient investment and affected economic growth. We are not concerned with this aspect. What, however, is important for us is that the situation as described is incompatible with the institutional definition of the enterprise. It is plain why this state of affairs was sharply criticised and why measures were urged, especially once the economic reform got under way, to hand over the investment function to the enterprises themselves.[5] This is the economic meaning of the so-called de-centralisation and de-bureaucratisation which have been so widely written about and discussed in Yugoslavia in recent years.

Will all the problems be solved, however, once the state withdraws from this field? Enterprises will have greater financial means for investment; but the problem of the concentration of these means has to be faced. One possible answer is concentration through business banks; another is 'integration', over a range from co-operation to mergers. Both solutions, the latter especially, have many inherent difficulties, since the basic problems of controlling investments in another enterprise (by participation in management) and of participation in the distribution of the resulting income have not yet been solved. The situation will be further complicated by possible foreign investment in some Yugoslav enterprises.

---

[5] This is still one of the proclaimed goals of the economic reform. However, it has not come about, since the practical economic policy measures were, more often than not, at variance with this aim.

All these eventualities are under study and various practical steps are being taken.[6] However, it seems that, if practical solutions are to be achieved, the institutional definition of the enterprise will have to be modified so that invested capital can be taken as a claim to participation in managing another enterprise and sharing in its income. On the other hand, it is too early to say whether and to what extent any of these modifications will be realised in the near future.

'MANAGEMENT'

By defining the interest that the enterprise is supposed to serve we are also giving a definition of the enterprise itself. If the enterprise is deemed to serve the interests of shareholders, we may define it as a coalition of capital. On the other hand, if it is supposed to serve the interests of the working collective, we may define it as a coalition of people or, to use the marxist term now used in Yugoslavia, an 'association of producers'.[7] The first definition may be taken as an economic definition with important sociological implications, the other as a sociological definition with important economic implications.

The basic institutional definition of the enterprise determines the main function of management. When the enterprise is a coalition of capital, the task of the management is to organise and run the enterprise in such a way that they may maximise profits, or ensure the stability of profits in the long run, in order to provide the shareholders with maximum or stable dividends. In cases where the enterprise is an association of producers, the management's main task is so to organise it as to provide for the maximum level of self-determination for the members of the association. Management thus becomes self-management. Thus, the former definition has sociological implications— a satisfactory level of performance of the enterprise's social system; the latter has economic implications—a satisfactory economic performance. It is in these 'implications' that the problems of both definitions lie.

The basic managerial function defines the structure of managerial actions. In the coalition of capital, managerial action leads to or—as we are still on the institutional level—is supposed to lead to a rational and functional system of behaviour; the 'logic of efficiency' and an orientation of action towards the formal structure prevail. In the association of producers, managerial action—leaving aside technical actions closely connected with production— leads to a 'micropolitical' system of behaviour; what prevails in this case is the 'logic of politics' and an orientation towards 'natural' social structures. The different structures of managerial action will, of course, determine the typical manager: the 'bureaucrat' or 'professional expert' on the one hand and the 'politician' on the other.

---

[6] This problem has been paid some attention in a study made by the group of authors from the Institute of Economics, Zagreb (the author of this chapter being one of the joint authors), under the title Problemi dugoročnog proizvodno-financijskog povezivanja privrednih subjekata s posebnim osvrtom na mješovita (Problems of long-term links between production and finance in the economic area with special reference to joint ventures). Zagreb, Ekonomski Institut, 1966, duplicated document. In the event, little progress along these lines has been made so far.

[7] The notion of 'association' is much more complex in marxist theory. We cannot go into this problem here.

It is also plain that the structure of actions will determine the formal structure of management. In a capital coalition the source of authority is at the top, and authority itself is thus executed downwards by delegation. The supervisor is the last step; no further delegation is possible. In short, management is a hierarchy imposed upon the employee. In an association of producers the source of authority is at the bottom, that is, in the 'natural' basis of the association, and is thus delegated *upwards*. Such a pattern of delegation is well known in political organisations, from which it may be said to be borrowed. Thus, the Enterprise Management Act of 1950 stipulated that the members of the working collective should elect representatives to the Workers' Council, which in turn should elect members of a narrower body, the Management Board. The Workers' Council and the Management Board are both management bodies, which means that the elected representatives of all employees perform the functions of 'managers', in the usual capitalist sense.

But what has happened to the executive branch of management? If it is to tally with the institutional definition of the enterprise it should be organised (to use Professor P. Novosel's apt term) as an 'inverse hierarchy'.[8] Roughly, an inverse hierarchy entails (*a*) the election and dismissal of all managers from the foreman to the director-general by those managed by them; and (*b*) a group model of organisation, somewhat similar to the 'motivation approach' of Professor Rensis Likert, with the proviso, in contrast with Likert's model, that the final authority lies with the group. However, even after the introduction of the 'upward' pattern of delegation into management the executive branch has still been organised along traditional hierarchical lines. The resulting dualistic structure has caused a vast problem of co-ordination. True enough, the new Federal Constitution passed in 1963 brought about important changes. The director-general is elected by the Workers' Council and the election of other executives is subject to autonomous regulation by the enterprise itself. This has enabled Yugoslav enterprises to approach an institutionally consistent structure of authority ('authority by acceptance'), and some enterprises have come very close to such a solution, at least on paper. Even in these cases, however, there remains a kind of hierarchical responsibility which further complicates the already intricate problem of co-ordination in such a structure.

The model of 'inverse hierarchy' would accord best with the present institutional definition of a Yugoslav enterprise. If the definition were modified by the introduction of capital as one of the criteria of management, a dualistic or even pluralistic model might prove even better. In both cases the problems of co-ordination are vast. Instead of embarking on a complicated theoretical discussion, we shall limit ourselves to one very pertinent problem: is such a model viable in practice?

No satisfactory *a priori* answer can be given. The difficulty is twofold. In the first place, organisational structures are indeterminate:[9] the same functions of the enterprise can be successfully performed within different

---

[8] The idea of 'inverse hierarchy' is being elaborated by Professor Novosel in a yet unpublished work; the author learned of it from Professor Novosel himself.

[9] See Jacques Lobstein, 'Structure et l'organisation de l'entreprise', in Friedmann and Naville (eds.), *Traité de Sociologie du Travail*, Paris, Armand Colin, 1962, Vol. 2, pp. 56–7.

structures. It is therefore hazardous to maintain, *a priori*, that a certain structure is not viable. Secondly, the model itself is in a state of flux. As we have seen, it is neither sufficiently worked out nor has it approached a final form. It is therefore difficult to determine to what extent the difficulties and drawbacks should be attributed to the essential institutional properties of the model, or to its, as yet, primitive state.

An empirical approach is therefore required; the phenomenon must be regarded not as a controlled experiment but as a developing process. Above all, we need much more empirical data than we have at the moment. A few observations on certain problems and tendencies, without any pretention to conclusions or forecasts, however tentative, will seek to illustrate some of the relevant phenomena.

Some of the functional problems and tendencies of this model of enterprise structure may be well illustrated by 'managerial behaviour', the response to basic organisational dilemmas. One of these, in an enterprise defined (in marxist terms) as an association, is the dilemma between the self-determination of those who form the association and economic performance. Self-determination is, of course, the main aim of an organisation defined in such a way; on the other hand, a certain return ('profit' or 'surplus') must be yielded by the financial means of the enterprise although these are not functioning as capital. If there is no return the enterprise will be unable to function and to survive. Financial return is therefore second in priority to self-determination.

These two aims do not necessarily conflict, but neither are they necessarily in harmony. It often happens in practice that one aim is pursued at the expense of the other. The organisation must then make a choice; this is the organisational dilemma. In the absence of detailed studies concerning the way these choices are made, we may suppose that the balance will be tipped according to whichever pressure is stronger. The pressure for financial return will be strongest if an enterprise continuously runs at a loss.[10] When this occurs, the institutional imperative is to resolve the dilemma in favour of financial return; in such a case the public authority (the local community council) dissolves the Workers' Council and appoints a trustee. This also means that for the time being democracy in the enterprise is abolished and the power of one man, with dictatorial authority, is put in its place.

The pressure for financial return comes mostly from the competitive market. The intensity of that pressure is in proportion to the level of competitiveness and/or 'freedom' of the market. Minimising the chances of resolving the dilemma in this direction (that is, to the disadvantage of self-determination) also implies minimising the market pressure upon the enterprise. The investment role of government, already described, is part and parcel of such a scheme, very appropriately termed by Professor D. Gorupić 'state re-insurance of business'.[11] The unavoidable results of such a govern-

[10] Not necessarily, for the market pressure could be (and quite often is) cushioned by the 'state re-insurance of business' policies which, though officially condemned, still persist in various more or less disguised forms. It is a plain fact that an enterprise continually operating at loss extremely rarely goes bankrupt.

[11] Drago Gorupić, 'Proizvodjac i samoupravljanje u poduzeću' ('The producer and the self-management of an enterprise'), *Naše teme*, No. 3, March 1966, p. 547.

mental role are a lessening of the autonomy of the enterprise and consequently fewer self-determining opportunities within the working collective. Self-determination does therefore demand a certain 'freedom' in the market. It follows that it is not always inconsistent at one and the same time to stress both the greater pressure of the market and the stronger development of self-management.[12]

Thus, the organisational dilemma is linked with a wider dilemma within the framework of the economic system as a whole. It also follows that this dilemma is not absolute:[13] self-determination and 'profit' do not inevitably cancel each other out. Taking all this into account, it is plain that the dilemma cannot be instantly resolved by an ingenious institutional scheme. According to circumstances, practical solutions will be impermanent and imperfect and, of necessity, always a matter of degree.

Different resolutions of the organisational dilemma will set different courses for managerial action. If priority is given to financial return, action must be directed towards a rational and functional system of behaviour; if self-determination is given first place, action must be directed towards a micro-political system. However, not all parts of the enterprise structure can orient themselves with the same ease towards one system or the other. For example, line management can more easily be guided towards a rational and functional system of behaviour than can the working groups or the Workers' Council. There need be no problem in the fact that, because of this, one part of the structure will play a more important role than another in one situation, and that in a different situation the roles will change.

Problems may arise when one decisively orientated part of the organisational structure tries to impose its own orientation on the other part, in all organisational situations. Conflict will then break out between different parts of the structure and its inherent logic will cause the problem of power to be the dominant factor; organisational aims (the resolution of the organisational dilemma) and action orientation will become of secondary importance. This may perhaps explain some of the tendencies noticed in the behaviour of line management. When the latter, in pursuit of financial return, tries to impose a rational and functional system of behaviour as the only answer to all kinds of organisational situations, it is really trying to re-establish its former traditional function of 'boss'. If it succeeds—not a foregone conclusion since such an attempt will be strongly opposed—it may establish *control* over the whole structure but not *authority*, since any such control, under the given social and institutional conditions, can be neither stable nor legitimate. In a case like this, control becomes the sole preoccupation—the obsession, even—of line management, which may then itself deteriorate into a punitive bureau-

[12] Such an emphasis is understood under the circumstances of the Yugoslav economic reform.

[13] For some sociologists of co-operation in the West (A. Meister and H. Desroches, for example), this dilemma is absolute in character. They draw, on the basis of the historical experience of the co-operative movement, a general conclusion that the economic success of an association is inversely related to the participation of the members and that 'association' must of necessity become an 'enterprise'. This general hypothesis underlined A. Meister's research in a Yugoslav factory in 1960. Some of his results were published in his book *Socialisme et l'autogestion: expérience yougoslave*, Paris, Editions du Seuil, 1964.

cracy (according to A. W. Gouldner[14]) or an informal, clique-dominated oligarchy. This, naturally, is just one of a number of tentative hypotheses; no systematic study has yet been made of the mechanism of the behaviour of executives in Yugoslav enterprises. It is also difficult to judge how much these tendencies are encouraged by autocratic traditions in industry, by inadequate systems of recruitment and management training, or by the structural drawbacks of the model itself.

Another fruitful method of studying the functional problems of our model is to review the functions and roles of a chief executive. As he forms the main link between the two basic branches of management, his behaviour directly and essentially influences the functioning of the whole structure. According to the institutional definition, the functions of a 'director' are fourfold. (i) To ensure the legality of decisions made in the enterprise. Previously, he had the authority to postpone the implementation of any decision of the Workers' Council or Management Board he considered incompatible with the laws (suspensive veto) while awaiting the final decision of the competent public authority. Although he has lost this prerogative he is still responsible for the legality of decisions made in the enterprise. In this particular function the director acts, as it were, as a civil servant. (ii) To promote the interests of the local community in the enterprise. It has already been mentioned that the influence of the local authority in electing the director-general is still quite substantial. In former years it was the local authority which had the decisive voice in the appointment of directors. 'Interests' of the local authority often meant that the enterprise made contracts under unfavourable terms or even supplied financial means out of its own funds for the needs of the local community. By furthering local interests, the director often plays the role of a local politician. (iii) To prepare preliminary drafts of the decisions to be made by the Workers' Council and Management Board and to carry out these decisions. By performing this function the director is at the same time a staff adviser and an executive.[15] (iv) Independently to perform other necessary duties. The director has certain fields of authority based on the law that have nothing to do with delegation from the Workers' Council. In these areas the director is a 'manager' in the Western meaning of the term.

The role and function of the director do not, in fact, tally with the basic institutional definition of the enterprise, according to which the director should perform only the roles of staff adviser and of executive, as in (iii) above. In defining the director's role and function practical considerations have been taken into account. Not only are there different interests for the enterprise to consider but the institutional mechanisms for the co-ordination of these interests are either inadequately developed or simply do not work well enough. Though these practical considerations for a deviation from the basic institutional definition of the enterprise can be appreciated, the question

[14] See A. W. Gouldner, 'Organizational Analysis', in R. K. Merton, L. Broom, and L. C. Cottrell (eds.), *Sociology Today*, New York, Basic Books, 1959.

[15] This is an oversimplified account. The real situation is far more complex for the reason that the director is *ex offiico* a member of the Management Board. This body, on the one hand, elaborates proposals for the Workers' Council and, on the other hand, has an autonomous decision-making power in important matters. By participating in the autonomous decision-making within the Management Board, he performs the role of a manager.

remains whether such a multifunctional definition of the director's duties is feasible. The problem is not only that the director is supposed to represent different interests, but also that he has to play several roles demanding different patterns of behaviour. What is the real behaviour of a director likely to be?

It is altogether too logical to assume that a manager will consider one of these specific interests as the most important and will thus act mainly within the limits of one of his roles. In practice, the real behaviour of directors may be expected to vary widely. There are no empirical studies on the topic but casual observation indicates that this is in fact so. On the other hand, there are certain tendencies towards uniformity. Even if a director does emphasise one specific interest and adopts a social role (because of the institutional and social context of his activity) he must at least pay lip service to the other interests he is required to represent. This means that he plays several roles at once. This simultaneous and multiple activity forces the director to develop a 'key role'[16] of his own that will 'solve' the conflict between his different responsibilities. What is this key role? It might be defined as follows: the role of a manipulator with 'cover' provided for each of his actions. In putting his ideas into practice he is careful, when manipulating different interests and social groups, to justify each of his actions in institutional, legal and ideological terms. This key role is probably a factor contributing to uniformity of behaviour—and also to the emergence of a popular, caricature, stereotype. When the executive branch shows a tendency towards absolute command in the enterprise, such a key role shifts control from direct coercion to more subtle techniques of manipulation.

Of course, such a definition of the functions and roles of the chief executive is not only institutionally inconsistent but also inadequate as a practical solution. There is therefore an urgent need for redefinition. This should go further than finding an institutionally consistent solution, though to a certain degree this is clearly indispensable. Generally speaking, the role of the chief executive should be so defined that he devotes himself to the problems of formulating general policy objectives and plans. He would help to guide his organisation, as Selznick suggests, by embodying policy values in the structure of the organisation. There is no room here to elaborate these ideas further; but it needs to be emphasised that unless the role of the chief executive is redefined (with implications for the whole executive branch) no criteria for recruitment can be formulated nor can training and personnel development programmes, capable of producing individuals who may successfully fulfil the role defined in such a way, be established.

EMPLOYEE REPRESENTATION

After this brief survey of the status and role of 'management', we must turn our attention to the other side of the classical dichotomy of the modern enterprise—the 'employees'. To what extent are their interests represented and what is their position in the social system of the Yugoslav enterprise?

[16] On 'key roles', see Earl Rubington, 'Organizational Strains and Key Roles', *Administrative Science Quarterly*, Vol. IX, No. 4, March 1965, pp. 350–369.

The very institutional definition of the enterprise suggests that the interests, as well as the position, of the workers will be different from those in a capitalist company. It is, of course, true that 'sectional interests' exist in both types of enterprise. There are, however, two major differences. In a Yugoslav enterprise the 'sectional interests' are not so narrowly based on the division between management and employees; they are more diffuse. There is, moreover, no such thing as sectional bargaining, and consequently, no 'sectional representation'.

Accordingly, the Workers' Council does not represent the workers in negotiations with the management but is a representative of the whole working collective (including supervisors and executives) and, at the same time, a body of management. In other words, it does not represent a special sectional interest but certain interests of different groups. These interests are not harmonised through 'bargaining' but through participation in decision-making. For example, when a Workers' Council discusses the allocation of finance from the collective fund for the building of housing for those members of the working collective who live in urban areas, the final decision might depend upon the workers who live in the country. Their approach, in turn, might depend on whether the town-dwellers voted some time ago in favour of buying buses for the commuters. The behaviour of the representatives of these two groups would, in effect, demonstrate a kind of tacit inter-group bargaining, realised through participation. Here we can see the specific role of the Workers' Council: to be a sort of clearing-house for various inter-group and informal deals. In other words, the Workers' Council is not just a management body but is also an institution for bargaining through participation. Thus, the relative 'bargaining' position of certain groups may be expected to be directly related to the intensity of their participation in collective decision-making. The next logical step is to seek to determine the degree of participation of these groups.

The institutional set-up might lead one to imagine that participation would be evenly distributed among social groups and consistently high in all organisational situations. In practice, it is uneven, varying from time to time and from one situation to another. It is a statistical fact that some groups are 'over-represented' in the Workers' Councils (highly skilled workers, for example) while others (such as unskilled workers) are 'under-represented'. Besides, as suggested by recent research, representatives of some groups are much more active than those of others in the process of social interaction at the sessions of the Workers' Council. On the whole, it seems that the level of participation is directly related to the position of these groups on the social ladder. This also shows that 'bargaining through participation' gives some of the groups at the bottom of the scale less opportunity for promoting their interests than might have been the case had sectional bargaining existed. However, such a problem exceeds the limits of this survey. Recent investigations into the problem of participation in industry, though far from being systematic and comprehensive, seem to suggest the following tentative conclusions: (a) intensity of participation is normally higher in a 'crisis' than in 'normal' circumstances; (b) participation is more extensive when human relations and 'internal politics', rather than functional problems, are under

331

discussion; and (c) participation is more intensive when distribution of personal income, rather than production problems, are in debate.

Nevertheless, these considerations are less important than the fact that social stratification is the essential determinant of the participation of various groups. Participation, in other words, is closely connected with social power, power being the essential dimension of stratification. The more power a certain group enjoys, the more it participates in collective decision-making. It may be asked whether the converse is also true: does participation give the feeling of power? Probably not.[17] In some enterprises the Workers' Council obviously exercises a high degree of control, equal to that of the executive branch of management; people interviewed in the course of research have stated that the workers as a group enjoyed only a small influence. One possible explanation is given by the data on the distribution of influence in the Workers' Council itself: executives and staff are found to be the most influential groups; the workers' groups, according to their degree of skill, appear to have the least influence. Though we do not know to which sectors of industry these data can be applied,[18] they still allow for a more general hypothesis: representative democracy within an enterprise does not necessarily give the worker a feeling of power. A new approach is therefore needed, that of direct democracy and direct participation. This approach is evident in the recent trend towards decentralising the inner structure of the enterprise by the setting up of 'economic units'. Such decentralisation can rely upon the 'natural' process of spontaneous participation in 'face-to-face' groups. Nevertheless, there remains the problem of bridging the gap which, as suggested by some studies, exists between spontaneous and institutionalised participation. In other words, the problem is how (to a certain extent) to institutionalise spontaneous participation in a certain group and to make institutionalised participation in the Workers' Council more spontaneous. This might seem like squaring the circle, but real life does not always permit an 'either/or' solution.

There is another question related to the effects of participation. Does participation remove or relieve the unfavourable effects of modern technology and formal organisation upon the individual, and, if so, to what extent? Does participation help in getting rid of the alienation of human labour? The study undertaken by Dr J. Obradović in twenty-seven economic organisations suggests that technology has, in the main, the same alienation effect in Yugoslavia as in the West. Furthermore, no significant differences were found between the attitudes of members and non-members of the Workers' Council. The author concludes, therefore, that participation in the functions of the Workers' Council has no effect upon alienation at work.[19] These questions

[17] Josip Županov and Arnold S. Tannenbaum, 'The Distribution of Control in some Yugoslav Industrial Organizations as Perceived by Members', in Tannenbaum (ed.), *Control in Organizations*, New York, McGraw-Hill, 1968, Ch. 6.

[18] Subsequent studies carried out in various industries by the present author and by other research workers (notably Dr V. Rus and B. Kavčič) strongly support the conclusion that the power structure within the enterprise as reported by Županov and Tannenbaum represents a general pattern in Yugoslav industry.

[19] J. Obradović, Djelovanje tehničkog nivoa proizvodnje na radnika upravljača (The influence of technical levels of production upon the worker-manager), University of Zagreb, unpublished doctoral dissertation.

obviously cannot be answered on the basis of a single study; more investigation is needed, not least because, as is well known, the participation of members of the Workers' Councils is often merely formal and thus could hardly counteract the impact of technology.

Discussion about the relation of participation and the dehumanising effects of technological development raises not only the questions of whether participation weakens the tendency towards dehumanisation but also the converse—whether processes of dehumanisation undermine participation. Two factors arise: trends arising out of technological development, related and leading to average production units of greater size, to the centralisation of decision-making and to an emphasis on formal structures; and also mass consumption which is capable of exerting a considerable influence on the pattern of motives, interests and orientation.

Not even a tentative answer can be given to the first question because of the lack of systematic data. As far as the second question is concerned, the available evidence (particularly the investigation undertaken over an extensive period by Dr M. Jezernik in Slovenia) suggests that the movement towards the 'consumer's society' really does influence the relative strength of the motives of individuals; the drive to earn seems to be gaining in importance, the desire to participate to be dwindling.[20] Naturally, further long-term research and enquiries into the circumstances under which consumption has such effects are needed. Until then, we must beware of reading too much into the available data and of making premature generalisations.

Although the effects of participation, as so far observed, have not entirely fulfilled our hopes—which tend to be far ahead of real possibilities at this stage of development—it should be stressed that participation does play an important part in a Yugoslav enterprise. We have already mentioned that the empirical data suggest that the high degree of influence wielded in the enterprise by the Workers' Council does not, of itself, give the workers a feeling that they, as a group, enjoy high influence in the enterprise. However, when asked who should have most influence in the enterprise, all respondents pointed to the Workers' Council. This is not only the view of the workers but also of those belonging to other social groups in the enterprise, including managers. Opinions vary from group to group as to how much influence managers and workers should have in the enterprise. All seem agreed that the Workers' Council must enjoy the highest influence—even the average scores, computed on the basis of individual replies, scarcely differ. The high level of consensus, in spite of the fact that the real position of different groups in the Workers' Council is not and cannot be equal, implies that the Council has been accepted as the legitimate government of the enterprise. Its legitimacy means that it offers opportunities equal to all groups and members of the working collective to participate in decision-making. Thus, participation becomes the legal basis for authority in a Yugoslav enterprise. Participation represents a better and more durable basis for the legitimacy of authority within industry (it being also the basis of democracy) than 'peace treaties' or 'armistices' within sectional bargaining can ever be.

[20] M. Jezernik, Hijerarhija motivacijskih faktorjev (The hierarchy of motivation factors), University of Ljubljana, unpublished doctoral dissertation.

THE FIRM AND THE LOCAL COMMUNITY

The main part of this survey has been devoted to internal problems—'management' and 'employee participation'. We must now consider some external problems of the enterprise: its relationship to the local and national community and to consumers. With regard to the latter, the question is whether they are, or should be, protected by means other than market competition. This problem becomes particularly important in a seller's market, as was the case for many products in Yugoslavia during the earlier period described in this survey. The institutional structure of the Yugoslav economy, with its system of councils, offers some opportunities for non-market protection. For example, consumers' councils were set up in connexion with retail organisations but they did not prove successful. The councils were in the end abolished and the only protection for consumers at the moment is through the market.

Of greater importance is the relationship of the enterprise with the local community. The point has already been made that such relations are more intensive and more important for both sides in Yugoslavia than in the West. They do not merely mean that the local community creates general conditions favourable for the smooth running of the enterprise and that the latter provides employment and income for the local people. Things are changing in certain respects but the overall situation could be summed up as follows.[21] The local community often acts as an important 'investor' in founding new firms and guarantees the bank loans of enterprises. To a certain extent, it protects 'its' firms (and not infrequently the monopolistic practices of some of them) in the local market. The community also pursues a sort of 'insurance' policy with regard to local firms, lessening the difference in economic power between the stronger and the weaker enterprises and helping the latter to survive. The distribution of income within enterprises and the appointment of their directors-general have been strongly influenced by the local community. Finally, the latter has been generally able, because of its responsibilities in overseeing the legality of the day-to-day management of the enterprises, as well as by the existing political system, to widen its influence on the business and personnel policies of the enterprises through formal and, to a greater extent, informal means.

Such a situation provided fertile ground for the elaboration of various theories of the overall integration of the enterprise into the local community that were fashionable some years ago. In fact, such an overall integration—a perfect co-ordination of interests—is possible only with smaller firms working solely for the local market. But in the case of a larger enterprise covering a national and/or international market, any insistence on 'full integration' might lead to a number of undesirable consequences. The enterprise might be forced to prop up the smaller firms within the commune and to come to the rescue of those that could no longer survive by merging under political influence. It could be compelled to accept a local 'man of confidence' as director, regardless of his abilities, and to make financial contributions to

---

[21] Changes in the relationship between the enterprise and the local community that have so far occurred have been minor in scope and formal in character and have not substantially affected the overall picture given here.

local 'needs'. The unjustifiable (and informal) requirement that nobody in the enterprise is entitled to a salary higher than that of the chairman of the commune could distort its own internal income structure. On the other side of the coin, it would be equally possible—and equally undesirable—for the enterprise (or rather its director) to acquire a dominating position in the life of the community.

The relations between the enterprise and the local community require a reappraisal. They should not be pushed back into the traditional framework, as a certain level of involvement of the enterprise in the local community is both possible and necessary. The enterprise must, to some extent, participate in the life of the local community as a responsible collective citizen. However, the determination of the level, form and means of such participation is a matter for further discussion, scientific investigation and practical experience.

THE FIRM AND THE NATIONAL COMMUNITY

If the question of the responsibility of the enterprise towards the national community is now being considered in Western countries, it is *a fortiori* a matter of debate in socialist countries such as Yugoslavia. The following problems must be solved: to what extent do Yugoslav enterprises meet the tasks set by social plans, the targets of national economic policy, the recommendations of the Federal Assembly and so on. If a systematic quantitative study of the behaviour of enterprises were undertaken from these aspects, it is probable that not a few would show a rather poor record. Why would this be so?

There is, of course, the problem of personal responsibility, but a lack of such responsibility on the part of some of the members of a firm does not provide a satisfactory answer. The key lies in the pattern of relations between the government and the firm. Until recently, the government has chiefly relied upon a mass of regulations to direct the activities of enterprises. These regulations are mostly mandatory rather than indicative.[22] In other words, the government has followed a policy of direct rather than indirect control. It could be said that the enterprises are 'conditioned' to this treatment. Some influences which are not mandatory (recommendations of the Federal Assembly, for example) often have no effect. The authorities have therefore come to the conclusion that enterprises can be brought into line only through mandatory regulations. This in turn means that the relations form a closed system of behaviour. Other factors contributed to backsliding on the part of enterprises: there were too many regulations; they were frequently changed; minor amendments could radically alter the situation of an enterprise, so that one, for instance, could all of a sudden be switched from being 'profitable' to 'non-profitable' or vice versa; some of the solutions did not go far enough and themselves necessitated further changes in the regulations. Last but not least, communications between the government and the firms have been one-way. One of the reasons why some solutions were inadequate was that

[22] This statement still holds true though some changes worth noting have occurred. For example, regulations on depreciation rates have been 'liberalised', giving almost complete freedom to firms to set their own rates as they see fit.

official bodies have consulted enterprises far too little on measures that were about to be taken and decisions have often been made without considering previous ones. But these poor communications have another and more important implication: how can one expect the enterprise, within the system of workers' self-management, to behave responsibly in relation to national economic policy targets unless it participates in the formulation of that policy?

Naturally enough, such a state of affairs has aroused severe criticism. Today, it is plain to everybody that things cannot go on as they are; already there are signs of change. But bureaucratic rigidity in the relations themselves has led to a similar rigidity in outlook—and not only in the state administration, where the logic of bureaucratic control was safely entrenched, but also among its critics. Thus, some people believe that all government direction of the enterprise must be abandoned *en bloc*; they fail to distinguish between direct control and indirect guidance and forget that there are some responsibilities the government cannot easily shrug off.

This, of course, is only one of the many facets of the problem of enterprise responsibility. Another side has recently developed—responsibility towards public opinion. The social climate of Yugoslavia favours this trend and enterprises are increasingly sensitive to public criticism. It would probably not be an overstatement to say that Yugoslav enterprises are more exposed to public criticism than their counterparts in, say, Britain. It must be remembered that a Yugoslav enterprise is not a private enterprise that can hide behind a dead wall of silence and secrecy. However, it would be too optimistic to say that such tendencies are not found in Yugoslav enterprises; indeed, they could be even more dangerous, as by its by-laws an enterprise can declare certain matters to be 'economic secrets'. Legal regulations would be appropriate here.

Appendices

Appendix A

BELGIAN ATTITUDES TO REFORM

A. TRADE UNIONS

Although Belgian trade unions have no legal status (they are so-called '*de facto* organisations'), the three largest—the CSC (Confédération des Syndicats Chrétiens), the FGTB (Fédération Générale des Traveilleurs Belges) and the CGSLB (Centrale Générale des Syndicats Libéraux de Belgique)—are considered by the government to be representative of all the workers in the country. They are represented in economic, social and financial institutions and consultative bodies and have the right to put forward candidates for election to health committees and works councils and for nomination to the joint committees at sector level where a major part of the collective bargaining is done. The FGTB, like the Belgian Socialist Party, is based on the principles of democratic socialism. It groups together fourteen national industrial unions each of which is an independent organisation accepting the basic socialist principles of the FGTB and engaging itself to abide by all the decisions made by the latter's statutory bodies. Each affiliated union is free to take what industrial action it chooses so long as it is done in accordance with the basic principles and statutory rules of the FGTB. The latter, which is decentralised at regional and local level, may take only general action in the workers' interests. The CSC has much the same structure, with seventeen national unions based on industries and is also decentralised at regional and local level. Its aim is to defend the interests of workers in accordance with Christian social doctrine and the principles of democracy. It has special national organisations for economic, cultural and educational action.

The point of view of the more important trade unions on company reform is on the whole realistic and pragmatic. They recognise that the present law is no longer up to date and regard gradual reform as necessary, although none of them has so far put forward any detailed proposals. The FGTB and CSC are ideologically opposed and consequently their ultimate long-term goals diverge. As far as company reform is concerned, however, they are in general agreement.

The unions are concerned first of all about the aims of the enterprise. They feel that the profit motive should be replaced by new principles aiming at more effective service to the common good. Secondly, they are concerned with the

339

way in which decisions affecting the workers' interests are made. Their main criticisms are directed against insufficient control over the power of decision of the representatives of capital; the dearth of information on the economic and financial state of the company (and the impossibility of understanding what is available); the low level of co-management and the absence of joint decisions on social problems which primarily interest the workers (such as recruitment and dismissal, working conditions and shut-downs); and less than adequate recognition of labour's part in the enterprise. Thirdly, they are anxious to preserve the union's fighting spirit and their right of 'contestation'. If ever joint management and joint responsibility were realised in a new company structure, the unions would not want to lose these powers.

The nationalisation of private firms is not advocated by the major unions. The FGTB, in its 1956 programme, suggested the nationalisation of several basic sectors (such as power) but no serious action was taken and the programme has in the meanwhile been largely forgotten. (No parliamentary majority could be found to favour the plan nor could any government bear the heavy burden of compensation.) Moreover, the socialists would not want to start a nationalisation experiment with industries (such as coal) that are in serious structural crisis. More importantly, however, the unions do not regard present-day government as efficient in the management of industry nor do they consider that nationalisation would guarantee either a better social climate in the enterprise or an improvement in the real rights of workers. The aim of Belgian socialists is not so much the nationalisation of property as its better management.[1]

No more is co-management (in the sense that the representatives of labour, together with those of capital, should be partly responsible for all management decisions in the firm) an objective of Belgian unions. One of their chief arguments is that unity of authority is necessary for the efficient operation of the enterprise. For the workers to share the responsibility of management decisions would weaken the unions' spirit of vigilance and right of contestation. The FGTB has made the further point that in the Belgian economy many important decisions are not made by companies themselves but are dictated by dominant financial pressure groups—the holding companies (see p. 244).

The reforms favoured by the leading unions are as follows: (a) the reorganisation and improvement of information for (and its supervision by) the workers, which the CSC regards as co-management without any lessening of the necessary authority in the enterprise; (b) a right of joint decision in matters which especially concern employees; and (c) the regulation of the decision-making process in the controlling bodies of the enterprise by reform of the present legislation and by joint agreements on a national, regional and industrial level. The unions are anxious that they should be heard on economic planning, regional development and area planning and that they should be given adequate representation on the mixed industrial boards. They also claim a right of joint decision on the governing boards of the SNCI (Société Nationale du Crédit à l'Industrie) and the SNI (Société Nationale de l'Investissement), the semi-public institutions which provide credit to and participate

[1] H. Janne, 'L'avenir du socialisme', *Socialisme*, May 1960, pp. 261–265, and R. Evalenko, 'Réformes de structure: lesquelles, pourquoi, comment', ibid., January 1966, pp. 4–30.

in private firms. Furthermore, they wish to take part in the decisions of the supervisory boards for the electricity and gas industries, in the legal supervision of holding companies and so on.

This programme would be realised gradually either by legislation or by agreements that covered the whole nation, an industry, a region or an enterprise. Such a gradualist approach is based upon the different situations of the companies involved and the time needed to train suitable employee representatives.

As regards management the unions make distinctions according to the size of firm. In the case of large companies they agree with the proposals to strengthen the legal position of management as the highest expression of authority and responsibility, with a limitation on the powers of the board of directors and the general meeting of shareholders. In this respect the unions are concerned about the real exercise of authority and the permanent presence in the enterprise of competent and responsible negotiators and intermediaries on behalf of the employees. According to a study committee of the CSC, a tripartite supervising and authorising organ in which capital, labour and government would be represented should be set up alongside the administrative board.[2]

The unions also seek full and objective economic and financial information in all large companies, legislation on the general principles of accounting and on the form of the annual accounts—balance sheet and profit and loss account —and a legal status for the workers in the firm. Employees and employers, they claim, should be represented in the institution that controls the *reviseurs d'enterprises* (see pp. 36 and 164).

A reform of works councils is also sought by the unions. They grant that the councils have served as forums for negotiation and discussion and are responsible for the great reduction in paternalism; but they do not agree that they have made it possible for workers to be true partners in decision-making or that they have had much or any influence on the economic and financial development of firms. The unions would like works councils to become supervisory bodies without interfering with the authority vested in the enterprise or assuming responsibility for financial or economic management. Their power should be extended to the right of supervision and gradual joint decision-making in social matters which have a bearing on recruitment, appointment and dismissal, and also in personnel and medical services and the organisation of work. The unions also seek a right of recourse to a competent authority in such matters as the closing down of a firm.

Belgian unions are not enthusiastic about profit-sharing. Their main concerns remain wages, fringe benefits, social security, working hours and conditions, employment and the reforms of company law already mentioned. They are somewhat suspicious of any regulations whereby social provisions are made by firms in favour of their employees, or whereby bonuses and profit-sharing schemes in relation to earned profits are contemplated. They fear that the expectation of higher profits could lead to accelerated work schedules; that discrimination in remuneration might result from the varying productivity of firms; that an undesirable flow of labour from less to more

[2] *Onderneming en syndicalisme*, Brussels, CSC, 1964, pp. 146–152.

profitable companies might follow; that employees might then be committed too strongly to particular firms; and that the fighting spirit of the unions might be weakened because, in a certain sense, their members would become capitalists. Measures which stress the 'community' aspect of the firm and which relate it to greater entities such as the town, region or state are strongly favoured by the unions.[3,4]

B. EMPLOYERS' ORGANISATIONS

The Federation of Belgian Industries, the leading employers' organisation in Belgium, has not so far defined its position on company reform but can hardly be said to have shown much enthusiasm. Employers in general have voiced no clear opinions on final business objectives. Most of them believe in economic 'liberalism' and in traditional conceptions of company management and organisation.[5] However, some change of thought is apparent. Although leading businessmen defend the principles of free enterprise and of profit as its reward, some have looked farther afield[6] and consider that the essential motive and function of the company is the promotion of social and economic progress by raising productivity and the creation of new jobs. In exchange, the enterprise has a right to a return that enables it to maintain its productive capacity and to a level of profit that makes it possible for it to adapt itself to wage movements and to social, economic, technological and scientific progress. Profit is no longer the sole motive of economic activity but is justified by wider social aims.[7]

The Union of Catholic Employers,[8] the members of which are mainly heads of small and medium-sized businesses, has devoted several congresses

[3] I. Lindemans, 'Naar convergentie tussen economie, ethica en recht inzake de onderneming', *De Gids op Maatschappelijk Gebied*, November 1963, pp. 945–976.

[4] For general trade union attitudes towards company reform, see their annual reports, *passim*, and also the following: *Holdings et démocratie économique*, Brussels, FGTB, 1956; and (for the views of the Katholieke Werkliedenbond, a member of the CSC) L. de Witte, 'De Onderneming van morgen', *De Gids op Maatschappelijk Gebied*, October 1963, pp. 857–874, 'Besluiten uit de inhoudsbesprekingen van het ontwerp-manifest uit Nationaal KWB Congres 1964', ibid., 1964, No. 6, pp. 547–556, and *Ontwerp-manifest: KWB'ers op zoek naar een nieuwe ondernemingsvorm*, October 1963.

[5] R. Goris, 'Het concept en de structuurhervorming van de grote onderneming', *De Christelijke Werkgever*, August/September 1966, pp. 287–303.

[6] R. de Staercke, 'De beloning van de onderneming', *Medelingen van het VBN* (Federation of Belgian Industries), 1 June 1966, pp. 7–18. For other opinions of the Federation of Belgian Industries, see 'De Belgische industrie straks', *Medelingen*, special issue, 1966, and the following articles in *Industrie*: P. Bolle, 'Où va le patronat?', February 1964, pp. 146–150; L. Jacques, 'La direction de l'entreprise', May 1964, pp. 340–345; Baron Boel, 'L'entreprise privée, catalyseur de progrès', September 1964, pp. 590–597; J. Horn, 'Contre une réforme inutile de l'entreprise', November 1964, pp. 756–762; P. Holoffe, 'Réflexions d'age mûr d'un chef d'entreprise', December 1964, pp. 824–829; and R. de Staercke, 'A quoi sert l'entreprise?', June 1965, pp. 344–349.

[7] Goris, op. cit.

[8] For the views of the Catholic employers, see *De deelneming aan de verantwoordelijkheden in de onderneming*, Verbond van Katholieke Werkgevers van België, National Congress, 1965, Reports and Conclusions; and J. Raes, 'L'homme et la société: essai de synthèse doctrinale en vue de la participation', Fédération des patrons catholiques de Belgique, *Documents et opinions*, 1965, No. 22.

and publications to company reform. It stresses the need for strong and unified leadership but is nevertheless in favour of co-operation and discussion at all levels of the firm and especially when working conditions and methods are at issue. The union is not fundamentally opposed to a gradual institution-alisation of these contacts and to some form of joint decision-making in the domain of work policy and personnel management. It believes the reform of the works council to be the best way towards the reform of the company.

C. THE NATIONAL COMMITTEE FOR INVESTMENT IN SECURITIES

The Committee is a non-profit-making institution set up to promote share investment. Its members include banking, industrial, stockbroking and insurance institutions, chambers of commerce and the like. It believes that shareholders should get more and better information from annual reports (balance sheet, profit and loss account, general commentary, etc.), from the general meeting of shareholders and from data on the progress of the firm during the financial year. Although it expects the situation to improve of itself, by companies taking the initiative, and does not necessarily demand legal reforms, it does support some reform of the legal status of limited liability companies along the lines advocated by the official committee on company law reform. These include the issue of shares without voting rights which are, however, privileged when profits are distributed or the company is liquidated; more authority for a 'management board' and a revision of the functions of the existing board, which would become a supervising and authorising organ; more protection for dispersed small shareholders; a requirement that auditors be *reviseurs d'entreprises*; and more precise legal requirements concerning book-keeping, annual reports and the publication of accounts.[9]

D. POLITICAL PARTIES

The political parties have not shown much interest in company reform during the last decade or so, though the Belgian Socialist Party did emphasise, in the period from 1956 to 1960, the need to reform economic structures and advocated flexible democratic planning, the nationalisation of key industries and control over holding companies. Neither the government nor parliament, however, have taken any important initiatives on company law reform.

Christian Democratic Party

The CDP paid a good deal of attention to company law reform in the years immediately after the war.[10] (See Introduction, p. 20, above.) In 1964 the party's research centre (CEPESS) published a document on company law reform[11] which formed the basis of the party's position in the general election

[9] For the views of the National Committee for Investment in Securities, see Nationaal Comité der Beleggingen in Effecten, *Een betere voorlichting voor de aandeelhouder: praktische suggesties*, 1958, and *Verslag van de beheeraad aan de algemene statutaire jaarvergadering*, 1966.

[10] See CDP, *Kerstprogramma 1945*, pp. 53–62 and 70–79.

[11] 'De hervorming van de onderneming', *CEPESS-documenten*, 1964, No. 4; see also 'België 1970', ibid., 1964, Nos. 5 and 6.

of 1965. The following measures were suggested: (a) better information for shareholders, employees and the public on company activities; (b) protection of small shareholders; and (c) labour co-partnership through the works council. The reforms would take into account the different needs of various industrial sectors and regions and also the size of firms. The programme did not propose legislation as the only means of reform; its authors clearly had enterprise agreements in mind and, as far as key sectors were concerned, the existing electricity and gas agreements.

Belgian Socialist Party

In the post-war period the BSP (in coalition with the CDP) supported the Official Organisation of Industry Act of 1948, which, among other measures, provided for the setting up of works councils. As already mentioned, the party (supported by the socialist trade union) concentrated on the reform of economic structures in the 1950s. The results were: (a) the establishment of the Bureau for Economic Planning under the CDP-Liberal government in 1959; (b) the institution of the Coal Industry Directorate under the CDP-BSP government in 1961 (see p. 59); and (c) the originally private 'joint' gas and electricity agreement of 1955 into which the government entered in 1964 (see p. 59). BSP members of parliament have introduced a number of draft bills on the setting up of a unified accountancy plan.

Socialist authors[12] have recently taken a renewed interest in company reform, in the light of changes in the economic and social scene and the actual working of large firms (the separation of management and ownership and employee co-management within the enterprise) and also the results of nationalisation in other countries. They lay special stress on the need for flexible economic planning. At the level of the firm the workers should use the works council to make sure that 'the company adjusts itself to national planning in such a way as best to realise its own objectives'. This, however, could not come about unless company law were changed to make possible 'more genuine participation, a greater feeling of self-determination and happier results than the transformation of companies into nationalised services'. Nationalisation is seen to have the following disadvantages: (a) the state is not organised in such a way that it is capable of the efficient management of industry; (b) the social climate is not necessarily better for workers in a nationalised enterprise nor do they necessarily enjoy more rights; (c) the compensation of private shareholders is likely to be a heavy financial burden on the state.

In fact, there are other and better ways of attaining the desired objectives. The ownership of the means of production is rather less important than a real power of control. The aim should therefore be to strive for the 'nationalisation of management' within those industrial sectors and companies which have been set and must achieve planning targets. Arrangements should be worked out to guarantee efficiency and responsibility, taking into account the functional, technical, economic and social problems which would face such 'national' enterprises. The Coal Industry Directorate and the Agreement on Gas and Electricity are examples of this type of arrangement.

[12] See Janne and Evalenko, op. cit.

Liberal Party

Until the end of the 1950s the party (now called the Party for Liberty and Progress) maintained its nineteenth-century 'neo-liberal' attitude towards the structure and function of the enterprise. It supported neither the Official Industry Organisation Act of 1948 nor the later draft bills already mentioned. A change occurred in 1959 when, in coalition with the CDP, the party agreed to the formation of the Bureau for Economic Planning. About the same time, in an analysis of the Belgian social climate, J. Rey called for a new 'social pact', the success of which would depend on a profound change of outlook on the part of both employers and unions with regard to the ultimate purpose of the enterprise.[13] Debates within the party have brought it round to a new conception of the enterprise as a community of interests and activities in which personal aspirations may be attained by greater individual responsibility and better communication between workers and management. The party now seems to hold views on company reform not fundamentally dissimilar from those of the CDP and the BSP, although it has so far taken no parliamentary initiative to put them into effect.

[13] J. Rey, 'Vers un nouveau pacte social?—Contribution à une solution des problèmes belges', *Cahiers du Centre Paul Hymans*, No. 2. See also E. C. Klein, 'Pour une politique des cadres,' ibid., No. 7.

Appendix B

THE COMPANY IN SCOTLAND

The Companies Acts 1948 and 1967 apply with a few minor exceptions[1] to both England and Scotland thus providing a certain basic uniformity for both countries. However, the Acts do not constitute a comprehensive codification of company law and many areas have been left to be developed by the Courts such as the fiduciary duties of promoters and directors, dividends and the protection of creditors. Nevertheless, there has been little disagreement between the English and Scottish Courts in these areas and uniformity has been secured generally by the fact that the House of Lords represents a common appeal court whose decisions in this area are regarded as binding upon both legal systems regardless of the country of origin of the appeal.

Minor differences on various points do exist because of the different institutions of the two systems. Thus, for example, the floating charge was unknown to Scottish law, but this has been remedied by the Companies (Floating Charges) (Scotland) Act 1961. At present the English Courts take a different view from their Scottish brethren on the question of the availability of an unrealised capital profit for distribution by way of dividend. In *Dimbula Valley v. Laurie*[2] the English Court held that such a profit was available for dividends, although distribution could not normally be regarded as a wise commercial practice. On the other hand the Court of Session (the Scottish Court) has decided[3] that it cannot be distributed.

Occasionally the Court of Session has taken a different line of approach from the English Courts and has interfered with transactions which it regarded as being contrary to the public interest. Thus in *A. and D. Fraser Ltd.*[4] it refused to sanction a reduction of capital which was designed to avoid payment of profits tax, although this case was later overruled.[5] Similarly in *ex parte Westburn Sugar Refineries Ltd.*[6] the Court of Session refused to sanction a scheme whereby the company removed part of its undertaking from its own control in an effort to keep this part free from any possible danger of nationalisation. One of the reasons given by the Scottish Court for refusing to approve the scheme was that it was contrary to the public interest. However, this decision was reversed by the House of Lords who stated that the motive

---

[1] See for example 1948 Act Sections 245(4), 246–251, 252(1) and (2), 263, 270 and 275.
[2] [1961] Ch. 353. [3] In *Westburn Sugar Refineries Ltd. v. IRC*, 1960 T.R. 105.
[4] [1951] S.C. 394. [5] David Bell Ltd. 1954 S.C. 33. [6] [1951] A.C. 625.

for entering into the scheme was completely irrelevant and gave a very narrow interpretation to the public interest, in effect limiting it to the public interest in the maintenance of a company's capital. As Professor Gower states,[7] 'Although the Scottish courts have proved somewhat bolder, their efforts have been effectually frustrated by the House of Lords.'

[7] *Modern Company Law* (2nd edn), at p. 568.

Appendix C

ABBREVIATIONS OF ORGANISATIONS MENTIONED IN SECTIONS DEALING WITH FRANCE

ACADI   Association des cadres dirigeants de l'industrie pour le progrès social et économique. (Association of industrial senior salaried staff for social and economic progress.)

ANACACI Association nationale des Commissaires aux comptes indépendants du ressort des Cours d'Appel de France. (National association of independent accountants within the jurisdiction of the French Courts of Appeal.)

ASSEDIC   Association pour l'emploi dans l'industrie et le commerce. (Association for employment in industry and commerce.)

CADIPPE   Comité d'action pour le développement de l'intérêt des personnes au progrès de leurs entreprises et professions. (Action committee for personal involvement in industry and the professions.)

CFDT   Confédération Française Démocratique du Travail. (Democratic French Confederation of Labour.)

CFPC   Centre Chrétien des Patrons et Dirigeants d'Entreprises Françaises. (French Christian Employers' and Executives' Centre.)

CFTC   Confédération Française des Travailleurs Chrétiens. (French Confederation of Christian Workers.)

CGC   Confédération Générale des Cadres. (General Confederation of Salaried Staff.)

CGPME   Confédération Générale des Petites et Moyennes Entreprises. (General Confederation of Small and Medium Firms.)

CGT   Confédération Générale du Travail. (General Confederation of Labour.)

CJP (CJD) Centre des Jeunes Patrons. (Young Employers' Centre.) This organisation has now adopted the new name of Centre des Jeunes Patrons et Dirigeants d'Entreprises (Young Employers' and Executives' Centre.)

CNPF   Conseil National du Patronat Français. (National Council of French Employers.)

CREE   Centre de Recherche sur l'Evolution des Entreprises. (Business Development Research Centre.)

FDES   Fonds de Développement Economique et Social. (Economic and Social Development Fund.)

ORGECO   Organisation Générale des Consommateurs. (General Consumers' Organisation.)

SFIO   Section Française de l'Internationale Ouvrière. (French Section of the Workers' International.)

SICAV   Société d'Investissement à Capital Variable. (Variable Capital Investment Company.)

UFC   Union Fédérale de la Consommation. (Federal Consumers' Union.)

UNR   Union pour la Nouvelle République. (Union for the New Republic.)

Appendix D

THE CONTRIBUTION OF THE SOCIAL SCIENCES TO THE UNDERSTANDING OF THE DEVELOPMENT OF THE ENTERPRISE IN FRANCE

INTRODUCTION

This appendix is based on a study of the available literature and on a series of interviews with social scientists. The interviews had as their starting point a questionnaire which had three objectives: (*a*) to seek a definition of the enterprise, from psychologists and sociologists, which would distinguish it from other forms of organisation; (*b*) to determine the groups involved in the enterprise, their formal or informal structure and their modes of representation; and (*c*) to describe the relationships between these groups, using, among other concepts, those of power, responsibility, opposition and participation. The questions themselves were very open (more a list of subjects for discussion) in order to leave the person interviewed the greatest freedom. One reason for this was that early investigation showed that researchers usually studied the enterprise from a particular angle (unions, management, salaried staff, etc.) rather than as a whole. It thus seemed appropriate to give the discussion a direction by making the definition of the enterprise a 'lead-in' question to determine the respondent's frame of reference. Those interviewed were sent the questionnaire before the discussion, to allow them to think the problems over. Thus, in general, every interview covered one or more precise points from a predetermined angle. Consequently, the sample is qualitative rather than quantitative, its chief concern being to gather a variety of views on the enterprise.

Economists were not included in the sample—not because they are not 'social scientists' but for the very reason that their studies are much more complete and their conclusions better known. It would also be a mistake, in this context, to distinguish between psychologists and sociologists, particularly in France where, much more than in other countries (especially the United States), theoretical studies and practical action take place more at group level than at that of the individual. It therefore seemed better to distinguish either between practitioners and theoreticians or between 'interventionists' and descriptive observers. In fact, these distinctions overlap and we have adopted the second, which seemed more precise and more relevant to our purposes.

350

The authors of descriptive (and explanatory) studies have concentrated on the problems such as union representation, the place of salaried staff and the authority of the employer; their position is clearly quite different from that of a psycho-sociologist on the staff of a firm or of an outside expert working for a private or public organisation. However, it seemed to us, when choosing our sample, that the dynamics of the mechanisms described by the former and the methods of working employed by the latter both shed light on the direction of the development of the enterprise and the forms it takes.

THE FRENCH SITUATION

The enterprise has not been a popular subject with French sociologists, at least not until very recently. This neglect is evident in other countries as well,[1] but a number of factors, some peculiar to France, seem to have deterred French sociologists in particular.

The earliest sociological work was concerned with society in general and the development of systems capable of accounting for its evolution. With a few notable exceptions, sociologists quickly abandoned vast explanatory theories and the search for universal laws to cover more limited ground. Nevertheless, the social sciences in France have remained affected by nostalgia for the broad panoramas of the early days and have come relatively late to the study of particular phenomena or narrowly defined sectors of social reality.[2] It can be said, for instance, that the sociology of work was introduced shortly after the war by the researches of Georges Friedmann[3] and that its development in France dates only from that time. This tendency in French sociology has been intensified by the close links between sociology and philosophy in French higher education,[4] not to mention the gulf between the academic world and industry, which is only now beginning to be crossed. Consequently, students and research workers have shown little enthusiasm for empirical studies in the field. (It is true that the scarcity of resources, about which research teams often complain, is quite largely responsible for this situation.[5])

Approaching the question from the other side, it is true that most businessmen are still very distrustful towards all scientific research within their enterprises. The tradition of the 'business secret', the tendency of small and medium firms to keep themselves to themselves, the fear of the unknown represented by research are all partial explanations of this attitude. Moreover, experience in the United States seems to show that it is the big corporations that are most

---

[1] See, for instance, Paul Lazarsfeld, 'Reflections on Business', *American Journal of Sociology*.

[2] Gaston Bouthoul, *Histoire de la Sociologie*, Paris, Presses Universitaires de France, 1961.

[3] Georges Friedmann, *Le Travail en Miettes*, Paris, Gallimard, 1958.

[4] French degrees in sociology have been awarded only since 1959 and in psychology since 1948. Until 1966, the former required four papers, of which only one (General Sociology) was 'sociological' in a strict sense. The other three papers (Social Psychology, Political and Social Economics and one left to the candidate's choice) were part of other degree courses.

[5] See 'Sociologie du travail sociologique', in *Revue de sociologie du travail*.

disposed to co-operate with sociologists; and there are few businesses in France of a comparable size. Finally, there are certain ideological difficulties: social science research workers often tend to what we will call 'the left', while the average businessman tends to 'the right'. There are, of course, some notable examples of successful co-operation between businessmen and sociologists;[6] but the improvement of the last few years in the relations between the universities and industry will continue only if sociologists are properly trained. Their education must be more intensive, both on the theoretical side and (perhaps even more importantly) in equipping them to deal with the concrete problems and social realities of which the enterprise is the arena. As Raymond Aron has written:[7] 'The social sciences have a function as pure knowledge. Further, they have a philosophical function, they transform the modes of thought of those who practise them, as of those who are their object, they help society to be conscious of itself and to resolve its problems less imperfectly. But applied science, far from being harmful to theoretical sociology, is a source of its enrichment and progress.'

THE ENTERPRISE AS AN ORGANISATION

The enterprise cannot be considered a sociological concept in itself. Its legal and organisational forms and, above all, the part it plays in society vary considerably; moreover, the way a society is organised affects the importance of the enterprise. The more a society is industrialised, the greater its importance; yet it seems that the concept of the capitalist enterprise—since they see it as an economic rather than a social concept—is the one to which sociologists have given small attention. However, if the relationship of the sociologist to the enterprise is not comparable, say, to that which the ethnologist has towards the village he is studying, this fact should not eliminate the enterprise as an object of sociological study.[8] For if an enterprise is not a specifically sociological entity, it is nevertheless an arena where many factors of social life, and the values and norms of cultural life, act and interplay. It is, perhaps, one of those 'total social phenomena' through which sociologists may apprehend 'society in action'.[9] This complexity emerges quite clearly from sociological studies based upon investigations carried out in enterprises. It is evident that, from a sociological point of view, the enterprise is 'a concrete organisation, whose limits only coincide with a unitary analytic system ... it is not a unitary system of values, does not pursue a single and exclusive object and is not characterised by a collection of norms'.[10]

Thus it is that sociologists study the enterprise only from the point of view

[6] Pierre Bourdieu, *La Photo, Art Moyen*, with preface by Philippe de Vendœuvre (Paris, Editions du Minuit), may be consulted on this topic.

[7] In a special number of *L'expansion de la recherche scientifique*, November 1963.

[8] Howard R. Bowen, *The Business Enterprise as a Subject for Research*, New York, National Science Council, 1955.

[9] Georges Gurvitch, *La vocation actuelle de la sociologie*, Presses Universitaires de France.

[10] Arnold S. Feldman, 'The Interpenetration of Firm and Society', in Conseil International des Sciences Sociales, *Les implications sociales du développement économique*, Paris, Presses Universitaires de France, 1962. (Quoted by Maurice Montuclard in 'Le comité d'entreprise', *Sociologie du Travail*, 1965, No. 2.)

of organisation, a general concept upon which much work has been done. Organisation in the business world may be briefly defined as 'a system of positions and roles, of group powers and of individuals with individual or group strategies. It is a type of social system, comprising inter-individual and inter-group relationships, which constitutes a collection of social rules.'[11] Psycho-sociologists seem to go no further than thinking of the enterprise as a 'social organisation composed of groups and individuals' and consider that 'everything that happens in an enterprise is determined by inter-group or inter-personal relationships which are themselves affective'. Others think that such a limited view gives too much emphasis to an internal concept of the enterprise and stress its specific organisational aspects, its 'clear frontiers' and 'regular structure' which society usually places on it by official and institutional means. 'Like all organisations it is an arena of conflict, but there are conflicts peculiar to the enterprise.' Such people maintain that to reduce the sociological study of the enterprise to the sociology of organisation is both inadequate and misleading.

The organisation of the enterprise is of equal interest to the sociologist because the enterprise is an institution, 'a collection of means organised for certain legitimate or, rather, legitimised objectives'. These objectives are much less explicit in France than they are, for example, in the United States. A distinctive characteristic of the enterprise, according to Etzioni, is the fact that of the three reasons for discipline which he finds in all organisations (calculation of interest, constraint and normative discipline), the first plays a much more important part in the enterprise than the others. Alain Touraine has often stressed the attraction of power for its own sake which is to be found in many directors of big French firms—a factor which, though it should not be exaggerated, partly explains the similarity of outlook shared by the higher echelons in government and big business. Thus, while American business is underpinned by a real 'philosophy' (as, for example, the works of Dr Peter Drucker[12] show), French business is not nowadays guided as rigorously by any ideology of profit. The attempts at a 'rehabilitation' of the concept of profit (the expression itself is significant), especially in the writings of Octave Gélinier,[13] should, however, be noted. Finally, although the enterprise in France is indeed an organisation, its peculiarities with regard to those of other organisations are less clear cut than in some other countries. This perhaps partly explains why French sociologists have been slow in approaching the study of the enterprise.[14] However, organisation theories have, in France as elsewhere, done much to improve the understanding of business.

Industrial developments at the end of the nineteenth century and the beginning of the twentieth resulted in efforts to rationalise business organisation. At a theoretical level, Max Weber elaborated his ideal type of bureaucracy; more practically, the celebrated studies of F. W. Taylor in the USA

[11] Quotations without reference are from conversations with French social scientist during the preparation of this appendix.

[12] Jean-Daniel Reynaud, 'La philosophie du management de P. Drucker', *Sociologie du travail*, 1960, No. 3.

[13] Octave Gélinier, *Morale de l'entreprise et destin de la nation*, Paris, Plon, 1964.

[14] Friedmann, 'Quelques problèmes de définitions et de limites', *Sociologie du travail*, 1959, No. 1.

and of Henri Fayol in France contributed to the spread of the idea that technical progress went hand in hand with rationalisation in the organisation of work and in the functioning of firms. These ideas had a great influence on French management but were not in general seriously studied by sociologists at the time of their application.

The sociology of work, chiefly developed in France since 1945, has been able to draw upon research done mostly in the United States since 1930. The discovery of the 'human factor', the role of informal groups (as opposed to the formal groups explicit in the 'official' structure of the firm), made it possible to explain why technical rationalisation did not necessarily improve performance, as those who held mechanistic theories had predicted. This comparatively new understanding of 'human relations' has stressed the importance of reducing tensions in the firm by techniques such as group discussion, interviewing and 'business psychotherapy'. This trend, however, has not escaped vigorous criticism. Max Pagès, for example, has shown how dubious can be a policy of 'human relations' if it is not balanced by a proper policy of 'industrial relations'.[15] The point here is that the power of the employer should be matched by organised trade union power, so that 'psychotherapy' in the firm is not always used to the advantage of one party only.

The human relations movement, while helpful, is not enough in itself. What is needed is a considerable development in the sociology of organisation. An outstanding contribution to this aspect of the problem is the work of Michel Crozier. His book *Le Phénomène Bureaucratique*[16] analyses the dysfunctions of French business bureaucracy. (The term 'dysfunction', borrowed from Merton, refers to the inadequacies and irrelevancies of the functioning of organisations.) In both content and methodology (a reliance on empirical research and field investigation by interviews in depth and detailed questionnaires), this book is a landmark in the development of French business sociology. Crozier approaches the study of bureaucracy (taking the term in its everyday sense) in a clinical manner which exposes the unwieldy complexity of modern administrative or business organisations. He adopts, as he himself says, 'a method which consists in considering particular cases and generalising only from a thorough comprehension of these cases'. This approach, familiar enough in the English-speaking world, is relatively novel in French research, which more often relies on documentary evidence and on the analysis of a large number of 'facts' in order to achieve a broad synthesis. There is a strong case for arguing that the business world is most appropriately studied by empirical research; if business is a social fact, it surely gains from being observed 'live' in all its complexity.

Although the two organisations studied by Crozier in this book were not private firms, certain characteristic traits of modern bureaucracy emerge which, in broad outline, seem to be valid for companies of a certain size.[17] Four

[15] See his article in *Sociologie du travail*, 1964, No. 1.
[16] Paris, Editions du Seuil.
[17] Crozier has, however, also studied some large insurance companies in the Paris region from the same point of view. See his *Le monde des employés de bureau*, Paris, Editions du Seuil, 1965.

essential features characterise the bureaucratic organisation and set up a vicious circle, from which the only means of escape (into a new vicious circle) is a crisis, often violent and resolvable only by outside intervention.[18] The first characteristic is the development of impersonal rules: functions are classified as are also the people chosen to carry them out—the competitive system. Secondly, decisions are centralised: those decisions which are not implicit in the impersonal rules are taken by persons at a level in the hierarchy where they are sheltered from the pressures which fall upon those who are affected by the decisions. Thirdly, the categories in the hierarchy are isolated from each other and it is comparatively difficult for an individual to pass from one category to another. The fourth characteristic feature is the development of 'parallel power' relationships: where certain areas of decision are not clearly classified, informal networks of decision and power grow up which allow individuals at various levels to enjoy powers out of proportion to their status in the official hierarchy.

The confrontation of the organisational structures of the French economy with the acceleration of technological change has highlighted the obsolescent and inflexible nature of these structures. Moreover, the difficulties of adaptation seem largely to stem from the behaviour of businessmen and from what we may call social habits which have a strong influence in the 'economic' world. For the characteristics of bureaucratic organisations are in fact found in business: the importance of rank, the delays and difficulty of promotion and scrupulous equality between members of the same category; an avoidance of face-to-face relations; a desire to avoid direct confrontation between superior and subordinate, or between company and union (at company rather than regional, national or sectional level); and a similar reluctance to achieve direct contact with consumers.[19]

Thus, the bureaucratic system seems somewhat lost when faced with the hallmark of our time: rapid technological change forcing organisations to make constant efforts to adapt their structure, methods and modes of thought and action to new circumstances. The French business world has reacted to these harsh facts by relying more and more on the state (considered a necessary evil) to protect it both against competition and against the trade unions. Moreover, it is the state alone which can, in exchange for its protection, impose the changes made indispensable by technological progress. As Crozier says, 'we have reached the paradoxical situation in which the class of bourgeois entrepreneurs, which made itself indispensable as the only group capable of introducing necessary innovations at the right time, has become generally opposed to all innovation and progress, while the incompetent and workday state has taken up the role of *animateur*, exhorting and scolding'.

The originality and interest of the views of Michel Crozier are everywhere recognised; but not all sociologists agree with them. In the present context it may be useful to summarise the criticism made by Alain Touraine of the application of the model of bureaucratic behaviour to business. Touraine believes that such a model cannot by itself account for the functioning of an

[18] See Crozier, *Le phénomène bureaucratique*, Chapter 7.
[19] ibid., Chapter 10. See also Hoffman, Pitts, Duroselle and Wylie, *A la recherche de la France*, Paris. Editions du Seuil, 1964.

organisation. He prefers Weber's approach, which consists in working out an ideal type and then in analysing its relationship with actual organisations, rather than Crozier's method of studying actual bureaucracies and their dysfunctions. 'It is necessary', he has written,[20] 'to consider bureaucracy, in whatever sense one takes this term, as a theoretical model which does not fully explain a real situation, only one of whose dimensions it explores.' Other criticisms have been made of Crozier and especially of his theory of bureaucratic behaviour as an interpretive factor of French society and the optimism to which his analysis finally leads.[21] Nevertheless, his views on the theory of organisations and business have stimulated a great deal of other very interesting research, as Octave Gélinier has shown.[22] One example is a book by Pierre Naville[23] on automation as a social fact which is transforming the habitual concepts of industry and of work itself. Forms of management are being modified, terms such as productivity or remuneration for performance no longer mean what they used to and the relationship of man to machine has ceased to be that of employer to employed. Automation can thus be defined by the changes it brings about: its object, says Naville, is 'to contribute to the autonomous functioning of complete and ever more extensive production cycles at a very high rate of performance'. This autonomy is characteristic of automation with regard to both equipment and workers.[24] A social transformation results from a new interdependence between workers, a new 'collectivisation' of work. Claudine Marenco has studied[25] the introduction of a computer into a financial establishment. She sees this as a result of mechanisation: not a simple rationalisation of administrative structures but rather a renewed injection of interdependence into hierarchical relations. Automation does not, however, diminish the distance between employees and management, for its effects are different according to the category of personnel to which it is applied.

GROUPS IN THE ENTERPRISE

The enterprise as an organisation is a theatre of confrontations, oppositions and coalitions. Distinctions develop between different groups, continue for a while and then disappear. Sociologists are very interested in the nature of these groups and distinctions but they answer the questions that arise in very different ways. Any analysis requires that the groups be examined one by one. The classic breakdown is now the object of much lively criticism but since no new dominant theory has yet emerged it seems the simplest to keep to the traditional typology.

[20] Alain Touraine, 'Entreprise et bureaucratie', *Sociologie du travail*, 1959, No. 1.

[21] Jacques Lautman, 'Sur le phénomène bureaucratique', *Annales*, March/April 1965.

[22] Gélinier, 'Le secret des structures compétitives', *Hommes et techniques*, 1966.

[23] Pierre Naville, *Vers l'automation social? Problèmes du travail et de l'automation*, Paris, Gallimard, 1963. See also *Cahiers d'étude sur l'automation et des sociétés industrielles*.

[24] Pierre Rolle, 'Nouvelle classe ouvrière et nouvelle technologie', *Critiques*, February 1965.

[25] Claudine Marenco, *L'introduction de l'automatisme dans les bureaux: l'administration du changement, les modalités d'adaptation des individus et des groupes*, Paris, Institut des Sciences Sociales du Travail, 1963.

The traditional typology of groups

The holders of capital own the enterprise and, legally, have power vested in them. The role of this group may be called episodic, for it seems to intervene only from time to time and usually at moments of conflict. Unlike the shop-floor workers or salaried staff, the capital holders tend to assume a marginal role which cannot be objectively defined. For this reason, they are not of prime interest to psycho-sociologists studying the enterprise. Moreover, as a group they are extremely heterogeneous. Three sub-groups can be identified, each with different economic purposes: (*a*) those in family or quasi-family businesses, whose behaviour is essentially directed towards preserving the good name of the firm and realising high profits; (*b*) those in companies with highly fragmented capital ownership; and (*c*) dominant controlling groups such as banks (a form of ownership which is developing rapidly) or foreign interests. There are hardly any studies on the holders of capital in France, partly, no doubt, because of the difficulty of research in this area. One result is the perpetuation of myths, of which the famous legend of the 'two hundred families' is a celebrated example.[26]

Much more research has been done on the role of *managers and salaried staff*, because of their increasing importance. If there is general agreement about the importance of salaried staff in industrial societies, conflicting views are held about their position in the enterprise. Some see their role as 'analogous to that of the overseer', at once intermediary and marginal; others put them on the side of the capital owners; yet others contrast, among salaried staff, the bureaucratic character of administrative staff with that of technical or production staff. There are still few academic studies on the salaried staff group itself, its social origins and its education, though many journalists have written about these subjects. On the other hand, its role in business and society has caused a great deal of controversy, especially to do with the problem of 'technocracy'. In Touraine's view, for instance, technical progress, by the increasing rationalisation of decisions, considerably enhances the power of those who take the decisions—i.e. management and salaried staff. 'The great social problem . . . in advanced industrial societies is the un-controlled power of economic managers.'[27] Here he agrees with Crozier and his 'zones of uncertainty'—the areas in which informal power networks develop (see p. 355, above). Individuals strategically placed in relationship with these zones can come to considerable power. Other studies have drawn attention to the shifting on to the political level of the role which salaried staff are conscious of playing in business. An example is the importance assumed in recent years in French political life by clubs, alongside the official parties. Some people see the salary earners as the real bourgeois of the twentieth century. Nevertheless, there are as yet few scientifically based French studies in which the category of salary earners is identified and contrasted with, for example, the working class.[28]

It is, indeed, the problems of *employees*—the 'working class'—in which

[26] Among the scant literature, the work of the polemicist H. Colson may be noted.
[27] Touraine, 'Les chances du progrès technique', *Revue Française du travail*, October/December 1965.
[28] See Jean Meynaud, *La technocratie*, Payot.

French social researchers have shown the greatest interest and about which there is a great number of studies. In particular, the question of the development of the working class has been debated with some bitterness—though everyone seems to agree that 'a man is not a worker in a firm but is "working class" '. In other words, the working group is defined outside the enterprise. Of special interest is the research which has been done on workers faced with changes brought about by the introduction of new techniques and industries. Serge Mallet[29] has studied the problems posed in, for example, the electronics industry and by the introduction of new methods of oil refining. He believes it is necessary to link 'the working activity to the work situation, defined in terms of the economic relationships between man and what he produces'.[30] Mallet does not go deeply into the vocational and social transformation of industrial workers in recent decades and does, in a way, leave his reader somewhat up in the air. His references to traditional unionism and his allusions to revolution seem to conflict strongly with the facts that the analysis of working society clearly reveal—there is a wide gulf between revolutionary unionism and the 'new workers'.[31] However, in Mallet's scheme economic development and the extension of the power of the workers go hand in hand. His central idea can be stated as follows: the labour movement takes on new forms and a new direction when its action is concerned immediately with economic development, when its struggle is no longer conducted in the name of one category against another (i.e. in the name of one set of private interests against another) but aims at once at developing the forces of production and at resisting all private appropriation of the means and results of this development.

Pierre Belleville, the author of another book with an almost identical title,[32] reaches the same conclusion. His object is to demonstrate the obstacles which hinder the growth of modern unionism in the world of labour. In many cases collective labour relations are often prevented from developing in their proper framework, that is to say, in the enterprise, where the most important economic decisions are taken. He sets out to prove that various policies at high sectorial level—such as authoritarianism in the iron and steel industry, neo-paternalism in textiles, state bureaucracy in coal and the railways—are all impediments to the unions' rightful power of opposition. Like Mallet he concludes that there should be a valid framework for the development of 'enterprise syndicalism', supported by a large union of workers. Belleville notes the appearance of new forms of labour initiative and would like to see a new type of unionism which could be called 'participational and oppositional' or, more simply, 'bargaining'.[33] His discretion does not, however, completely mask the solution which he would himself prefer: a neo-liberalism which would aim at creating the conditions for true negotiation and at increasing bargaining power (which implies that firms should be fully masters of their economic decisions).

[29] Serge Mallet, *La nouvelle classe ouvrière*, Paris, Editions du Seuil, 1964.
[30] Quoted by Touraine in *Sociologie du travail*, 1964, No. 1.
[31] ibid.
[32] Pierre Belleville, *Une nouvelle classe ouvrière*, Paris, Juillard (in *Les Temps Modernes* series), 1963.
[33] Quoted by Touraine, loc. cit.

Typologies other than the traditional one just outlined have been proposed but none of them seems fully satisfactory. They attempt to categorise groups by the objectives ascribed to them. For example, 'career personnel' can be contrasted with 'non-career personnel'. The former would be salary earners and white-collar workers, with group strategy directed towards personal advancement and mutual competition. The latter would be manual workers, interested in 'having a job' and keeping it—a very different outlook. Other distinctions may be drawn, within a firm, between 'capitalists' and 'non-capitalists' and the wielders and subjects of bureaucratic power; but these do not get us very far. A more interesting contrast is that between the various groups' different attitudes to change. These can extend from the 'progessive' to that which resists all innovation. The objectives of the various groups' strategies can thus be explained, as they ally with and oppose each other according to their interests and play a game with no clear outcome. It could be possible to develop a theory of games based on group strategies within the firm.

Representation in the enterprise

Works councils were set up in France in 1945 with the declared object of bringing greater democracy into the economic, technical and social management of firms. They have been chiefly studied from a legal point of view (i.e. in labour law) or with regard to their functioning and decision-making processes. Sociologists have rarely investigated works councils and the latter's practical results have undoubtedly made people feel pessimistic about them. The weakness of their influence has various complementary causes. They are limited to firms employing more than fifty; the heads of firms who are obliged to preside over them and ensure a time and place for meetings are often reluctant to do so; the necessity for secrecy concerning certain technical and financial matters makes complete and objective information well-nigh impossible; the members of the councils are often of a low educational standard. Generally speaking, their concrete achievements seem to be limited to the field of welfare.

Maurice Montuclard has studied the efficacy of works councils from the point of view of an industrial sociologist.[34] He maintains that the limitations of their procedure demonstrate the 'dominant and privileged' place held by 'the firm' in relation to the council and to social and labour matters. The distinction between 'dispute' and 'participation' has no longer any meaning when the latter is defined as 'the collective attitude according to which the employees' representatives feel themselves involved in the enterprise, its functioning, its internal equilibrium and its results beyond the level that the contractual exchange of work given and wage received demands'.[35] But even if there is no immediate practical expression, the interest shown by the members of the councils in the condition of firms is undeniable, as is witnessed by increasing requests for information on accounts, orders and other matters which is in the

---

[34] Maurice Montuclard, *La dynamique des comités d'entreprises*, Paris, CNRS, 1963; 'Pour une sociologie de la participation ouvrière dans les comités d'entreprises', *Sociologie du travail*, October/December 1960; and 'Le comité d'entreprise: A propos d'une hypothèse concernant son effet sur l'évolution de l'entreprise', ibid., April/June 1965.

[35] *Sociologie du travail*, April/June 1965, art. cit.

management's possession. But interest shown in the enterprise does not imply any lessening in the will or power to dispute; on the contrary, these go together. 'Instead of the expected contradiction between participation and demands, a type of participation through conflict has most frequently been encountered. (One would have preferred to be able to write "through contestation".) On the one hand, demands are more firmly based on economic information and, on the other, more and more stress is put on seeking the means to greater participation.'[36]

The councils seem to be contributing to a breaking up of power within the enterprise which has lost the strictly unitary character it appeared to have, in law, before 1945. There is now a Social Fund which originates in the firm but is not administered by the management and which, by training employees, can even be used to make them better fitted to press their claims in problem areas which demand a higher level of education if they are to be properly understood. Furthermore, the councils receive a certain amount of non-confidential information and can thus put pressure on the management. They may also make suggestions which can affect decisions taken by the firm. Montuclard thus identifies a double hierarchy and therefore a double dynamic within the enterprise: a functional hierarchy based upon authority and responsibility for organisation, production and management and an ethico-cultural hierarchy based upon human needs for improvement and integration in society as a whole. The contempt formerly shown for such needs resulted in violent union action. The works council represents an institutionalisation of the conflict between the two hierarchies, making this conflict inevitable but giving it a better chance of being resolved. Montuclard arrives at the following functional definition of the council: 'an apparatus organised in an industrial group to allow the manifestation and real confrontation of the social tensions underlying labour relations; to develop by this confrontation the participation of all the elements composing the industrial group and thus to provide the conditions for a more democratic functioning and administration of the enterprise'.[37]

If we now turn to French trade unionism, we see that it has characteristics which distinguish it both from other national representative institutions and from the forms of unionism found in other countries. Since the Amiens Charter of 1906, the unions have considered themselves solely the spokesmen of the workers. They are not political parties which aim to represent citizens and to express common interests. Furthermore, the membership of the various unions is only a minority of the total relevant work force. They are comparatively weak financially and in number of officials, in striking contrast, for instance, with American unions. Their effectiveness is further reduced by lack of discipline and above all by the ideological differences between those of communist (CGT), anarcho-syndicalist (CGT-FO) and Christian (CFTC and CFDT) allegiance.

However, as Frederic Meyers notes in the conclusions of his study on two collective negotiations in France,[38] American unions are not usually considered

---

[36] ibid.   [37] Montuclard, *La dynamique des comités d'entreprises*, op. cit.
[38] Frederic Meyers, 'Deux aspects du rôle des négotiations collectives en France', *Sociologie du travail*, January/March and April/June 1965.

by society in general as any more than the representatives of their paid-up members. In France, on the other hand, the unions, taken collectively, are recognised as representing 'the interests of all workers against the state and the employers, also taken collectively'. French society implicitly accepts that the workers place their trust in the unions without belonging to them. Jean-Daniel Reynaud, however, concludes that their minority character makes the recognition of the union branch (the precondition of representation) an impossibility. In present circumstances, French unions oppose without taking responsibility, content themselves with saying 'no', while their American counterparts are able actually to reach agreement with managements.

Not that psychological or sociological research any longer considers opposition and participation as contradictory. Gérard Adam has written that 'to a certain extent the act of opposition implies the necessity of presence. . . . Participation even facilitates the exercise of opposition.'[39] Union action expresses itself by demands which are at the same time opposition and participation. It is therefore at this level that it is possible to distinguish the various forms taken by union strategy. Ideological demands (peace in Algeria, for instance) may be distinguished from demands for better pay or conditions. A union may be acting for external or internal motives. Some demands constitute true objectives; others are purely formal and may be no more than tactical moves during negotiations. Finally, there is a distinction between 'professional' and 'social' action. The former applies to specific categories of workers; it tends towards corporatism and can just as easily split the labour movement as set a good example. The 'social' claim 'is one which concerns wage earners irrespective of their grade or sector'[40] and is thus more comprehensive and 'political'.

The paradox of French unionism lies in the fact that although it is both a minority movement ('unionism is an impulse of active minorities'[41]) and divided, it is universally recognised as the representative of the working class against the employers and the state. To quote Montuclard: 'It is a strange but inescapable fact that the sociologist must recognise at once the disparities, the opposition amongst themselves of the great trade unions, and the identity of some of their basic reactions and behaviour.'[42]

Relationships between groups

Yves Delamotte[43] has listed the various forms of employee participation and their inter-relationships as a preliminary to studying their position with regard to industrial conflict. Delamotte distinguishes two types of participation which he calls 'instigated' and 'combative'. The former is so called because it emanates from the power of the employers. This introduces a fresh element but at the same time the presence of a psychologist on the staff ensures the scientific character of the operation while allowing rigorous

[39] Gérard Adam, 'L'action syndicale et les types de démocratie', roneoed document.
[40] ibid.
[41] Reynaud, *Les syndicats en France*, Paris, A. Collin, 1963.
[42] In *Revue Française de sociologie*, July/September 1964.
[43] Yves Delamotte, 'Conflit industriel et participation ouvrière', *Sociologie du travail*, 1959, No. 1.

control and description. A typical example is provided by an American experiment,[44] from which it emerged that once it is admitted that the power of the employers is used only when based on understanding and that the employees have nothing to lose by change, the goodwill of the workers is assured. (This is why this participation is also called 'idyllic'.) 'Combative' participation, on the contrary, results from union action and is the confrontation of two powers. In this case there is direct 'contact through conflict', made possible by the institutionalisation of conflict in collective bargaining. (It should be noted that these two types of participation, far from being mutually exclusive, are quite complementary.) Delamotte also studies the works council—a type of participation provided for by law and of fixed form. It is an observable fact, however, that both combative and idyllic participation are impossible in the councils. In fact, they have no effective responsibility (what they do have is as general as that of the employers) and cannot reach agreements because there is only consultation, without any recognition of the power of labour. Delamotte concludes that both 'combative' and 'instigated' participation can be applied only to problems of little importance. He maintains that attempts made to provide for 'total participation' in works councils show that it is not possible 'to graft the scheme of participation on to industrial conflict'.[45] With regard to negotiation (in connexion with which the study by Frederic Meyers on union organisation has already been mentioned[46]), two facts may be noted. First, the dominant influence of the state of the labour market on collective agreements fixing wage rates and, second, the success of negotiations on questions such as unemployment benefits in circumstances where employers and workers are both wary of state intervention. On the other hand, the common front made by the unions against the employers has resulted in their being considered by the latter and by the state as the representatives of all workers. This has made it possible to establish an effective negotiating relationship between the two sides.

CONCLUSIONS

This appendix has taken a brief look at the changes that have taken place in the concept of the enterprise within a comparatively short period. Future trends are uncertain but it is possible to identify some of the factors which might contribute to a transformation of inter-personal and inter-group relationships and, consequently, of the enterprise itself.

Many scholars, in refusing to consider the enterprise of today as a phenomenon—the superstructure shall we say—of industrial capitalism, contrast it with other forms of productive organisation characteristic of earlier phases

[44] J. R. P. French, J. C. Roos, S. Kirby, J. B. Nelson and P. Smyth, 'Employees' participation in a program of industrial change', *Personnel Magazine*, November/December 1958. A new method was being introduced into the firm and interested personnel were asked to make suggestions on the practical application of the innovation.

[45] Delamotte, art. cit.

[46] Meyers, art. cit. This study examines union action with regard to the relationship between real wages and those resulting from collective bargaining and an unemployment benefit scheme worked out by the Conseil National du Patronat Français (the main French employers' organisation) and the big unions.

of this same capitalism. The entrepreneur of the Schumpeter type—the representative, it seems, of a phase of liberalism, of laissez-faire much more than of free competition—has to yield to the enterprise in which the links between the various ranks of the hierarchy tend to become depersonalised. The economic transformation of capitalism, marked by a growth in the size of productive units and by changes in the relationship between the enterprise and the market, has made problems of internal organisation more important. This fact has led to the development of rules institutionalising relationships in the enterprise—and makes it legitimate to talk of 'bureaucratisation'.

Twin and opposing forces are now evident. Economic facts are compelling enterprises to grow and adapt themselves to national and international markets. Small units still exist but become further and further removed from the market, coming within the orbit of big firms as subsidiaries or, more loosely, as subcontractors. The 'central organiser' thus becomes ever more important. On the other hand, the dehumanisation of industrial bureaucracies has become so blatant that they are themselves seeking to reforge the links between persons and groups which they neglected in their exclusive concern for efficiency.

It is tempting, but of little value, to speculate on the future of the enterprise in ideological terms. If we wish to be scientific, it is as well to limit our examination to the observable factors which are likely to determine the uncertain shape of things to come.

The first of these factors are of a technical nature and have been the subject of much research. It has been said, for example, that automation is strengthening functional rather than hierarchical relationships since it creates a need for specialists and that the element of 'subordination', therefore, appears more objective because it is based on needs and skills. The increase in the number of personnel concerned with the gathering and processing of information and the replacement of 'non-informative' workers by machines also lie behind this idea. Similarly, it may be argued that centralisation will become less effective as information becomes more abundant and that organisations will have to be more flexible and allow more autonomy to the various levels of their hierarchies.

But those factors within the enterprise which may be called psycho-sociological need to be studied more intensively. Many sociologists, as we have seen, do not believe that the enterprise is evolving towards the ideal of a field of conflicting or 'combative' relationships. They see its dynamic of change in a dialectic: participation no longer excludes the making of demands because it is no longer regarded as synonymous with collaboration. Put most succinctly, the role of the unions is to say 'no'. In France, moreover, the minority position of the unions in relation to the total number of workers forces them to oppose without a corresponding assumption of responsibility, unlike the more fully representative unions in the United States.

Finally, the works councils. These allow participation, in the sense that employees are able to demonstrate a concern with what happens in the enterprise over and above that demanded by their contract of labour. But this participation is of a 'combative' type, evolves in step with the making of demands and is based on better information. It thus appears that the business theoreticians and the 'interventionist' company psycho-sociologists (who join in conflicts in order to further their fruitful outcome) are on common ground. For both, confrontation is the prime mover of the future transformation of the enterprise.

Appendix E

GERMAN ATTITUDES TO REFORM

This appendix seeks to amplify the German sections of this book, which were mainly concerned with law and with legal and social history. It is based on discussions with leading businessmen, academics and politicians who were asked to answer questions on a number of immediately important issues of company law, with freedom to put the accent where they themselves wished according to their own point of view and interests. In this way it was possible through a large number of interviews, over and above the discussion of important individual questions, to arrive at a general assessment of the importance of the different problems.

THE GERMAN SYSTEM OF COMPANY LAW

The range of legal forms made available by German law for the establishment of commercial organisations (more extensive than that allowed by the law of any other country) was generally regarded as satisfactory. If this range is considered systematically—from the point of view of the important distinction between capital and personal associations, each with their own principles and problems—it is striking that one of these forms, the combined GmbH and KG company should have been so easily accepted by the courts and allowed to develop. This form of association aims at gaining tax advantage without limited liability and is, in fact, contrary to the general pattern of the company law. In it the members of GmbH form an association of such a kind that the GmbH itself becomes a 'personally responsible' member of the KG, while the members of the GmbH become its sleeping partners. The increasing preference for the GmbH-KG (which can now be said to be fully established in law) can further be explained by the opportunity it gives to new companies to offset initial costs against the profits of the sleeping partners. Many lawyers believe that GmbH have increasingly been converted into GmbH-KG since the abolition of the former organic relationships between GmbH and one man firms or 'personal companies'. It was also remarked that in the case of family firms, the GmbH-KG were given a supervisory board that makes it possible to separate management from the family, as is especially necessary when the latter cannot provide a sufficient number of persons qualified for top management. It was frequently said that the GmbH-KG has from many points of view already acquired considerable significance as a mixed form between 'personal' and 'capital' companies.

A variety of opinion was expressed on the question whether the strengthened disclosure provisions of the new company law have led to a flight to the GmbH, and so to a marked preference for this type of company. Certainly there are cases of recent conversions to this form which have given the GmbH an additional significance over and above its proper function as the right form for companies with limited capital and for holding companies. In general, however, it is thought that the forthcoming reshaping of the law on the GmbH (in which stiffer disclosure rules, at least for the larger companies, may certainly be expected) will contain attempts to avoid the increased publicity requirements of the new Act.

THE ORGANISATION OF THE COMPANY

Two questions loomed large with regard to organisation, one concerning the organisation pattern as such, the other the relations of company organs to one another. The two sets of problems are closely linked.

The great majority of those questioned approved the threefold division laid down in the Companies Act—between shareholders' meeting, supervisory board and administrative board—as reasonable and consonant with economic conditions and needs. However, some representatives of the academic world and the banks, and also of the trade unions, showed marked sympathy for a more 'concentrated' type of constitution. Their main reason was a desire for more effective control over management, though they made it clear that this was not so much a question of principle as of technique.

In contrast to the widespread approval of present company constitution and practice, the trade unions felt there was a need for a 'functional organisation of authority within the company related to social and economic facts'. This view was based on the opinion that none of the three company organs can, on their own, fulfil the functions laid down for them by the legislature in the actual economic and social conditions of today. The shareholders' meeting, the unions believe, is far from being democratic since a true and undistorted expression of shareholder opinion is no longer possible, not least because of the proxy system and the collaboration between banks and major shareholders. In the larger companies, for instance, a small proportion of the vote can often effectively control the firm. Given the present machinery of authority in the company, the supervisory board, elected by the shareholders' meeting, can under circumstances like these no longer genuinely represent the outside shareholders, while the intended independence and separate responsibility of the administrative board becomes largely a fiction. The unions think that the proposals put forward at one time by the Friedrich Ebert Stiftung would inject some realism into the pattern of company authority laid down by the law and regret that they have been given so little consideration. The Stiftung suggested that (a) appropriate means for the representation of shareholders should be provided at the shareholders' meeting in order to make possible a valid expression of opinion; (b) the supervisory board should be so composed that the group of shareholders' representatives should include a number of representatives of the general mass of outside shareholders corresponding to their share in the capital; (c) the administrative board should be protected from outside interests and its position strengthened against shareholders who pursue interests foreign to those of the company.

Parallel to this, but much more fundamental to the organisation of companies, are the ideas of the DGB[1] on the future form of company organs. These start from the conception that the substantial structural change which is taking place in German company law will lead to a far-reaching integration of the persons involved in an enterprise, and so advance from co-determination to the idea of an 'enterprise constitution'. They have therefore proposed the establishment of enterprise management, enterprise councils and enterprise assemblies in which representatives of the workers and the trade unions would have a powerful voice. The aim would be self-determination for the workers allied to efficient production—in short, economic company democracy.

This concept could be achieved only at the price of profound changes in the entire economic, legal and social order. A less revolutionary concept put forward from the trade union side is therefore particularly interesting. This is the suggestion that the interests of shareholders, workers and public should be built into the constitution of the enterprise in such a way that these three streams of interest are expertly represented 'in proportion to their true economic and social significance' in a shareholders' meeting re-entitled an 'enterprise assembly'. The shareholders' meeting would be reconstructed in such a way that under a system of elected delegates, 40 per cent each of the votes would go to the representatives of shareholders and workers and the remaining 20 per cent to the public interest. The supervisory board would be composed in like manner.

The functions and responsibilities of the executive board would remain basically unchanged; there would be no question of 'parliamentary organisation' of the plant. Trade union representatives added in discussion that, depending on the structure of the enterprise and contrary to the present law, it should become possible through greater flexibility in articles of association to widen the authority of the supervisory board and allow it to take managerial decisions—for example, on prices. Union representatives were not yet ready to set a definite percentage relationship between those employed in the company itself and union representatives, in the proposed enterprise assembly. The method suggested for the election of representatives of the public interest was the provision for the eleventh man in the supervisory boards of coal and steel companies: representatives of both shareholders and workers would have to agree on the public delegates, whose task would be not only to neutralise conflicting interests but also to overcome the tendency of the other parties to 'wear the blinkers of their own firm'.

The structure of this type of constitution, in the opinion of the trade unions, is particularly appropriate for the so-called 'mammoth' enterprises. If it is assumed that an enterprise becomes a mammoth only when it has around

[1] The central trade union organisation.

20,000 employees or, as the unions would prefer, reached a certain level of turnover or volume of assets, about fifty companies would be likely to be affected by the proposal. The union view is that it would be desirable to allow firms of a certain size to take only one particular legal form (as is already the case with insurance companies) not only in Germany but also in the whole of the EEC. Considering the effort that is being made to establish a European company law, these proposals for a modern company constitution are also a contribution to the solution of this problem as well.

The unions were not alone in believing that bringing all large undertakings under a single legal form is desirable or even, in view of recent developments in the German economy, necessary. Yet the union proposals met with strong opposition. The tendency of the unions to pursue an extension of co-determination over the whole field of enterprise constitutions (though in the first place only in the case of 'mammoth' enterprises) was the first target of criticism. The great majority of our informants rejected 'democratisation' of the economy by an extension of co-determination. This opposition is based on the conviction that private property (including ownership of the means of production) together with untrammelled free enterprise constitutes the main pillar of the legal and economic order. They believe that an extension of co-determination, as variously advocated by the unions, would destroy this order, not least because an economy so democratised must, in fact, become a vast, uncontrollable combination of central, economic and trade union power. They also maintain that it would prevent companies from satisfactorily fulfilling their real social functions—service to the consumer and the production of goods needed by the economy—and would weaken the national and international capital markets and the international competitiveness of the German economy, as well as the economic integration of Europe. Furthermore, 'the demand for equal rights for capital and labour is pointless, for it is already fulfilled. The worker is socially integrated in the civic and political as well as the social and economic sense, not least through company constitutional law and autonomous collective bargaining. Social integration through the extension of co-determination means integration of the trade unions and their representatives, not of workers themselves.' (Wietholter, *Juristen-Jahrbuch* 1966–67.)

Götz Briefs, writing in the *Frankfurter Zeitung* in October 1965, declared that an extension of co-determination 'would in the end lead to a syndicalist transformation of the economy into a labour-based economy which would drive out of existence today's productive and moderate capitalism with its tension between enterprise and trade union which guarantees freedom'.

Suggestions on the relation between company organs were confined almost entirely to strengthening the position of the supervisory board as begun by the reform of company law, the results of which are still to be seen. How far the board could fulfil the supervisory function entrusted to it by the law was, it was recognised, partly a question of the personalities involved. It was generally expected, however, that the innovations made by the Act of 1965 (limitation of the number of supervisory board seats which may be held and of interchange of members between boards) would help to improve their performance.

THE REFORM OF 1965

In tune with the legal and social policies of the German government, the main purpose of the 1965 reform of company law was to strengthen still further the position of shareholders and at the same time to discourage the concentration of capital in the hands of a few large shareholders. It is generally held that the most important of the new regulations—and those most likely to be effective—provide for greater disclosure in the interests of shareholders. Academic specialists and others have also stressed that radical disclosure provisions are necessary (and wholly to be supported) in order to put companies under public supervision. Closely connected with this are the new valuation provisions which make it much harder arbitrarily to create hidden reserves and thereby conceal the true profit position (Sec. 153 ff).

Special disclosure provisions are also desirable in order to make clear the complex of linkages between companies, which have hitherto been difficult to pin down and which have now for the first time been dealt with by law. The third chapter of the Act on controlled undertakings is regarded as the second basic innovation, over and above the general extension of disclosure requirements, although it is still too early to judge the effectiveness of these provisions. Nevertheless, the preparatory reports on 'concerns' and the auditors' reports on relations with subsidiaries were expected to meet with difficulties and, in the provisions of the third chapter, are considered to be meaningful and to take a realistic view of the facts as they are. Indeed, the whole conception of the reform of company law has been favourably received in Germany. In the words of one of its main authors: 'The purpose was no to introduce revolutionary innovations but to maintain the line of development and set the points in some new directions.' It is, however, understandable that the banks should not only criticise the amount of extra work involved in the change of law on proxies but also ask, with some scepticism, whether many shareholders are not likely, in view of the complexity of the new procedure, to ignore the documents sent to them. This could result in accidental majorities at shareholders' meetings—an outcome much less satisfactory than the fiduciary administration of proxies by the banks. Discounting the presumably prejudiced views of the banks themselves, and the common trade union opinion that proxies are a false solution designed to maintain existing power relationships, the prevailing attitude seems to be as follows.

It cannot be overlooked that the use of proxies gives the banks a certain position of power and that clashes of interest are obviously possible, though these are likely to be kept within bounds by the equilibrium between various interests which the investment banks must maintain. Indeed, it is precisely this possibility and achievement of equilibrium of interests that gives the bank proxy system its value, in spite of certain drawbacks; nor should it be forgotten that the system has a long history and that people are accustomed to it. The banks have generally managed both to render good service to shareholders and to achieve a satisfactory balance of interests. An organisation such as the Shareholders' Protection Society—the officials of which themselves sit on a number of supervisory boards—is regarded as a useful adjunct to the system. On the other hand it is hardly surprising in the circumstances that shareholders' associations have made so little headway. A common argument for preserving the bank proxy system was that there was no alternative to it—no doubt because none had ever been necessary.

Although there is little experience as yet to go on, various opinions were expressed on a number of other changes made by the Act of 1965. It remains to be seen, for instance, to what extent shareholders' meetings will decide to place more than half the profits at the disposal of administrative boards (by amending the articles of association). In general, however, it is clear that this regulation will in the end lead to a marked reduction in self-financing and some of our informants therefore regarded this point as very important— unlike the new provisions allowing for easier issue of shares for employees. It was sometimes remarked, however, that any preference given to workers might one day have to be considered in connexion with the extension of co-determination. Finally, it was noted that the right of shareholders to demand information, which has been more closely defined rather than widened, should not be overestimated since it bears little relation to what actually happens at shareholders' meetings.

CO-DETERMINATION AND THE PLAN FOR A EUROPEAN COMPANY[2]

Full-scale co-determination is likely to be further extended under the present coalition government. It is now provided that full-scale co-determination shall end in those coal and steel firms in which coal and steel output drops below 50 per cent of total production, not as hitherto two, but five years after the point at which this happens. It may be surmised that the trade unions hope by then to be able to extend 'economic co-determination' to all large enterprises, irrespective of their industrial sector. The debate on the extension of co-determination has therefore become acute once again and at the same time other problems raised by this contentious social experiment have become apparent. ('Economic co-determination' is defined on p. 216.)

In the efforts to establish a European company law—whether in the form of European companies established under national or supranational law, or by way of point-by-point harmonisation—the obstacles raised by German legislation on co-determination have become strikingly clear. There has been a general readiness to overcome the many various difficulties in the way of establishing a European company law, and thus to allow the formation of large European firms capable of matching American competition. It has always been clear that the harmonisation of company law is one of the most complicated tasks facing the European Community; but the vigorous efforts both inside and outside the Community justify the hope that a common basis will be found.

The German law on co-determination, however, is unlike any other and is therefore a hindrance. Although company law differs from one member

[2] It should be noted that this text was written before the publication of the Sanders proposals for a European company statute. (These are discussed in a paper in the joint Chatham House/PEP European Series, by D. Thompson, published in 1969.) On 'co-determination', see pp. 213 ff above.

state to another, it is only in Germany that workers are so closely involved with matters of social policy and labour law, or have a general right to participate in administration and supervision. The difficulties caused have emerged clearly in the discussions on the 'European company' and on so-called 'international mergers' that have taken place within the framework of the EEC.

The aim of the special agreement on international mergers is to permit mergers between companies 'which are subject to the legal rules of different member states'. This means, in the first place, that in a merger the company rules to be applied will be those of the member state in which the company making the take-over has its registered office. Thus, a German company taken over by a foreign company would legally cease to exist and consequently employee co-determination would come to an end. Conversely, where a German company took over a foreign company, German law would be applied. Given that the other states would reject the direct, or, as in this case, the indirect introduction of co-determination along German lines, there is clearly a danger that international mergers across frontiers will be between firms in other community states or between them and firms in third countries. The serious economic and political disadvantages that this would imply for Germany are obvious.

A similar situation arises in the plans to set up a European company. Even if it could be arranged that national provisions on co-determination would not be affected by the formation of such companies, the question would remain whether the Federal Republic would gain more from co-determination or from full and unreserved participation in the European market. Given the attitude of the other members of the EEC, the chances that European companies will be set up with bases in Germany appear slim.

Union representatives commented that, although European trade unions were following different roads towards influence over companies, a marked increase of interest in the German idea of co-determination was notable in the last three years or so. It was, therefore, reasonable to assume that within a foreseeable time European trade unions would be able to agree on a minimum area of co-determination. The German unions would reject any attempts to narrow down the area of co-determination—which they now regard as a minimum achievement—in a system of European company law. These two factors combined would mean that a European company law would be regarded throughout the EEC as hostile to the workers, and spontaneous unity on the question among all West European unions could well follow. Other models of the enterprise—the Yugoslav, for example—would then inevitably become increasingly attractive to the workers.

That this should be the attitude of important union leaders (who claim, in general, to be interested in a single company form for all European enterprises above a certain size) illustrates the possibly insuperable difficulty of the problems. German employer circles have therefore discussed a compromise: to include in the proposed European company statute the co-determination rules of the German Industrial Constitution Law. This appears the most constructive and realistic contribution so far, and it is regrettable that the unions have not responded favourably to it, since the hostility of the other community states towards any kind of co-determination will in any case make it difficult enough to get them to agree even to European regulations equivalent to those of the German Industrial Constitution Law.

Appendix F

CORPORATION GIVING IN THE UNITED STATES

Corporation giving in the United States has become a substantial part of the total philanthropic giving in recent years. This total, from all sources and for all purposes for the United States in 1965, was $11,300 million, or 1·66 per cent of the nation's gross national product of $681,200 million. Total philanthropic giving for that year amounted to 2·11 per cent of personal income ($535,100 million) and 2·41 per cent of disposable personal income ($469,100 million). The percentages have tended to increase since the war, and corporation giving has risen both in percentages and in dollar amounts. The American Association of Fund-Raising Counsel has estimated that philanthropic giving for 1965 was derived from the sources shown in Table 1.

TABLE 1. US Philanthropic Donors in 1965

Source	Amount	Percentage
Individuals	$8,662 million	76·6
Foundations	1,125 million	10·0
Bequests	780 million	6·9
Business Corporations	733 million	6·5
	$11,300 million	100·0

SOURCE: *Giving: USA*, 1966 edn., published by American Association of Fund-Raising Counsel, Inc., New York, NY.

These figures do not take into account the fact that some foundation gifts originate with business corporations. Nor do any of the standard tables show the full scope of corporate support in non-cash aid, which is substantial. It should be noted, too, that the recipients of most American philanthropy are not the usual recipients of corporate aid. The Association's estimates for the distribution of total American philanthropy in 1965 are shown in Table 2.

It is possible to give only estimates for a comparable breakdown of corporate giving. The best estimates we have are from the National Industrial Conference Board, which conducted in 1965 a survey of 448 companies, which gave 0·68 per cent of their pre-tax income to various types of donees

373

TABLE 2. Recipients of US Philanthropy in 1965

(Percentages)	
Religion	49
Education	17
Welfare	13
Health	11
Foundations	4
Civic, cultural, etc.	4
Other	2
	100

SOURCE: *Giving: USA.*

during 1965. The companies in this sample were mostly manufacturing firms with a heavy concentration of electrical and non-electrical machinery makers, fabricated metal firms, and chemical and allied companies. Most of the non-manufacturing companies in the sample were in banking, finance and real estate. Some of the 448 were of modest size, but the majority controlled assets of $100 million or more. Table 3 shows the breakdown of the 1965 corporate contributions dollar according to the results of the sample survey.

TABLE 3. The Corporate Contributions Dollar, 1965

(Percentages)	
Health and Welfare	41·5
Education	38·4
Culture (cultural centres, performing arts, orchestras, little theatres, libraries, museums, and the like)	2·8
Civic causes (municipal and community improvement, good government, and the like)	5·8
Other (religious causes, groups devoted solely to economic education)	9·2
Non-identifiable (because the donee is unknown)	2·3
	100·0

SOURCE: John H. Watson III (Manager of Company Donations Department, Division of Business Practices, The National Industrial Conference Board), 'Report on Company Contributions for 1965', *The Conference Board Record*, October 1966, pp. 45–54.

Comparison of these figures with those of previous years shows a decided shift in corporate emphasis toward the support of cultural organisations and activities. The Board began these studies in 1955. Corporate giving was then predominantly for health and welfare. In 1962, for the first time in the series of surveys, company gifts budgeted for education exceeded those for health and welfare. Funds allocated to civic and cultural purposes also figured more prominently than before. On average, companies in 1962 set aside 17·2c out of every contribution dollar for other causes than health, education, and welfare. About 5·3c went mainly to cultural and civic projects. This level represented a high point for these cultural and civic types of contributions; earlier surveys had averaged only 3c for these categories. In the cultural-civic sector, the performing arts accounted for about two thirds of all projects in 1962. This shift in corporate giving towards cultural and civic projects is not yet a strong trend, but it is a significant one.

There are important differences among companies in the weight given to 'civic and cultural' contributions. The NICB report for 1962 shows that companies with the largest number of employees (10,000 and over) averaged only 4·45 per cent of their contributions budgets for this support area, while all others gave more: 7·48 per cent for example, in the case of companies with 5,000–9,999 employees, and as much as 12·11 per cent for those with 500–999 employees. Clearly some of the smaller companies were moving more actively into this area than the larger ones. There were differences, too, between companies with and companies without foundations. Companies with foundations gave more (5·7 per cent of their contributions dollar) than those without foundations (4·9 per cent). Industry classifications may also be significant. Highest in the list for 'civic and cultural' were textile-mill products (31·04 per cent); stone, clay and glass products (14·37 per cent); and paper and like products (7·12 per cent). Electrical machinery and equipment (3·42 per cent) and chemical and allied products (3·81 per cent) are examples of classes of industries that fell below the average of more than 5 per cent of the contributions dollar from corporations for 'civic and cultural' activities and organisations.

Corporate giving often has been precedent-bound and generally unimaginative, though certainly of substantial help to health, welfare and education. Corporate giving to higher education has risen because of concerted efforts by business leaders and the colleges and universities to rescue institutions that were in dire need a decade ago. The need is still great, but national education legislation has now provided large appropriations. The arts and the humanities are now coming to the centre of attention, both for federal and state support and for corporate giving. While some companies now have staff components to put company contributions on a planned and systematic basis there is still need for more wisely designed policy in this area of corporate management.[1]

[1] See R. Eells, *Corporation Giving in a Free Society*, New York, Harper & Bros., 1965, and 'Corporate Giving: Theory and Policy', *California Management Review*, Vol I, no. 1, Fall 1958, pp. 37–46.

Appendix G

THE MULTINATIONAL CORPORATION IN THE INTERNATIONAL SYSTEM

The most useful way to define the functions of the multinational corporation may be to specify its role in world affairs, broadly conceived in terms of an international system. The term 'international system' is used because of current studies by political analysts under this heading. While traditional ways of thinking about the law of nations and international relations tend to exclude business corporations almost completely from a central place in the international system and to treat only of sovereign states as 'subjects' of international law, it is now becoming evident to many scholars[1] that realism requires a more comprehensive view.

It is true, of course, that the multinational corporation, as the term is used in this instance is essentially a private-sector organisation[2] but as such cannot simply claim the right to autonomy, to be left alone to carry on business without political involvement of any kind, and the right to participate centrally in the decision processes of national and international public organisations. The 'primacy of politics' tends naturally to rule out organisations

---

[1] On the emergence of non-state organisations as 'subjects', and not mere 'objects', of international law, see Myres S. McDougal, 'International Law, Power and Policy: A Contemporary Conception', *Recueil des Cours*, Hague Academy of International Law, 1953—I, Vol. 82, pp. 137–258, esp. pp. 249 ff on 'Transnational Private Associations as Participants in the World Power Process'; Phillip C. Jessup, *Transnational Law*, New Haven, Yale University Press, 1956; C. W. Jenks, *The Proper Law of International Organizations*, London, Stevens & Sons, and Dobbs Ferry, NY, Oceana Publications, 1962; Georg Schwarzenberger, *The Frontiers of International Law*, London, Stevens & Sons, 1962; Wolfgang G. Friedmann, *The Changing Structure of International Law*, New York, Columbia University Press, 1964; Morton A. Kaplan and N. Katzenbach, *The Political Foundations of International Law*, New York, John Wiley & Sons, 1961.

[2] Mixed public-private corporations and consortiums of the Comsat type are, however, properly within the purview of a comparative analysis of multinational corporations. See Herman Schwartz, 'Governmentally Appointed Directors in a Private Corporation—The Communications Satellite Act of 1962', *Harvard Law Review*, Vol. 79, December 1965, pp. 350–364; and John McDonald, 'The Comsat Compromise Starts a Revolution', *Fortune*, October 1965. So also joint ventures that may involve public as well as private corporations. See Richard D. Robinson, *International Business Policy*, New York, Holt, Rinehard and Winston, 1964.

other than the latter from major roles in the world arena. The corporation is not, and cannot be, a state or even a quasi-sovereign entity. As a basically different kind of organisation and legal entity the business corporation has to be defined in its own terms. It may not be a *mere* 'object' of international law, while the centre of the stage in world legal forums is occupied by states as the primary 'subjects'; important parts of international law of the future will undoubtedly be formed in commerce as the law merchant was by use and wont as well as by more formal methods of contract and convention. Yet it is the nation-state that stands today as the dominant institutional type in the world and not the multinational corporation.

The multinational corporation is not, on the other hand, of minor importance in the international system, and it is not unreasonable to hypothesise types of future international systems[3] in which it may play a major role—though not necessarily of co-ordinate significance in relation to nation states. The future role of the nation state, however, is not entirely free from doubt. We have come a long way from Hegel for whom the nation state was the ultimate embodiment of the world spirit. As Shotwell once remarked, the world arena of nation states presents a picture of anarchy—'the most dangerous since the fall of Rome'. Ours is an age of vast uncertainty about all institutions of public order. Ours may be 'a civilisation whose roots have rotted until they will no longer sustain the great weight of its trunk and the vast spread of its branches', or simply a transitional one that 'still contains much sound timber'.[4] The multinational corporation could turn out to be some of this sound timber.

There may possibly be a true *civitas mundi* far in the future but there is no functioning world community, no reliable world order under law, in sight. We have to use the timber we know about. Yet today's transitional period makes it extremely difficult to distinguish the transient from the permanent. Changes since World War II have been rapid. The 'historic' multipolar international system was transmuted briefly into a bipolar system, and now seems to be in process of further transformation towards a complex pattern exhibiting both bipolarity and polycentricity.[5] The polarisation is always assumed to be about sovereign centres, and especially the power centres of superstates. The mini-states and the medium-sized states in the contemporary international system are often less significant than some large corporations. Could it be assumed by hypothesis that these larger entities may themselves be 'sound timber' to be used in an emergent system of world order, or even of systems of regional order?

The question demands systematic enquiry into international systems and the role of the multinational corporation in the form most likely to emerge

[3] Modelski, whose two models of international systems called 'Agraria' and 'Industria' are discussed in Part III, Chapter 3 of this book, points to the necessity of keeping in mind 'the universe of international systems, past, present, future, and hypothetical for the proper study of international relations' including 'a large number of hitherto ignored species' that are 'exotic' to the Westerner with eyes fixed on the nation-states system which emerged at the end of the Middle Ages.

[4] John M. Clark, *Alternative to Freedom*, New York, Vintage Books, 1960, p. 126.

[5] Harold and Margaret Sprout, *The Ecological Perspective on Human Affairs with Special Reference to International Politics*, Princeton University Press, 1965, p. 205.

in a generation or two. The literature[6] on 'the international system' is extensive and rapidly growing. No attempt is made here to indicate its scope. The immediate problem—little treated in this literature—is the place of the corporation in it.

It is interesting to note that Easton, an authority on 'the political system', is critical of most current theories of international politics for the tendency to ignore 'the development of new kinds of actors', namely individual members of the system.[7] But his definition of the political system leaves the impression that the actors in the international system—which, for him, is 'just another kind of political system cognate with any national system'— might not include corporations. He writes that 'a political system can be designated as those interactions through which values are authoritatively allocated for a society; this is what distinguishes a political system from other systems that may be interpreted as lying in its environment'.[8] He distinguishes the 'intra-social' from the 'extra-social' environment, the former consisting of 'those systems in the same society as the political system but excluded from the latter' by his definition of the nature of political interactions.

Easton's attempt to unify the theory of political systems so as to include international politics as well as national politics is subject to attack from several quarters. Some students of international relations have insisted that the theory of this highly specialised field cannot be made into a segment of the theory of political systems generally. The argument is that the large aggregates involved in international politics require a different approach, that the 'political' is not the same at national and international levels, and that one cannot realistically set up categories that distinguish 'political acts' from economic acts, cultural acts, and so on. There is not, from this point of view, anything inherent by nature in an act or interaction that makes it political or otherwise. Nor is there any 'fixed hierarchy of analytical categories'[9] which places political acts above all others in order of importance.

One may thus see all acts and interactions in the world arena from quite diverse points of view, and the result is that the right approach to the study of 'international relations' and world affairs is a thoroughly interdisciplinary one. The world of transnational[10] affairs, most broadly conceived in all of its reactions of men and organisations at every level, is a big, buzzing universe

[6] See Klaus and Sidney Verba (eds.), 'The International System: Theoretical Essays', a Special Issue of *World Politics*, Vol. 14, No. 1, October 1961; Stanley Hoffman (ed.), *Contemporary Theory in International Relations*, Englewood Cliffs, NJ, Prentice Hall, 1960; Charles A. McClelland, *Theory and the International System*, New York, The Macmillan Co., 1966; Myres S. McDougal and Harold D. Lasswell, 'The Identification and Appraisal of Diverse Systems of World Order', *American Journal of International Law*, Vol. 53, January 1959, pp. 1–29; Wm. D. Coplin, 'International Law and Assumptions about the State System', *World Politics*, Vol. 17, July 1965, pp. 615–634; Gabriel A. Almond, 'A Developmental Approach to Political Systems', *World Politics*, Vol. 17, January 1965, pp. 182–214; J. David Singer and Melvin Small, 'The Composition and Status Ordering of the International System: 1815–1940', *World Politics*, Vol. 18, January 1966, pp. 236–282.

[7] David Easton, *A Systems Analysis of Political Life*, New York, John Wiley & Sons, 1965, p. 486.

[8] ibid., p. 21.

[9] McClelland, op. cit., p. 19.

[10] For the use of this word, see Part III, Chapter 3, pp. 253–254 above.

of multifarious interactions that we categorise only artificially as analysts; and many kinds of analysts are at work in this arena, which is far more than an arena of power-seekers, profit-seekers, and so on. But if 'the political' can be reasonably determined, not as an inherent quality of nature but as a point of view, then political relations can be said to occur locally, nationally and internationally. In this sense, Easton stands on solid ground in the same way as does Lasswell in making his distinction between 'public order' and 'civic order', both of which are regarded as components of 'social order': the 'public order' embraces not only the 'value patterns and institutions of the power process', but also the 'distinctive values, patterns, and institutions of the whole society'.[11] These are all protected by a process of authoritative decision. Political institutions for this purpose sustain themselves and also other fundamental patterns in the market, the family system, and other components of the culture. As Lasswell puts it, 'The scope of civic order is no less inclusive; but civic order employs mild, not severe, sanctions.' The 'civic order' is based generally on persuasion rather than coercion, while the power elite concentrates its efforts where the severer sanctions of the public order are available. The authoritativeness of value allocations bears a close relationship to this use of the more severe sanctions.

In this way, the observer sharpens his focus to whatever interests him most. For the political scientist it is undoubtedly true that the power elite and its practices stand at this focus, even though some analysts may deal primarily with peripheral influences that lead eventually to the authoritative allocations and sanctions. The narrowing down is from a very broad view of the entire range of phenomena in the international system broadly conceived. International relations so conceived embrace '*all* of the exchanges, transactions, contacts, flows of information, and actions of every kind going on at this moment of time between and among the separately constituted societies of the world', as well as 'the effects created within societies from all such interflowing events in earlier times, both of the immediate and the remote past', and in addition the stream of these actions and responses conceived 'as moving on to the future of tomorrow and beyond, accompanied by the expectations, plans, and proposals of all observers of the phenomena'.[12] This total picture is the reference intended by McClelland in his use of the term 'the international system'.

Easton, obviously, is talking about something more limited when he speaks of the international *political* system. For, as he points out, there is an 'international society' which is more than a sum of its component national cultures, and an international economy, both seen as aspects of international life. But political life at the international level can be seen separately as an international political system that is equivalent in all respects but one to the political systems of national societies: 'the component units of the international system consist of large and powerful subsystems that we call national political systems, and regional groupings of them'.[13]

[11] Harold D. Lasswell, 'The Study of Political Elites', in Lasswell and Lerner (eds.), *World Revolutionary Elites: Studies in Coercive Ideological Movements*, Cambridge, Mass., The MIT Press, 1965, p. 11.
[12] McClelland, op. cit., p. 20.   [13] Easton, op. cit., p. 486.

McClelland has a similar view in stating that 'the parts or components of the international system are *national systems*',[14] a rather surprising position after his sweeping definition of the international system just quoted. The implication is that only 'national actors' are involved directly in the international system, though other groups and individual actors might be involved indirectly in 'national subsystems'. These non-state actors, in other words, are not directly at work in the international system. He also speaks of public opinion as a kind of national subsystem. This follows from his definition of 'system': 'an ensemble of parts or subsystems capable of changing from one state to another state' and 'a structure that is perceived by its observers to have elements in interaction or relationships and some identifiable boundaries that separate it from its environment'.[15] He discusses the inputs and outputs of the international system in terms of some contemporary theories of international relations, notably that of Morton A. Kaplan,[16] who is also concerned with the national actors.

Kaplan's six models of international systems are called balance-of-power, loose, bipolar, universal, hierarchical, and unit-veto systems. These models provide hypothetical interrelationships for conceivable as well as existent and historical systems. An example of a non-existent and unprecedented, but conceivable system is the unit-veto model, since it is one that might exist some day were all the national actors in the international system to have 'weapons of such a character that any actor is capable of destroying any other actor that attacks it even though it cannot prevent its own destruction'.[17] Under such conditions every national actor would act to stand off every other member in order to preserve the existing steady state of the unit-veto international system, while the steady state of the system could be sustained only if every actor, without exception, will resist threats of destruction and will be prepared to retaliate if attacked. The instability of such a system arises from the circumstance that a national actor could start a chain reaction by attacking or by succumbing to blackmail (such as the threat of nuclear destruction), thereby transforming the system into one with a different structure.

Forays of this kind into the theory of the international system are probably too abstract for use in the study of the multinational corporation as a part of the system. But, as McClelland has shown, there are many contemporary approaches that do provide more immediate use. He discusses, for example, theories of transformations in the international system, notably the studies of Toynbee, Herz, Haas, Deutsch, Boulding and Sorokin. They all help one to get the proper historical perspective on the Western state system that now has expanded to the whole globe but may in the process undergo fundamental change. One such change is indicated in a perceptive observation of Kenneth Boulding: 'Everywhere is now accessible to everybody; there are no nooks, corners, or retreats left, and no snugly protected centres of national power. The great continental heartlands are as exposed to aerial warfare as are the

[14] McClelland, op. cit., p. 21.
[15] ibid., p. 20.
[16] Morton A. Kaplan, *System and Process in International Politics*, New York, John Wiley & Sons, 1957, p. 50.
[17] ibid.

coasts to naval bombardment. The result is a sudden and dramatic collapse of unconditional viability.'[18] The 'conditional viability' of all transnational institutions such as the multinational corporation leaps to mind. John Herz speaks of the 'permeability' of the protective boundaries of states.[19] An international system without the national system of nation states as the basic protective units may be hard to envisage; but the communicational revolution has perhaps changed the basis profoundly. And with that change the hitherto protected institutions will have to find new kinds of protectors.

But multinational corporate managers, looking for some unifying theory of transformation in the international system to guide them in the search for the right kind of protector for transnational enterprise, will look in vain, at least in the contemporary state of theory. McClelland makes the useful observation that historical sociologies, theories as sets of answers that get popular followings but generate no solutions and no controls in the face of massive problems, are not to be depended upon if they appear; and it is doubtful that they will appear in the form of a blueprint or prescriptive code of the form: do this, then that, and after that, the following. Creative formulations that will take into account all of the various approaches, probings, trends, indications and forewarnings that he includes within his monograph are not to be expected, McClelland adds. To get at the crucial variables and the facts behind the facts it is necessary to simplify in theory; yet the simplification may lead to distortions and even the ignoring of wide ranges of observed experiences. And not the least difficulty is that, when knowledge takes new shapes, a neat theory in the books may fail us if we overlook changes in form; and he asks: 'What if theory in the future should be only the pattern of instructions given to computers? The very wide span of relevant changes and the large size of the international system may not allow the development of any unitary theory but may encourage, instead, the formulations of clusters of theoretical questions and statements.'[20] This is not to say, of course, that anything short of comprehensive perfection will be useless to corporate managers in the baffling world arena now changing at such a rapid pace, and so full of dangers. For the time being one must be satisfied with the clusters of questions and statements, and then go on to the judgmental types of decisions that executives have always had to make anyhow.

The need for global answers to global questions, however, is sometimes most urgent, and more than hunches are required for rational management. In this connexion and bearing in mind the constant need for corporate attention to public policy as it affects transnational business, some comments by Ernst Haas are of interest. He has said that 'cumulative innovation is intolerable for a minimal stability in our environment' and one of the disturbing ratios is technological capability as compared with social and political design. Technology seems, in principle, to be able to meet the demands of the revolution of rising expectations. 'But what happens if in the underdeveloped

---

[18] Kenneth E. Boulding, *Conflict and Defense*, New York, Harper & Row, 1962, p. 272.

[19] John H. Herz, *International Politics in the Atomic Age*, New York, Columbia University Press, 1959, and 'The Rise and Demise of the Territorial State', *World Politics*, July 1957, pp. 473–493.

[20] McClelland, op. cit., p. 55.

countries the expectations outstrip the capacity of the political and social system to meet them?'[21] In the developed nations themselves, he asks, what happens 'when the "objective" need of sharing affluence with the needy in order to head off their revolt against the West—whether under communist or some other aegis—meets a pervasive and democratically legitimate insistence on husbanding affluence at home and investing it in the domestic revolution of still higher expectations. . . ?'

The implications of these questions for the managers of transnational business are many, and some of the more important ones are not immediately obvious. One needs a theory of the international system, and of the place of the multinational corporation in that system to expose these questions. Economic development, at home and abroad, can lead to political chaos as well as to peace, democracy and welfare. As Haas says, 'managerial and administrative skills, social mobility and literacy, an inquiring mind as well as a full belly, are essential to economic progress',[22] and we dare not gloss over the destabilising social consequences of economic growth when unmatched by development in other-than-economic sectors. In another context, Haas has made the plea for functionalism as a promising road to the solution of some of these problems.[23] And it is the functionalist approach that one must take in order to see and emphasise the role of the multinational corporation in the evolving international system.[24]

[21] Ernst B. Haas, 'Toward Controlling International Change: A Personal Plea', *World Politics*, October 1964, pp. 3–12.

[22] ibid., p. 11.

[23] E. B. Haas, *Beyond the Nation-State: Functionalism and International Organization*, Stanford, Calif., Stanford University Press, 1964.

[24] The functional approach is used to some extent in Robinson, op. cit. (footnote 2).

BIBLIOGRAPHIES

BELGIUM

R. Clémens. *Contributions à l'étude de l'entreprise et de la distribution des pouvoirs de décisions*, Liège University Press, 1961.

P. Coetsier. *Organismen voor medezeggenschap in de onderneming: een socio-psychologisch onderzoek*, Standaard, Antwerp, 1966.

E. de Barsy. *Raisonnement sur l'entreprise*, Société d'Economie Politique de Belgique, No. 312, December 1965.

'De positie, betekenis en ontwikkeling van de vrije onderneming in de hedendaagse economie', *Tijdschrift voor sociale wetenschappen*, 1957, No. 1, pp. 3–19.

E. de Barsy and R. Henrion. 'L'entreprise et le progrès social', *Cahiers économiques de Bruxelles*, No. 19, pp. 319–332.

Ph. de Woot. *La fonction de l'entreprise: formes nouvelles et progrès économique*, Nauwelaerts, Louvain, 1962.

'L'entreprise dans son milieu', *Industrie*, December 1963, pp. 818–852.

'Croissance et progrès des entreprises', *Industrie*, May 1963, pp. 300–312; October 1963, pp. 654–669; May 1965, pp. 306–315.

R. Evalenko. 'Réformes de structure: lesquelles, pourquoi, comment,' *Socialisme*, No. 73, January 1966, pp. 4–30.

R. Henrion. 'L'entreprise et les apporteurs de capitaux', *Cahiers économiques de Bruxelles*, No. 22, 1964, pp. 227–235.

'L'évolution du droit de l'entreprise', *Bulletin social des industries*, August/September 1965, pp. 400–407.

'Système économique et statut de l'entreprise', *Annales de sciences économiques appliquées*, August 1965, pp. 337–365.

L. Morissens. 'Les résponsibilités de l'entreprise et son statut', *Cahiers économiques de Bruxelles*, No. 28, 1965, pp. 477–482.

A. Priem. 'Medezeggenschap in de onderneming', *Rechtskundig Weekblad*, 31 October 1965, pp. 418–430.

R. Vandeputte. *Le statut de l'entreprise*, Brussels, Bruylant, 1965.

'Juridische problemen in verband met de ondermening', *Rechtskundig Weekblad*, No. 40, 1962.

P. van Ommeslaghe. 'De hernieuwing van het vennootschapsrecht in België', *Sociaal-Economische Wetgeving*, October/November 1965, pp. 573 ff.

'De hervorming van de naamloze vennootschap', *Sparen en beleggen*, July/August 1965, pp. 1–47.

La réforme des sociétés anonymes, Centre d'études bancaires et financières Conference, Brussels, December 1965, No. 108.

A. Vlerick. 'De onderneming als drager van de economische groei', Zesde Vlaams Wetenschappelijk Economisch Congres, Antwerp, April 1963. *Report*, pp. 15–39.

FRANCE

G. Adam. 'L'action sociale et les types de démocratie'. (Roneoed document.)

Bassoul, Bernard and Touraine. 'Retrait, conflit, participation', *Sociologie du travail*, 1960, No. 2.

P. Belleville. *Une nouvelle classe ouvrière*, Juillard, Paris, 1963. (*Les Temps Modernes* series.)

O. Benoit. 'Statut dans l'entreprise et attitude syndicale des ouvriers', *Sociologie du travail*, 1963, No. 2.

F. Bloch-Laîné. *Pour une réforme de l'entreprise*, Paris, Editions du Seuil, 1963.

Boltanski and Chamboredon. *Une banque et sa clientèle: éléments pour une sociologie du crédit*, Paris, Centre de Sociologie Européenne.

G. Bouthoul. *Histoire de la sociologie*, Paris, Presses Universitaires de France, 1961.

R. P. Boyer, OP. 'Recherches doctrinales sur la nature et les finalités de l'entreprise', *Cahiers chrétiens de la fonction publique*, 1963, No. 54.

C. Bruclain. *Le socialisme et l'Europe*, Paris, Editions du Seuil, 1965.

R. Capitant. 'Vers la réforme de l'entreprise . . . enfin trois premiers pas en avant', *Notre république*, 21 May 1965.

M. Crozier. 'A propos de la réforme de l'entreprise', *Sociologie du travail*, 1963, No. 4.

Le monde des employés de bureau, Paris, Editions du Seuil, 1965.

Le phénomène bureaucratique, Paris, Editions du Seuil, 1964.

P. de Calan. *Renaissance des libertés économiques et sociales*, Paris, Plon, 1964.

Y. Delamotte. 'Conflit industriel et participation ouvrière', *Sociologie du travail*.

M. Demonque. 'La firme et son role dans les systèmes économiques françaises', *Revue d'économie appliquée*.

G. Friedmann. *Le travail en miettes*, Paris, Gallimard, 1958.

'Quelques problèmes de definitions et de limites', *Sociologie du travail*, 1959, No. 1.

O. Gelinier. 'Le secret des structures competitives', *Hommes et techniques*, 1966.

Morale de l'entreprise et destin de la nation, Paris, Plon, 1965.

G. Gurvitch. *La vocation actuelle de la sociologie*.

Hamblin. 'Les fonctions de la maîtrise', *Sociologie du travail*, July 1963.

Hoffman, Pitts, Wylie and Duroselle. *A la recherche de la France*, Paris, Editions du Seuil, 1964.

J. Lautman. 'Sur le phénomène bureaucratique', *Annales*.

J. Lautman and J. Annie. 'Roles de syndicalisme patronal et évolution économique' (Colloque de la Société française de sociologie, Paris, 1965).

S. Mallet. *La nouvelle classe ouvrière*, Paris, Editions du Seuil, 1964.

C. Marenco. *L'introduction de l'automatisme dans les bureaux: l'administration du changement, les modalités d'adaptation des individus et des groupes*, Paris, Institut des sciences sociales du travail, 1963.

F. Meyers. 'Deux aspects du role des négotiations collectives en France', *Sociologie du travail*, January, March and April 1965.

M. Montuclard. 'La comité d'entreprise: à propos d'une hypothèse concernant son effet sur l'évolution de l'entreprise', *Sociologie du travail*, April/June 1965.

La dynamique des comités d'entreprise, Paris, CNRS, 1963.

'Pour une sociologie de la participation ouvrière dans les comités d'entreprise', *Sociologie du travail*, October/December 1960.

Morin. 'Contraintes sociales et communications dans l'entreprise', *Sociologie du travail*, 1965.

P. Naville. *Vers l'automatisme social? Problèmes du travail et de l'automation*, Paris, Gallimard, 1963.

J.-D. Reynaud. 'La philosophie du management de P. Drucker', *Sociologie du travail*, 1960, No. 3.

Les syndicats en France, Paris, Armand Colin, 1963.

R. Sainsaulieu. 'Pouvoirs et stratégies de groupes ouvriers dans l'atelier', *Revue français de sociologie*, 1966.

R. Salmon. *L'information économique, clé de la prospérité*, Paris, Hachette-Entreprise.

F. Sommer. *Au-delà du salaire*, Editions Robert Laffont.

A. Touraine. 'Entreprise et bureaucratie', *Sociologie du travail*, 1959, No. 1.

'Psychologie de l'entreprise et sociologie du travail,' *Revue française du travail*, November 1962.

Sociologie de l'action, Paris, Editions du Seuil, 1965.

Willener. 'L'ouvrier et l'organisation', *Sociologie du travail*, 1962, No. 4.

GERMANY

K. Ballerstedt. Gesellschaftsrechtliche Probleme der Unternehmenskonzentration, in *Die Konzentration in der Wirtschaft*, Berlin, H. Arndt, 1960.

F. Böhm. 'Es geht um die Menschenwürde: ein Plädoyer gegen die Mitbestimmung', *Frankfurter Allgemeine Zeitung*, 22 October 1966.

O. Buhler. *Steuerrecht der Gesellschaften und Konzerne* (3rd edn), Berlin and Frankfurt a. M., 1956.

R. Dietz. *Das wirtschaftliche Mitbestimmungsrecht, insbesondere seine Auswirkungen in den Aufsichsraten der Handelsgesellschaften*, Karlsruhe, 1958.

Gadow-Heinichen. *Grosskommentar zum Aktiengesetz* (2nd edn), Vol. I, Berlin, 1961.

Goldmann (ed.). *Aktiengesetz—GmbH-Gesetz*, Textausgabe, 1966.

Hachenburg. *GmbH—Kommentar* (6th edn), Vol. I, Berlin, 1956.

A. Hueck. *Gesellschaftsrecht* (13th edn), Munich and Berlin, 1965.

Kunze-Christmann. *Wirtschaftliche Mitbestimmung im Wiederstreit*, Wirtschaftswissenschaftliche Institut der Gewerkschaften, Cologne, 1964.

H. Lehmann. *Gesellschaftsrecht* (12th edn), Frankfurt a. M. and Berlin, 1959.

W. Strauss. *Grundlagen und Aufgaben der Aktienrechtsreform*, Tübingen, 1960.

W. Stützel. 'Aktienrechtsreform und Konzentration', in *Die Konzentration in der Wirtschaft*, Berlin, H. Arndt, 1960.

W. Vallenthin. *Das Aktienwesen* (4th edn), Frankfurt a. M., 1966.

H. Würdinger. *Aktienrecht*, Karlsruhe, 1959.

JAPAN

Shozo Akazawa. *Keieisha no Shakai-teki-sekinken to Kasen Keizak* (*The Social Responsibility of Business and the Oligopolistic Economy*), Fabian Studies, Vol. XVI, No. 11.

Yoshindo Chigusa (ed.). *Sangyo-Taisei no Sai-hensei* (*The Reorganisation of Industrial Structure*), Shunju-sha, 1963.

Sachio Hon-i-den. *Shin Kigyo Genri no Kenkyu* (*A Study of the Principles of the New Enterprise*), Seimeikai Series, Vol. III, 1965.

Hiroshi Kato, Yutaka Hara and Naomi Maruo. *Gendai no Keizai wa Do Kawaru Ka?* (*How will the Modern Economy Change?*), Kodansha, 1963.

Kenzo Kiga, Masao Komatsu and Hiroshi Kato. *Keizai Seisaku-ron* (*Economic Policies*), Sekai-shoin, 1966.

Mitsuro Muto. Keizai Keikaku to Keikakusha (Economic Planning and Planners), in *Government*, Vol. V, Chapter 3, Chuo-Koronsha, 1960.

YUGOSLAVIA

Note. Many books relevant to the topics discussed in Part IV, Chapter 3 of this book are not published in English or any other 'world' language. The following works in English and French are of interest.

I. Adizes. The Effect of Decentralization on Organizational Behavior—An Exploratory Study of the Yugoslav Self-management System, New York, Columbia University, unpublished (roneoed) doctoral dissertation.

A. Deleon. *33 Questions, 33 Answers on Workers' Self-government*, Belgrade, Yugoslav Publicity Enterprise, 1956.

J. T. Dunlop. *Industrial Relations Systems*, New York, Holt, 1959, Chapter 8.

J. Kojala. *Workers' Councils: The Yugoslav Experience*, London, Tavistock Publications, 1965.

R. Lang and D. Gorupić. 'La décision d'investissement dans le système économique yougoslave', Zagreb, Ekonomski Institut, 1963, roneoed paper.

G. Macesich. *Yugoslavia: The Theory and Practice of Development Planning*, Charlottesville, The University Press of Virginia, 1964.

O. Mandié. 'Yugoslavia', in A. M. Rose (ed.), *The Institutions of Advanced Societies*, Minneapolis, University of Minnesota Press, 1958.

A. Meister. *Socialisme et l'autogestion: expérience yougoslave*, Paris, Editions du Seuil, 1964.

A. Sturmthal. *Workers' Councils*, Cambridge (Mass.), Harvard University Press, 1964.

B. Ward. 'The Firm in Illyria: Market Syndicalism', *American Economic Review*, Vol. XLVIII, No. 4, September 1958, pp. 566–589.

J. Županov and A. S. Tannenbaum. 'The Distribution of Control in some Yugoslav Industrial Organizations as Perceived by Members', in Tannenbaum (ed.), *Control in Organizations*, New York, McGraw-Hill, 1968, Ch. 6.

International Labour Office (ILO). *La gestion ouvrière des entreprises en Yougoslavie*, Geneva, 1962.

Organisation for Economic Co-operation and Development (OECD). *Economic Studies*, The Federative Socialist Republic of Yugloslavia, Paris, 1966.

Yugoslav League of Communists. *Yugoslavia's Way: The Program of the League*, New York, All Nations Press, 1958.

INDEX